CONTEMPORARY
CZECHOSLOVAK
COMPOSERS

Edited by Čeněk Gardavský

PANTON

PRAGUE • BRATISLAVA

1965

INTRODUCTION

The Oldest Czech musical mementos are today a thousand years old. Czech musical culture achieved a very individual character at the beginning of the fifteenth century in the pre-Hussite and Hussite folk songs. Intonations, peculiar to Hussite songs, appear in Czech music even up to the present.

As early as the sixteenth century the work of Kryštof Harant of Polžice and Bezdružice *(was beheaded by the Habsburgs in 1621) achieved a standard set for outstanding works of that day. After the battle of the White Mountain (1620), which saw the loss of Czech independence, a period of darkness prevailed in the Czech lands. Political and cultural growth in the previous centuries gave way to the despotic pressure brought to bear by the Roman Catholic Church, Germanization of the people and the economic improverishment of the Czech lands.*

The end of the seventeenth century and the beginning of the eighteenth century witnessed in music the commencement of a new creative era. The work of Bohuslav Matěj Černohorský *(1684—1742) and* Jan Dismas Zelenka *(1679—1745) attracted the attention of the great among European masters. Despite the persecution of all cultural activity of a national character, the people retained their native tongue. Folk music creativeness during this period of oppression took on greater vigour and became the basis for compositional work of numberless country teachers and many Czech musicians-instrumentalists who, in large numbers, left their native land to seek work and recognition in the orchestras of various European cities.*

During the eighteenth century Czech musicians were active in Germany, Russia, France and in Italy, in England and in Poland, but most of all in Vienna. The Czechs made a considerable contribution to the formation of the classical musical style and even today this contribution has not yet been fully appreciated.

A comparison of the compositions of the Mannheim masters of Czech origin, as for instance of their representative Jan Václav Stamic *(1717—1757) with the work of Joseph Haydn and W. A. Mozart is sufficient evidence of the quality of their work. This is true as well of the compositions of* Josef Mysliveček *(1737—1781) as compared to the work of his contemporaries, or of the work of* Jiří Benda *(1722—1795),* Jan K. Vaňhal *(1739—1813),* Jan Ladislav Dusík *(1760—1812),* Vojtěch Jírovec *(1730—1813),* Antonín Rejcha *(1770 to 1836),* Jan Hugo Voříšek *(1791—1825) and many others.*

It was not chance that made Prague the first to understand and unreservedly acknowledge the genius of Mozart and Beethoven, nor was it due to chance that these two great masters found so many friends in Bohemia.

The first half of the nineteenth century saw the first efforts for the creation of a national Czech music. The Czech nation at that time was in the ardour of a reawakening, despite the fact that political independence became a reality only in 1918 with the birth of the Czechoslovak Republic.

Czech cultural activity was undergoing a new growth which, in music, culminated in the work of Bedřich Smetana. *The pre-Smetana period is particularly fruitful in its collections of folk songs, patriotic songs and choirs as well as operas. The song by* František Škroup "WHERE IS MY HOME?" *(1833) falls into this period. It took on the character of a folk song and became the national anthem.*

Efforts to create a national Czech opera did not result in works of lasting values, but on the other hand the choir music of the period serves as a model even today. Its most outstanding writer was Pavel Křížkovský *(1820—1885), the teacher of* Leoš Janáček. *The establishment of the Prague Conservatory in 1811 became the portent for new unsuspected achievements in Czech music.*

6

Czech Modern Music

As a point of fact it is interesting to note that similarly as in other European countries, endeavours to bring into being Czech national music were concentrated in the creation of national opera.

Bedřich Smetana *(1824—1884)* is not however, only its creator but the founder of Czech modern music as well. Smetana did not imitate the Czech folk song but wrote in its spirit, did not create national music in the fact that he simplified expressive mediums, but that he was able to go his own way and forge his own path in a musical world represented by Chopin, Liszt, Berlioz and Wagner, the avantgarde of that day.

All of Smetana's creative work as well as his activity as an outstanding piano virtuoso and conductor was his contribution to the national independence movement and the cultural development of the Czech nation. It was his conviction that the highest cultural mission of an artist is in the service to his nation. His compositions are exacting but understandable, have a high artistic standard but are still a model of simplicity; they are rich in expression, mood and content and manifold and authentic as life itself—they are realistic.

Antonín Dvořák *(1841—1904)*, Smetana's greatest successor gained world popularity for Czech music, particularly with his symphonic and chamber works. The sound folk foundation of Dvořák's music was a potent artistic strength, especially at the end of the nineteenth century.

Zdeněk Fibich *(1850—1900)* significantly influenced the development of Czech music with his scenic and concert melodramas.

The work of these masters is closely tied up with the National Theatre which the people as a nation had built for themselves, not once but twice, first in *1881* and after the fire of the theatre in *1883*. Antonín Dvořák, *due to his pedagogical activity* at the Prague Conservatory, laid the foundation for a highly ramified school of composing which produced Vítězslav Novák *(1870—1949)*, Josef Suk *(1874—1935)*, Oskar Nedbal *(1874—1930)*, Rudolf Karel *(1880—1945)* and others. Novák and Suk, together with Josef Bohuslav Foerster

(1859—1951) became the teachers of a large body of Czech, Slovak and foreign composers.

Leoš Janáček *(1854—1928) represents a completely individual personality in modern Czech and contemporary world music. His entire work, particularly his operas, are gaining greater and greater recognition.*

The bulk of the work of Smetana's contemporaries such as Karel Bendl *(1838—1897),* Jan Malát *(1843—1915),* Karel Šebor *(1843—1903),* Josef Richard Rozkošný *(1833—1913),* Zdeněk František Skuherský *(1830 to 1892) and others is today almost forgotten. Despite this fact however, the concert, music-educational and music-theoretical movement in which they were outstanding factors, represented the first steps of Czech musical art in the acquiring of an international reputation.*

The foundation of the CZECH PHILHARMONIC *and of the* CZECH QUARTET, *as well as the work of many Czech singers, virtuosos, conductors and pedagogues* (Emmy Destin, Karel Burian, František Ondříček, Jan Kubelík, Otakar Ševčík *and others) demonstrated that the old glory of "Bohemia— the Conservatory of Europe" had not been destroyed in the eighteenth century.*

Contact between Russian and Czech music had seen considerable development. Tens of Czech musicians were active in Russia and took an effective part in the development of Russian musical culture. The most outstanding of these were Eduard Nápravník *(1839—1915), who was chief of the Petrograd Opera, and* Váša Suk *(1861—1933), the chief of the Great Theatre in Moscow.*

Czech Music Before 1945

The distinct and fundamental lines of development are evident in the work of Czech composers in the first half of the twentieth century. Their sensibilities and forms of expression had been influenced by the two World Wars. One group worked toward the further evolution of Czech national musical culture on the basis

8

of the classic heritage of the nineteenth century while the others oriented themselves to the various modernistic trends of west European music. Both these trends however, were mutually interwoven.

The natural process of expressing in music the life about us in its entirety demanded a coherence in form and content. And for this reason, in this constant turmoil, the perfection of the work of the classic composers stood as a model.

The largest group in the period between the two World Wars was the pupils of Vítězslav Novák, *who however, were not adherents, even as teachers of the next generation, of one evolutionary artistic trend. Among them are such writers as* Ladislav Vycpálek, Alois Hába, *pupils of Leoš Janáček, the Slovak composers and a large group of contemporary Czech composers.*

Of many pupils of Josef Suk, *mention should at least be made of* Bohuslav Martinů *and of the pupils of J. B. Foerster,* Emil F. Burian. Alois Hába *created a large school of composition. Many of the composers had several teachers and in their work a great number did not evidence the typical characteristics attached to the "school" from which they originally came.*

In the period before 1945, the most outstanding composers of Czech music include Emil Axman, Boleslav Vomáčka, Otakar Jeremiáš, Otakar Ostrčil, Jaroslav Řídký, Jaroslav Křička, Pavel Bořkovec, Jaroslav Kvapil, Vilém Petrželka, *a few of the last named having created many schools of composing.*

The years of the Nazi occupation left definite traces on the development of Czechoslovak music. The war itself, even the Munich betrayal of Czechoslovakia and the attack on the Soviet Union, the victorious battles of the Red Army freeing many nations of Europe from barbaric fascism, the underground, the Slovak national uprising and the Prague revolution repulsing the fascist forces, news of the suffering of martyrs in concentration camps and of the persecuted heroes of the national movement—all this was reflected in the work of Czechoslovak composers. Many works by J. B. Foerster, Otakar Jeremiáš, Vítězslav Novák, Jaroslav Řídký, Václav Dobiáš,

9

Jaroslav Doubrava, Jan Hanuš, Osvald Chlubna, Milo-
slav Kabeláč, Jan Kapr, Rudolf Kubín, Jaroslav Kvapil,
Jan Seidel, Klement Slavický, Josef Stanislav, Boleslav
Vomáčka *and others spoke in a manner understood by all.*

*Even the youngest composers in Czechoslovak music are
constantly giving of their best so that musical art growing out
of life is returned again to life, enriching the sentiments and
thoughts of the people themselves in their fight for the building
up of a better life and society.*

Slovak Music

*The creative ability of the Slovak people who, for a thousand
years, lived under extremely unfavourable social and cultural
conditions, is particularly evident in the development of an out-
standingly rich musical and poetic folk music, a living concept
even today.*

*The history of the Slovak people shows a repeated intensive
musical development as in the sixteenth century, when parallel
to church music, the renaissance polyphonic vocal music is zeal-
ously cultivated, and in the seventeenth and eighteenth centuries
we see the development of Baroque church music. During the
period of classicism, Bratislava (the birthplace of Johann N.
Hummel) becomes, so to speak, a branch of Vienna, attracting
such masters as Haydn, Mozart and Beethoven.*

*In the nineteenth century, new romantic elements are brought
to Slovakia by Heinrich Marschner, and later particularly by
Ferencz Liszt and Johannes Brahms. In the second half of the
nineteenth century the idea of Slovak national music begins to
take concrete form. The most outstanding artistic figures of
Slovak musical rebirth are* Ján Levoslav Bella *(1843—1936)*
and Ludovít Vansa *(1835—1873), oriented to the German
and Czech neoromantic schools; but neither of these two composers were able to realize fully their creative ideas.*

*With the new century, Slovak music sees a new generation of
composers, pupils of the Conservatories in Budapest, Vienna,
Prague and Leipzig, such as* Mikuláš Moyzes *(1872—1944),*

Viliam Figuš-Bystrý *(1875—1937)*, Mikuláš Schneider-Trnavský *(1881—1958)*, Frico Kafenda *(1883—1963)* *and* Alexander Albrecht *(1885—1958)*. *These composers begin to lay the foundations for the creation of a European oriented and artistically mature national music.*

After the First World War a liberated people began to build their own professional musical institutions (opera buildings, musical schools, orchestras). At the beginning of the thirties, the first representatives of modern Slovak music come to the fore, having completed their compositional study with Vítězslav Novák in Prague. They include, among others, Alexander Moyzes, Eugen Suchoň, Ján Cikker, Ladislav Holoubek, Desider Kardoš, Andrej Očenáš, Šimon Jurovský, Jozef Kresánek *and* Tibor Frešo.

Their work creates a widely differentiated type of musical expression, synthetizing subjects of Slovak folklore (Vítězslav Novák as well as Béla Bartók had already tied up with this genre), showing a tendency to a European musical development. The work of this generation climaxes in the period after the Second World War in both symphonic music and modern opera.

Under the new social conditions, Slovak musical life is considerably intensified and strengthened, new artistic ensembles come into being as the SLOVAK PHILHARMONIC *and its mixed choir, the* SLOVAK FOLK ARTISTIC ENSEMBLE *and* LÚČNICA, *today known and recognized abroad as well.*

New opera buildings have been built as well as Conservatories and the High School of Musical Arts in Bratislava. Parallel to this, Slovak music has had an increased share in the growth and international importance of Czechoslovak music.

At the end of the forties, new composers appear on the horizon, pupils of the representatives of the generation of the thirties. Whereas Oto Ferenczy, Ján Zimmer *and some of the young composers have displayed a leaning to the style orientation of the older generation, the youngest composers are in the main seeking their own characteristic style within the tendencies of the progressive European avantgarde.*

THE PRONUNCIATION
OF CZECH AND SLOVAK WORDS

a	short	as in	*alphabet*
á	long	as in	*father*
c		as in	*Hudson*
č		as in	*child*
e	short	as in	*let*
é	long	as in	*fair*
ě		as in	*yes*
g		as in	*get*
h	is only a breath	as in	*help*
ch		as in	*loch*
i		as in	*fit*
í	long	as in	*feel*
j		as in	*yet*
n		as in	*singing*
o	short	as in	*shop*
ó	long	as in	*order*
q		as in	*quarter*
ř		as in	*Dvořák*
s		as in	*less*
š		as in	*sugar*
t		as in	*tube*
u		as in	*put*
ú and ů		as in	*root*
v and w		as in	*venture*
x		as in	*mix*
y		as in	*fit*
ý		as in	*feet*
z		as in	*zeal*
ž		as in	*leisure*

The stress is always laid on the first syllable of a word.

THE COLLECTIVE OF CONTRIBUTORS

The list of contributors to this volume, which was edited by Čeněk Gardavský (with indication of their initials):

BARVÍK Miroslav	M. B.
BERKOVEC Jiří	J. B.
BRACHTL Josef	Br.
ČERNOHORSKÁ Milena	M. Č.
ČERNUŠÁK Gracián	-k
GARDAVSKÝ Čeněk	Č. G.
HERZOG Edvard	E. H.
JANÁČKOVÁ Irena	J.
MOKRÝ Ladislav	L. M.
MUSIL Vlastimil	V. M.
PETRŽELKA Ivan	P.
ŠTĚDROŇ Bohumír	B. Š.
TROJAN Jan	J. T.
VACHULKA Ladislav	L. V.
VÁLEK Jiří	jiva
VANICKÝ Jaroslav	J. V.
VETTERL Karel	K. V.

These initials were interpolated into the *Survey of Composers* on following pages.

SURVEY OF COMPOSERS

(with initials of the contributors)

Aim Vojtěch Bořivoj	Č. G.	19	*Brož* František	M. B.	71
Albrecht Alexander	L. M.	21	*Burghauser* Jarmil	Č. G.	72
Alvín František	L. M.	23	*Burian* Emil		
Ambros Vladimír	Č. G.	23	František	Č. G.	74
Andrašovan Tibor	L. M.	26	*Burlas* Ladislav	L. M.	78
Aust Alois	Č. G.	27			
Axman Emil	-k	28	*Ceremuga* Josef	Č. G.	79
			Černík Josef	K. V.	81
Babušek František	L. M.	31	*Černík* Vilém	Č. G.	83
Bakala Břetislav	B. Š.	32	*Červený* Jiří	Č. G.	84
Balatka Antonín	B. Š.	33	*Chlubna* Osvald	M. Č.	85
Balcar Milan	Č. G.	34	*Cikker* Ján	L. M.	88
Balling Karel	Č. G.	36	*Cmíral* Adolf	Č. G.	91
Bárta Lubor	Br.	37			
Bartoš František	Č. G.	38	*Devátý* Antonín	Br.	93
Bartoš Jan Zdeněk	Č. G.	40	*Dobiáš* Václav	Č. G.	95
Bartoš Josef	Č. G.	43	*Dobrodinský* Bedřich	Br.	98
Bartovský Josef	Č. G.	45	*Donátová* Narcisa	L. M.	99
Barvík Miroslav	Č. G.	47	*Doubrava* Jaroslav	J. B.	99
Baur Jiří	Br.	49	*Doubravský* Petr	Č. G.	101
Bayerle Pavel	Br.	50	*Drejsl* Radim	jiva	102
Bažant Jaromír	jiva	51	*Ducháč* Miloslav	Br.	103
Bažant Jiří	Br.	51	*Ducháň* Jan	M. Č.	104
Bázlik Miroslav	L. M.	52	*Dusík* Gejza	L. M.	105
Bedřich Jan	Č. G.	53	*Dvořáček* Jiří	M. B.	106
Beneš Bedřich	Č. G.	54	*Dvorský* R. A.	Č. G.	107
Berg Josef	Č. G.	55			
Berkovec Jiří	E. H.	57	*Eben* Petr	E. H.	108
Bezubka Ladislav	Br.	59	*Elbert* Karol	L. M.	110
Bláha Václav	Č. G.	60			
Blahník Roman	Č. G.	60	*Fadrhons* Jan	Č. G.	111
Blatný Josef	B. Š.	61	*Feld* Jindřich	Br.	112
Blatný Pavel	Č. G.	63	*Felix* Václav	Č. G.	115
Blažek Zdeněk	B. Š.	64	*Ferenczy* Oto	L. M.	116
Boháč Josef	Č. G.	67	*Fiala* Jaromír	Br.	118
Bořkovec Pavel	J. B.	68	*Fiala* Jiří Julius	Br.	120
Borovička Antonín	Br.	70	*Fischer* Jan F.	Br.	121

15

Koštál Arnošt	Č. G.	243	*Martinů* Bohuslav	E. H.	293
Koštál Erno	Č. G.	244	*Máslo* Jindřich	Č. G.	298
Kovaříček František	Č. G.	245	*Maštalíř* Jaroslav	Br.	299
Kowalski Július	L. M.	245	*Matěj* Josef	Č. G.	301
Kozderka Ladislav	Č. G.	246	*Matuška* Janko	L. M.	302
Koželuha Lubomír	B. Š.	248	*Matys* Jiří	Č. G.	303
Kratochvíl Jiří	Č. G.	249	*Meier* Jaroslav	L. M.	304
Krautgartner Karel	jiva	250	*Mihule* Jiří	Č. G.	305
Krejčí Iša	Č. G.	251	*Mikoda* Bořivoj	Č. G.	306
Krejčí Miroslav	E. H.	253	*Mikula* Zdenko	L. M.	308
Kresánek Jozef	L. M.	255	*Mlejnek* Vilém		
Křička Jaroslav	Č. G.	257	Prokop	Č. G.	308
Křivinka Gustav	Č. G.	261	*Modr* Antonín	Č. G.	309
Křížek Zdeněk	Č. G.	263	*Móry* Ján	L. M.	311
Krombholz Jaroslav	E. H.	263	*Moyzes* Alexander	L. M.	311
Krotil Zdeněk	Č. G.	264	*Móži* Aladár	L. M.	314
Kubín Rudolf	Č. G.	265	*Móži* Július	L. M.	315
Kučera Václav	Č. G.	268			
Kunc Jan	B. Š.	269	*Nečas* Jaromír	Č. G.	316
Kupka Karel	Č. G.	271	*Nejedlý* Vít	Č. G.	316
Kupkovič Ladislav	L. M.	272	*Németh-Šamorinsky*		
Kvapil Jaroslav	B. Š.	273	Štefan	L. M.	318
Kyral Vilém	Br.	275	*Neumann* Věroslav	Č. G.	319
			Nikodem Bedřich	Č. G.	320
Langer Adolf	Br.	276	*Nováček* Blahoslav E.	Č. G.	321
Lenský Ctibor	L. M.	277	*Novák* Jan	Č. G.	322
Leopold Bohuslav	Č. G.	277	*Novák* Jiří F.	Č. G.	323
Letňan Július	L. M.	278	*Novák* Milan	L. M.	325
Lídl Václav	Br.	279	*Novosad* Lubomír	Č. G.	326
Lieskovský Andrej	L. M.	280			
Liška Zdeněk	Č. G.	280	*Oborný* Václav	Č. G.	327
Lucký Štěpán	Č. G.	281	*Obrovská* Jana	E. H.	328
Ludvík Emil	Č. G.	283	*Očenáš* Andrej	L. M.	328
Macák Bohumil	Č. G.	284	*Pádivý* Karol	L. M.	331
Mach Sláva			*Páleníček* Josef	Č. G.	331
(Pravoslav)	Č. G.	285	*Pálka* Dušan	Č. G.	333
Mácha Otmar	J. B.	286	*Palkovský* Oldřich	Č. G.	333
Macourek Karel	Č. G.	287	*Palouček* Alois	Č. G.	335
Macudzinski Rudolf	L. M.	289	*Parík* Ivan	L. M.	336
Malásek Jiří	Č. G.	289	*Parma* Eduard	Č. G.	337
Malina Jaroslav	L. V.	290	*Pauer* Jiří	Č. G.	338
Malovec Jozef	L. M.	291	*Pečke* Karel	Br.	340
Marat Zdeněk	Č. G.	292	*Pek* Albert	Č. G.	341
Martinček Dušan	L. M.	293	*Pelikán* Miroslav	Č. G.	343

16

Tausinger Jan	Č. G.	460	*Vipler* Vlastislav A.	Č. G.	490
Těšík Jan	J. T.	462	*Vlach-Vrutický* Josef	Č. G.	491
Thomsen Geraldine	Č. G.	463	*Vodák* Josef	Č. G.	492
Tichý František A.	Č. G.	463	*Vodrážka* Karel	Č. G.	493
Toman Josef	Č. G.	464	*Vogel* Jaroslav	Č. G.	494
Tomášek Jaroslav	Č. G.	465	*Voldán* Jiří	Br.	495
Tonkovič Pavol	L. M.	467	*Vomáčka* Boleslav	Č. G.	496
Trojan Václav	E. H.	467	*Vomáčka* Jaromír	Č. G.	499
Tylňák Ivan	Č. G.	469	*Vorlová* Sláva	Č. G.	499
			Vostřák Zbyněk	J. B.	502
Uhlíř Jan	Br.	470	*Vrána* František	J. B.	504
Ullrich Josef	Br.	471	*Vycpálek* Ladislav	E. H.	505
Urbanec Bartolomej	L. M.	472	*Vycpálek* Vratislav	Br.	508
Urbanec Rudolf	Br.	474	*Vyhnálek* Ivo	Č. G.	509
Vacek Karel	Br.	474	*Wolf* Alois	Br.	509
Vacek Karel Václav	Č. G.	475			
Vacek Miloš	Č. G.	477	*Zahradník* Zdeněk	Č. G.	510
Vačkář Dalibor	Č. G.	479	*Zelenay* Pavol	L. M.	511
Vačkář Václav	Č. G.	481	*Železný* Lubomír	Č. G.	512
Valašťan-Dolinský Ján	L. M.	483	*Zelinka* Jan E.	J. B.	512
Valdauf Karel	Č. G.	493	*Zeljenka* Ilja	L. M.	515
Válek Jiří	-k	484	*Zich* Jaroslav	Br.	516
Vignati Miloš	Br.	486	*Zimmer* Ján	L. M.	518
Vilec Michal	L. M.	489	*Zrno* Felix	Č. G.	520

CONTEMPORARY CZECHOSLOVAK COMPOSERS

A survey of individual composers in alphabetical
sequence (according to English alphabet)

AIM, Vojtěch Bořivoj

[born Rovné, 13 April 1886]

MERITED ARTIST

Aim studied at the Prague Conservatory piano and
organ, later composition under VÍTĚZSLAV NOVÁK.

He became director of the Music School at Tábor,
then inspector of music schools in Bohemia and, since
1935, professor of singing and choral conducting at the
Prague Conservatory. He was also in charge of radio
musical programmes for schools, chairman of the examination commission of teachers of music and voice
adviser of the Army Artistic Ensemble Vít Nejedlý.

He directed a number of conducting and singing
courses. Aim's long activity as a choirmaster, particularly of the Prague ensemble TYPOGRAFIA (with many
successful tours abroad—first prize in International
Competition of male choirs in 1948), had a strong
influence upon his creative work.

Instrumental Works

The core of Aim's creative work was in vocal compositions; but nonetheless his intrumental works are noteworthy. Amongst them are *The First Leaves* (1910
to 1911) and *In the Rain* (1917) both for piano, a cycle

of compositions for violin and piano *The Life* (1917) and further piano cycles *About a Little Urchin* (1928), *Rebirth* (1928) and in later years *Three Valses* (1951 to 1952), *Four Spring Polkas* (1952) and *From My Piano Diary* (1952).

Vocal Works

Songs: His other creative work includes song cycles *The First Songs* (1910—17), *The Pilgrim Bids Farewell* (1958) and *Towards New Spring* (1959).

Female choirs: Aim enriched Czech choral literature for women's voices particularly by the following cycles—*Three Four-part Female Choirs* (1916—18), *Flora Capricciosa* (1918), *The Storm* (1920), and in later years *Sparks* (1949), *Nature both Disturbed and Lovely* (1956), *Three Female Choirs* with piano accompaniment to words by Petr Bezruč (1957), *A Woman Sings* with piano accompaniment (1958), *Simple Songs About a Great Love* (1961) and *Mother and Children* (1964).

Male choirs: most outstanding of them are *Spring Songs from My Notebook* (1904—07), *Six Choirs* (1907—25), *From the Years of War* (1915), *Genuine Gaiety* (1907—27), *The Man* (1919—33), *A New World Rises* (1927), *World and Matter* (1937), *From French Poetry* (1938), *Twilight* (1938—39), *To the Depths* (1938—39) and then, after the war, *Tighten the Rigging—Let the Banners Wave!* (1945—48), *For My Country and a Better Life* (1949), *Forward!* (1949—51), *To Black-art and its Workers* (1956), *Sunny Old Age and Joyous Youth* (1956), *The Poet's Bitter Path* (1956), *Songs of Autumn of Life* (1957), *The Token of My Thanks* (1959), *To Prague* (1961), *My Home* (1961), *Songs* (1960—64) and *An Open Heart* (1964).

Mixed choirs: Noteworthy amongst them are *Centaurs* (1924), *The Lads from the Upper Hron* (1930), *Two Madrigals* (1930 and 1938), *The Triumphal Arch of May Day* (1945), *Lullaby* (1947), *A Starlit Evening* with piano accompaniment (1949), *The Day* for mixed choir and double choir (1957), *The Year* (1958), *An Eternal*

Return (1960), *Tabor Regions* (1960), *Fly Away, White Dove!* (1962), *Lillies-of-the-valley* (1962) and *The Mission* (1963).

Cantatas: Aim's three-movements composition *Suffering, Subjugation and Victory*, without text for solos, female choir and double choir (1939), the ten-section cycle of songs on suffering and redemption of man *Ecce homo*, for soprano, alto, tenor, baritone, bass baritone, bass and piano (1944—46), and the dramatic poem *To People All Over the World*, for solo voices, recitative, male choir and double choir (1960) occupy a special place in Czech vocal music.

Arrangements

Aim utilized his knowledge of vocal music in a large number of arrangements of folk songs and in children's choirs.

Writings

Aim applied his broad experiences as a pedagogue and choirmaster in his literary work *The Technique of Beating Time* (1952) and in his work, still in manuscript form, *The Rudiments of the Art of Singing*.

ALBRECHT, Alexander

[born Arad, Roumania, 12 August 1885—died Bratislava, 30 July 1958]

Albrecht belonged among the most significant personalities in the musical life of Slovakia during the period between the First and the Second World War. He studied the piano (ISTVÁN THOMÁN), composition (HANS KOESSLER) and conducting (F. SZANDTNER) at the Budapest Conservatory.

After graduation from the Conservatory as well as from the Law Faculty, he became a teacher of piano and theory of music at a music school and the organist at the Bratislava Cathedral. From 1921 until his retirement he was director of the City School of Music and choirmaster at the Cathedral. In the latter function, he was chairman of the Society for Church Music (an organization that played an important part in the pre-war musical life of Bratislava).

Albrecht was a personality with many broad interests. As a composer he endeavoured to arrive at a balanced use of new media of expression, particularly of harmony, and to preserve a continuity of late romanticism on a new level. In the last period of his creative work he began to respond actively to folklore stimuli.

Chamber and Orchestral Compositions

After the youthful *Piano Quintet*, Op. 6 (1913), Albrecht's work acquired a maturity, particularly in the *String Quartet* in D major, Op. 19 (1918), a composition performed very frequently both at home and abroad.

The symphonic suite *The Sleeping Beauty* (1921) is a romantically poetic work, inspired by personal experiences. On the other hand, The *Sonatina* for eleven solo instruments (1926), Albrecht's most vigorous composition from the point of view of tone and expression, is free from any subjective romantic traits.

In *Three Poems* from the cycle Marienleben by R. M. RILKE (1928) the composer returns to the underlying thought appearing in the Sleeping Beauty but achieves here a greater emotional intensity and depth of expression. In the symphonic poem *Longings and Recollections*, Albrecht wrote once more a large programme composition with a profound philosophical content.

After many years he returned to his earlier compositions with a *Concert Suite* for viola and piano (1952).

Vocal Works

His other creative work includes numerous song compositions, as well as the cantata *Šuhajko* (Country

Lad, 1950) which together with *Eight Slovak Folk Songs* for female (children's) choir (1950) are the most characteristic expression of his interest in Slovak folklore.

Music for Children

Albrecht wrote several cycles of compositions for children, stressing execution: eleven small *Instructive Compositions* for three-fourth violins (1953) and small compositions for piano for four hands *To Small Artists* (1957).

ALVÍN, František

[born Brno, 13 November 1898]

For many years he was active at the Bratislava Radio as a pianist, a member of the staff charged with musical programmes and later as their manager. In his compositions he has been a pupil of ALEXANDER ALBRECHT and of EUGEN SUCHOŇ.

He is one of the successful composers for children and youth, as is shown by his *A Day in a Pioneer Camp*.

He has composed as well songs for community singing, marches and cantatas (the small cantata *The May Song*) and cycles of songs for solos and orchestra (*Four Songs about Bratislava*, *Three Songs* and others).

AMBROS, Vladimír

[born Prostějov, 18 September 1891—died Prostějov, 12 May 1956]

Ambros graduated from the School for Organists in Brno as a pupil in composition of LEOŠ JANÁČEK.

He was opera accompanist in Frankfort-on-Main, where he studied simultaneously music under IVAN

KNORR. After eight years as conductor with an opera company in London, he returned home. He taught music at Prostějov and for several years he was director of the school of music at Břeclav. Later, he was active as conductor of the Moravian Philharmonic.

Stage Works

His creative activity as a composer was influenced particularly by LEOŠ JANÁČEK, JOSEF SUK and VÍTĚZSLAV NOVÁK. He composed three operas in which he gave expression to his musical dramatic sensibility.

His first opera *Stolen Happiness* (1924—25, première in Brno 1926) was set to a gloomy peasant drama from the Carpathian Ukraina, according to I. FRANKO.

His second opera *El Christo de la Luz* (1926, première in Bratislava, 1930) was inspired by one of the Three Legends About the Crucifix by JULIUS ZEYER.

The third opera *Maryla* was composed according to a tale of the same name by ALOIS JIRÁSEK (1951, première in Olomouc 1953).

Instrumental and Chamber Music

Ambros' temporary fondness for an exotic style and admiration for ALBAN BERG and IGOR STRAVINSKY were reflected in his *Four Exotic Dances* for chamber orchestra (1933), in his cycle of songs with chamber orchestra *Moods from Atlantis* (1940) and in his *Symphonic Poem* for nonet (1943).

Further, we should mention his *Episode* for chamber orchestra (1931), a *Spring Serenade* for small orchestra (1933), a *Puppet Suite* for chamber orchestra (1934) and a fantasy for wind quintet *Piccadilly* (1935).

His following works are in keeping with the expressive media of the period: three *String Quartets* (1936, 1940, 1945), a piano trio *Love* (1947), a piano *Quintet* (1949), *Three Compositions* for violin and piano (1949), a *Fantasy* (1949), a *Small Suite* for violoncello and piano (1950), a *Sonata* for violoncello and piano (1951), *Meditations to*

AMBROS

a Ukrainian Folk Song for string quartet (1952), *Two Moods* for violoncello and piano [*Lament—Joy*] (1952), six quartet *Miniatures* (1952), a *Small Quartet* (1953), a *Nonet* (1955) and a *Suite* for violin and piano (1955).

Orchestral Works

Ambros' orchestral forms are represented by a *Fantasy* set to folk songs from Moravian Slovakia for orchestra (1936), a *Sinfonietta* (1938—39), written under the impression of the Munich ultimatum, by three *Symphonies* [No. 1 (1941), No. 2 *The Symphony of Nature* (1944) and No. 3 *About our Beautiful Country* (1954)].

His works of smaller forms were *The Ballad of an Unborn Child* (1927, originally a melodrama to a poem of the same name by JIŘÍ WOLKER), the trilogy *Beskid Mountains* [*The Beskids* (1928)—*Fantasy* for violin and orchestra (1931)—*Spring of Life* (1932)], a *Concertino* for piano and orchestra (1948), a *Song of the Mountains* for small orchestra (1948), a *Peasant Suite* for full orchestra (1952), a *Comedy Overture* (1954) and a symphonic fantasy *Fairy-tale,* according to HANS CHRISTIAN ANDERSEN (1955).

Melodrama

The review of Ambros' compositional activity should be rounded out by a reference to his melodrama *May,* inspired by the poem of the same name by K. H. MÁCHA (1936).

Vocal Works

Of his numerous vocal compositions mention should be made of the songs *A Little Swan,* to words by PETR BEZRUČ (1934), of the song cycle *Adieu and A Little Kerchief,* set to words by VÍTĚZSLAV NEZVAL (1935), a *March Preludium* to words by ZDENĚK SPILKA for female choir with orchestra (1939), *The White Act* (1940), *Letters to the Sun and to the Beloved One* for soprano, flute, violin, viola, violoncello and harp (1948), *Humility* to

AMBROS

words by Jiří Wolker (1948), the cantatas *The Grand Return* (1950) and *The Mother* (1956), and a *Concerto* for violin and coloratura soprano with small orchestra (1952).

ANDRAŠOVAN, Tibor

[born Slovenská Ľupča, 2 April 1917]

Andrašovan is one of the most prolific and successful Slovak composers in the field of operetta, folk, film and scenic music. He studied at the Bratislava Faculty of Philosophy and at the Conservatory where he graduated from composition and conducting sections. For a short time he also studied musicology and conducting in Prague.

He was active as conductor of the Bratislava Opera and Ballet, in 1957—60 was artistic director of the Slovak Folk Art Ensemble and since that time has devoted himself completely to composition.

Stage Works

His sense for the scenic application of music led him to compose the ballets *Orpheus and Euridice* (1948, première in Bratislava, 1948) and *The Song of Peace* (1950, première in Bratislava, 1950), the successful operetta *Gentlemen Choose Your Partner!* and the comic opera *The Wag Geľo* (1958, première in Bratislava, 1958) as well as a great variety of incidental music.

Film Music

He has been equally successful in writing music to films (*The Native Land*, *Interrupted Song*).

Folklore Works

The essence of his creative work has been the many compositions for folklore ensembles which have become standard works of this genre in Slovak music. By their accentuated elemental nature, optimism and characteristic poetry of Slovak art, his folklore inspired compositions have gained great popularity. His most successful cyclic works in this genre include *The Tale About Jánošík*, *Detva Merry-making*, *The North Hron Country Feast*, *The Poprad Songs*, *Hey, Fishermen, Fishermen!*, *The Hrochot Songs* and others.

In 1949 Andrašovan was awarded the Czechoslovak National Prize for his music to the film *The Song of the Machines*. He also has been awarded the State Decoration of the Mongolian People's Republic for guest conducting. In acknowledgement of his compositions for youth, the Decree of Recognition was conferred upon him by the People's Republic of Poland.

AUST, Alois

[born Prague, 26 September 1889—died Prague, 11 November 1961]

Aust studied music privately. He has written about three hundred compositions.

Stage Works

He composed an operetta *Ondráš and Maryna*, based on Slovak folk songs, music to LADISLAV ŽILINSKÝ's comedy *The World at the Crossroads*.

Orchestral and Instrumental Works

An overture *In the Current of Life*, *The Libverda Serenade*, *The Last Romance* for violin with orchestra, and a *Cavatina* for violoncello and orchestra.

Dance & Incidental Music

A *Polonaise di bravura*, a concerto polka *For Pleasure*, a *Country Dance*, a *Dance of the Mountaineers*.

Of his valses, *Love's Gift*, a *Wish Fulfilled*, a *Silver Surface*, *Carlsbad Porcelain Figurines* and a *Spring Breeze*, together with many others, have become popular.

He has written as well a number of well-known polkas (*My Marietta*, *At Parting*), successful marches (*The Honours Man*, *In Union is Strength*, *Seven Years*, *The Film Star*, *At the Goal*, *Joyous Youth*, *Barandov*, *God-Speed!*)

Aust composed many musical medleys (*From Fairy-tale to Fairy-tale*, *Recollections of* KAREL HAŠLER, *Melodies of* VÁCLAV VAČKÁŘ, *Melodies of* BEDŘICH NIKODEM) and music to many gymnastic exercises.

Arrangements

He has made over five hundred arrangements for variety orchestra and brass band.

AXMAN Emil

[born Rataje, 3 June 1887—died Prague, 25 January 1949]

Axman studied musicology at Charles University, simultaneously devoting himself to the study of singing (FRANTIŠEK SPILKA) and of composition (VÍTĚZSLAV NOVÁK). After taking his doctor's degree, he became musical archivist of the National Museum in Prague and in 1948 was made chief of its administration.

After the First World War he was organizationally active in the Prague Society for Chamber Music.

In both his compositional and research interests, his creative efforts soon found expression in creative work, having their foundation in the spirit of the folk song, in the legacy of PAVEL KŘÍŽKOVSKÝ and ANTONÍN DVOŘÁK, and growing out of the school of VÍTĚZSLAV NOVÁK and the example of LEOŠ JANÁČEK. Axman arrived at an individual expression of virile lyricism and of dramatic conflicts.

With the exception of opera, his creative work embraces every compositional field.

Orchestral Works

His six *Symphonies* [first *Tragic* (1926), second *Giocosa* (1927, produced at the Festival of Contemporary Music in Frankfort-on-Main 1928), third *Spring* (1928), fourth *Eroica* (1932), fifth *Dithyrambic* (1936) and sixth *Patriotic* (1942)] and four *Concertos* [for violin (1936), for piano (1939), for violoncello (1940) and double-concerto for violin and violoncello with full orchestra (1944)] brought to Czech symphonic literature a new quality.

Further we have to mention the symphonic poems *Sorrows and Hopes* (1919—20) and *A Bright Sky* (1921—22), *Sinfonietta* (1923) and an orchestral *Dumka* and *Gay Rondino* (1933).

Axman's other compositions for smaller orchestra include a suite *From the Beskids* (1934), *Fantasy on a Moravian Folk Song* (1934), two series of *Moravian Dances* (1935 and 1939), a *Serenade* (1937) and *Three Concert Valses* (1945). The *Suite* in the form of variations (1948) was Axman's last orchestral work.

Chamber Music

In his work, the chamber music is represented by following compositions: piano *Sonatas* No. 1 and 2 (both 1922) and piano *Sonatina* (1922), a *Sonata* for violin and piano (1924), a *Sonata* for violoncelllo and piano (1924), piano *Sonata* No. 3 (1924), a *Trio* for violin, violoncello and piano (1924—25), *String Quartet* No. 1 (1924), No. 2 (1925), a piano cycle *Moravia Sings* (1925, instrumented 1935), *String Quartet* No. 3 (1929), a *Quintet* for wind instruments (1938), a *Suite* for string quartet (1940), a *Divertimento* for nonet (1944), *Three Moravian Dances* for a nonet (1944), *Variations*, a fantasy for string quartet (1944) and *String Quartet* No. 4 (1946).

Vocal Works

Axman's songs are imbued with an ardent vigour. They include the song cycles with orchestra *Recollections* (1918) and *Rainbow* (1921), *The Night* with string quartet (1924, reworked in 1929 for voice and piano), *Psalms* (1928), *At the Flame* (1930), *Autumn Bathing* to words by JAROSLAV KOLMAN-CASSIUS (1937), *Songs of Home* (1946) and a *Bouquet from Moravia* (1947).

In his choirs, particularly in his male choirs, Axman enriched his inspirational flow by a new technique and a captivating vigour of expression, as witnessed by the *Two Choirs From the War* [*(Medinia Glogowska)* to a poem by PETR KŘIČKA and the *Report* to words by FRÁŇA ŠRÁMEK (1916)], and the choirs *The Voice of the Earth* (1926), and *On Mother's Grave* (1928).

His cantatas have exceptional musical value. They include *My Mother* to an elegy by Otakar Březina (1926), *A Ballad on the Eyes of a Stoker* to words of a compassionate poem by Jiří Wolker (1927), *Ilonka Beniačová*, according to a poetic tale by J. V. Rosůlek (1930), *The Cemetery of Sobotka* to words by Fráňa Šrámek (1931) and *Stabat Mater* (1938) in which the text of religious sequence is only an allegory expressing the sufferings of the author's native country.

Arrangements

They are an important supplement to the composer's creative work. They include *A Wreath of Songs from Moravian Slovakia*, *A Bouquet of Czech Songs*, *Russian National Songs* and *Eleven Songs from Moravian Slovakia*.

Writings

As a musicologist Axman occupied himself with the problems of musical life in Moravia [*Moravian Operas of the Eighteenth Century* (1912)]; the edition of the Haná song-play *Jora and Manda* (1912); *Moravia in Czech Music of the Nineteenth Century* (1920); further he has taken up the creative work of *Bedřich Smetana, Antonín Dvořák, Zdeněk Fibich* and *J. B. Foerster.*

He is as well the author of an essay on *Leoš Janáček* in the Almanac of the Czech Academy (1929) and of many articles and essays written for various periodicals.

BABUŠEK, František

[born Bratislava, 5 November 1905—died Bratislava 13 October 1954]

Babušek was originally a member of Bratislava and Prague Radio Orchestras. In 1939, after completing the study of conducting (PAVEL DĚDEČEK) and composition (VÍTĚZSLAV NOVÁK, JOSEF SUK, JAROSLAV KŘIČKA) at the Prague Conservatory, he became conductor of the Symphonic Orchestra of the Bratislava Radio (in 1942 to 1952 as chief conductor).

Orchestral & Instrumental Works

His intense conducting activity interfered with his promise as a composer; this was evident in his *Fantasy* for organ and orchestra, *Prelude* for strings and in his *Nonet.* In these works he indicated an inclination to exacting counterpoint work and a clear and straightforward expressive media.

The breadth of Babušek's talent was, however, demonstrated in the works written during the last years before his premature death: a *Piano Concerto* in D minor (1950), a cantata for choir and orchestra *The Song of Life* (1951) and a symphonic poem *Hail, the People!* (1952).

Radio & Popular Compositions

His further compositions came into being in connection with the needs of radio transmissions—scenic music, popular symphonic compositions (*Valse triste,*

a small *Overture*, a *Slovak Dance*, a *Polish Dance*); but
in particular he made extensive arrangements and fantasies based on Slovak folk songs (*A Slovak Rhapsody* for
orchestra, a *Slovak Family Sings*, for children, female and
male voices and orchestra, and a symphonic idyll *Slovak
Merry-making*).

BAKALA, Břetislav

[born Fryšták, 12 February 1897—died Brno, 1 April 1958]

MERITED ARTIST

He was a pupil of LEOŠ JANÁČEK (composition), FRAN-
TIŠEK NEUMANN (conducting) and VILÉM KURZ (piano).

Bakala was an excellent accompanist (he toured
abroad with the Dutch violoncellist HANS KINDLER)
and choirmaster, directing the VACH Choir of MORAVIAN
WOMEN TEACHERS.

With the exception of a one-year stay in the United
States (with Kindler) he was active in Brno as opera
conductor, the conductor and later chief of the Radio
Orchestra and eventually chief conductor of the State
Philharmonic.

As a conductor he was an enthusiastic propagator of
Czechoslovak contemporary music, particularly of the
works of LEOŠ JANÁČEK and VÍTĚZSLAV NOVÁK.

Instrumental Compositions and Chamber Music

He devoted himself only occasionally to composition;
he wrote a *Sonata* for violoncello and piano (1915—18),
a *String Quartet* in C major (1919) and orchestral *Scherzo*
(1922, arranged for small orchestra in 1927).

Vocal Works

His most mature and best known creative work was
a *Christmas Lullaby* for soprano and piano [or orchestra]
(1946). He was as well the author of many Moravian

folk songs arrangements: Four folk songs for female choir with piano *From Our Slovácko* (Moravian Slovakia), ten *Wallachian Songs* for mixed choir with piano, thirty-three folk songs from the Zlín region for male choir, a montage of carols for solos, female choir and children's choir with orchestra.

He arranged and revised compositions of LEOŠ JANÁČEK.

BALATKA, Antonín

[born Prague, 27 October 1895—died Brno, 25 June 1958]

MERITED ARTIST

After a short career as a teacher, Balatka devoted himself to the study of music at the Prague Conservatory. He studied the organ under ONDŘEJ HORNÍK and JOSEF KLIČKA and composition under KAREL STECKER and JAROSLAV KŘIČKA. At the Master School of the Conservatory he was a pupil of VÍTĚZSLAV NOVÁK.

In 1919, he became accompanist of the opera in Ljubljana in Yugoslavia, where he became later conductor and manager. Simultaneously he taught at the Ljubljana Conservatory and at the School of Vocal Art.

From the year 1929 he has been conductor of opera in Brno, where he introduced many new Czech and Yugoslav operas and ballets and translated and produced numerous other operas. He also taught at the Brno Conservatory.

After the Second World War he was appointed administrator of the Brno Opera and in 1951 senior lecturer at the Janáček Academy of Musical Arts.

Stage Works

Due to Balatka's theatrical activities, he wrote numerous scenic compositions for various plays, the opera *Holy Spring* (1952), the ballet *Morning Land* (1927,

première in Ljubljana in 1927) and music to K. J.
ERBEN's *The Bouquet* (1943).

He has written also music to the radio montage, set to
words of the poet K. H. MÁCHA entitled *Long Is My
Journey—Vain Is My Cry* (1936).

Chamber Music and Orchestral Compositions

Of his chamber music works, the *Piano Trio* (1919)
and *Suite* for flute, clarinet and bassoon (1927) attracted
considerable attention, the same being true of his
orchestral compositions *Scherzo* (1926) and *The Serbian
Round* (1926).

Vocal Works

Balatka achieved success as a composer with his cantata
A Song About the Supreme Commander (1952) and by the
female choir *A Weaver Sings*, set to words by F. SEMERÁ-
KOVÁ (1950). Furthermore he has written *South Bohemian Songs* for mixed choir (1940), male choir *Lidice*
(1955), numerous youth and pioneer songs, arrangements
of Slovenian folk songs and others.

Writings

Balatka wrote many articles on music and it was due
to his efforts that Czech music became well-known in
Yugoslavia.

At home, Balatka's musical literary activity for
HUDEBNÍ ROZHLEDY (Musical Review) and other
publications is important as well.

He was chairman of the Brno branch of the Guild of
Czechoslovak Composers.

BALCAR, Milan
[born Ostrava, 13 December 1886—died Místek, 16 April 1954]

Balcar studied the Technical College but early
matriculated at the composition section of the Prague

Conservatory. After graduation he was active in Zara (Dalmatia) as teacher and choirmaster. After the First World War he returned to his native town where he was active as a pedagogue, appearing as well on concert platforms as a concert pianist.

Instrumental and Chamber Music

Balcar's instrumental chamber music is represented by two *String Quartets*, Op. 1 in C minor (1908) and Op. 2 in D minor (1909), a violin *Sonata* in B major, Op. 4 (1910), piano compositions *The Three Voices of My Life*, Op. 8 (1921), *The Sonata of the Heart*, Op. 23 (1933) and the *Jáchymov Suite*, Op. 25 (1937), a *Sonata* in E minor for violoncello and piano, Op. 33 (1943), a *Suite* in D major for violin and piano, Op. 34 (1943), *Variations* on the composer's own theme for string quartet, Op. 35 (1943), *The Frenštát Idyll* for wind quintet, Op. 31 (1943), *Dance Suite* for wind quintet, Op. 37 (1945), *Spring Sonata* for clarinet and piano, Op. 40 (1945), *Variations* on the composer's own song for piano, Op. 41 (1945), a suite for oboe and piano *Female Portraits*, Op. 46 (1952) and a *Piano Trio*, Op. 48 (1952).

Vocal Works

His work is marked by song lyricism, tying in with the creative work of ZDENĚK FIBICH and J. B. FOERSTER, as testified to by these compositions: *An Evening Ballad*, Op. 3 (1910), *Simple Motifs* set to a poem by JAN NERUDA, Op. 5 (1909—12), *With Awakened Spring*, Op. 7 (1911—13), *Songs of a Recluse*, Op. 9 (1922), *A Wedding Song* to words of the poem Madame von Stein by J. W. GOETHE, Op. 10 (1923), *Three Prayers*, Op. 12 1920—1925), *Longing*, Op. 13 (1909, 1926), *Cosmic Songs* set to poems by JAN NERUDA, Op. 14 (1920—26), *A Three Leaf Clover*, Op. 18 (1930), *The Avowal*, Op. 32 (1943), *The Betrothal*, Op. 36 (1945), *Melancholy*, Op. 42 (1948), *Czech Songs* set to poems by JAROSLAV VRCHLICKÝ, Op. 44 (1948).

BALCAR

Reflections on Balcar's native countryside are among others his *Beskid Songs* to poems by PETR BEZRUČ, *Songs from Horečky* (Little Hills) to words by JOSEF KALUS, a cycle of songs *The Wallachian Muse* and the *Miners' Songs*.

Numerous choirs complete this survey of Balcar's compositional work.

BALLING, Karel
[born Rakovník, 17 December 1889]

Balling was a pupil of J. S. SYCHRA and JAROSLAV KŘIČKA. He is inseparably associated with the history of the Czech cabaret (founded the cabaret group IGNOTUS and in 1911—20 was one of the originators of the famous literary and political cabaret THE RED SEVEN).

In the period between the two World Wars he was one of the outstanding representatives of the popular trend in Czech music. This is evidenced by the large number of successful chansons and dance music he wrote during that time.

Stage Music

Balling occupied himself with the operetta (*My Heart for a Smile, Aunt Agatha, Barnabas Rages*, the operetta burlesque *Anatol Is Getting Married* to a libretto by the famous Czech opera singer EMMY DESTIN). The ballet *The Christmas Present of the Composer Sesadílek* is his last musical dramatic work.

Orchestral Music

In the field of orchestral music he wrote a *Fantastic Overture* in D minor, a *Small Overture* in C minor, *Czech Dances*, a *Ballet Suite* and a suite *The Old Town*.

Instrumental Music

Balling composed two violin serenades, *Variations* for harp and the *Glass Fountain* for harp and flute.

●

Particular note should be paid to Balling's sustained activity on behalf of the Authors' Association for Protection of Rights on Musical Works.

BÁRTA, Lubor

[born Lubná, 8 August 1928]

Bárta studied musicology and aesthetics at Charles University in Prague and simultaneously composition at the Academy of Musical Arts in the class of JAROSLAV ŘÍDKÝ.

Chamber Music

His initial works were in the field of chamber music and include *Sonata* for violin and piano (1949), *String Quartet* No. 1 (1950), *Divertimento* for wind quintet (1950), *Sonatina* for trombone and piano (1956), *String Quartet* No. 2 (1956), *Wind Quintet* (1958), *Sonata* for clarinet and piano (1958), the *Second Sonata* for violin and piano (1958, awarded in the artistic jubilee competition in 1960) and *Concertino* for trombone and piano (1964).

Instrumental and Orchestral Works

Sonata for piano (1956), *Second Sonata* for piano (1959), a symphonic suite *From Eastern Bohemia* (1961), *Concert Overture* (1963) and *Ludi* for orchestra (1964).

Vocal Music

Five Love Songs to verses by Italian renaissance poets

(1955), *Children's Songs* for voice and piano (1957) and a cantata for mixed choir and full orchestra *A Song of the New Age*, inspired by flights into the cosmic space (1962).

Various

He is as well the author of compositions for youth and variety ensembles.

Prizes

In 1951, Bárta was awarded a prize at the Second Festival of Youth in Berlin for his *Komsomol Cantata* to words by VLADIMIR MAJAKOVSKY; in 1957 for his *May Sonnet* in the competition at the Festival of Youth in Moscow; his *Concerto* for chamber orchestra (1956) was awarded the principal prize in the Canadian International Competition in 1963.

For his *Second Sonata* for piano and the *Song of the New Age* he was awarded the State Prize in the artistic jubilee competition 1965.

BARTOŠ, František

[born Brněnec, 13 June 1905]

Holder of the decoration FOR OUTSTANDING WORK

Bartoš studied composition at the Prague Conservatory under K. B. JIRÁK and at the Master School under J. B. FOERSTER.

As a composer he has found a path for a contemporary style while at the same time respecting a clear formal arrangement, with voices not overtaxed and maintaining a musical flow with a proper rhythmic cadence. An inclination towards musical grotesqueness is also characteristic in his creative work.

Instrumental and Chamber Music

Among his chamber music works are to be mentioned: *String Sextet* (1926), two *String Quartets* (1928 and 1935), *Orchestra Suite* for music to a farce (1928), *Radio music* for chamber orchestra (1936), suite for wind quartet *The School of Women* (1936), *Duo* for violin and viola (1937) and *Trio* for oboe, clarinet and bassoon (1958).

The suite for wind quintet *The Bourgeois Nobleman* (1934), well-conceived from the point of view of invention and sound, has for the time being the greatest success of all his compositions.

Vocal Works

His compositional development is evident from the following works:

Songs: song cycles *Bouquet de l'amour* (1924), *Three Songs* set to texts of French poetry (1928), *Burlesques* (1934), *Rainy Pictures* (1945) and the *Black...* (1959);

choirs: *Music on the Square* (1927), *"1917" and Love* (1939), *Two Female Choirs* to words of JAN NERUDA (1942);

melodrama: *Spring* (1925).

Arrangements and Incidental Music

The composer's musical personality is best proved by his arrangements of folk songs (*The Rusava Songs*, programmes of carols *Christmas* and *Songs of Old France*), incidental music and music for the film *The Castle of Prague* by ALEXANDER HACKENSCHMIED.

Writings

A deep admiration and esteem for the founder of Czech national music BEDŘICH SMETANA has prompted Bartoš to undertake the editorial work on a study publication of the scores of Smetana's works and on a revision of the piano arrangements of Smetana's operas.

Equally meritorious and significant is his activity as

chairman of the editorial committee for the publication of ANTONÍN DVOŘÁK's complete works.

Bartoš has been instrumental also in the publication of a number of important musical documents, such as *Mozarts in Letters, The Autobiography of Vojtěch Jírovec* (Girowetz), a documentary picture of Smetana's personality *Smetana in Memories and Letters*, the most popular book about a great artist and man (in addition to nine Czech editions, it has appeared as well in English and German) and *Gustav Mahler's Correspondence*.

Formerly, Bartoš was also active as critic and editor of the review TEMPO. As organizer, he was active in the Czech Philharmonic and took part at the inception of the *Prague Spring Music Festival*.

BARTOŠ, Jan Zdeněk

[born Dvůr Králové on Labe, 4 June 1908]

Holder of the decoration FOR OUTSTANDING WORK

Bartoš studied at the Prague Conservatory under OTAKAR ŠÍN and JAROSLAV ŘÍDKÝ and at the Master School under JAROSLAV KŘIČKA. At present, he is professor of the theory of music and of composition at the Prague Conservatory.

He is an author of extensive and varied compositional work. His development was first influenced by his long activity as an instrumentalist.

Stage Works

He has composed a one-act opera, taken from contemporary life, entitled *The Cursed Castle* (1951, première at Ústí on Labe 1951 and at Neustrelitz [German Democratic Republic] in 1963), the four-act opera *The Sky Attacked* (1955) on a theme of the Paris Commune; then a full-length melodramatic ballet *Hanu-*

man (1941), a full-length ballet *Mirella* (1962) and a shorter ballet *The King of the Manège* (1963); further a three-act operetta *Pineapples, If You Please* (1956) and a dramatic montage *We, the Miners* (1950), as well as two musical plays and several scenic compositions.

Orchestral Works

His compositional work has reached new hights in his two symphonies: *The First Symphony*, op. 65 (1949 to 1952) and the *Second Symphony* (Chamber), op. 78 (1956).

A mention should be made about two *Feuilletons* for symphonic orchestra, op. 6 (1935), and a *Students' Suite* for string orchestra, op. 25 (1941); then three symphonic poems *St. Matthew's Song*, op. 37 (1945), *Events of a Single Day*, op. 80 (1958) and *Intermezzo* for full orchestra, op. 89 (1961); further *Fantasy* for flute and orchestra (1964) and the *Third Symphony* for string orchestra (1964—65).

Instrumental and Chamber Music

Bartoš has applied his innate compositional talent with the most effectiveness for the time being in his chamber music.

This is shown in his *Sonata* for violoncello and piano, op. 17 (1938), in a *Nonet*, op. 19 (1939) and in his nine *String Quartets* (1940—62), as well as in his three *Wind Quintets* (1946—63).

After a temporary accentuation of chromatics— a *Concertino* for bassoon and orchestra (or piano), op. 34 (1943) and a *Sonatina* for viola and piano, op. 46 (1947) —a turning point occured in his creative work with an emphasis on a balance in the choice of harmonic means, even though he sometimes arrived at complicated harmmonic combinations, as for inst. in *String Quartet* No. 5, *May the Whole World be a Garden*, op. 66 (1952).

His recent works show the same phenomenon; these are: a *Divertimento* for nine wind instruments, op. 79

41   BARTOŠ J. Z.

(1957), a *Harp Trio* for violin and viola with harp, op. 91 (1961), a *Sonata* for doublebass and piano, op. 93 (1962), a *Concerto* for oboe and string orchestra, op. 95 (1962), a *Concerto da Camera* per oboe ed archi, op. 97 (1963), *Prelude* for flute and piano, op. 98 (1963), a *Concerto* for viola and instrumental ensemble, op. 99 (1963) and a *Suita Concertante* (chamber) for viola, double-bass and nine wind instruments (1964).

Among these are solo compositions, as a *Partita* for viola, op. 36 (1944), a *Sonata* for piano, op. 70 (1955) and a *Sonata Giocosa*, op. 82 (1959).

Vocal Works

His compositions in vocal field did not lack the melodic trends of the day; they are, first of all,

songs: a song cycle *About Jack* (O Honzovi), op. 14 (1937), *Three Intimate Songs* for baritone and piano, op. 26 (1941), three meditations for mezzosoprano, viola and piano *My Pilgrimage*, op. 28 (1943) and the song cycle *The Song of Springs*, op. 35 (1944); then follow

cantatas: they were written in the same form— *The Peace Runner*, op. 47 (1948), *To Live in Peace*, op. 61 (1951), a meditation on Štursa's statue *The Wounded* op. 76 (1956), a *Message*, op. 84 (1960, which was awarded in the artistic jubilee competition in 1960), the *Country of Comenius* for baritone, female choir, two oboes, two horns, two fagots and piano, op. 90 (1961), and *Sonnets about Prague* for tenor and instrumental ensemble (1964).

●

His manifold musical creation is shown in numerous song cycles and choirs, instrumental and instructive compositions, light and dance music.

He wrote also music to the First Spartakiad (1955).

Writings

Bartoš compositional work is supplemented by his pedagogic, organizational, editorial and critical activities. In an entertaining manner he has written about musical forms in his book *Reading on Musical Forms* (1960).

For the Television Conservatory he wrote a treatise *The Development of Musical Forms and Genres* (1963—64).

BARTOŠ, Josef

[born Nová Paka, 10 February 1902]

After completing the secondary school, Bartoš entered the Prague Conservatory, graduating from the sections of piano, conducting and composition and from the Master School under VÍTĚZSLAV NOVÁK. He continued the study of composition with VINCENT D'INDY in Paris at the Schola cantorum. He graduated as well from Charles University in Prague where he studied musical science.

Bartoš was a pianist in the trio of the Slavonic Institute in Paris, choirmaster of the choral society at Nový Bydžov, director of musical school in Těšín and accompanist and later choirmaster at the theatre in Olomouc and Pardubice.

From 1939 he has been professor of obligatory piano at the Prague Conservatory as well as of the study of melodrama at its dramatic school and since 1945, professor of musical theoretical subjects.

Stage Works

Bartoš has composed a three-act opera *The Rebels* (1953—56), and has written a melodrama on verses of contemporary poets *Meeting with Time*, op. 47 (1961).

Orchestral Works

He has written a *Theme with Variations* for piano and orchestra, op. 5 (1935) and four orchestral *Suites*.

43

Chamber Music

Of his many compositions we mention only a few ones: a piano *Trio*, op. 10 (1932), *Concertino* for accorddion, accompanied by string orchestra, op. 37 (1958), a *Sonatina* for violin, viola and violoncello, two wind *Quintets*, *Four Compositions* for violin and piano, op. 44 (1960), a *Cassation* for wind quintet, op. 45 (1961), a *Bucolic Suite* for oboe and piano, op. 47 (1961), a *Sonatina* for flute and piano, op. 48 (1962), a *Serenade* for flute, guitar, viola and violoncello, op. 50 (1962) and a *Village Serenade* for wind instruments, op. 52 (1964).

Instrumental Works

Among his compositions for one instrument are to be mentioned: three *Sonatinas* for piano, the piano cycle *Music for Youth*, op. 27 (1947) and several other cyclic compositions for piano, furthermore *Small Preludes* for organ, op. 38 (1958), *Fantasy and Toccata* for piano, op. 41 (1959), and a *Small Dance Suite* for accordion, op. 42 (1960).

Vocal Works

He composed several cycles of songs and choirs, among which we mention the following:

Songs—*Joyous Songs of Youth* with piano accompaniment, op. 36 (1958);

male choirs—*The Songs of the Beskid Mountains*, op. 14 (1947), *To the Land of the Mountaineers*, op. 19 (1947) and *May Days*, op. 28 (1949);

mixed choirs—*Three Songs of Peace*, op. 39 (1958) and

cantatas—*The Heroic Ballad*, op. 13 (1934), *The Unknown Soldier*, op. 18-1 (1940), *Kitty*, op. 18-2 (1940 to 1941) and a *Song of the Homeland*, op. 30 (1951) were inspired by social themes.

Deserving mention among his recent works are *Love Songs* to words by SYLVA KAPUTIKJANOVA, op. 49 (1962).

Bartoš has also written numerous arrangements of folk songs and folk dances.

Writings

He elaborated theoretical surveys on musical instruments, on the general theory of music, on harmony, counterpoint and musical forms.

BARTOVSKÝ, Josef

[born Stupno, 3 December 1884—died Pilsen, 19 November 1964]

MERITED TEACHER

Bartovský studied composition at the Master School of the Prague Conservatory under VÍTĚZSLAV NOVÁK. He became professor of musical subjects at the Teachers' Training College in Pilsen and has written more than eighty compositions.

Stage Works

Bartovský's extensive compositional activity includes three one-act operas: *At the Golden Sun* (1911), *The Bishop's Niece* (1938—40, première in Pilsen 1946) and *The Burdock* (1938—40), four full-length operas: *The Song of the Blue Mountains* (1923—24, première in Pilsen 1925), *Wenceslas of Michalovice* (1926—27, première in Pilsen 1928), *A Woman in a Triangle* (1931, première in Pilsen 1937) and *The Ways of Reconciliation* (1950—52), the ballet pantomime *The Primroses* (1932—33) and four melodramas.

Chamber Music

In this field he composed ten string quartets, two piano quintets, a wind quintet, two trios, a sextet, four violin sonatas, sonatas for wind instruments (oboe,

English horn, clarinet), a viola suite, three violoncello sonatas, three concertinos for piano, violin and trombone, and a number of piano compositions.

Orchestral Works

In addition to two *Symphonies* [in A major (1922) and in C sharp minor (1942)], he wrote eight symphonic poems: *The Song of Life* (1912), *Confiteor* (1915), *Kačerov* (1920), *Per aspera ad astra* (1933), *Ex Ponto* (1940) and a trilogy *Ars longa, vita brevis* (1944).

He also wrote two piano *Concertos* [first in 1934 and the second in 1950 (for left hand only)], a *Concerto* for flute (1954), three suites, four rhapsodies and a sinfonietta.

Vocal Works

Bartovský enriched the Czech vocal literature by five cantatas [*Our Song, The Spirit of Žižka, Ritornellos, Mácha's May, In Honour of Work*), a full-length cycle of nine cantatas *I Sing to Thee, my Country* (1939—45), seventeen cycles of songs and ten cycles of choirs, three ballads set to words of Moravian and Slovak folk poetry, The *Portuguese Sonnets* for mezzosoprano and chamber music accompaniment, three series of *Songs from the Pilsen Region* for male, female and mixed choirs, *Gay Polkas* from Rokycany region for two-part choir and orchestra, and a number of arrangements of folk songs.

●

For brass band Bartovský composed ten *Pilsen Polkas*.

●

In the years 1954—62 he worked over his opera *At the Golden Sun*, wrote a two part *School for String Orchestra* (for the needs of the People's Schools of Art), composed a number of smaller vocal and chamber music compositions and revised his orchestral and chamber music works.

BARVÍK, Miroslav

[born Lužice, Moravia, 14 September 1919]

Holder of the KOREAN ORDER OF THE STATE BANNER

Barvík studied composition under VÁCLAV KAPRÁL and JAROSLAV ŘÍDKÝ and privately with VÍTĚZSLAV NOVÁK. Because of his compositional, pedagogic, lectorial, journalistic, musicological and organizational activities, he became one of the significant personalities among the younger Czech musical generation.

From 1948 he taught history of music and since 1957 composition at the Prague Conservatory.

Stage Works

In 1960, Barvík completed the opera "1944" (The Partisans), set to a libretto by STEFAN LADIŽINSKY, and in 1962 the oratorio *The Argonauts*.

He has written as well scenic music to the plays *Dukla* by JAN MAREŠ, *Dalskabáty* by JAN DRDA "...As We Forgive Others", and to the Korean play *South of the 38th Parallel*.

Orchestral Works

Barvík has composed a *Sinfonietta* for orchestra and organ (1942), an orchestral suite *Dances from Moravian Slovakia*, a *Symphony* (1944—47), a rhapsody for full orchestra *Dimitrov* (1952) and music to the dance pictures *Recruiting the Gallant* [symphonic dances] (1956—57).

Chamber Music

Among his works noteworthy are two violoncello *Sonatas* (1940 and 1943), a *Sonatina* for oboe and piano (1956) and four *String Quartets*.

Instrumental Works

He devoted himself to piano compositions, as a two-movement piano sonata *Lidice* (1943), three *Sonatinas* (1944) and a cycle of small instructive compositions.

Vocal Works

The core of Barvík's compositional activity lies in vocal music in which he often draws on some characteristic trait of Moravian Slovak folk songs:

Voices and songs — a cycle *Gardener*, set to words by RABINDRANATH TAGORE (1947), a song about Julius Fučík *He Shall Be With Us* (1953), a cycle *I Shall Find You*, to words by STIEPAN SHCHIPACHOV (1954), and a cycle *About Love and Faithfulness*, set to Vietnam folk poetry for soprano and piano (1964).

Female choirs: *A Song About the Soviet Land* for solo, female choir and piano (1951),

Male choirs: three choirs *Žermanice*, set to poems of PETR BEZRUČ (1942—43), a cycle *Before the Coming of the Red Army* (1945), *A Song of the Native Land*, set to words by JOSEF HORA (1945), *Salute to the Soviet Union* and *Peace* (1950), *To Prague*, set to a poem by JAROSLAV SEIFERT (1953) and a *Wish* (1954), *We shall March Together* (1956), *My Sweet Home* (1956), a two-movement *Vocal Symphony* for male choir to words by A. SURKOV and J. SEIFERT (1959), *The Party* (1962) and *Love Song* (1964).

Mixed choirs: *Two Songs about Stalin* (1949).

Children choir: *For the Republic* (1949).

Cantatas: *Thanks to the Soviet Union*, written on the occasion of the thirtieth anniversary of the Great October Revolution (1947), a popularized cantata-ballad *Hands Off Korea* (1950), a *Cantata about Gottwald* (1952), *Prague Spring*, set to words by VÍTĚZSLAV NEZVAL (1952), a small cantata *Dukla* (1957), and many community songs, military and pioneer songs and arrangements to folk songs.

His song *My Dearest One* was awarded in the artistic jubilee competiton in 1960.

Film Music

He composed music to the film *A Weekday* and *A Great Opportunity* (1949—50).

Writings

Recently, Barvík embarked on an extensive drive in the field of educational concerts and popularization of music, particularly in the radio and television. As a result of this activity are his publications *How to Listen to Music* and *Discourses on Music*; both were awarded in the artistic jubilee competition in 1960.

Of his other publications, mention should be made of *The Theory of Music* (second edition in 1946), *I Want to Learn how to Modulate* (1947), *Aesthetic Appreciation of Music* (1948), *A Survey of Musical Acoustics* (1949), *A Musician's Tour of the Soviet Union* (1956), *Milan Harašta—Unfinished Life and Work* (1956), *One Hundred Famous Composers* (1963) and *Music of Revolutions* (1963).

In cooperation with KAREL TAUŠ, he worked over *Malát's Brief Musical Dictionary* (the fifth edition in 1960).

He is chief-editor of PEOPLE's CONSERVATORY (issued by the Publishing House of the Guild of Czechoslovak Composers PANTON), for which he wrote a treatise *Don't Be Afraid of Musical Theory* (1964).

For the School Edition of SUPRAPHON he elaborated *Lessons on Sounds from Musical Science*.

He is chairman of the collective that is preparing a *Musical Encyclopedia*.

Barvík is a member of the Committee of the PRAGUE SPRING MUSIC FESTIVAL.

BAUR, Jiří
[born Prague, 15 July 1923]

After the Second World War he founded the dance ensemble *Swing Stars* together with VLASTIMIL HÁLA. In 1946 he joined the orchestra of KAREL VLACH.

His work is entirely oriented to jazz music: *Mambo*; ¶ the blues *Who is Whistling Here?*; ¶ the foxtrots: *If I*

Did not Love You, When the Alarm-Clock Rings, The Black-bird and the Shoemaker, A Little Lie, The Song about the Double Bass, I Got a Letter, Such is Life, Now and Tomorrow Forever, Always in a Hurry, Vindobona, The Most Beloved of All; ¶ the rock: *My Son Peter* (in collaboration with Vlastimil Hála); ¶ the waltz *A Few Words,* and others.

Baur and Vlastimil Hála collaborated in the musical comedies *The Circus Orion, A Woman on Wednesday, Let Susanne Sing, Three Oranges* and *I Love, I Love.*

He composes as well incidental music for films and television and collaborates in making arrangements for the orchestra of Karel Vlach.

BAYERLE, Pavel

[born Trutnov, 31 March 1925]

Graduated from the School of Pharmacy. His keen interest in music prompted him to study composition with JAROSLAV KOFROŇ, JAN RYCHLÍK and ALEXEJ FRIED.

At present, he is chief conductor of the dance orchestra which is a part of the Military Variety Ensemble in Prague.

As a composer, he achieved success with his dance and variety music including the following: ¶ the slow foxtrot *The Story of Our Love*; ¶ the foxtrots: *The Ostrich Adventure* and *About Us Two* (published and recorded in the German Democratic Republic), *The Morning March*; ¶ the lipsi: *Count to Six, A Náchod Polka*; ¶ the valse: *To Be Spring,* a *Cuban Dance,* the trumpet solo *Meditation*; ¶ the twist *A Little Song Inside Out*; ¶ the blues *A Sad Bunch of Flowers* and *A Dusty Road*; ¶ the charleston *The New from the Old.*

Bayerle has composed as well music to several short films and is a competent arranger for modern dance orchestras.

BAŽANT, Jaromír

[born Krásný Dvůr, 8 August 1926]

Bažant studied composition at the Prague Conservatory under EMIL HLOBIL and MIROSLAV KREJČÍ and oboe under VÁCLAV SMETÁČEK and ADOLF KUBÁT. He studied piano as well, taking the State examination. He was a member of the City Symphonic Orchestra at Mariánské Lázně and at present is teaching theoretical subjects in music at the Pilsen Conservatory.

In addition to chamber music compositions such as *The Small Suite* for oboe and piano (1948), the *First Piano Sonata* (1958), four compositions for violin and piano (1958), the *Second Piano Sonata* (1958) and *Czech Dances* for piano (1962), he has written the following symphonic works: *Czech Dances* for full orchestra (1956), a *Concerto* for violin and orchestra (1959), a *Symphony* (1960), a *Concerto* for oboe and orchestra (1961) and a ballet *Maryčka Magdónova* (1962).

From 1951—53 he arranged a number of folk songs and dances for the Army Artistic Ensemble Vít Nejedlý.

BAŽANT, Jiří

[born Semily, 27 September 1924]

Bažant is a pianist of the foremost dance orchestras and ranks among the significant of Czech composers of dance and light music.

Of his creative work up to the present the following dance compositions have gained popularity: *Beautiful Metamorphoses*; ¶ the sambo *Sunday in the South*, ¶ the slow foxtrots *When Snow Falls* and a *Little Song*; ¶ the foxtrots *Before Dawn, Afternoon in the Park, The Peep Show, The Real Reason, Little Red Slippers, A Girl with a Bouquet, I Wish I Had a Band, Prague Chimney Sweep,*

The Moon and Advertisements, She is Grey-Eyed, This Guitar I Have Bought because of You, Rain Drops, If I Were an Angel; ¶ the waltzes *My Boat, A Declaration of Love in Kisses, Secretly*; ¶ chanson *A Duck in Reeds*.

His music for variety programmes includes *The Lyric Intermezzo, An Excursion into the Mountains, In the Meadows* and *Slow Night Music*.

Together with JIŘÍ MALÁSEK he has written music to tens of short films (advertisements, popular-scientific and animated cartoon), to the full-length film *A Castle for Barbara*, to several television plays (*Three Chaps in a Cottage*) as well as to stage productions.

With JIŘÍ MALÁSEK and VLASTIMIL HÁLA he composed music to the first Czechoslovak film musical *Old Hops Pickers*.

BÁZLIK, Miroslav
[born Partizánská Ľupča, 12 April 1931]

Bázlik studied piano at the Bratislava Conservatory as a pupil of ANNA KAFENDOVÁ and while studying mathematics at Komenský University he began to devote himself to composition, being completely self-taught. At the suggestion of JÁN CIKKER he became his pupil at the School of Musical Arts in Bratislava, at the same time filling a post of a lecturer at the Bratislava Technical University.

His early compositions—a *Piano Sonata* (1955) and the piano bagatelle *The Palette* (1956)—show the influence of the late romanticism and impressionism of Brahms. In his subsequent creative work he deviated from this way and tended to neoclassicism as is evident in his *Baroque Suite* for string orchestra and winds (1958).

In his works such as *Songs* set to Chinese poetry for alto, flute, violoncello and piano (1960) and *Music* for violon and orchestra (1961), he ascertained his individual path, occasionally marked by the dodecaphonic style. This search for an individual expression is characteristic of the efforts of the young generation of Slovak composers. In *Three Pieces* for eleven instruments he uses in an expressively redundant music a serial technique.

At present he is working on the television opera *Peter and Lucia*, according to the novel by ROMAIN ROLLAND.

BEDŘICH, Jan

[born Kralupy, 16 December 1932]

After completing the secondary school Bedřich entered the Academy of Musical Arts where he studied composition under PAVEL BOŘKOVEC. On completion of his studies he became musical advisor for the Czech Music Fund. Since 1958 he has been conductor of the East Bohemian Theatre at Pardubice.

He has composed a cycle of lyric songs *Tranquil Love-making* (1954), variations for children's choir and orchestra *The Calendar* (1955), *a Concerto* for piano and orchestra (graduation work 1956), a *Wind Quintet* (1956), a *String Quartet* (1957), a *Violoncello Sonata* (1957), a ballet *The King has New Clothes* [according to ANDERSEN] (1957), a cantata *February and Roses* set to words by JAN NOHA (1958), a *Concertino* for oboe and orchestra (1959), *May Symphony* (1960), a *Concerto* for violoncello and orchestra (1961), a cantata *The Astronaut* to a poem by MICHAL SEDLOŇ for solos, mixed choir and orchestra (1962) and *Serenade* for strings, flute and oboe (1962).

He has written considerable scenic music for the theatre and television, musical comedies *What Love Can Do*, *It Happened in Granada*, *The Petřín Romance*, *The Dancing Teacher*, *Three Musketeers*, musical *Bel Ami* and music to the films *Attention*, *The Building of Peace*,

Little Red Riding Hood, The Iron Hat, Reason and Feeling, Red Footprint and *Moment of Decision*.

Bedřich is also the author of variety and instructive compositions and of pioneer songs.

BENEŠ, Bedřich

[born Kosmonosy, 2 March 1903]

Beneš studied composition privately with ANTONÍN MODR.

Stage Works

He composed music to operettas *The Magic Veil, The Infantry, A Gay Comedian, A Lone Wolf, A Girl From the Mountains*.

Instrumental and Orchestral Works

Beneš, inspired by themes from Kladno coal region, composed a musical picture *In the Realm of Permons* (1948) and *The Miner's Legend* for full orchestra (1951).

In the spheres of other kinds of instrumental music he has written a cycle of small piano compositions *Our Children* (1947), *Pictures from the Mountains* (1953), *Sonatina* (1954) and *Four Folk Aquarelles* for piano (1962), as well as orchestral compositions which include a *Serenade*, a *Russian Romance*, a *Canzonetta*, an *Overture* on a Czech folk theme (1959), an *Autumn Romance* and *Meditation*.

Vocal Works

Beneš composed many march songs as *Our Czech Land, The Songs of the Tourists, Fathers-Mothers, Watch Us!* His songs *The Miners' Pony, Below the Shaft* and a *Song of the Miner's Davy Lamp* were inspired by the coal mines and their workers. Then followed a cycle of songs *The Calendar* (1943) and *Four Songs for Youth* (1962).

Marches

He is the author of successful marches as *A Victorious March, The March of the Tankists, Hail to the Post! The March of the Artists, Silver Wings* and others.

Dance Music

He wrote dance music especially for the young generation. Thus a mazurka *With Us in the Mountains*, a slow folk waltz *From Šumava*, a valse *Recollection from Youth* and *Valse Impromptu*, a grand valse *Summer Moods*, then a *Czech Polka* and *Two Czech Folk Dances*.

Various

Recently, Beneš has composed a paraphrase on a Czech folk song *My Horse is Saddled* for violin and orchestra, a musical picture *The Slovak Countryside*, an orchestral grotesque *Felix, the Tom-cat* and a *Fantasy* in the Czech folk style (1963).

BERG, Josef
[born Brno, 8 March 1927]

Berg graduated from the section of composition at the Brno Conservatory under VILÉM PETRŽELKA, studying simultaneously musicology.

In the years 1950—53, when he was music editor of the Brno Radio, he oriented his creative work mainly for the ensembles of Folk Art and for the Radio Orchestra of Folk Instruments.

Folk Art Music

Berg wrote almost one hundred compositions and arrangements for this orchestra, including the following: *The Spring Suite* (1953), *Winter Suite* (1953) and *Autumn Suite* (1964), *Heavenly Music* (1954) and a folk play *A Fairy-tale for the Cabbage Patch* (1959).

Orchestral Compositions

His creative work for folk instruments and his romantic inclinations had an influence on the style of his symphonic compositions in those years. They include *The Cantata of my Country, the Second Symphony*, a *Comedy Overture* and the overture *People, Be on Guard!* (all in 1952), an overture *Jan Žižka* (1953), music to KUNDERA's text *The last May* (1954), music to HOLAN's *Theresa Planetová* and the *Third Symphony* (1955).

Chamber Music

In 1953, when he devoted himself only to composing, a change occurred in his style; it is to be noted from the *Five Fugues* for wind quintet (1957), *Sonata* for viola and piano (1958), a *Capriccio* about a meeting of two friends in Prague (1958), a *Sextet* for piano, harp and string quartet (1959), a *Nonet* for two harps, harpsichord, piano and percussion instruments (1962), *Renaissance Folk Suite* for chamber orchestra (1962) and a *Sonata* for harpsichord and piano *in modo classico* (1962).

Instrumental Compositions

The piano cycle *Something About Oneself* (1953), piano cycle *The Months* (1956), *Three Improvisations on a Summer Day* (1957), *Three Improvisations after Reading the Illiad* (1957), *Fantasia* in C major for two pianos (1958) and *Seven Preludes* for piano (1959).

Vocal Works

After a change, with occurred in his style in 1953, he composed a song cycle *You Gave me Bread with Burning Lips* (1955), *Carols* (1955), *Christmas Songs of the Polish People* (1956), *Janské Songs* [ceremonial dances in Central Slovakia] (1958), song cycle *The Strophes of Love* to words by STIEPAN SHCHIPACHOV (1959), a cycle of male choirs *The Fires* and a *Song of New Werther*, set to his own text for bass baritone and piano (1962).

BERG

His song *The Burning Birch* was awarded in the artistic jubilee competiton in 1960.

In the field of cantatas he composed *Choral Singing* (1953) and an oratorio *Today the Sun Still Sets Over Atlantis*, set to the dramatic poem by VÍTĚZSLAV NEZVAL.

Radio Music

Berg also composed music to a number of radio plays. He demonstrated his aptitude for characterization especially in the melodrama *Lucullus' Interrogation*, according to BERTOLD BRECHT, in the musical dramatization *Mystery-Buffa* of VLADIMIR MAJAKOVSKY and in music to BRANDSTAETTER's comedy *Markolt's Pranks*.

●

His theoretical activity is aimed at questions dealing with folklore and contemporary art.

●

For his work he was awarded the Prize of the South Moravian Region (1965).

BERKOVEC, Jiří

[born Pilsen, 22 July 1922]

Berkovec graduated from the piano section of the Prague Conservatory in the class of EMIL MIKELKA. He completed as well the study of musicology and psychology at the Faculty of Philosophy at Charles University.

Since 1949 he has been active at the Cezchoslovak Radio where he was editor-in-chief in the field of symphonic, vocal and chamber music. He is a member of the scientific advisory boards of the SMETANA and DVOŘÁK MUSEUMS and of the editorial advisory council for the publication of the complete works of ANTONÍN DVOŘÁK.

Stage Works

As a composer Berkovec has expressed himself most significantly in three operas: (1) *Twelve Little Months*, according to a fairy-tale by Božena Němcová (1956 to 1957), (2) *Krakatit* after Karel Čapek's novel of the same name (1959—60, première in Brno 1961) and (3) *The Inn at the Stone Table*, on a story by Karel Poláček (1961—62).

He is also the author of the musical comedy *Hadrián z Římsu*, according to a play of the same name by V. K. Klicpera (1953, première at the Czechoslovak Radio in Prague 1953).

Orchestral Works

Berkovec's orchestral creative work includes an *Overture* (1944), a symphonic poem *The Silver Wind*, according to Fráňa Šrámek (1943—45), a fantasy *A Merry Day Has Come*, based on Christmas song of the Hussite historical period (1951), *Three Sonatinas* (1956), *Intermezzos* (1958), *Capriccio* [flute, oboe, clarinet, bassoon and orchestra] (1961) and a *Grand March* (1962).

Chamber Music

His chamber music is represented by the piano suite *July* (1943), a *Sonata* (1944), a *Rhapsody* (1946), a *Sonatina* for viola and piano (1947) and a *Small Suite* for nonet (1954).

Music for children

In an individual manner Berkovec has elaborated topics for children: *Sing With Us* (1943), *Welcome, May!* (1952), a *Pioneers' Suite* for small orchestra (1953), five miniatures *Jane Plays the Piano* (1956, awarded a prize in the Jubilee Competiton of the Czechoslovak Guild of Composers and the Czech Music Fund in 1956) and the musical comedy *Robbers from Veseličko*, according to F. Egner (1961, première in Prague 1961).

Radio Music

For the radio he has composed a number of scenic compositions, as *The Epic of Gilgamesh* (1951), OTAKAR THEER's *Faethon* (1962) and SHAKESPEARE's dramas *Tempest* (1962), *Macbeth* (1963) and *Coriolanus* (1964).

Writings

Berkovec has written a study on *Kryštof Harant* (his diploma thesis, 1951), a compositional portrait to *Josef Suk* (published in 1956), a publicity booklet *The Smetana Quartet* (published in 1956), a monograph on *F. V. Hek* [the principal figure in Alois Jirásck's novel F. L. Věk] (published in 1958), *The Influence of Music and the Dance on the Contemporary Theatre* (1957), WEBER's *Der Freischütz* (1958), KOVAŘOVIC's *The Dog-Heads* (1962) and a number of publications on Czech music of the eighteenth century [in particular Czech Pastorales] (1957 to 1963).

BEZUBKA, Ladislav

[born Kostelec, 8 May 1926]

Bezubka has occupied himself with dance music from his fifteenth year. As leader of a popular dance orchestra he has devoted himself to the composition of dance music.

His songs, which have met with success, include ¶ the foxtrots *The Bumblebee's Breakfast, Why Not, The Kerchief, All Round, A Magical Letter-Carrier, Three Girls, L B 3*; ¶ the slow foxtrots *An Evening With a Fairy-tale, Beyond the Blue Hill, a Wet Rendez-vous, A Journey for a Gift* ¶ the beguines *Two Heels of a Girl's Shoe, A Happy Day*; ¶ the valses *A Little Song about Vienna* and others.

His music to short films attracted attention both at home and abroad.

BLÁHA, Václav

[born Křečov, 4 May 1921—died Prague, 22 March 1959]

Bláha ranks among the best known Czech authors of popular music. His work as a composer was influenced by a long activity as a practicing musician.

Some of his dance music has become popular the world over and is played or sung up to the present. This is true, for example, of his polkas *A Little Clover* and *Yesterday I Waited for You*; the valse *A Little Red Skirt* and others.

After 1945 Bláha devoted considerable attention to songs for children as is evidenced by his *Children's Songs* to words by MILOŠ VESELÝ (published 1951), a cycle of nine songs (published 1953), in which the composer tied in with old dances, and his *Songs for Children* (published 1957).

His polka *The Earthworm Dancing* became extremely popular.

BLAHNÍK, Roman

[born Pilsen, 2 February 1897—died 15 September 1964]

Blahník graduated from the organ section of the Prague Conservatory. After his return from the First World War he continued the study of composition under J. B. FOERSTER and later under JOSEF SUK and was a piano pupil of JAN HEŘMAN.

He was accompanist at the Pilsen Theatre, was active as a pedagogue at the Cairo Conservatory, had the opportunity to acquaint himself with musical life in Barcelona and in 1954—56 directed the School of Music in Karlovy Vary.

He is the author of an orchestral suite *In Nature* (1933), of musical accompaniments to the films *Morality Above All*, *Virginity*, *A Night Butterfly and a Dancer*, of the operettas *A White Cavalier, A Stroke of Luck* and *A Masked Sweetheart,* of the ballets *Primroses* (1948—51) and *Nagaina* (1961), *Legends 56* (given an award in the competition of the Paris Television and Radio in 1956), *Rhapsody* for piano and orchestra (1957), *Oriental Suites* (1961), *Second Rhapsody* for orchestra (1963) and *Third Rhapsody* for orchestra (1964).

His dance music includes ¶ the foxtrots: *A Great Miracle, With What—With What?, Why I Dream Sometimes;* ¶ the slow foxtrots: *Before You Go to Bed, The Most Beautiful Night, My Native Country* and ¶ the march *Forward and Onward.*

Some of Blahník's compositions have been successfully produced and published abroad.

BLATNÝ, Josef
[born Brno, 19 March 1891]
MERITED TEACHER

Blatný graduated from the School for Organists in Brno. He studied piano under VILÉM KURZ. Then he taught organ and theory at the Conservatory and at the School for Organists, both in Brno. At the Conservatory he first filled the post of secretary; later he was appointed professor of organ and of organ subjects. He taught as well at the Janáček Academy of Musical Arts. He is an outstanding improvisator on the organ.

Chamber Music

Blatný composed a *Sonata* for violin and piano, op. 6 (1926), *Song and Rondo* for clarinet and piano, op. 17 (1942), and three *String Quartets;* furthermore a *Suite* for two flutes, clarinet and bassoon, op. 26 (1947), a *Piano Trio,* op. 32 (1950), the second *Sonata* for violin and piano, op. 47 (1957), *Sinfonia brevis* for string orchestra, op. 45

BLATNÝ J.

(1956—57), two *Symphonic Dances*, op. 49 (1958—59) and a *Chamber Symphony*, op. 53 (1961).

Organ Works

Among his compositions for organ are three *Pastoral Preludes* (1916, 1917—18 and 1928), a *Sonata*, op. 11 (1938), *Variations on a Christmas Carol*, op. 15 (1942), *Te Deum* and *Alleluia*, op. 16 (1942), which was inspired by his unshakable faith in the liberation of his people; furthermore *Easy Preludes*, op. 20 (1944), *Prelude and Fugue*, op. 22 (1943—44), *Preludio festivo e Fuga*, op. 36 (1954) and *Toccata* and *Scherzo*, op. 38 (1955).

Vocal Works

During the German occupation of Czechoslovakia he demonstrated his courageous and undaunted attitude, as is witnessed by his mixed choirs *Our Fields* and *Advent*, op. 14 (both of 1941). In his male choir *Be Lauded In Song* (1942) he expressed his social feeling with the working man.

In anticipation of postwar peace, he composed *The Introduction*, *Heroic Song* and *March* for trumpet and piano, op. 21 (1944).

His other works include the song cycles *The Confessor of Souls*, op. 8 (1931), *The Moon and the Sun*, op. 19 (1943), children's, female, male and mixed choirs, a cantata *La Saletta*, op. 30 (1949), an oratorio *The Thief on the Right Hand*, op. 35 (1953) and *Spring*, op. 44 (1956).

He composed also the melodrama *Kyjov* to words by PETR BEZRUČ (1928).

Instructive Compositions

He is also the author of a number of successful instructive compositions for piano and other instruments. His piano compositions include *Études*, op. 33 (1951), *Prelude, Fugue* and *Toccata*, op. 43 (1956) and *Sonata*, op. 51 (1960).

BLATNÝ, Pavel
[brno Brno, 14 September 1931]

A son of the composer JOSEF BLATNÝ; studied piano at the Brno Conservatory under VILÉM VAŇURA, conducting under BOHUMÍR LIŠKA and composition under THEODOR SCHAEFER. He became an outstanding piano improvisator.

He continued compositional work in Prague with PAVEL BOŘKOVEC, completing there as well the study of musicology.

Blatný's music shows an admiration for the creative work of BOHUSLAV MARTINŮ, but he composes as well in the technique of the second Viennese school.

Stage Works

He is the author of four musical fairy-tales *The Wolf and the Fox* (1956), *Three Musical Instruments* (1960), *How the Grindstone Went Awandering* (1962) and *The Enchanted Forest* (1962); then of a children's opera *The Little House* (1959) and a ballet in four movements *Ophelia* (1964).

Orchestral Works

Symphonic music is represented in Blatný's creative work by *Music* for piano and orchestra (1955), *Concerto* for orchestra (1956), a symphonic *Finale* (1956, worked over in 1962), a *Fairy-tale Suite* for small orchestra (1956), *Piccola Suita Italiana* (1958) and *Prologue* for full orchestra (1959).

Chamber Music

Chamber music as well represents a significant artistic expression in his work and includes a *Sonata* for clarinet and piano (1954), *Miniatures* for chamber orchestra (1957), *Small Classical Variations* (1958); several suites supplement these works, such as two *Small Suites* for winds (1958—59 and 1962), a *Suite* for winds (1959), a *Suite* for flute and harp (1960), and a *Suite* for bass-clarinet and piano (1961); *Wind Quintet* (1958), *Concerto* for chamber orchestra (1958) and a *Trio* for flute, bassclarinet and piano (1962).

Recently, he composed *Three Poems* for reciter and bassclarinet (1964), *Canto a sonori* for chamber ensemble (1964), *Tre per due* (for two pianos, 1964) and *Tre per quatro* (for four pianos, 1964).

Instrumental Works

Variations for harpsichord (1954), *Passacaglia* (1955), *Ballets* (1955—56), a *Suite* for piano (1957), *Prologue and Scherzo* for two pianos (1959), and *Meditation and Passacaglia* for organ (1960).

Various

Next to these works he composed scenic music, vocal compositions, chansons and dance music.

In the field of *"the third stream music"*—which is characterized by a synthesis of modern compositional technique with some specialized jazz elements—belong his polyphonic *Prologue* (1962), *Models* for Karel Krautgartner (1963), *Rhythmus and Nuances* (1964), *Dialogue* for soprano saxophone and orchestra (1964), as well as a *Study* for quarter-tone trumpets and jazz orchestra (1964) and the composition *Per Orchestra Sintetica* (1964).

In frequent articles for the daily press and for specialized periodicals Blatný deals with problems pertaining to contemporary music.

BLAŽEK, Zdeněk

[born Žarošice, 24 May 1905]

MERITED ARTIST

In composition, Blažek was a pupil of VILÉM PETRŽELKA at the Brno Conservatory; he studied at the same time the science of music, completing his study of composition at the Master School of Prague Conservatory under JOSEF SUK.

He became director of the Brno Conservatory. At present he is senior lecturer of music theory at the Faculty of Philosophy of Purkyně University in Brno.

Blažek ranks among the significant composers of songs and choral works. During the German occupation his songs and choirs fortified the nation in its resistance against the reign of terror (*The Simplest, God's Mills*); at that time he also expressed his faith in the liberation of his country in the cantata *Song to the Native Land* for baritone, mixed choir and orchestra, set to words by JOSEF HORA, op. 17 (1938—39).

Stage Works

Blažek expressed his musically dramatic feeling in his opera *The Highlands* to the libretto by JAROSLAV ZATLOUKAL (1950—51, première in Brno 1956).

Cantatas

His cantata *The Ode on Poverty* to a text by PABLO NERUDA was awarded the second prize in the Jubilee Competition of the Czechoslovak Guild of Composers and the Czech Music Fund (1956). Recently, Blažek has written a further cantata *Home* to a text by FRANTIŠEK NECHVÁTAL for soprano, baritone, mixed choir and orchestra, op. 71 (1962).

Chamber and Instrumental Compositions

He has also composed a number of instrumental works, which include a *Piano Intermezzo*, op. 26 (1945), *String Quartet* No. 1 (1945), *Divertimento* for flute, oboe, clarinet, and bassoon, op. 28 (1946), *String Quartet* No. 2 (1946 to 1947), a *Quintet* for two violins and violoncello, op. 34 (1949), a *Sonatina giocosa* for clarinet and piano, op. 35 (1949), *Music at Home* for string trio, op. 44 (1953), *String Quartet* No. 3 (1956), a *Sonatina* for bassoon and piano, op. 60 (1958), a *Sonatina balladica* for violoncello

BLAŽEK

and piano (1962) and a *Sonata* for French horn and piano, op. 75 (1964).

Vocal Works

Of his extensive vocal creative work *The Ballad of an Unborn Child* for alto and male choir, set to words by JIŘÍ WOLKER, op. 8 (1933) deserves special attention. Furthermore there are song cycles *In a Pensive Mood*, op. 10 (1933—34), *The Last Spring*, op. 14 (1936), cycles of male choirs *Anxieties and Hopes*, op. 16 (1938 to 1939), a cycle of female choirs *Song of Spring*, op. 19 (1940), song cycles *To my Native Region*, op. 20 (with orchestra 1942), *The Blessings of Summer*, op. 22 (with orchestra 1942 to 1943), *Sung Far Away* op. 24 (1944), two ballads for mixed choir and orchestra, set to texts of Moravian Slovak folk poetry *Slain—Near Strážnice*, op. 32 (1948), a song cycle *Simple Strophes*, op. 36 (1949), a cycle of male choirs *For Peace*, op. 37 (1950), the choral trilogy *To Mother Land*, op. 49 (1953—54), which deserves a special attention, then song cycles *Ten Brigands' Songs and Ballads* to texts of Slovak folk poetry, op. 51 (1955), *Home*, op. 52 (1955), *Echoes of Days*, op. 58 (1958) and *Love Songs*, op. 62 (1959), *Nursery Rhymes* for children choir and piano, op. 76 (1964) and *Four Nocturnettes* for female choir and piano, op. 77 (1964).

Various Compositions

Blažek has written numerous scenic compositions for radio, arrangements of folk songs and instructive compositions.

Writings

He was the first theoretician in our country to occupy himself with the problems of the method of upward and downward alternation (1949).

He has an unfailing interest in and has made a systematic study of the theoretical doctrine of LEOŠ JANÁČEK.

•

For his work he was awarded the Prize of Liberation
of the City of Brno (1965).

BOHÁČ, Josef

[born Vienna, 25 March 1929]

Boháč worked in the factory Sázavan at Zruč,
attended the workers' preparatory school for university
study and became a student of composition at the Janáček Academy of Musical Arts under VILÉM PETR-
ŽELKA.

After graduation he was appointed conductor of the
Military Artistic Ensemble in Prague (1956—57). In
1958 he founded in Prague the Central Pioneers'
Ensemble as the representative body of the Pioneers'
Organization of the Czechoslovak Union of Youth. At
present he is secretary and member of the composers'
section of the Guild of Czechoslovak Composers.

Up to the present, Boháč has devoted himself to
creative work in the field of songs for children, youth
and military ensembles. His best known works are:
At the Lipník Village Green, *A Song About an Accordion*,
May March, *A Song About Fučík*, *When Soldiers March*,
A Gay Song, *A Soldier's Saturday*, *The Path Before Us*, *Sing
My Song*, *Children's Laughter* and others.

His pioneer song *The Path Before Us* was awarded in
the artistic jubilee competition in 1960. He has also
composed incidental music for the New Year pioneers'
festivities at the Prague Castle (1959 and 1960). In
addition, he has written a number of compositions for
the Military Artistic Ensemble Vít Nejedlý in Prague as
well as three *Lyric Songs* for middle voice and piano
(1952), a *Suite* for string quartet (1953), a *Violoncello
Sonata* (1954), a *Rhapsody* for full orchestra (1955),
a cycle of songs *Had I to Defend My Love* for baritone
(1956), a cycle of female choirs *The Rings* (1957), a cycle

of mixed choirs *Young Love* (1960), a symphonic *Over-ture* (1963) and a song cycle *The Blossoms of Jasmines* for soprano and piano, set to Old Indian poetry (1964).

BOŘKOVEC, Pavel

[born Prague, 10 June 1894]

LAUREATE OF THE STATE PRIZE, MERITED ARTIST

Bořkovec studied composition first privately with J. B. FOERSTER and JAROSLAV KŘIČKA, then entered the Master School and studied under JOSEF SUK, who exercised the greatest influence on his early work. This is evident in his *First Symphony*.

His orientation towards European musical circles of that time and his efforts to arrive at an idependent ex-pression is markedly shown in his further orchestral compositions. After the Second World War his work is characterized by a simplification and purification of his style and a further expansion of the melodic line.

Since 1946 Bořkovec is professor of composition at the Academy of Musical Arts.

Stage Works

One of his most typical works is the opera *Satyr*, composed on a theme by J. W. GOETHE (1937—38, première in Prague 1942); on the same day was the première of his ballet *Rat-Catcher* (1939). A further work in the field of musical drama is his opera *Tom Thumb* (Paleček), composed on the occasion of the six hundreth anniversary of the foundation of Charles University in Prague (1945—47, première in Prague 1948).

Orchestral Works

The first was the romantic symphonic poem *Growing*

Dark (1920), the *First Symphony* in D flat major (1926 to 1927), a symphonic allegro *The Start* (1930), *First Piano Concerto* with orchestra, notable for its definitely formed stylization (1931), a *Violin Concerto* (1933), an orchestral *Partita* (1936), *Concerto Grosso* for two violins, violoncello, orchestra and piano (1941—42).

After the war he composed the *Second Concerto for piano and orchestra* (1949—50), the *Concerto for violoncello and orchestra* (1950—51), the *Second Symphony* (1955), written in honour of the sixtieth anniversary of the founding of the Czech Philharmonic, and the *Third Symphony* (1959), which received the second prize in the artistic jubilee competition in 1960.

Chamber Music and Instrumental Works

Piano Quartet (1922), *First String Quartet* (1924), *Second String Quartet* (1928), a *Wind Quintet* (1932), *Third String Quartet* (1940), a *Nonet* (1940—41), a *Sinfonietta* for chamber orchestra (1944), *Fourth String Quartet* (1947) and *Fifth String Quartet* (1964).

His further development toward neoclassicism is presented by following instrumental works:

Piano solo compositions: *Suite* for piano (1930), *Partita* for piano (1935); violin and viola compositions: *Sonata* for solo viola (1931), *First Violin Sonata* (1935), a *Violin Sonatina* (1942) and *Second Violin Sonata* (1956).

Vocal Works

Voices: lyrical pictures for alto and piano *The Animals* (1961) and a cycle of songs for lower voice and piano *Dreams* (1962).

Melodrama: *Only Once* (1921), set to words by Petr Bezruč.

Madrigal: six *Madrigals About Time* (1957.)

Songs: song-cycles (with a chamber orchestra) *The Stadium*, set to words by K. Wierzyński (1929), *Capri-*

BOŘKOVEC

cious Songs, set to words by J. W. Goethe and François Villon (1932), *Seven Songs* to words by Vítězslav Nezval (1932—33), *Five Songs* to words by Boris Pasternak (1935) and *A Chat* to words by Jaroslav Seifert (1937).

Female choirs: *Six Songs* to words by Jaroslav Seifert for female or children choir (1949).

Male choirs: *From Ancient Chinese Poetry* set to words by Bohumil Mathesius (1925) and *The Folk Nursery Rhymes* to words by K. J. Erben (1936).

Various

For the Prague Spring Music Festival 1965 he composed a symphonic movement for alto and orchestra *Silentium turbatum*.

BOROVIČKA, Antonín

[born Davle, 4 November 1895]

Borovička acquired a thorough musical background during the First World War in the field of military band music. After returning to civil life, he devoted himself exclusively to folk music as composer and bandmaster of the Davle string and brass ensemble Vltavan, which he led for forty years. In his compositions he ties in with the tradition of Czech popular musicianship, represented by František Kmoch.

His best known compositions are ¶ the polkas: *In the Garden, The Prettiest Corner, When The Trumpet Sings, Vltavanka* (When the Band Played), *The Davle Polka, The Sázava Polka, Joyous Youth, I Shall Not Implore You for Love, Perhaps You Will Remember* and the *JAWA Polka*. His ¶ valses include: *Sweet Recollections, The Rose Blossom, For Your Happiness, May Evening* and *The Native Village*.

He has also composed a number of successful ¶ march songs such as *Greetings from the Forests* (published also in Switzerland), *For Freedom, Down the Stream, The Sports March* and others.

BROŽ, František

[born Prague, 10 April 1896, died Prague, 21 July 1962]

Brož first studied violin at the Prague Conservatory and after the First World War continued his studies of composition under J. B. FOERSTER and later at the Master School of composition under VÍTĚZSLAV NOVÁK and conductiong under OTAKAR OSTRČIL and VÁCLAV TALICH.

He was a violist in the Czech Philharmonic and choirmaster of various Prague choral societies. For a number of years he was active at Hranice in Moravia, where he founded a music school and performed with the local choir and orchestra many significant works of Czech and world masters. He became professor of composition at the Prague Conservatory.

Among his best compositions are a *String Quartet* (1928), a wind *Quintet* (1944), a *Spring Sonata* for viola and piano, op. 18 (1946) a *Fantasy and Fugue* for organ, op. 20 (1948), three piano *Capriccios* (1952, 1956), a *Symphony*, op. 22 (1953), *In Commemoration of Heroes*, prelude and double-fugue for orchestra (1954), *Chromatic Variations* for accordion and orchestra (1956) and a *String Quartet* (1960).

He also composed a number of vocal works; for instance the song for coloratura soprano with orchestra *The Skylark*, *Three Love Songs* with piano (orchestra), then choirs, a chamber music cantata *The Vigils*, op. 5 (1928), and songs for community singing.

The musically dramatic field is represented by his

ballet *Temptation*, op. 7 (1934, première in Ostrava 1937).

Brož composed as well several compositions for children.

He wrote a book entitled *Generalbass et Continuo* (1948).

BURGHAUSER, Jarmil
[born Písek, 21 October 1921]

Burghauser studied musicology and psychology at Charles University and at the same time privately composition with JAROSLAV KŘIČKA and OTAKAR JEREMIÁŠ. Later he studied at the Prague Conservatory conducting under METOD DOLEŽIL and PAVEL DĚDEČEK and at the Master School under VÁCLAV TALICH.

At the Academy of Musical Arts he held the post of lecturer and at the National Theatre in Prague he was choirmaster and conductor. From the year 1953 he has devoted himself completely to creative work.

Of his many compositions, the following have achieved noteworthy success.

Stage Works

He has written two operas: *The Miser* (1950, première at Liberec 1950) and *Carolina and the Liar* (1955, première at Olomouc 1955).

Of his two ballets he composed *Jack and the Devil* (1954, première in Ostrava 1954, worked over 1960) and *A Servant of Two Masters* (1958, première in Prague 1958).

Orchestral Works

Of many of his orchestral compositions should be mentioned *Toccata* for small orchestra (1947), symphonic variations *Hail Spring!* (1952), a *Sonata* for orchestra (1954), a *Symphonic Suite* (1955), a *Symphony* in D minor

(1959). His *Seven Reliefs* for full orchestra (1962) make the turning point of his creative work, which represents the first synthesis in serial compositional technique, tested in scenic and film music. This technique crystallizes into a modification of seriality. Thus he composed the antiopera *The Bridge*, set to libretto by JOSEF PÁVEK (1963—64) and a cycle of eight small symphonic movements for bow, string and percussion instruments, called *The Ways* (1964).

Chamber Music

Consists of a *Concerto* for wind quintet and strings (1942) and of five string quartets and five wind quintets.

Vocal Works

Burghauser composed fifteen song cycles and five choral cycles and following cantatas: *The Eternal Skies* (1942), *A Mysterious Trumpeter* (1944), *Suffering and Resurrection* (1946), *Czech Cantata* (1952) and children's cantata *Sekora's Alphabet* (1955).

Film and Scenic Music

He wrote as well many scenic works and music to films.

Writings

He is the author of many articles and extensive studies as *A Quantitative Analysis of Musical Structure* (1950), *How to Write for the Guitar* (1954), *Janáček's Chamber and Symphonic Work* (1954) and the *Orchestration of Dvořák's Slavonic Dances* (1959). In 1960 he set up a *Thematic Catalogue of Works by Antonín Dvořák*. Together with PETR EBEN he has written a textbook entitled *The Reading and Playing of Scores* (1960).

In his booklet *Renowned Czech Conductors* (1963), he rendered a conscise development of the conducting art.

Burghauser is a member of the editorial committees for the publication of the *Complete Works* ... Dvořák and *Zdeněk Fibich*.

He has prepared as well a critical edition of the librettos of Dvořák's operas *The King and the Collier* (1957) and of *Dimitri* (1961).

International Prizes

His *Toccata* for small orchestra (1947) was awarded a prize in an International competition in the Netherlands (1957).

BURIAN, Emil František

[born Pilsen, 11 June 1904—died Prague, 9 August 1959]

NATIONAL ARTIST, holder of the ORDER OF WORK and of the ORDER OF THE 25TH OF FEBRUARY, LAUREATE OF THE STATE PRIZE

The son of the prominent Czech baritone EMIL BURIAN (1876—1926) and nephew of the famous Czech tenor KAREL BURIAN (1870—1924), E. F. Burian was a versatile artist, founder of a vanguard theatre and of a chamber opera, composer, dramatist, poet, fiction writer, piano accompanist, jazz singer, actor, stage-manager, film producer, journalist and a member of the National Assembly.

He graduated from the Prague Conservatory and from its Master School in the composition class of J. B. FOERSTER.

His compositional development was influenced by jazz, Negro spirituals, French modern music, Czech folk songs and by stimuli stemming from the creative work of VÍTĚZSLAV NOVÁK, JAROSLAV KŘIČKA and LEOŠ JANÁČEK.

Stage Works

His musical dramatic work is represented by following works: Fai   opera *Alladina and Palomid*, according to the lyric drama by MAURICE MAETERLINCK (1923), the opera —one-act musical drama *Before Sunrise* to a libretto by BEDŘICH BĚLOHLÁVEK (1924, première in Prague 1925); the jazz opera *Bubu from Montparnasse*, asserting the drama of the disinherited by CHARLES PHILIPPE (1927), the buffa *Mister Ipokras*, a melodrama according to VÍTĚZSLAV NEZVAL (1925, première in Prague 1926; reworked in 1956 into an operatic farce *I Beg Your Pardon*, première in Prague 1956), the fanciful singspiel *Opera from the Pilgrimage* (1955, première in Prague 1956), the ballets *The Bassoon and The Flute* (1925, première in Prague 1929), *Wooden Soldiers* (1926), *The Manège* (1927) and *The Motorcoach* (1927, première in Prague 1928), the musical comedy *Lovers from the Market Stall*, according to the play of the same name by VÍTĚZSLAV NEZVAL (1935), a musical-poetic montage *Paris Plays First Fiddle*, according to a text by FRANÇOIS VILLON (1938) and an operatic parody *The Emperor's New Clothes* (1947).

The opera *Maryša*, according to the well-known drama by BROTHERS MRŠTÍK (1938, première in Brno 1940, and in Lübeck 1964), represents the peak of E. F. Burian's musical dramatic work; in this opera he presented a moving picture of a Moravian village and of the fettered life of a village woman.

Folk Plays

In the folk plays with songs and dances Burian pointed out the theatrical effect of ancient Czech folk art. This includes the plays *War*, set to texts of folk songs from the collection of K. J. ERBEN (1935, première in Prague 1935), the first *Folk Suite* (*A Play About Saint Dorothy*, 1938), *Salička* (1938), *The Mendicant Bakus* (première in Prague 1938), the second *Folk Suite* (*Soldiers of Saint Gregory, A Comedy About Frances and Johnny, How One Went Formerly About Haunting in Bohemia*, 1939), an old Czech comedy *Esther* (1946), *Love, Defiance and Death* (1946) and *Christmas Plays* of the Czech People (1946).

Orchestral Works

His most characteristic works include: a *Symphony* with piano solo (1948), the five-part *Suita Poetica* (which came into being 1925—53), *Suite* for full orchestra (1926), *Suite* for oboe and string orchestra (1928), the suite *Reminiscence* (1930), a *Concerto* for accordion and orchestra (1949) and *The Overture to Socialism* (1950), which is the musical introduction to the film *The Team of Grinder Karhan*.

Chamber Music

His graduation work at the Conservatory was a *Trio* for flute, viola and violoncello (1924). His most inner self is expressed in eight string *Quartets*, composed in the years 1927—51, in his string sextet *From Youth* (1924), in *Variations* on folk songs for wind quintet (1928), in a suite for violin and piano *Of Warm Nights* (1928), in *Sonata* in C major (1928) and in the *Lost Serenade* for flute and piano (1940).

He also composed *Duo* for violin and violoncello (1925), *Passacaglia* in C for violin and viola (1929), *Four Pieces* for wind quintet (1929), a *Wind Quintet* (1930), *Suite* for violoncello and piano (1935), a *Nonetto* in D (1938) and a romantic *Sonata* for violin and piano (1938).

Instrumental Music

The *American Suite* for two pianos (1926), *Echoes of Czech Dances* for piano (1953) and others.

Vocal Music

In his numerous songs, choirs and melodramas, set to verses by contemporary Czech poets, Burian followed up the rich tradition of his native country. He wrote many songs for community singing, of which we note the following: *I Know the Country Near the Pole, The Red Tractor-driver, No Passeran!, Two Songs of the Five Year Plan, Pioneer's Song, Harvest-home Song*.

Voice Band

In 1927 Burian founded a voice-band (an ensemble for speech set to music) with which he appeared successfully at the International Festival of Music in Siena (1928). His most effective new work in this ensemble was the production of *The Baptism of Saint Vladimir* by KAREL HAVLÍČEK BOROVSKÝ and *The Ballads* by JIŘÍ WOLKER.

Film Music

Into Czech film Burian introduced a new conception of the function of sound: film music is not only an accompaniment or a musical background but an equal dramatic factor.

Full-length films to which Burian wrote the music include: *Golden Bird* (1931), *Taking the Examination of Maturity* (1932), *From the World of Forest Solitudes* (1933), *A Lane in Paradise* (1935), *Jan Výrava* (1937), *Věra Lukášová* (1939), *The Chicories* (1940), *Rhythmus* (1941), *A Career* (1948), *Beasts of Prey* (1949), *The Murderer's Gorge* (1950), *The Team of Grinder Karhan* (1949), *The Warning* (1953), *The Dog-heads* (1954).

Burian wrote as well the music to the short experimental film *November*, to the documentary film *Our Army*, and to the animated cartoons *The Cockroach* (1947) and *Who is the Most Powerful* (1950).

Writings

E. F. Burian wrote *Reminiscences of* his father *Emil Burian*, the famous Czech baritone (1947), made vivid the portrait of his uncle in a booklet *Karel Burian*, a Czech singer of World Renown (1948) and prepared *The Memorial Volume of Brothers Burian*.

He is as well the author of the following books: *Polydynamics* (1926), *Modern Russian Music* (1926) and *Jazz* (1928).

International Prizes

For his music to the film *The Siren* [after a novel by

MARIE MAJEROVÁ] he was awarded a gold medal for the best film music at the Bienale in Venice 1947; with the co-author of this film he shared the State Prize.

BURLAS, Ladislav
[born Trnava, 3 April 1927]

Burlas studied musicology at the Bratislava University and composition at the Conservatory under ALEXANDER MOYZES, with whom he completed his studies at the High School of Musical Arts.

At first he was active as a scientific worker at the Institute of Musicology of the Slovak Academy of Sciences and later as senior lecturer of musical theory at Comenius University in Bratislava; in 1961, he has returned to the Institute of Musical Science; since 1964 he is director of this Institute.

In his early compositional creative work the influence of his teacher ALEXANDER MOYZES can be felt but just as evident is the fact that he endeavoured nonetheless to follow up a non-conventional elaboration of Slovak folklore. In this effort he was greatly stimulated by BÉLA BARTÓK.

Orchestral Works

In the orchestral field he is the author of a *Symphonic Triptych* (1957) and the *Epitaph* (1958), awarded the second prize on the occasion of the fifteenth anniversary of the Slovak National Uprising.

Chamber Music

Burlas' efforts to achieve an original style in expression is evident in its most mature form in the string sextet *The Singing Heart* (1960, awarded in the artistic jubilee competition in 1960). He has written also the *Bagatelles* for string orchestra (1960).

Vocal Works

His *Wedding Songs of the Upper Hron* (1955), *Military Folk Songs* for solos, choir and orchestra (1958) and *Young Girls' Songs from Myjava*, inspired by a poem of VOJTECH MIHÁLIK (1958) are characteristic of the results he achieved in his striving for a new attitude to folklore.

Various Compositions

Of his other works, *The Miners' Cantata* for solos, choir and orchestra (1955), a small cantata *To the Party* (1961), children's songs *Children From Our House* (1961) and music to several films deserve mention.

Writings

As a musicologist, Burlas treats a wide range of problems from the history of Slovak music (he is co-author of the work *Music in Slovakia in the seventeenth Century* and *History of Slovak Music*), to problems of contemporary Slovak music (a *Monograph on Alexander Moyzes*) and problems of music theory (the book *Forms and Kinds of Musical Art*).

CEREMUGA, Josef

[born Ostrava-Kunčice, 14 June 1930]

Ceremuga studied composition at the Academy of Musical Arts under JAROSLAV ŘÍDKÝ and VÁCLAV DOBIÁŠ and quarter-tone music with ALOIS HÁBA. He is senior lecturer in the film section of the Academy of Musical Arts.

In his creative work he inclines to the folk elements of Eastern Moravia but strives to attain an individual expression.

Stage Works

He composed the one-act opera *Juraj Čup* (1958 to 1960), to own libretto, according to a story of the same name by KAREL ČAPEK.

Orchestral Works

His graduation work, *Symphony* in B major (1952—53) foreshadowed the path which the composer intended to follow. Of his symphonic compositions mention should be made of the symphonic poem *Childhood* (1954), according to the novel of MAXIM GORKY, a *Violin Concerto* (1955), three *Symphonic Frescoes* (1957—58) on a freely conceived theme from the Slovak national uprising, a *Piano Concerto* in C major (1961—62) and an overture *The Salute to Students* (1964).

Chamber Music

His works in this field include the suite *The Most Cherished Recollections* (1953), a *Serenade for Strings* (1956) a *String Quartet* in E minor (1956), a *Sonata* in D minor for violoncello and piano (1957), *Pictures from Youth* (1958), a *Piano Trio* (1959), a *Sonata Elegica* for viola and piano (1961), a *Trio* for two violins and viola (1962) and a *Wind Quintet* (1964).

His second string quartet *Creation* (1962) Ceremuga composed in the twelve-tone system.

Instrumental Works

Amongst his instrumental compositions we mention the *Spring Sonata* for violin (1952), a piano *Sonata* (1953), *Five Short Compositions* for piano (1961) and *Toccata* for piano (1962).

Vocal Works

Songs: Moravian folk influences are to be seen in his three vocal cycles called *Three Lyric Songs* for soprano with piano accompaniment (1952), *Song of Love* for baritone with orchestra (1955), and six songs *Love to*

One's Beloved to words of Moravian folk poetry (1957).

Female choirs: three choirs *Czech Motifs* to verses by JAROSLAV SEIFERT and VÍTĚZSLAV NEZVAL (1959).

Mixed choirs: three choirs *My Song* (1960).

Cantatas: *The Song of Love for Life*, set to a poem by FRANTIŠEK HRUBÍN for recitative, mixed choir and orchestra (1960).

Various Compositions

Ceremuga is also the author of film music. For the Spartakiads he composed music to the exercises for girls *The Little Red Balls* for the second one and for exercises *To Learn by Play* and *My Country is a Blooming Meadow* and two symphonic marches—*The March of Pioneers* and *Spartakiad Youth*—for the third one.

ČERNÍK, Josef

[born Staříč, 24 January 1880]

Holder of the decoration FOR OUTSTANDING WORK

After graduation from the Teachers' Training Institute, Černík studied composition under LEOŠ JANÁČEK at the School for Organists in Brno, continuing his studies under VÍTĚZSLAV NOVÁK in Prague and again with LEOŠ JANÁČEK at the Brno branch of the Master School of the Prague Conservatory.

He became teacher and later professor of music at the Teachers' Training Institute and lecturer at the Janáček Academy of Musical Arts in Brno.

Instrumental and Orchestral Works

Černík composed piano cycles, as *From a Chidren's Album* (1931), *Passing Moods* (1931—32), *Spring Flowers —Summer Flowers—Autumn Flowers* (1933), *Beetles— From Fields and Meadows—Birds—Little Animals—Trees*

(1935—36), *What the Flails Say* (1936), *Play of Colours* (1939) and the *Student Intermezzo "1939"* (1947).

His chamber music compositions include *Intimate Sonata* for violin and piano (1934—35), a piano trio *Intention* (1942) and a string quartet *From the Slovak Leas* (1932—33).

The orchestral compositions present *For Eternity* (1928), *The Handrlak Suite* (1930), a *Concerto Prologue* (1936) and *Silesian Dances* (1937).

Vocal Works

Černík's creative work was strongly influenced by his profound interest in folk poetry and music.

His cycles of songs include *The Silesian Songs* set to words by PETR BEZRUČ (1921—28), *Beggars' Songs* to words of JAROSLAV DURYCH (1926—27), *Lullabies* (1928), *From the Herbarium of Petr Bezruč* (1929), *Under the Slavonic Sky* (1930). *From the poetry of Jiří Wolker* (1933), *Love Songs* to words by JAN NERUDA (1937), *The Patriotic Songs* to words by ZDENĚK SPILKA (1939 and 1948), *With a Song on Lips* to words by ZDENĚK SPILKA (1941), *A Revolutionary March and Soldiers' Songs* (1945), *Sokol* and *Pioneer Songs* (1950), *Songs from Gruň*, set to words by PETR BEZRUČ (1950, 1952—53), *Military Songs* (1954), *Through the Universe* (1958) and *Three Slogans* (1961).

Of his choirs for female voice mention should be made of *Love* (1916 and 1926), *From Slovak Poetry* (1932) and *From Time to Time* to words by ZDENĚK SPILKA (1937).

Černík's male choirs include *The Land of Poetry* (1914), *The Path of Life* (1915), *The Country below the Mountains* to words by PETR BEZRUČ (1916), *When You Come to Us* (1930), *Defiance* (1932 and 1935), *From Saturday to Sunday* to words by JIŘÍ WOLKER (1933), *The Recruits* to words by JIŘÍ WOLKER (1935), *At a Father's Grave* to words by JAN NERUDA (1937), two male choirs *"1938"* (1938), *In the Native Village* (1941), *From My Native Region* (1942) and *Greetings to the Soviet Union* (1959).

Černík's cantatas include *The Beloved Poisoner* (1926), *The Murderous Lover* (1927) and *About an Unborn Child* (1933—34).

Folk Songs

Černík ranks among our most prominent collectors and connoisseurs of folk songs (he collected nearly three thousand various songs).

From 1898 he collected and later arranged *Songs of the Moravian Dwellers, Gypsy Songs, Slovak Songs* for female choir and solos, *Brigands' Songs, From the Poprad Hills, From the Marikov Hills*.

For the radio Černík has arranged medleys of folk songs *From Our Břeclava Region, Through the Wallachian Region, In Moravian Slovakia, Through the Silesian Region* and others.

He has also made collections of songs *As We Do It, A Bouquet of Folk Songs from the Brno Region* and *Songs from Beyond the Woods* (Luhačovice).

For publication he has prepared an enlarged edition of *The Songs of the Moravian Hill Dwellers* (about one thousand seven hundred songs).

Writings

Černík has done a great deal of literary music work as well, specializing in folk music dealing with questions of musical education. He has been awarded The Prize of Liberation of the City of Brno.

ČERNÍK, Vilém

[born Brandýs on Labe, 20 May 1909]

After graduation from the Teachers' Training Institute in Prague, Černík taught in his native town. At the same time he studied composition privately with

VLADIMÍR POLÍVKA. He is now a headmaster of a school at Brandýs. He is very active as choirmaster and conducductor of Folk Art Ensembles.

Stage Works

His most important works are the musical fairy-tale *The Mermaid* (1937) and the full-length ballet *The Flower Princess* (1943).

Chamber and Instrumental Works

Amongst his instrumental compositions are the quartet *May Suite*, then *The Work, My Love, The Song of the Land* and *Peace and May 1945*, as well as compositions for piano (*Happiness, Pas de deux* and others).

Vocal Works

The songs *Tell Me My Love* for tenor, soprano and mixed choir with accompaniment and a number of songs for pioneers; then mixed choirs *Our Song, In One's Own, Our Fields, The Proletarians, Follow the Red Flag, The May Country, My Fatherland, To Lenin's Country*.

Dance Music

¶ The valses *For Mummy, The Golden Ears, Monday Valse, Ultramarine, Love pas de deux, The Wedding Gavotte, the Little Gamin*; ¶ the polkas *Teachers' Polka*; ¶ the intermezzos *The Lady-bird* and ¶ marches *The Festival March, We All, Spartakiad March* and *The Radio March*.

ČERVENÝ, Jiří

[born Hradec Králové, 14 August 1887, died Prague, 6 May 1962]

Červený studied law at Charles University. He founded the first Czech literary and political cabaret THE RED SEVEN.

He wrote many popular songs of which *The Hradec Little Songs, Songs from Youth, Mister Bandmaster, Play that Song of Mine* were among the most popular of his day.

For many years he was an official of the Authors' Association for Protection of Rights on Musical Works.

CHLUBNA, Osvald

[born Brno, 22 July 1893]

Holder of the decoration FOR OUTSTANDING WORK

Chlubna studied composition under LEOŠ JANÁČEK at the School for Organists and at the Brno branch of the Master School of the Prague Conservatory.

He was active as a teacher at the School for Organists in Brno, at the Brno Conservatory and at the Janáček Academy of Musical Arts. He is a member of the committee of the Prague Spring Music Festival and chairman of the Janáček Society in Brno. In 1958 he was awarded the Leoš Janáček medal. Chlubna ranks amongst the foremost composers of Moravia, vocal and programme compositions holding a prominent place in his creative work.

Stage Works

In his two operas *The Courtships of the Master of Heslov* (1939—40, première in Brno 1949) and *George of Kunštát and Poděbrady* (his own libretto, 1941—42) Chlubna elaborated themes from Czech history.

In his other operas he drew mostly on dramatic plays: *Catulle's Vengeance*, set to words by JAROSLAV VRCHLICKÝ (1917, première in Brno 1921; in the reworked version produced at the Janáček Academy of Musical Arts 1959), further *Alladina and Palomid*, according to MAURICE MAETERLINCK (1921—22, première in

Brno 1925), *Nura* by Osip Dymov (1930, première in
Brno 1932), *How Death Came to the World* by Alexander
Hartley (1935, première in Brno 1936), *The Cradle* by
Alois Jirásek (1952, première in Brno 1953) and
Eupyros, own libretto (1962).

The ballet *Frolics on Wire*, on his own libretto (1955),
supplements this survey.

Chamber Music

A picture of Chlubna's work is incomplete without
mention of his significant chamber compositions, a field
to which he devoted himself particularly in the twenties
and thirties, at which time the following came into
being: a *String Quartet* No. 1 in G minor (1925), *Sonata*
for violin and violoncello (1925), *String Quartet* No. 2 in C
(1928), *String Quartet* No. 3 in E flat (1933), a *Wind
Quintet* (1936), a *Sonata* for violoncello and piano (1948)
and string quartet *E morta* (1963).

Orchestral Works

Initially Chlubna's orchestral whole work was
inspired by an embittered subjectivism and pessi-
mism: the symphonic poems *Distance and Dreams*
(1916), *Before I Become Silent* (1918), *Two Fairy-tales*
(1920), *A Song of Longing* (1922) and his first *Symphony
of Life and Love*, set on poems of Otakar Březina (1927).
Little by little, however, his compositions have acquired
a character of natural lyricism: the symphonic poem
From the Hillsides, Mountains and Woods (1934), a three-
part cycle of symphonic poems *Nature and Man* (1949
to 1953), a six-part cycle of symphonic poems *This Is
the Land of Mine* (1956—62), a part of which was awarded in 1959 the Prize of the Liberation of the City of
Brno, and two *symphonies*: the *Second* [called Brno
Symphony] (1946) and *the Third* in G (1960).

Instrumental Works

Attached to his chamber music are a piano cycle

Nocturne (1933), *Prelude, Toccata and Fugue* (1933), *Passacaglia* for organ (1934), three piano *Preludes* (1935), an organ *Finale* on a theme of the Jistebnice Hymnbook (1944), *Sonata* for violin (1948), *Sonata* for violoncello (1948) and a *Sonata* for piano (1959).

Vocal Works

Songs: the cycle *Those Asleep Speak with Death* set to poems by OTAKAR BŘEZINA (1918), *A Quiet Reconciliation* set to poems by OTAKAR BŘEZINA (1919), *Three Songs of One Far Away* (1928); during the German occupation Chlubna composed a cycle of songs *The Czech Resurrection* (with orchestra), a part of which contains a hymn of pain and thanksgiving *Hallelujah* to words by OTAKAR BŘEZINA (1943), followed by a song-cycle *Lights Out!* to words by JAROSLAV SEIFERT (1943); after the liberation he has written song-cycles *Eulogies on Liberation* (1945).

From his songs following have a character of social defiance: *Two Ballads* to words by JIŘÍ WOLKER (1925), *The Beggar's Songs* to words by JAROSLAV DURYCH (1927) and *New Year's Eve Song* to words by VÍTĚZSLAV NEZVAL (1932).

Male choirs show his inspirational sources: *A Miner's Ballad* to words by J. V. SLÁDEK (1949), A *Worker's Ballad* (1952), *No, I Cannot Return* to words by JIŘÍ HAVEL (1959), *Hail! Life* (1959) and *A Ballad of the Street* (1962).

Other Works

Chlubna gave expression to his gratitude to LEOŠ JANÁČEK particularly by his instrumentation of the third act and the arrangement of the first and second acts of the opera *Šárka* (1918—19, 1924).

In cooperation with BŘETISLAV BAKALA he instrumented and made compositional arrangement of JANÁČEK's last opera *From the House of the Dead* (1930). In 1940, he completed JANÁČEK's symphony *The Danube* (1948).

Writings

He wrote numerous articles dealing with Janáček's compositional style and personality.

CIKKER, Ján

[born Banská Bystrica, 29 July 1911]

MERITED ARTIST, LAUREATE OF STATE PRIZES,
LAUREATE OF THE CZECHOSLOVAK PRIZE OF PEACE

Cikker is one of the leading personalities of contemporary Slovak music. He began to compose music already as a secondary school student, having been well grounded in the piano by his mother, herself a piano pedagogue.

After completing the secondary school he studied composition at the Prague Conservatory under JAROSLAV KŘIČKA, the organ under B. A. WIEDERMANN and conduting under PAVEL DĚDEČEK. At the Master School he was a pupil of VÍTĚZSLAV NOVÁK. After graduation (his graduation work being a symphonic *Capriccio*) he continued studying conducting under FELIX WEINGARTNER in Vienna.

Since 1939 he has been active in Slovak musical life as professor of the theory of music at the Bratislava Conservatory and after the liberation of Czechoslovakia he was also dramaturgist of the Bratislava Opera. Since 1951 he has continued teaching composition at the High School of Musical Arts where he has trained many talented members of the younger generation of composers.

Stage Works

He used extensively the folklore dance elements in his first opera JURO JÁNOŠÍK, set to libretto by ŠTEFAN HOZA (1953, première in Bratislava 1954; new version 1956). This heroic opera was the first, but Cikker's creative work is now oriented almost exclusively to operatic works where every aspect of his talent can be fully developed.

The second opera *Beg Bajazid*, to a text by JÁN SMREK (1956, première in Bratislava 1957) is a balladic tale of the love for one's native land.

Folklore inspiration, which plays a less important role in *Beg Bajazid* than in the first opera, ceases to fill the function of a symbol and refrains from being a characteristic element in Cikker's third opera *Mr. Scrooge* [Shadows (1959, première in Bratislava and Kassel 1963)], in which the composer formulates a tale inspired by DICKENS' *Christmas Carol*. A profound humanity and a penetrating psychological characterization are combined here with a dramatically effective expressiveness.

Up to the present, Cikker has achieved his finest creative operatic work in his opera *The Resurrection*, to a libretto according to L. N. TOLSTOY's novel (1961, première in Prague 1962 and in Stuttgart 1964). This opera, which has been compared by foreign critics to Allan Berg's opera Wozzeck, clearly demonstrates the strides that Cikker's musical development has made. Above all it manifested a broadening of the composer's ability to express in contemporary musical drama thoughts on the moral greatness and strength of man.

Cikker's operatic work means a high point in the postwar development of Czechoslovak opera and as such has met with outstanding success not only at home but also abroad.

Orchestral Works

Cikker's explosive and emotionally rich personality expressed itself—for a relatively long time—mainly in instrumental compositions. His early works, as his first *Symphony* in C (1930), the symphonic poem *The Epitaph* (1931), the symphonic *Prologue*, op. 13 (1934) and *Capriccio* for full orchestra, op. 14 (1936), all of them dating from the period of his studies, were already note-

CIKKER

worthy; they were followed by *The Spring Symphony*, op. 15 (1937), where Cikker's individual and spontaneously expressed style is characterized by an accentuation on tone quality and intricate harmony.

Cikker's cantata *Cantus Filiorum*, op. 17 (1940), contains the same quality and is a passionate protest against war.

In succession he wrote the first two compositions of the trilogy of symphonic poems entitled *About Life, The Enduring Summer*, op. 19 (1941) and the dramatic poem *The Battle*, op. 21 (*The Soldier and Mother*, 1943), where his work was enriched with impressionistic expressive elements.

The youthfully fresh and optimitic *Concertino* for piano and orchestra, op. 20 (1942, performed in Vienna, Budapest, Berlin and London), *The Slovak Suite*, op. 22 (1942) [awarded a National Prize 1945] and the ballet music *The Bucolic Poem*, op. 23 (1944) are evidence of the composer's inclination to Slovak folklore which not only enriched his imaginative faculty but became as well a source of strength and optimism.

After the war Cikker completed the third poem of his trilogy *About Life*, by the symphonic poem *Morning*, op. 24 (1946).

Soon thereafter Cikker wrote one of his most beautiful scores *Recollections* for five winds and string orchestra, op. 25 (1947), a work of rare intimacy and fervent lyricism.

Orchestral variations on the theme of the choral *Blissful are the Dead* is one of his latest works.

Instrumental Works

In addition to the works referred to, Cikker devotes himself occasionally to instrumental compositions, as are—among others—the virtuosic piano études *The Tatra Streams* (1954) and the piano composition entitled *What Children Told Me* (1957).

Folklore Music

A new intensive contact with folklore material in connection with Cikker's first compositions for the Slovak Folk Artistic Ensemble and Lučnica (*Dupák*, a folk dance with rhythmic stamping, 1950), *The Encounter* (1953), *Songs and Dances of Lučná* (1954), *On Saint John's Day* (1954) were reflected in the extensive use of folklore dance elements in his first operas.

Film and Scenic Music

In the years after the war he wrote notable scenic compositions and accompaniments to films (for inst. music to the film *The Wolves' Dens*).

CMÍRAL, Adolf

[born Roztoky, 12 April 1882—died Prague, 17 September 1963]

MERITED TEACHER, holder of the decoration
FOR OUTSTANDING WORK

Cmíral ranked among the finest pedagogues in school and extracurricular music education in Czechoslovakia.

On completing his studies at the Prague Conservatory (organ and composition) he became organist, music pedagogue and from 1920 professor at Conservatory, where he created a pedagogic section; after the war he became professor at the Academy of Musical Arts.

He propagated intensively progressive trends in musical education. In the early period of the Czechoslovak Radio he helped substantially to realize musical transmissions for youth.

Vocal Works

He composed many songs: among them *Three Tetrads of Gay Songs*, *Baroque Carols*, *A Song to Cremation*;

further three *Old Czech Prayers to Saint Wenceslas* and *Two Prayers of J. A. Comenius*.

For youth he has written instructive vocal compositions as *Songs for Youth*, *A Christmas Lullaby*, *Choral Songs*, one-voice choir *Saint Wenceslas* to words by J. V. SLÁDEK, *Kožíšek's Songs*, *Spring Songs*, *Ditties and Rhymes*, *Pebbles* (rhymes for nursery schools), a military songbook entitled *Song, the Way to the Heart* and *Joy and Love*.

During the German occupation Cmíral created several cantatas: *Balbín's Prayer for the Czech Nation*, *Balbín's Motto "In silentio ac spe fortitude mea"*, the song *Everything But Fear* to words by FRANTIŠEK HALAS, the cantata *We are Winning by Song*, a *Czech Stabat Mater* and others.

In connection with his activity as a collector of songs the following cycles came into being: *Rakovník and Křivoklát Songs*, *Poříč Songs*, *From Suk's Region*, *Songs from Below Blaník*, *Moravian Songs*, *Znojmo Sings*, *Merry Carols from the Giant Mountains*, *Slavonic Carols*, *Old Czech Songs and Carols*, *Our Christmas* and others.

Instrumental Compositions

He has devoted himself as well to instructive compositions for piano: *Three Little Dances*, *Plaveč Moments*, *A March of Little Lead Soldiers*, *Both a Gay and a Sad Song*, *Autumn and Winter in Songs*, *Spring and Summer in Songs*, *How Our Ancestors Danced*, *The Piano Sings*, a cycle of Moravian Slovak and Slovak dances *Dance, Dance, Whirl About!*; for piano for four hands: *Old-time Songs and Dances* and *Old Czech Songs and Chorals*; for violin he composed *Minuets and Meditations*.

His work as organist led him to write smaller compositions for this instrument.

Dance Music

In connection with his instrumental activities, the orchestral *Zlenice Polka*, *Polka from Below Blaník*, *Folk Dances from Benešov Region* and ten *Folk Dances from the Sázava Region* came into being.

Arrangements

Cmíral has also arranged folk songs, *Hussite Chorals* and songs from *Comenius' Hymnal*, made a selection of songs from Škroup's *Bouquet* and from songs which acquired a national character.

Writings

He is the author of the first Czechoslovak textbook of singing *Spring* (1920); then he has written *Basic Concepts of Music* (1921), *Music Pedagogy* (first volume 1937, second volume 1940), *Musical Didactics* in the spirit of J. A. Comenius (1958).

He was editor-in-chief of the Hudební revue (Musical Review), founded and edited the periodical *Music and School* and elaborated and published a detailed syllabus for the teaching of singing. In many articles and essays he dealt with elementary methods in this branch of education.

For youth he has written a booklet on *Bedřich Smetana* (1924).

He published also the authentic text of the national anthem *Where is My Home?* and the facsimile of Škroup's manuscript.

DEVÁTÝ, Antonín

[born Skuteč, 12 June 1903]

Devátý acquired his initial musical education at Žerotín School of Music in Olomouc; later he studied organ at the Prague Conservatory under Bedřich Wiedermann, composition under Jaroslav Křička and conductiong under Václav Talich and Otakar Ostrčil. Besides he studied privately violin with Jindřich Feld and conducting with Pavel Dědeček.

For years he was active as a violinist in Prague and

abroad. In 1938 he became conductor of the Radio Orchestra in Ostrava, from where he went to Brno in the same capacity. In 1951—63 he was chief conductor of the Pilsen Radio Orchestra.

His first attempts at composing produced the *March* for orchestra No. 1 (1925) which was followed by the *Scherzo*, the *Piano Quintet*, *Bagatelles* for piano and the song cycle *In Love*.

In the years 1939—44, he devoted himself to the study of folk songs, resulting in a number of potpourris for choir, solo voices and orchestra [*Through the Moravian Countryside, Under Our Windows, Ho-Slavs!, God Speed, A Bouquet of Polish Songs* and *In the Manner of People of the Haná Region.*

The operetta *All Women Are Alike* also dates from this period.

From 1944—49, Deváty made a more thorough study of the technique of composition with VÍTĚZSLAV NOVÁK and we find then among his works such compositions as the *Humoresque* for piano (orchestra), a *Spring Song* for choir and orchestra and the cantata *Towards the Sun*.

The last few years have produced such works as a march *The Guardians of Peace, Danse Suite, Bumble-bees* for two clarinets, bassclarinet and orchestra, a *Heroic Overture* for orchestra, *Dances of Eastern Bohemia* for choir and orchestra, a *Fantasy* for oboe and orchestra, the suites *Ivana's Toys* and *Pictures from My Native Skuteč, Three Compositions* for flute and orchestra, a *Concerto* for viola and orchestra (première in Tokyo, 1963) and the cantata *To My Beloved Country* for choir and orchestra.

DOBIÁŠ, Václav

[born Radčice, 22 September 1909]

Thrice named LAUREATE OF THE STATE PRIZE,
LAUREATE OF THE INTERNATIONAL PRIZE OF PEACE,
holder of the ORDER OF WORK

Dobiáš studied composition under J. B. FOERSTER,
VÍTĚZSLAV NOVÁK and ALOIS HÁBA.

Since the foundation of the Guild of Czechoslovak
Composers he worked in this organization and became in
1955 its chairman. He is, since 1950, professor of composition at the Academy of Musical Arts.

Chamber Music

His earlier creative work of merit includes *String
Quartet* No. 1 (1931), *Sonata* for violin and piano (1936),
String Quartet No. 2 (1936), *Rhymes* for nonet (1938),
String Quartet No. 3 (1938), *Chamber Symphony* (1939),
String Quartet No. 4 (1942); *Pastoral Wind Quintet* (1943),
intimate *Quartettino* (1944), *Dance Fantasy* for nonet
(1948), and four-movement nonet *Of the Native Land of
Mine* (1952) mark his path towards an individual style.

Orchestral Works

In the first half of 1943, his *First Symphony* for full
orchestra came into being, the three extensive movements of which are filled with the tragic oppressiveness
in the period of German occupation. Then followed the
Sinfonietta for full orchestra (1946—47, reworked 1962),
Sonata for piano, strings, wind quintet and timpani (1947,
reworked in 1958), and a symphonic picture *The
Grande Procession* (1948). His warm sympathy for the
Czechoslovak Army is expressed in his compositions
The Young Symphonists, dedicated to the military school
of music (1948), and *The Festive March* (1951).

In the *Second Symphony* [the State Prize] (1956—57)
the composer aims at creating on the one hand a clean-

cut picture of world and nature, visions, grief and of faith in life-giving peace and on the other hand at finding a new form of musical expression.

Instrumental Works

His first instrumental compositions which we should mention are *Violoncello Sonata* (1938), *Piano Sonata* (1940), *Three Toccatas* for piano (1941) and *Violoncello Suite* (1942) which show an individual style of his own.

In *Three Poetic Polkas* for piano (1950) Dobiáš revalues the traditional intonations of the typical Czech dance.

In the quarter-tone system he composed a *Concertino* for violin and a *Piano Suite* (both 1940).

Vocal Works

Voices: his *Czech Shrovetide* for voice and chamber orchestra (1940) is imbued with a vivid folk quality.

Songs: After the war, he embodied his affection for the Army in his song *Under the Banners* (1945). The tragedy of a small village was personified by his *Songs of Lidice* (1948). In cooperation with the poet FRANTIŠEK HALAS he composed *Little Songs of Our Days* (1949), of which the songs *Forging Ahead, Come With Us on a Brigade* and the *Polka of Peace* have become widely popular.

In addition to songs for community singing Dobiáš has composed cycles of concert songs of which *Dreams* to words to Chinese folk poetry (1956), *Song of Love* (1958) and *Only Prague* (1961) to words by MARIE PUJMANOVÁ are of outstanding character.

Male choirs: During the last years of the Second World War a turn towards folk melody and a more simplified harmony made itself manifestly felt in his creative work and particularly so in his choirs *Oh, Lord, Show Us Your Grace* (1944) and *The Slavonic Linden* (1945).

Children choirs: His understanding of the vivid folk quality is reflected in his two children's choirs *From Spring* and *The Whistle* (both in 1941).

Mixed choirs are best represented by his composition *God's Warriors* for baritone and mixed choir (1952).

Cantatas: In a number of compositions Dobiáš arrived at a musical expression of a living reality, which is particularly shown in his cantata *Stalingrad* (1945) and *The Order No. 368* (1946), emphasizing in a magnificent gradation the merits and sacrifices of the soldiers of the Red Army—the liberators of Prague. His third cantata, the Czechoslovak polka *Build-up Your Country, Thus You Strengthen the Peace*, set to FRANTIŠEK HALAS' poem (1949—50), indicates the road towards a better world.

Popular Music

Dobiáš concentrates serious artistic efforts to the composing of folk music as testified by his popular *Polka of Peace* (1949) and the marches *Tomorrow is Ours* and *Into Further Years* (both 1955).

Various Music

Further arrangements of folk songs, scenic music, music to films and Spartakiads complete Dobiáš's compositional activity; there are to be mentioned: music to the exercises of school gymnasts for the First Spartakiad (1956) [State Prize in 1956] and music to the exercises of the more advanced school gymnasts (both boys and girls) *Set the Fire Aflame on the Mountain Tops* for the Second Spartakiad.

For the Prague Spring 1965 he composed a *Festive Overture*.

International Prizes

Dobiáš's cantata *Build-up Your Country, Thus You Strengthen the Peace* was awarded a gold medal at the World Congress of Peace in Warsaw (1950).

DOBIÁŠ

DOBRODINSKÝ, Bedřich

[born Kunžak, 13 February 1896]

Dobrodinský studied harp, flute and choral singing; in composition he was pupil of JAROSLAV ŘÍDKÝ.

He played flute with the Šak Philharmonic (where he founded a wind quintet). During the years 1922—62 he was solo harpist of the Czech Philharmonic. At the same time he was active as pedagogue at the Academy of Musical Arts.

Instrumental Works

As a composer, Dobrodinský enhanced harp literature with a *Concerto* (1943), a *Baroque Suite* (1947, published also in Moscow) and with an *Impromptu* (1959).

His other works include a *Dance Suite* and ten *Small Compositions* for piano, a *Serenade* for two bassoons, a *Suite* for bassoon and piano, a *Sonata* and *Concertino* for oboe and piano, a *Prelude* and *Capriccio* for flute and piano, a *Bagatelle* and *Rondo* for French horn and piano, a *Prelude* for full orchestra, two *Masses* and a *Wedding March* for organ.

Instructive Works

His instructive music includes a *Suite* for harp (1945), *Duets* for two violins (awarded the second prize in the Jubilee Competition of the Guild of Czechoslovak Composers and the Czech Music Fund in 1956), two *Concertinos* for violin and piano, a *First Performance of a Young Violinist*, *Three Little Dances* for violin and piano, a *Legend* and a *Burlesque* for violoncello and piano, the cycle of songs for children *We Welcome Spring*, an *Overture* for violin divisi and four-hand piano.

He is also the author of cadences to concertos for harp and arrangements of various piano compositions for harp.

Dobrodinský has written a number of technical

articles and studies pertaining particularly to harp playing, as well as a booklet of humorous incidents entitled *The Philharmonic Laughs*.

DONÁTOVÁ, Narcisa

[born Uherské Hradiště, 8 May 1928]

Donátová studied composition at first privately with DESIDER KARDOŠ, later at the Bratislava Conservatory and at the High School of Musical Arts under ALEXANDER MOYZES.

She is at present active in the department of music at the Czechoslovak Television in Bratislava.

Her work, showing the influence of her teacher and of folklore motifs, embraces practically all genres.

In her symbolic music (*First* and *Second Symphony*, an overture "*1921*", *Dances of Eastern Slovakia*) she has aimed at a programme moulding of themes from contemporary life.

She has written the operas *The Forester's Wife* and *Inez* as well as a one-act ballet *The Weiner Case* and a considerable number of vocal compositions (*Three Lyric Songs* for tenor and piano, six revolutionary songs *Liberty to All Peoples*, three patriotic choirs *For Eternal Glory*, eight *Children's Choirs à capella*, arrangements of folk songs, songs for community singing, and the cantata *The Slovak Land of Mine*).

DOUBRAVA, Jaroslav

[born Chrudim, 25 April 1909—died Prague, 2 October 1960]

Doubrava was a private pupil of OTAKAR JEREMIÁŠ (composition). Since 1945 he worked in the musical division of the Prague Radio, later as a dramaturgist.

In his creative work he was influenced by progressive traditions of Czech and world music, which led to an individual compositional expression.

Orchestral Works

Doubrava arrived at a conception approaching an individual expression of his works; his search for this original path led to the evolvement of his three *Symphonies*: the first (choral) 1938, the second (Stalingrad) 1943—44, and the third 1958.

Instrumental Works

In this field he concentrated on a small instrumental form as a piano *Suite* (1937), a piano *Sonatina* (1938), a *Sonata* for solo violin (1942) and several cycles of charming and witty instructive *Miniatures*, destined for young pianists [*The First Polka, Bagatelles, For Five Fingers, Ten Fingers* (1949, 1953 and 1956)]; then the piano *Sonata* (1949) and the second violin *Sonata* (1959).

Vocal Works

Doubrava's sense for abbreviation in song is particularly pronounced. This is most convincingly evident in his *Epigrams* (1939), *Understanding* (1941), a cantata *A Ballad about a Beautiful Death* (1941), *Three Female Choirs* (1942), *Nights* (1944); then children's rhymes to texts by FRANTIŠEK HRUBÍN *Let's Sing Together* (1946), *The Plain Truth* (1952), the cycle *Youth, Enchanting Love* and the *Paradise of Home* (all 1956), *The Tales* to folk texts (1958) and *Five Songs about Love* (1958).

Stage Works

Doubrava's attitude to satire led him to themes particularly suitable for musical dramatic works: following the Shakespearean *Mid-Summer Night's Dream* (1945) he chose the satirical poetic allegory of KAREL HAVLÍČEK BOROVSKÝ *The Baptism of Saint Vladimir*, which served as a model for Doubrava's opera of the same name (1950, unfinished).

HavlÍČek's poem *King Lávra* inspired him to write a ballet (1951, première in Olomouc 1955), which demonstrated the composer's sense for stage forms as well as his attempt to arrive at a new, unconventional conception of ballet pantomime.

The principles and forms of expression contained in this ballet were even more consistently worked out in Doubrava's second ballet *Don Quixote*, according to CERVANTES (1955, première in Brno 1957).

His last work, confirming his strong dramatic talent, was the opera *The Ballad About Love*, on composer's own theme, set in verse by JAN WENIG (1960, unfinished); the final arrangement was carried out by JAN HANUŠ (première in Prague 1962).

DOUBRAVSKÝ, Petr

[born Vienna, 10 April 1925]

Doubravský completed his study of conducting at the Prague Conservatory in the class of ALOIS KLÍMA; he studied composition under MIROSLAV KREJČÍ and FRANTIŠEK PÍCHA.

He was conductor of the theatre orchestras at Olomouc and České Budějovice and of the symphonic orchestra in Ostrava. At present he is conductor of the opera in Liberec.

His *Sonata* for violin (1946), *First String Quartet* (1946) and *Four Meditations* for mixed choir (1947) date from his student years. Furthermore he wrote a lyric cantata *Blossoms of Joy* (1950), a cycle of male choirs (1954), a *Romance* for orchestra (1955) and *Five Compositions* for violoncello and piano (1957).

Within the last few years he has composed the *Pilgrimage Song* (1958), the *Second String Quartet* (1959), *First Symphony* (1959), *Rondo capriccioso* for flute and harp

(1959), a *Small Fantasy* for piano on folk songs of the Iron Mountains (1959), a musical dramatic sketch *In the Name of Life* (1960) and a *Concerto* for violin (1962).

In addition, he has written successful scenic music for the radio, compositions for the variety theatres, dance music and has found his place as well as an arranger of folk songs.

DREJSL, Radim
[born Dobruška, 29 April 1923—died Prague, 20 April 1953]

LAUREATE OF THE STATE PRIZE

After completion of his studies at the Prague Conservatory, Drejsl entered the Academy of Musical Arts as a pupil of PAVEL BOŘKOVEC.

In 1949, he became the artistic chief of the Army Artistic Ensemble Vít Nejedlý, to which he devoted his artistic and organizational aptitudes.

Orchestral Works

His talent was revealed in his *Symphony* for strings (1948) and in *Concerto* for piano and orchestra (1948).

Chamber and Instrumental Music

In this field he has written a *Sonatina* for flute and piano (1947), a wind quintet *Spring* (1948) and *The Harvest-home Suite* for oboe and piano (1949—50).

We should mention his children's ballet *The Negro Boy* and a *Monkey* (for piano, 1945), two piano *Suites* (1945 and 1946), two piano *Sonatas* (1946 and 1947) and a *Sonatina* for bassoon (1948).

Vocal Works

Drejsl has also written fine vocal works of which a cycle of songs for soprano and piano *The Countryside of Childhood* (1946) aroused particular attention. Other vocal compositions following this cycle include *Four Drinkers' Songs*, set to Chinese poetry for baritone and piano (1947) and *Spring Choirs* for female voices (1947 to 1948).

The year 1949 represented a milestone in his creative work; it was then that he wrote his dance compositions on national motifs for solo, choir and orchestra entitled *Karičky*, the popular songs *A Day Abloom*, imbued with fresh lyricism as well as other compositions.

He wrote numerous military songs for the Army Artistic Ensemble (*Hail to the Army!*, *Glory to Tanks!*, *The Candidate* and others), lyrical songs (*Lullaby*, *A Song about Fučík*, *Letter to a Soldier*) and concert songs (*A Letter to the Frontier*, *A Song about a Child*).

The small cantata *In the Name of Jan Žižka* is one of Drejsl's finest compositions.

His last compositions include the songs *A Beautiful Land*, *A Song About the Dearest One*, *A Song About the Dream of a Driver* and *The Song of the Machine-gun Squads*.

Drejsl's creative activities in the field of songs were awarded the State Prize.

Arrangements and Montages

Successful were the arrangements of folk songs *My Beloved Took a Peacock to Pasture* and *Black Mountains*, the montages *Dances* from Velká Kubra and melodramatic montages *The Five Year Plan*, *The Hussite Songs* and *The Oath of Peace*.

DUCHÁČ, Miloslav

[born Prague, 27 January 1924]

Ducháč participated in many amateur orchestras during his secondary school studies. His first compositions were published and recorded in 1942. After graduation he cooperated with several prominent professional ensembles. In 1945, he joined the orchestra of KAREL VLACH as pianist and arranger.

He is co-author of music to several short and medium-length films and to the full-length film *The Star Travels South*. He wrote music to the revue *For Whom?—For You!* (1960).

In the field of dance and jazz music Ducháč has composed ¶ foxtrots: *Happy Day, A Morning Song, When You Are Mine, It Will Be Six, The Empty Frame, Love Without Quarrels, I Don't Know, Finally, Solitude; Amo, Amare; I Open the Window Wide for You, Upon My Soul;*

¶ slow foxtrots: *The Empty Corner, I Would Never Have Dreamed, An Evening Recollection, They Always Say It, A Seat at the Jasmine Tree* (awarded first prize in the competition of the Czechoslovak Radio and the Czechoslovak Television for the best chanson and dance song in 1957), *What Happened to Our Street, I Did Not Love You, Merry Christmas, A Romantic Song, Be Only a Wind;*

¶ slow rock: *I Am Walking along a Quiet Street;*

¶ blues: *Far is the Morning, Laces of Neons;*

¶ waltzes: *I Write You a Letter, Bright Eyes, The Camomile, My Darling Is Not Here;*

¶ twist: *Normally,* the song *A Night Romance;*

¶ orchestral compositions: *A Summer Dream, Promenade, Concertino* for piano and orchestra, *The Roulette, Studio "A", Prazdroj-Urquell 12°, Spring Mood, Something for Richard, Improvisations* and a *Wedding Ha-Ha.*

DUCHAŇ, Jan

[born Šlapanice, 13 May 1927]

Ducháň completed the study of law at the Brno University and studied composition in the class of THEODOR SCHAEFER at the Brno Conservatory, at the

Advanced School of Music in Warsaw and privately with PAVEL BOŘKOVEC.

He was a teacher at the music school in his native town and at Teplice, later becoming a teacher of theory of music and composition at the Brno Conservatory, a post he occupies at present.

His creative work includes *Variations* for piano in an old style (1953), a *Sinfonietta* concertante (1955), a ballet *Pygmalion*, to his own libretto (1955—56, première Ostrava 1963), a *Concerto* for bassoon and orchestra (1956), a three-act comic opera *Canterbury Tales* (1958), a cycle of *Songs* on folk texts (1953), *Variations* for trumpet and piano, *String Quartet* (1954), *Prelude and Toccata* for violoncello and chamber orchestra (1960) and others.

DUSÍK, Gejza
[born Zavar, 1 April 1907]
MERITED ARTIST

After completing the secondary school, Dusík began to study medicine but his interest in music predominated and he transferred to the Neues Wiener Konservatorium, where he graduated in composition, studying under JENÖ ZÁDOR.

Since 1939 he has been active in the Slovak Authors' Union and from 1949 has been its director. There he published in the years 1941—49 most of the dance music written by Slovak composers.

Beginning with the year 1935, Dusík has written many operettas, all of which have attained considerable popularity. They include *A Thousand Meters of Love*, *When the First May Comes Into Bloom*, *A Blue Rose*, *Under a Foreign Flag*, *Turkish Tobacco*, *The Fateful Valse*, *The Mysterious Ring*, *The Court Theatre Box*, *The Golden Fish* and *The Potters' Ball*. His last operetta is *Carneval on*

Rio Grande (1964 awarded the prize M. Schneider-Trnavský).

Many of the melodies from these operettas as well as his dance music have become very popular and some are known abroad.

Dusík is one of the creators of the so-called Slovak tango. Most of his tangos have become "evergreens": *I Am So Sad Without You, So Infinitely Beautiful, This Native Land of Mine, Marina, Two Unfaithful Eyes, Let's Beg the Stars, Light and Shadow, What Can Happen to Me.*

He has written as well many waltzes, foxtrots, polkas and compositions for small chamber orchestra (the suite *Idyllic Pictures*, the serenade *Recollections of Piešťany*, a *Slovak Dance*, a suite *Working People on Recreation*).

DVOŘÁČEK, Jiří

[born Vamberk, 8 June 1928]

Graduated from the organ class of the Prague Conservatory; at the Academy of Musical Arts studied composition under JAROSLAV ŘÍDKÝ and VÁCLAV DOBIÁŠ. At present he is senior lecturer at the Academy of Musical Arts (composition).

Orchestral Works

He attracted considerable attention by his graduation work *The Symphony* (1953); then followed a symphonic *Suite* (1958), an *Overture* for full orchestra (1958), a *Suita Concertante* for full orchestra (1962, awarded in the competition of the Czechoslovak Radio) and a symphonic movement for piano and orchestra *Ex post* (1963).

Chamber Music

During his studies he drew attention by his *Wind Quintet* (1951) and later by his *Sonata Capricciosa* for violin and piano (1956), the *Inventions* for trombone and piano (1961) and *Clarinet Meditations* for clarinets and percussion instruments (1964).

Instrumental Works

His other works include piano variations *The April Sketches* (1955). His *Etudes* for piano (1959) were awarded in the artistic jubilee competition 1960. We have to note still the *Sonatina di bravura* for piano (1960).

Vocal Works

His *Male Choirs*, set to words by FRÁŇA ŠRÁMEK and JAN NOHA, composed on the occasion of the tenth anniversary of the liberation (1955) are often sung at concerts. His songs in C—*Morning Monologues*, for baritone and piano or orchestra (1959), were awarded in the artistic jubilee competition 1960. Noteworthy are his mixed choirs set to verses by the Vietnam poet HO CHI MINH *From the Diary of a Prisoner* (1960), four lyric songs for solo voice and female choir *A New Spring* (1962) and *The Little Song* to verses by ZDENĚK KRIEBL for maiden (children) choir (1963).

Dvořáček has also written a number of variety compositions.

DVORSKÝ, R. A.

[born Dvůr Králové on Labe, 24 March 1899]

Dvorský [proper name Rudolf Antonín] ranks among the pioneers of new Czech dance music. In Prague he appeared at the legendary cabaret THE RED SEVEN and at the cabaret of the popular song writer Karel Hašler, was employed at the Springer's Publishing House and after a short activity on the BUM stage he was bandmaster and singer during the last era of THE RED SEVEN. He founded the ensemble MELODY MAKERS which later became the ensemble THE MELODY BOYS.

Dvorský became renowned due to his interpretation of Czech and foreign dance music. With his ensemble MELODY BOYS he made recordings, appeared on the radio, in many films and concerts in Czechoslovakia and abroad.

In 1936 he founded a publishing house of music. Due to his varied and intensive activity he represented a significant stage in the development of Czech dance music.

In his dance songs he tied in with the creative work of Czech popular composers and text-writers, such as JIŘÍ ČERVENÝ, KAREL HAŠLER (1879—1941), FRANTIŠEK HVÍŽĎÁLEK (1886—1955) and others. He had the ability of giving his compositions expressive melodics.

Early modern dance forms of this popular ballad-singer, conductor and pianist include ¶ the foxtrots *Bells of Cadiz* and *Who Knows* and ¶ the valse boston *Come Along, My Lad!*

Recently he has composed ¶ the foxtrots *It Was Like a Dream, Short-lived Happiness, Morning and Evening, Love Cannot be Dictated to, A Song for a Bumble-bee, Who is in Love, They Say, The Parachutists' Alphabet, Tomorrow*; ¶ the slow foxtrots *An Autumn Romance, I Feel Lonely*; ¶ the samba *Three Patrons*; ¶ a bolero *Far, Far Away*; ¶ the charleston *Tell Me More*; ¶ the song *Prague, I love You*, and others.

EBEN, Petr

[born Žamberk, 22 January 1929]

Eben graduated in composition from the Academy of Musical Arts, studying under PAVEL BOŘKOVEC and piano under FRANTIŠEK RAUCH.

At present, he is lecturer of musical science at Charles University. He is a skilled performer on the piano.

Eben is very prolific composer and decidedly ranks among the promising young talents. His work is marked by a wealth of invention and extraordinary technical aptitude.

Orchestral Works

Eben has mastered with success large forms as is shown by his *Concerto* for organ and orchestra (1954) and a representative *Concerto* for piano and orchestra (1961).

Chamber Music

His small forms are represented by following compositions: *Sonata* for oboe and piano (1950), *Suita balladica* for violoncello and piano (1955), *Duetti per due trombe* (1956), *Sonatina semplice* for flute and piano (1958), *Duettino* for soprano instrument and piano, *Concertino Pastorale* for three instrumental solos and string ensemble and a chamber suite *Ordo Modalis* for oboe and harp (1964).

Instrumental Works

Sonata in D flat for piano (1951), cycle of four compositions *Sunday Music* (Musica dominicalis) for organ (1958) and a cycle of organ compositions *Laudes* (1964).

Vocal Works

During his studies he already attracted attention to himself with his vocal compositions, particularly with *Six Love Songs* with piano (1951). In his compositions for voices are *Ballads* for solos, choir and orchestra to words of folk poetry.

Among his cycles of songs: are to be mentioned *Těšín Songs* (1960), children's songs *Green is the Branch* (1960), seven rhythmic songs *The Spring Tunes* for unison choir with piano and *Songs* set to words by R. M. RILKE (1961, published by Breitkopf & Härtel, Leipzig, 1965), vocal cycle *Songs Unkind* for mezzosoprano and six violas (1963) [a drama expressing the separation of two people] and a cycle a songs *Small Grief* for woman's voice and piano (1964).

Of his choral creative work, mention should be made of his male choir *Epitaph Hic Ego* to a Latin text by OVIDIUS (1957); female choir *About Swailows and Girls* (1960); children choir *Merry-go-round and Stars* for choir and piano (1964); mixed choir *Love and Death* (1959) and a five-voice choir *Ubi caritas et amor* (1964, published by Bärenreiter Verlag Kassel, 1965).

Cantatas: *Old Enchantments of Love* (1959, published by Breitkopf & Härtel, Leipzig, 1965), *The Bitter Earth* to a text by JAROSLAV SEIFERT (1960).

Montages: Lyrical montage *Strophies of Love* for tenor, male choir and recitative, set to words by STIEPAN SHCHIPACHOV (1963).

Instructive Compositions

Eben has also worked in the instructive field and the following have been published: *One Hundred Folk Songs* for piano in easy style, the piano cycle *The World of Little Ones* and the children's dance *Games In the Grass* (1960).

Writings

In cooperation with JARMIL BURGHAUSER he has written a textbook *Reading and Playing of Scores*.

International Prizes

The *Most Intimate Songs* were given an award in the competition at the World Festival of Youth in Vienna, 1959, and the cycle *Seven Love Songs* set to texts of the Middle Ages (1956) were awarded the gold medal in the competition at the Festival of Youth in Moscow, 1957.

ELBERT, Karol

[born Trnava, 19 December 1911]

Elbert is an outstanding writer of Slovak dance music. He studied composition at the Music and Dra-

matic Academy in Bratislava under ALEXANDER MOY-
ZES and conducting under JOZEF VINCOUREK. His graduation work was a *Sonata* for violin and piano.

He has been active as accompanist at the City
Theatre at Opava and conductor of the East Slovak
National Theatre at Košice. After the war, he conducted the Bratislava Musical Comedy and at present is
active at the Bratislava Radio as advisor on light and
dance music.

He devotes himself intensively and with success to
dance music: ¶ the swing *A Little Tear, In the Evening
at Half-past-five*; ¶ the waltz *Autumn Sings a Sad Song*;
¶ foxtrots *Wait Until Tomorrow, I Wouldn't Harm Even
a Fly, In the Rhythm of Happiness, A Scar on the Poplar*; ¶ the
charleston *The Dance in the Forest*; ¶ the slow rock
The Midnight Rendez-vous.

He writes as well music to radio and theatrical
plays, popular symphonic compositions (the suite
At the Circus, Mazurka for violin and orchestra, *The Pioneers' Suite*, the *First* and *Second Slovak Rhapsody*), songs
for children and youth (*Boys and Girls, Let's Go!*) and
political songs (*A Song About a Red Sun, A Song About
the Soviet Space Ship*).

He is also the author of two operettas, *From Harbour
to Harbour* and *Till We Meet Again, My Love*.

FADRHONS, Jan

[born Uherce, 14 February 1910—died Prague, 7 July 1963]

Holder of the ORDER OF WORK and of decoration
FOR MERIT IN THE BUILDING-UP OF THE COUNTRY

His father was a folk musician. At the Prague Con-
servatory he graduated from the instrumental section
(French horn), where he studied under ANTONÍN JA-
NOUŠEK and from the section of conducting under

Pavel Dědeček; in addition, he continued his compositional work with Alois Hába, Rudolf Karel and Jaroslav Řídký, studying instrumentation as well under the latter.

In 1939—45 he was active at the Czechoslovak Radio, first as a musical manager, later as a conductor.

During his long service in the army, he occupied in succession posts of a bandmaster, artistic director of the Military Artistic Ensemble in Prague, chief conductor of military ensembles, attached to the Army Artistic Ensemble Vít Nejedlý, and senior inspector of military bands.

His work in the field of instrumentation is extensive. For military ensembles he has arranged many compositions for wind instruments and symphonic orchestra. He did considerable work on the instrumentation of the Spartakiad.

The best known of his compositions are the marches *The Cavalry Trumpeter, Hail the Hunter, Company, Forward March!*, the *March of Submachine Gunners*, the *Victorious Start* and others.

In addition to works for brass band, Fadrhons wrote variety and symphonic compositions of which the most popular are: *The Polonaise*, a *Capricious Valse*, the intermezzo *A Fairy-tale Night, Elegy, Small Pieces* for violoncello and a *Folk Dance Suite*.

FELD, Jindřich

[born Prague, 19 February 1925]

Feld comes of a musical family (his father Jindřich Feld was a well-known violin pedagogue). After completing the secondary school he matriculated at the Prague Conservatory. But it was only after the German occupation that he could continue his study of composition under Emil Hlobil and then at the Academy of

Musical Arts under JAROSLAV ŘÍDKÝ, simultaneously completing a course of study of musicology at Charles University.

Stage Works

He dedicated his radio opera *A Fairy-tale About Budulínek* to children (1955); his children's opera *The Postman's Fairy-tale* on a theme by KAREL ČAPEK (1956) was awarded a prize in the jubilee competition (1960).

Chamber Music

He devoted himself predominantly to instrumental music; special notice deserve: a *Suite* for clarinet and piano (1948—49), *String Quartet* No. 1 (1949), a *Wind Quintet* (1949), *String Quartet* No. 2 (1952), a *Sonatina* for two violins (1952—53), *Elegy and Burlesque* for violoncello and piano (1954—55), a *Sonata* for viola and piano (1955, awarded the prize of the Guild of Czechoslovak Composers and the Czech Music Fund in 1956), a *Concerto* for chamber orchestra in C (1956—57), a *Sonata* for flute and piano (1957, published by Leduc, Paris in 1960), a *Prelude* and *Toccata* for two pianos (1960), a *Chamber Suite* for nonet (1960, published by Leduc, Paris in 1963), a *Suite* for string chamber orchestra (1960—61, produced as a ballet in Hannover 1963), a *Trio* for violin, viola and violoncello (1961), a *Duo* for flute and bassoon or bassclarinet (1962, published by Leduc, Paris in 1964), *String Quartet* No. 3 (1962) [this one was published in München 1965], a *Trio* for flute, violin and violoncello (1963), a *Capriccio* for wind quartet and guitar (1964) and *String Quartet* No. 4 (1965).

Orchestral Works

Two symphonic *Marches* (1948 and 1949), a *Divertimento* for string orchestra (1950), *Furiant* (a Czech folk dance) for symphonic orchestra (1951), a *Concerto* for orchestra (1951, worked over in 1957), a *Comedy Overture* (1953, awarded a prize in the jubilee competition), a *Concerto* for flute, string orchestra, piano, harp and percussion instruments (1954, awarded a prize in the competition at the World Festival of Youth in Moscow 1957), a *Rhapsody* for violin and orchestra (1956), a dramatic overture *"May 1945"* (1959—60, which was awarded in the artistic jubilee competition in 1960), *The Thuringia Overture* for symphonic orchestra (1961), *Three Frescos* for symphonic orchestra (1963), and *Concerto* for oboe, bassoon and orchestra (1964).

Instrumental Works

Noteworthy among them are *Four Pieces* for solo flute (1954, published by Leduc, Paris in 1964), a *Violoncello Concerto* (1958), a *Bassoon Concerto* (1958—59, published by Leduc, Paris in 1961), *Rhapsody* for organ (1963) and performing compositions for trumpet and piano, oboe and piano, clarinet and piano (1963—64, published by Leduc, Paris in 1964).

Instructive Compositions

They are a *Suite of Seven Small Instructive Compositions* for violin and piano (1955) and an *Instructive Suite* for clarinet and piano (1960).

Vocal Works

Considerable note deserve: a cycle of male choirs *War*, set to a text by Fráňa Šrámek (1954) and a *Song of Peace* (which was given an award in the artistic jubilee competition in 1960) and a number of small songs.

Various Compositions

Feld has composed several scenic works, mainly to fairy-tales, popular compositions for variety performances and others. His gallop *Two Naughty Boys* for two flutes and orchestra has become particularly popular.

•

In his most recent creative work Feld uses many media of expression offered by new compositional methods (dodecaphonic and serial method).

FELIX, Václav

[born Prague, 29 March 1928]

Felix studied composition at the Academy of Musical Arts under PAVEL BOŘKOVEC and VÁCLAV DOBIÁŠ and theory under KAREL JANEČEK.

He was editor of HUDEBNÍ ROZHLEDY (Music Review) and secretary of the composition section of the Guild of Czechoslovak Composers. He is candidate of philosophical sciences and at present senior lecturer in theory of music at the Academy of Musical Arts.

His compositional trend was influenced by his long cooperation with folk art ensembles where his interest was stimulated especially in vocal and chamber music.

Chamber and Instrumental Music

In the field of chamber music Felix composed a *Sonatina* for double-bass and piano, op. 1 (1951), three *Piano Trios* No. 1, op. 3 (1955), No. 2, op. 5 (1957) and No. 3, op. 15 (1962), then a *Sonata* for violoncello and piano, op. 12 (1960), a *String Trio*, op. 14 (1961), a *Duo* for violin and violoncello, op. 19 (1962) and *Sonatina* for violin and piano, op. 20 (1963) and a *Quintet* for harp and strings, op. 23 (1963).

Orchestral Works

Felix' symphonic work is represented by a *Concertino* for violin, clarinet, harp and string orchestra, op. 2 (1953, his graduation work), a *Fantasy* for clarinet and orchestra, op. 9 (1959) and *Variations Concertantes* for symphonic orchestra, op. 16 (1962).

Vocal Works

His vocal works include a cycle of choirs *Three Ballads*, set to words of Chod folk poetry, op. 6 (1958), *Memento* op. 7 (1959), *To a Little Daughter*, op. 8 (1959), the song cycle *Battlefield*, op. 10 (1960), four *Cosmic Songs*, op. 11 (1960), the chamber music cantata *The Open House*, op. 13 (1961), a cycle duets *The Primer*, op. 17 (1962), the song *Boys and Men*, op. 18 (1962), *Black Country*, op. 21 (1963), *Three Male Choirs*, op. 24 (1963) and *All Day through I Sing* (1964).

Various Compositions

In addition, Felix has written a number of pioneer songs, choirs and incidental music. His pioneer song *The Days of Joy* received a special award in the artistic jubilee competition in 1960.

Writings

Of his theoretical works, the monograph *Smetana's Harmony* (1955—57) is of importance.

International Prizes

The oratorio *The Tale About Lenin*, op. 4 (1956) was awarded the bronze medal in the competition of the World Festival of Youth in Moscow (1957).

FERENCZY, Oto

[born Brezovice, 30 March 1921]

Ferenczy acquired basic musical education from OLDŘICH HEMERKA and developed it in study of his own.

After taking a doctor's degree he became chief of the music division of the Bratislava University Library, but since the foundation of the High School of Musical

Arts in 1949 he has been a lecturer at this school in aesthetics and theory of music. In 1954, he was appointed assistant professor. At the same time he was named a dean, then vice-rector and since 1962 rector of this school.

He began composing even during his studies at the University, orienting himself mainly to BÉLA BARTÓK nad IGOR STRAVINSKY. *The Music* for four string instruments [1947, given an award in the Béla Bartók International Competition in Budapest (1948)] and a *Concerto* for nine instruments in one part (1949) are the most significant works of this early phase of his development.

Orchestral Compositions

During the subsequent stage he composed several orchestral works based on East Slovak folklore elements: *Merry-making*, a dance picture from Šariš (1951) a symphonic fragment *A Picture From My Native Region* (1952), *The Hurbanesque Overture* (1952), a stylization of songs from the period of Slovak national renaissance, *The Dance Fantasy* (1953), and a *Rondo* (a round dance, 1954); in the middle 1950s Fcrenczy's work shows a concentration of expressive qualities, is free of pathos and clear of unnecessary content; this is true in particular of his *Capriccio* for piano and orchestra (1957), *Elegy* for full orchestra (1958) and *Finale* for full orchestra (1958).

Chamber Music

Beginning with *The Serenade* for strings, harp, flute, clarinet and bassoon (1955), Ferenczy brings in his work a qualitative expression, which is shown particularly in his *First String Quartet* (1961—62, awarded the prize J. L. Bella 1964).

Vocal Works

His vocal creative work is extensive as well and his most outstanding songs are the *Three Brigands' Songs* for baritone and orchestra (1952), a *Bouquet of Forest Flowers* for baritone and piano (1961) and a cycle of children's songs *The Alphabet* (1959).

His choral works include the male choirs *The Fragrance of the Mountain* (1951), *The Toast* (1951), *Children's Pictures* (four choirs à capella, 1951), *A Winter Song* (1952), *Three Male Choirs* (1959) and the mixed choir *The Ode* (1956).

In memory of the Norwegian humanist BJÖRNSTJERNE BJÖRNSON, Ferenczy wrote a cantata *The Northern Star* for baritone, mixed choir and orchestra (1960).

Writings

In addition to his activity as a critic, he has devoted himself as well to scientific work in the field of musical psychology, theory and aesthetics. He wrote numerous important works in these fields, the most outstanding of which is his *Aesthetics of Music*.

FIALA, Jaromír

[born Postoloprty, 30 December 1892]

Holder of the decoration FOR OUTSTANDING WORK

Fiala was professor at secondary schools at Domažlice and in Prague. At the Conservatory, he was pupil of ALBÍN ŠÍMA (piano), OTAKAR ŠÍN (composition) and ANTONÍN HEŘMAN (singing).

As a member of the Prague choral society HLAHOL and choirmaster of the Domažlice choral society ČERCHOVAN, he acquired considerable musical experiences. In the main, his interest was concentrated on musical education of the young generation and on the field of song. He wrote valuable contributions dealing with problems, presented by these two fields, translated texts of many songs and operas, lectured extensively on music for the general public and edited numerous musical publications.

Instrumental Compositions

In this field he wrote a *Souvenir* for violin with piano (1944), a lyric suite *A Summer Day* (1947—55), *Four Lullabies* and *Valse brillante* (1956) for piano.

Vocal Works

Fiala's compositional work embraces:

male choirs: *Lost* (1931), *In June* (1932), *From Heart to Heart* (For a Bit of Love—Christmas, 1942), *Give Away Your Heart* (1949);

female choirs: *Two Female Choirs* (Nocturne—A Shower, 1932), *I Know* (1936), *That Love* (Embroidering 1944, Deceived 1945), *Three Female Choirs* [A Love Song—A Little Russian Song—Eva Sings] (1960);

mixed choirs: *A Christmas Song* (1927), *A Slavonic Linden* (1930), *The National Flag* (1931), *At the Start* (1932), *Three Instructive Choirs* (1932—33) and a cycle of three choirs *With One's Heart for the Native Country* (1933—40);

children's choirs: *To a Young World, Four Seasons, Autumn, Dance of the Snowmen, God Speed! From a Children's World,* as well as canons;

solo songs: *Two Songs for my Little Son* (1930, 1944), *Two Wedding Songs* with organ (1952, 1954), *Come Infant Jesus!* (1955), *A Song About Prague* (1957);

songs for choirs: *Our Song* (1934), *For Liberty and Fatherland* (1937), *The March of Youth* (1946), *Hand in Hand to the Goal* (1948), *To Our Youth* (1950—55) [given an award in the Jubilee Competition of the Guild of Czechoslovak Composers and the Czech Music Fund, 1956].

Fiala is as well the author of military songs and of many arrangements of songs and folk songs, both Czech and foreign.

FIALA, Jiří Julius

[born Prague, 14 September 1892]

Fiala graduated from the organ and composition divisons of the Prague Conservatory as a pupil of ONDŘEJ HORNÍK, JOSEF KLIČKA, FRANTIŠEK SPILKA and KAREL STECKER. Then he studied composition under VÍTĚZSLAV NOVÁK.

He was conductor at various Prague and other theatres and later chief of the opera in České Budějovice.

Stage Works

Fiala composed the one-act opera *Love's Wonder*, according to JULIUS ZEYER (1924, reworked in 1962), and the romantic opera *The Respectable Matrons of Pardubice*, one of his latest compositions.

In the early stage of his work he has written a full-length ballet *The Ruler of the Yellow Poison*, to a libretto by J. JENČÍK (1912) and the ballet *Golem* (1920).

Among his operettas we should mention *The Kissing Baron*, *The Boys of the First Legion*, *Patriots from the Shanty*, *Strahováček*, *The White Infantry*, *The Musicians' Lillian*, *Babbie* and *Prague is Beautiful*.

In 1946 Fiala transcribed and instrumented the operetta *The Wedding in Malinovka* by the Soviet composer B. A. ALEXANDROV.

Chamber Music

With a long interval he composed following chamber music works: a *Suite of Polish dances* for piano trio (1913), a *Suite of Czech Dances* for wind quintet (1915), a *Serenade* (1920), *Miniatures* (1944) and *Piano Quintet* (1962).

Orchestral Works

He contributed to Czech orchestral works by such compositions as the *Symphonic Scherzo* (1912), a *Suite of Czech Dances* (1913), a *Comedy Overture* (1913), the symphonic poem *War and Peace* (1917, reworked 1944), an *Overture in an Old Style* (1922), a cycle of Spanish dances *A Spanish Grotesque* (1923), an *Optimistic Overture* (1945), a *Revolutionary Polonaise* (1947), *The Legend* (1949), a cycle of symphonic pictures in three parts *A Legend of Old Prague* (1960), and the symphonic triptych *Yesterday-Today-Tomorrow* (1962).

The works in this field include also a serenade *Con amore* (in various arrangements), a *Cavatina* for violoncello and orchestra, a *Nocturne*, three *Grand Valses*, a *Concertino* for trumpet, and a *Polonaise*.

Vocal Works

His vocal music is represented by a cantata set to a poem *May* by K. H. MÁCHA for solos, choir and orchestra (1924) and by *The Singing Fountain* for coloratura soprano, solo flute, violoncello, female choir and orchestra (1920).

Film Music

Since 1932, he has devoted himself mainly to film music. He is the author of music to 28 short and 35 full-length films (amongst others *The Musicians' Lillian, Grandmother, Jan Cimbura, The Respectable Matrons of Pardubice, A Little Town in the Palm of a Hand*).

FISCHER, Jan F.

[born Louny, 15 September 1921]

Holder of the decoration FOR RECONSTRUCTION SERVICES

Fischer studied composition with JAROSLAV ŘÍDKÝ. He was also active temporarily as secretary for small forms at the Guild of Czechoslovak Composers.

At present, he is chairman of the composers' section of the Guild of Czechoslovak Composers.

Stage Works

His stage creative work contains the operas *The Bridegrooms* (1956, première in Brno 1957) and *Romeo,*

Juliet and Darkness, according to the novel by Jan Otčenášek (1961, première in Brno 1962, Plauen 1962 and Stralsund 1964), and the ballet *Eufrosina*, on motives of J. K. Tyl (1951, première in Liberec, 1956).

He wrote incidental music to many plays. His music to the stage adaptation of Karel Čapek's play *The War with the Newts* by Pavel Kohout (première in Prague 1963) and Hašek's *Good Soldier Schweik* as well as music to the comedy *El Anzuelo de Fenisa* by Lope de Vega and the musical *A Black Cat Crossing the Street* have attracted considerable attention.

Orchestral and Instrumental Compositions

Fischer has composed a number of compositions for concert platforms, including the *Sonata* for piano (1944), a *Suite* for wind sextet (1944), a *Pastoral Sinfonietta* (his graduation work at the Conservatory, 1944), a *Ballad* for string quartet and clarinet (1949), a *Fantasy* for piano and string orchestra (1953) and a one-movement *Symphony* (1959).

A *Concerto* for viola and orchestra (1946), *Essay* for full jazz orchestra and solo piano (1947) and a *Dance Suite* for symphonic orchestra (1951).

Fischer's cooperation with the Army Artistic Ensemble Vít Nejedlý has also had outstanding results as testified to by the following compositions: *Nights over Prague*, *Dance of Friendship*, a *Meeting in Irkutsk*, *Physical Culture*, *Victory* and *The Tartars in Slovakia*.

Vocal Works

His original or adapted songs to the plays of the Spanish classics have become popular as, for instance, the songs in Cervantes' *Pedro de Urdemalas* or Lope de Vega's comedy *La Discreta Enamorada*, *El Acero de Madrid* and *Perro del Horiolono*.

Chansons and Dance Songs

He had created as well a new type of political and

satirical songs and chansons, such as *With a Bowler in Hand, Pardon, I Must, The Atomic Fairy-tale* and *The Prague Day.*

Fischer's dance songs are particularly successful; they include *How Shall I Say It, The Lad's Song* and others.

Film Music

He has written music to many films, of which the following are ¶ full-length: *Whereunto With It?, Cudgel, out of the Bag!, On the Silver Mirror, The Puppies, The Girl Robinson, Here are Lions, The Main Prize, The Uncomely Miss, Gazing Into Her Eyes, A Beautiful Ride, A Hunt for a Mammoth*; ¶ the animated cartoons *You Must Be Mine, A Fairy-tale About Trees and the Wind, The Devil and Kate, How Man Learned to Fly* and *Man Under Water*; for his music to the animated cartoon *A Hen Poorly Drawn-up* he received an award for the best musical work composed for Czechoslovak films in 1963.

International Prizes

First prize for a film for children *Little Pot, Boil!* at Bienale in Venezia 1953; second prize for the film *Grandfather Automobile* at the World Exposition in Brussels 1958; he composed also music to the first polyecran *Prague Spring*; for this music and his cooperation for the World Exposition in Brussels (1958) he was awarded a prize by an international jury.

FIŠER, Ján
[born Hronec, 9 May 1896—died Bratislava, 23 December 1963]

Fišer worked under a pen-name KVETOŇ; he studied composition and conducting at the Prague Conservatory (composition under J. B. FOERSTER and K. B. JIRÁK);

in 1948, he took his degree of Doctor of Philosophy at the Bratislava University. Since 1950, he was professor of theory and history of music at the Bratislava Conservatory.

Stage Works

His most important composition is the opera *Málka*.

Instrumental Music

He composed three string *Quartets*, a string *Sextet*, a piano *Sonata* in F minor and three piano compositions *The Drawings*.

Vocal Works

His other works include the cycle of choirs *Mother*, *The Rose Tree*, *Tree Shoots*, and the cantata *An Idyll on Highlands*.

For children he wrote a cycle of songs with piano *I Sing a Song*.

Writings

He was active also as a music critic and historian and wrote following professional books: *The History of Music* (1933), a *Monograph on Andrej Očenáš* (1955), *Music Theory* (1959), then a larger study of VIETORIZOV's *Tabularized Book* (1954) and *The History of the Opera of the Slovak National Theatre*.

FIŠER, Luboš

[born Prague, 30 September 1935]

Fišer graduated from the Prague Conservatory and the Academy of Musical Arts as a pupil of EMIL HLOBIL.

He has composed four piano *Sonatas*, the first of which (1955) was awarded second prize in the Grand

Jubilee Competition of the Guild of Czechoslovak Composers and the Czech Music Fund in 1956.

Furthermore, he has composed a violin sonata *The Hands* (1961), two *Symphonies* (1956 and 1960), an one-act opera *Lancelot* (1960, première in Prague 1961) and a musical *The Good Soldier Schweik* (1962, première in Prague 1962).

His latest creative works are represented by the three-part *Symphonic Fresco* (1962—63), a *Relief* for organ (1964) and a *Chamber Concert* for piano and twelve wind instruments (1964).

He has written as well considerable incidental music for the radio, television and films (*Cucumber Hero, The Length of a Kiss, The Lost Face*); with JARMIL BURGHAUSER and JIŘÍ STERNWALD he composed music to the film *The Place in the Crowd*.

FLEGL, Josef

[born Hořice, 7 December 1881—died Prague, 7 May 1962]

Flegl belongs among aknowledged composers of valuable instructive compositions for piano. After return to civilian life from military service he applied his experiences as a member of the Czech Philharmonic and other outstanding Prague orchestras. Later he decided to devote himself to the teaching profession for which he was prepared by the well-known piano pedagogue ADOLF MIKEŠ, the composer VOJTĚCH ŘÍHOVSKÝ and the music theoretician LUDVÍK BEZECNÝ.

The insufficiency of Czech piano literature for youth prompted Flegl to attempt to solve certain technical problems of piano playing. His pedagogic experiences, compositional dexterity and warm sympathy for folk songs resulted in a number of compositions which became very popular, particularly his *Pictures for Children*,

New Pictures for Children, Children's Suite, Czech Paradise (for four hands), *Gay Blossoms* and others.

He also made arrangements in an easy style of famous operatic arias and dance compositions, thus contributing to a great extent in acquainting students with them and giving them a more enduring popularity.

Flegl achieved considerable success with several of his vigorous orchestral marches and dances and by his expressive *Songs and Dances of Hořice* for middle voice with piano accompaniment.

He was also a keen student of piano compositions by Czech masters of the eighteenth century. In collaboration with the music historian VLASTIMIL BLAŽEK, he edited a collection of seventeen compositions by DUŠEK, MYSLIVEČEK, VAŇHAL, KOŽELUH, BEČVAŘOVSKÝ, DUSÍK and HELD.

FLOSMAN, Oldřich

[born Pilsen, 5 April 1925]

Flosman acquired a basic musical education from his mother and from JOSEF FLEGL and VLADIMÍR POLÍVKA, his teachers. He studied composition at the Prague Conservatory under KAREL JANEČEK and at the Academy of Musical Arts under PAVEL BOŘKOVEC.

He became artistic manager of the Army Artistic Ensemble Vít Nejedlý.

His creative work is characterized by wittiness with a bend to sarcasm and unsentimental lyricism and can be divided into three evolutionary periods:

In the first are grouped compositions from his student years, betraying modernistic influences, that climaxed in his *Double Concerto* for harp, clarinet and orchestra (the composer's graduation work of 1950). *The First Wind Quintet* (1948), *Bagatelles* for wind instruments and piano (1950), *The Preludes* (1950) and *The Sonatina* for harp (1951) belong to the same category.

The second period is characterized by strong folk influences and includes compositions for the ensembles of Folk Art, Army Artistic Ensemble Vít Nejedlý and the Czechoslovak State Ensemble of Songs and Dances (*The Chod Wedding, The Stamp Dance, Czech Masquerades, Vrtěná* (a folk dance), *Dance with a Rifle* and numerous arrangements of folk songs and dances, as well as the operetta *Ferkl is to Blame.*

This period reached its culmination point in *The Brigands' Sonatina* for clarinet and piano (1952).

In the third period (as yet incomplete) Flosman is seeking new paths. From past associations he has retained his fondness for LEOŠ JANÁČEK; in all else his creative endeavours have a tendency to SERGEY S. PROKOFIEV and DIMITRY D. SHOSTAKOVICH. This path is for the time being documented by a *Clarinet Concerto* (1954), *String Quartet* (1956) and *Concertino* for bassoon and orchestra (1956).

The most notable compositions of this period include *The Jeseníky Suite* for viola and piano (1956), a nonet *The Ghostly Suite* (1956) and *Violin Concerto* (1958), one of the best of his compositions.

Flosman also composed a full-length ballet *The Taming of the Shrew* (1960, première in Liberec 1961), and a pantomime *Pierrot and Colombine* (1957).

He collaborated in composing music for the First and the Second Spartakiad.

His cantata *Three Stoppings* for three solo voices, children's and mixed choirs and orchestra to words by ERICH SOJKA (1960), and his dance scene *The Woman Partisan* (1960) were given an award in the artistic jubilee competition in 1960.

The following compositions are his most recent ones: Sonata for piano *Butterflies Do Not Live Here* (1961), *Dances* for harp and string quartet (1961), a violin sonata *A Dream About the Violin* (1962), the *Second Wind Quintet* (1962) and the *Cuban Overture* (1962).

FOLPRECHT, Zdeněk

[born Turnov, 26 January 1909—died Prague, 29 October 1961]

Holder of the decoration FOR OUTSTANDING WORK

After completing the secondary school, Folprecht studied composition at the Prague Conservatory under J. B. FOERSTER and at the master School under VÍTĚZSLAV NOVÁK, simultaneously studying conducting under VÁCLAV TALICH.

He was opera conductor at the National Theatre in Bratislava and from the year 1939 of the National Theatre in Prague.

Stage Works

His musical dramatic work is comprised in the opera *The Fatal Game of Love* [according to a story by ČAPEK BROTHERS (1926, première in Bratislava 1926)] and in a scenic symphony to the composer's own libretto *A Broken Heart* (1934, première in Bratislava 1936). The melodrama *Meditation* to words by RABINDRANÁTH TAGORE (1961) belongs among his last compositions.

Orchestral Works

In his creative work he was influenced by the compositional style of his teacher VÍTĚZSLAV NOVÁK. He composed four *Symphonies* (1937, 1950, 1951, 1959), an orchestral fantasy set to Slovak folk songs *In the Forlorn Valley* (1934), *Scherzo fantastico* for full orchestra (1937), a *Piano Concerto* (1940), a *Festival Overture* (1948), a *Violin Concerto* (1951) and a symphonic poem *The Summer Solstice* (1956).

Chamber Music

His chamber music is represented by a *Suite* (1925), *Moods* for chamber orchestra (1926), a *String Quintet* (1930), a *Sonata* for piano (1933), three *String Quartets* (1933, 1949, 1955), a *Small Suite in an Old Style* for flute and harp (1937), a *Wind Quintet* (1938), a *Concertino* for nonet, one of his best compositions (1940), a *Rondo* for two pianos (1952) and *Capriccio* for violin and piano (1956).

Vocal Works

Of his numerous song-cycles *Songs* for baritone and orchestra (1920) and a *Secret Love* for baritone and orchestra (1945) are particularly significant. He is also the author of a cantata *The Hymn of Resurrection* (1929), of a lyrical cantata *Czech Spring* (1942) and of many choirs.

Scenic Music, Arrangements

Folprecht has written as well scenic music and music to radio plays. He has also made arrangements of Czech and Slovak folk songs (*Twelve Slovak Folk Songs* for middle voice and piano, *Mountain Songs*, *A Suite of Czech, Moravian and Slovak Songs and Dances*).

FOŘT, Vladimír

[born Vetlá, 5 February 1904]

Fořt wrote hikers' songs as early as at the time of his studies at the Law Faculty of Charles University. In 1927 he founded the ensemble the DICKEY CLUB TRIO and as a composer he collaborated with the SONG CLUB and the BAJO TRIO.

His most popular songs of that period include *Making-Believe We are Small Children*, ¶ the slow foxtrot *Indian Love* (The Lake Slumbers), ¶ foxtrots *I Shall Come after You*, *Hi—Ho—Sailors!*, ¶ a fox march *A Cottage on the Water*. His ¶ tangos *The Pine*, *You Know*, *My Beloved* and *Dájo, Don't Call!* belong to his most frequently played compositions.

Together with KAREL BALLING, under whom he studied composition, he composed the operetta *Deuce, Take the Aunt!* Fořt collaborated with BEDŘICH NIKODEM as a text writer (*Manuela, And the Violin Played, All Alone in a Canoe, Two Smiles, Cottage of Mine, Parting*).

Fořt has also written numerous texts for the composer FRANTIŠEK SVOJÍK, including ¶ the foxtrots *I Have a Rocking Horse at Home* and *The Fakir*, and ¶ the slow foxtrots *A Lullaby from Harlem* and *A Red Crinoline*.

Fořt is a director of the Author's Association for the Protection of Rights on Musical Works.

FRANCISCI, Ondrej

[born Tótkomlós (Hungary), 10 November 1915]

Francisci studied music at the Teachers' Training Institute at Miskolc and for a short time at the Academy of Music in Budapest. After his return to Czechoslovakia he entered the class of composition under ALEXANDER MOYZES at the High School of Musical Arts in Bratislava.

Since his graduation he has been active as choirmaster of the Children's Ensemble of the Czechoslovak Radio in Bratislava, well-known even abroad. He devotes himself mainly to vocal and instrumental creative work for children and youth, to chamber music and songs.

Francisci has written many popular songs for children, cycles of choirs (choirs à capella *To Make Children Happy*, six choirs with orchestral accompaniment *Children of Freedom*, twenty songs to children's games with accompaniment by a string quartet and flute), arrangements of folk songs, piano compositions *The Pioneers at the Piano*, music to puppet plays and to physical-cultural festivals.

For the smallest children he has arranged a col-

lection of songs with piano accompaniment entitled
Little Songs.

He is, as well, the author of several male choirs
à capella and of a small cantata for mixed choir and
orchestra called *The Beautiful Land.*

FRANCL, Jaroslav

[born Kutná Hora, 28 February 1906]

Francl graduated from the composition and conducting departments of the Prague Conservatory as pupil of
JAROSLAV KŘIČKA and PAVEL DĚDEČEK.

He was director of the music school at Kutná Hora
and later at Znojmo and became regional inspector of
music schools at Jihlava, headmaster of the music school
of Jaroslav Kvapil in Brno and at present he is inspector
of music schools for the Central-Bohemian region. He
cooperated also with E. F. BURIAN.

Stage Works

Francl wrote for the stage a children's play with songs
Schwanda, the Bag-piper (1930) and a ballet *Niobe* (1945
to 1946).

Chamber Music

His compositional work in chamber music includes
three *String Quartets* (1933, 1946, 1957), *The Nonetino*
(1938), a *Duo* for violin and violoncello (1940), a *Fantasy*
for clarinet, violin, viola and violoncello (1955),
a *Quintettino* for flute, oboe, clarinet, French horn and
bassoon (1962), a *Sonata* for violin and piano (1962),
Three Pieces for bassoon and piano (1962), *Reportages* for
wind quintet (1963) and *Suite* for clarinet, violin and
violoncello (1964).

Orchestral Compositions

In this field he has written an orchestral *Overture* (1960) and a *Concerto* for viola and orchestra (1961).

Instructive Compositions

They are popular and much sought after. They include three *Instructive Little Compositions* for clarinet and piano, a *Pastoral Suite* for flute, oboe and piano, *Instructive Little Compositions* for trumpet and piano, *Elementary Études* for clarinet (trumpet) and piano and five *Instructive Little Compositions* for violin and piano (1964).

Vocal Works

Francl composed *Songs* for alto and string quartet (1932) and later a cantata *A Meeting in a Meadow in May 1945* (1960).

His work as choirmaster for the Teachers' Mixed Choir at Kutná Hora led him to write numerous arrangements of folk songs and his post as conductor in the Uplands Chamber Orchestra at Jihlava stimulated his interest in writing *Folk Songs from the Moravian Uplands* for girls' choir and small orchestra, *The Upland Songs* for solo voice and chamber orchestra and *Variations on a Czech Folk Song* for French Horn and strings.

FREŠO, Tibor
[born Štiavnik, 20 November 1918]
Holder of the decoration FOR OUTSTANDING WORK

Frešo acquired training in compositional work in the class of ALEXANDER MOYZES at the Bratislava Conservatory, where he also studied the piano and conducting. He continued his study of composition at the Academia di Santa Cecilia in Rome under ILDEBRANDO PIZETTI.

After his return from abroad, he took up the post of accompanist and soon thereafter of conductor of the Bratislava opera. Then he was named chief of the Košice opera; upon his return to Bratislava, he assumed his present post as managing director of the opera of the Slovak National Theatre. He has also appeared several times abroad as an opera conductor.

Of particular importance is his production of premières of Slovak operas (JÁN CIKKER: *Juro Jánošík* and *Beg Bajazid*; EUGEN SUCHOŇ: *Svätopluk*).

Song lyricism is the main field of Frešo's creative work, represented by the cycle *The Most Beautiful Dream* (1940), *Meditation* for mezzosoprano and orchestra (1942), a cycle *A Child's Heart* for soprano and piano (1960) and *Three Songs* for mezzosoprano and orchestra (1960).

His orchestral music *A Concerto Overture* (1940), a *Symphonic Prologue* (1943), the symphonic poems *A New Morning* (1950) and *Liberation* (1955) are influenced by impressionistic and late-romantic expressive media.

Frešo has written as well three cantatas: *Stabat Mater* (1943), the lyric cantata *Mother* (1959) and a *Hymn on the Fatherland* (1960). He writes also compositions for children, choirs, arrangements of folk songs, scenic and film music.

FRIED, Alexej

[born Brno, 13 October 1922]

Fried first studied theory of music at the Brno Conservatory under THEODORE SCHAEFER and piano under ANNA SKALICKÁ. At the Prague Conservatory he continued his study in the composition class of EMIL HLOBIL, completing his musical education at the Prague Academy of Musical Arts as a pupil of PAVEL BOŘKOVEC.

During his studies he has organized in Brno a variety orchestra and continued in this activity in Prague, where he was artistic manager and conductor of the Folk Music Ensemble of the Conservatory, of the Orchestra of Jaroslav Ježek (LIBERATED THEATRE) and of the Artistic Ensemble of the Faculty of Law. In 1954, as a member of the editorial staff for light music at the Czechoslovak Radio, he founded the DANCE ORCHESTRA OF ALEXEJ FRIED. He has instrumented many compositions for all these ensembles.

At present he is the artistic manager of the Army Artistic Ensemble Vít Nejedlý.

Stage Works

His development in the field of musical drama is evident from his two musical comedies *The Devil Passed Through the Town*, to a theme by Charles de Coster (1956—57) and *A Fete in Harlem* (1959, awarded a prize of the Czech Music Fund in 1964). He composed as well songs to the comedy *Two Briefcases and an Attaché Portfolio*, to a text by J. R. PICK (1962); a further proof of his development is the ballet *Peter and Lucia*, according to ROMAIN ROLLAND (1965).

Orchestral and Instrumental Works

Among these are *Partita* and *Sonata* for piano (1950) and a piano *Trio* (1951). His graduation work at the Academy of Musical Arts was the symphonic poem *For a New Man* (1953). Recently he has composed a *Spring Overture* for brass band (1962).

Vocal Music

He wrote a number of small cantatas, songs for youth and community singing, as *Cantata about Gottwald, Song of Peace, May Cantata, The Rose of Friendship, For All People in the World* and a *Romance* for soprano and wind orchestra (1963).

Dance Music

His dance music includes: *Bashful, Do You Remember?,
A Pitch-Dark Day, The Prague Blues, Cacao Baby*. His song
A Message to America received a special award in the
artistic jubilee competition in 1960.

Jazz Music

Recently Fried has composed a programme composition *Maturing* for soprano saxophone and full jazz
orchestra (1962). In addition, he elaborated a jazz
arrangement of *Caravan and Solitude* by DUKE ELLINGTON.

He deserved well of the organization of the FIRST
INTERNATIONAL JAZZ FESTIVAL in Prague 1964 (he was
chairman of the festival committee).

Various

His other compositions include music to the children's
exercises for the Second Spartakiad, music to the film
Little Bear-leaders and scenic music to forty fairy-tales and
plays.

FÜRST, Jaromír Karel

[born Třtice, 30 December 1895]

Fürst was a pupil of the school of J. B. FOERSTER.
Initially he was active as a secondary school teacher of
musical education, later as professor at the Advanced
School of Music Pedagogy in Prague. He founded the
chamber music choir THE SINGING SIXTEEN and was
choirmaster of The Choral Society of Prague Typo-
graphers, as well as of the Prague Women Teachers'
Choir. At present he is advisor for vocal music of the
House for Adult Education of the City of Prague.

Fürst is primarily a composer of vocal music. He
has written ¶ song cycles (*The Wind and The Waves,
Sketches, L. W, Autumn Visit*), ¶ female choirs (*Lullaby,*

Wild Thyme, A Girl, Advent, A Jump-Dance, Our Water-falls), ¶ male choirs (*The Milky Way, Grass, When Day is Done, People, Native Land, Horses*), ¶ cantatas (*In the Czech Land, A Paradise Romance, Ballad of a Beautiful Death, The Return of Those Killed in War*) and ¶ community songs (*We Want to Live, On Guard of Peace*). He has also arranged scores of folk songs for male, female and mixed choir.

In addition, Fürst composed a *Lyric Suite* and *Evening Moods* for piano, a *Concertino* for violin and piano, an *Orchestral Suite* and concert valse *The Astronauts*.

GREGOR, Čestmír

[born Brno, 14 May 1926]

Gregor was a pupil in composition of his father JOSEF GREGOR and of JAROSLAV KVAPIL at the Janáček Academy of Musical Arts.

He is chief of musical programmes of the Czechoslovak Radio in Ostrava.

After a period of study during which he wrote, among others, his *Experiment* for piano and *The Sonata* (both in 1946), Gregor achieved a stability of style; in the field of invention he closely adhered to Moravian folk tonality, in expression to LEOŠ JANÁČEK and in technique to VÍTĚZSLAV NOVÁK.

Orchestral Works

This was evidenced in his suite for chamber orchestra *Once During a Spring Evening* (1955) and the *Tragic Suite* for chamber orchestra (1957); further he composed a *Suite* for strings (1959) and a *Trio* for flute, viola and bass clarinet (1959).

The same applies for his *Joyous Overture* (1951), symphonic picture *One of Us* (1952), the second symphony *Land and People* (1953), for his three-movement rhapsody for piano and orchestra *No One Is Alone* (1955) [awarded the Jubilee Prize in the competition of the Guild of Czechoslovak Composers and the Music Fund 1956]; this work tends to a modern compositional conception both from the point of view of its content and expression; the same is evidenced by the symphonic overture *May I Speak?* (1956), *Concerto semplice* for piano and small orchestra (1958), three-movement *Polyphonietta* for symphonic orchestra (1961) and symphonic poem *Stars Within Reach* (1961) [inspired by Gagarin's flight]; then balet-symphony *Dizziness* (1963), the symphonic-overture *If All the Chaps of the World* (1963) and two nocturnes for 18 string instruments *A Prague Pedestrian* (1963), the symphonic scene *The Discussion* (1963), choreographic *Symphony*—a concert version of the ballet *Dizziness* (1963, première Ostrava 1964) and *Concerto* for violin and orchestra (1965).

Instrumental Compositions

Two were chosen from several works: *Greetings to Friends in a Great Country* for piano (1954) and witty piano miniatures *Ash-Wednesday* (1962).

Vocal Works

The cycle of songs on folk tunes with small orchestra deserves special mention: *Below My Little Window* (1952), *Windy Breeze* (1953), *Little Horsie of my Beloved* (1952), *The White Dove* (1954) and *A Word for Mummy* (1955); then small cantata *The Czech Song* to verses by MARIE PUJMANOVÁ (1960).

Various Compositions

This is scenic and variety programe music and smaller choral and dance compositions.

International Prizes

The above mentioned *The White Dove* and a *Word for Mummy* were awarded medals in the competition at the World Festival of Youth in Moscow (1957).

GREŠÁK, Jozef

[born Bardějov, 30 December 1907]

Grešák began to compose relatively late. After graduation from the Teachers' Training Institute he was mostly active as pianist and accompanist and later as professor of musical education. At present he is secretary of the Košice branch of the Guild of Slovak Composers.

In his youth he had done some writing but it was only in 1951 when he began to devote himself intensively to composition, a field in which he was self-taught. His creative work attracts by its expressive strength and spontaneity, having a close affinity to musical folklore of Eastern Slovakia.

The most significant works of this original composer include *The Slovak Folk Ballads* for mixed choir (1953), a *Concertino* for violin and orchestra (1954), the ballet *Radúz and Mahuliena* (1954, première at Košice 1954), *The Emigrant Songs* for solos, male choir and orchestra (1961) and *Concerto* for piano and orchestra (1963).

At present, Grešák is reworking his opera *The Unawakened* (according to a tale by Martin Kukučín), his first compositional work.

GROSSMAN, Saša (Alexander)

[born Sarata, 15 June 1907]

Grossman studied trombone at the Prague Conservatory and composition under Fidelius Finke, completing it at the Prague German Academy of Music. At present he is a member of the editorial staff of the State Publishing House of Music.

In 1933, his first successful song *Boys, Today I Say Farewell to You* came into being. In 1935 he composed music to the film *The Fateful Moment* and in 1936—41 wrote eight *Russian Dances* for symphonic orchestra.

His work since 1945 includes *The March of Heroes* for male choir and orchestra, a grande overture *Victory*, six orchestra suites (*Slavonic Moods, Under the Banner of Peace, Cheer to the Members of Cooperatives!, Slavonic Dance Suite, Pioneers' Aurora* and *To the Brigade of Socialist Work*), then *The Ukrainian Rhapsody* for symphonic orchestra, *Song About Dukla* for solos, choir and orchestra, a cantata *Hail to the Fields!* for baritone, mixed choir and orchestra, and a *Song* (Dumka) *on Czech Partisans* for baritone and orchestra. Further he has written many marching songs, recitatives and dance compositions.

HÁBA, Alois
[born Vizovice, 21 June 1893]
MERITED ARTIST

Hába studied composition under VÍTĚZSLAV NOVÁK and after the First World War continued his studies in Vienna and with FRANZ SCHREKER in Berlin.

During the period between the World Wars he was one of the leading personalities of the vanguard generation of composers. In practice as well as in theory and in his pedagogical activity, he set forth and asserted his creative ideas in the field of quarter-tone and sixth-tone music and the athematic style.

Since 1923 he has been active at the Prague Conservatory where he founded the section of quarter-tone and sixth-tone composition. From 1945 to 1961 (when he retired) he was head of this section at the Academy of Musical Arts in Prague.

In the post-war years (after the second World War) Hába took a very active part in the building-up of our new musical life. He was chairman of the Board of the Authors' Association for the Protection of the Rights on Musical Works, co-founder and chairman of the

Syndicate of Czechoslovak Composers and founded the second Prague opera house.

Semi-tone Compositions

In this system Hába created several piano compositions, as fugue *Suite* for piano, op. 1a (1918), *Variations on Schumann's Canon* for piano, op. 1b (1918, published in Vienna), *Scherzo and Intermezzo* for piano, op. 2 (1918, published in Vienna), *Piano Sonata*, op. 3 (1919, published in Vienna), an *Overture* for piano and orchestra, op. 5 (1920, published in Vienna) and *Six Piano Compositions*, op. 6 (1920).

In later years he composed in the semi-tone system a symphonic fantasy *The Path of Life*, op. 46 (1933—34), and the opera *New Land* to a libretto by FERDINAND PUJMAN, according to a novel by FEDOR GLADKOV, op. 47 (1935—36).

Quarter-tone Compositions

His first large work in the quarter-tone system was *The Second String Quartet*, op. 7 (1920, performed in Berlin 1922), followed by suites and fantaisies for solo violin and violoncello (1922) and six suites and ten fantasies for quarter-tone piano (1923—28). In a number of further chamber music and piano works he discovered new possibilities, as in the *Third* and *Fourth String Quartets*, op. 12 and 14 (both 1923).

Hába experimented as well with the possibilities of the quarter-tone system in vocal music, as is evidenced in his *Suite* for male choir, op. 13 (1928); he also composed cycles of songs and choirs.

His main work was the opera *Mother*, written to his own libretto, op. 35 (1930, première in Munich 1931, 1947 in Prague and 1964 at Florence).

Sixth-tone Compositions

Beginning with the *Fifth String Quartet*, op. 15 (1923) he started to compose as well in the sixth-tone system.

His *Tenth String Quartet*, op. 88 (1952), was performed in Stockholm (1957).

For the stage he composed the sixth-tone opera *Thy Kingdom Come*, to his own libretto, revised by FERDINAND PUJMAN, op. 50 (1939—42).

Twelve-tone Compositions

His monothematic twelve-tone symphonic *Fantasy* for piano and orchestra, op. 8 (1921) amply demonstrate the tenacious development of his creative efforts. This was followed by two *Nonets*, op. 40 and 41 (both 1931).

Vocal Compositions

Besides a number of suites and sonatas he wrote during the war several cycles of songs, as *Poetry of Life*, op. 53 (1943) and *Moravian Folk Love Songs*, op. 58 (1944).

His songs and choirs for community singing, viz. the male choirs *Day by Day the World Grows Wider*, op. 65a, to poems by JOSEF HORA (1948), *The Scythe and the Dew*, op. 65b, set to poems by JOSEF HORA (1948), *Munich*, op. 65c (1948), *Peace* op. 67 (1948), mixed choirs *The Earth is Beautiful*, op. 71a (1950), *A Proud Song*, op. 71b (1950), *A Million of Smiles*, op. 71c (1950) and the cantata *For Peace*, op. 68 (1949) contributed to the building-up of a new life in those years.

Latest Compositions

Within the last decade, Hába has concentrated on chamber and orchestral works. He composed an orchestral *Wallachian Suite* op. 77 (1952), his *Third Nonet*, op. 82 (1953), a *Violin Concerto*, op. 83 (1954), a *Concerto* for viola, op. 86 (1956), the sixth to the fifteenth *String Quartets* (of which three are in quarter-tone and two in the sixth-tone system in the athematic style), then several *Suites* for solo violin, solo violoncello and piano, a *Fantasy* for quarter-tone piano, a three-movement *Suite* for cimbalom, op. 91 (1960) and the *Fourth Nonet*, op. 95 (1963).

Noteworthy are his children's choirs *From Popular Sayings of the Slav Peoples*, to words by F. L. ČELAKOVSKÝ, op. 84 (1955).

Construction of Musical Instruments

For many years, Hába has concerned himself with the construction of quarter-tone and sixth-tone instruments.

Writings

Hába laid down the theoretical foundations for compositions in ultra-chromatic systems in various treatises of which the most comprehensive is the *New Science of Harmony in Diatonic, Chromatic, Quarter, Third, Sixth and Twelfth-tone Systems* (1927, published in Leipzig). In 1942, he supplemented this work by another book on harmony in these same systems from the point of view of expression.

The first stimuli in the field of ultrachromatic system Hába sought in the folk song. From the folk song of his native Wallachian region he proceeded to the study of the music of non-European cultures.

●

Hába was for many years secretary of the section "International Society for Contemporary Music" in the Guild of Czechoslovak Composers. He is now an honorary member of the International Society for Contemporary Music (ISCM).

HÁBA, Karel
[born Vizovice, 21 May 1898]

Brother of Alois Hába. After completing the Teachers' Training Institute, he studied violin and composition at the Prague Conservatory under JAN MAŘÁK (violin)

Jaroslav Křička and J. B. Foerster (composition) and Alois Hába (quarter-tone composition). He continued his study at the Master School as a pupil of Karel Hoffmann (violin) and Vítězslav Novák (composition).

He was first active as a teacher and later as an orchestral artist (viola) and programme editor at the Czechoslovak Radio in Prague. In 1945, he founded the Radio children choir.

At present, he is assistant professor of the methodics of music education at the Faculty of Philosophy at Charles University.

Stage Works

Up to the present, the high point of his creative work has been reached in his operas *Jánošík* [to a libretto by Antonín Klášterský] (1929—32, première in Prague 1934), *The Old History* [to a libretto by Ferdinand Pujman, according to a theme from Julius Zeyer] (1934—37), *Kaliba's Crime* [after the novel by K. V. Rais] (1957—61), and the children's opera *About Smolíček* (a fairy-tale figure), set to a text by V. Čtvrtek (1949, première in Prague 1950).

Chamber Music

His chamber music is represented by *String Quartets* No. 1 (1921) and No. 2 (1924), a *Septet* (1928—29), a piano *Trio* (1940), a piano *Sonata* (1942), a *Wind quintet* (1943), *String quartet* No. 3 (1944), a *Nonet* (1948) and a *String trio* for two violins and viola (1954).

Orchestral Works

In his orchestral compositions he started with an *Overture* (1922); then followed a *Concerto* for violin and orchestra (1926), a *Scherzo* (1928), a *Concerto* for violoncello and orchestra (1934), an orchestral *Brigands' Suite* (1953) and orchestral *Suite* (1963); of Hába's other creative work of importance are his two *Symphonies* (1948 and 1954).

Instrumental Works

He has written *Piano Inventions* (1943), *Concerto Etudes* for the violin (1957) and works of similar character.

Quarter-tone compositions are represented in his creative work by a *Suite* for piano (1925) and *Trio* for piano (1926).

Vocal Works

Vocal music holds a special place in Hába's creative work. It includes above all compositions for children, as medleys of folk songs for children's choir and orchestra, the cycles *To the Smallest Singers*, *Children Sing*, *From a Children's World* and a cantata *The Golden Christmas Crip*.

The cycles *Children's Poetry*, *Summer Moods* and *Autumn Moods* as well as female and male choirs and the cantata *To Those Who Build Up Ostrava* (1950—51) are of similar genre.

Writings

On the educational field he published *Violin School in the Quarter-tone System* (1927) and *Modern Violin Technique*, in two volumes (1928).

HÁJEK, Maxmilián

[born Prague, 15 August 1909]

Hájek was a private pupil of OTAKAR OSTRČIL (composition). In 1943—44 he attended the conducting seminar of VÁCLAV TALICH at the National Theatre in Prague.

In 1945 he helped to found the opera at Liberec and was active in various opera houses in Czechoslovakia and from 1947 to 1948 in Sarajevo.

After his return from Yugoslavia he taught at the school of music at Liberec. At present he is devoting himself solely to composition.

Stage Works

He has composed the following three full-length operas: *Dornička* to a libretto by LADISLAV NOVÁK according to a novel by JULIUS ZEYER (1944—46, première at Ústí on Labe 1949), *Jan Výrava* according to a drama of the same name by F. A. ŠUBRT (1949—50, première at Ústí on Labe 1950, rewritten 1951, première at Liberec 1951) and the *Fishermen of Rožmberk* according to the play by VLADIMÍR MÜLLER (1955—56, première at Liberec 1958). His musical dramatic work is supplemented by the ballet *The Magic Tapestry* (1946, arranged 1952 as a five-movement suite) as well as the pantomime *The Glassblower's Dream* (1959—60).

Orchestral and Instrumental Compositions

Of Hájek's other creative works, mention should be made of an orchestral suite *Moravian Pictures*, a *Romance* for solo violin and orchestra, *Furiant* (a Czech folk dance) for full orchestra and a violin concerto bearing the title *The Song of Our Mountains* and dedicated to the town of Liberec on the occasion of the fifteenth anniversary of its liberation (awarded first regional prize). On the occasion of the fifteenth anniversary of the founding of the Liberec Theatre, Hájek wrote a *Grande Polonaise* (1960). *The Autumn Prelude* and *Jizera* for piano date from 1962.

In addition, Hájek has composed seventeen pieces of incidental music for the Liberec Theatre.

HÁLA, Kamil

[born Most, 1 August 1931]

Brother of the composer Vlastimil Hála. Graduated from a commercial academy in Prague. In 1949—55 he was a member of the dance orchestras of Ladislav Habart and Zdeněk Barták. In 1955—60 he had his own dance orchestra with which he made tours abroad. At present he is a member of the jazz orchestra of the Czechoslovak Radio in Prague.

His creative work, up to the present, has been oriented primarily to orchestral jazz, such as his foxtrots *We Are Going Home*, *The North Wind and Mateus*, a trombone fantasy *My Dream*, *Pianola*, a *Concertina* for alto saxophone and jazz orchestra, three-parts suite *Vienna at Night* for soprano saxophone and full jazz orchestra, as well as *Elegy*, *A Portrait*, a *Dance of the Dolphins*, *You*, the suite *Intensity* and rhapsody *The Cult of Jazz* for full jazz orchestra.

Hála devotes himself as well to making arrangements for the leading Czechoslovak jazz orchestras.

HÁLA, Vlastimil
[born Souš near Most, 7 July 1924]

Hála, brother of the composer Kamil Hála, has played in various amateur orchestras, in the orchestra of Zdeněk Lenc and from 1945 in the ensemble SWING STARS. From 1946—62 he was a member of Karel Vlach's orchestra, writing numerous compositions and arrangements for it.

In 1948—54 he supplemented privately his musical studies with JAN RYCHLÍK.

He wrote a number of popular dance music such as ¶ the foxtrots *A Nail in the Boot* (collaborating with JIŘÍ BAUR), *When You Are Mine*, *A Song About a Train*, *The Stage Coach*, *Our Flat*, *Three Lassies*; ¶ the rumba *Catana*, ¶ the slow foxtrots *A Simple Medicine*, *Perhaps Your Eyes Will Believe*, *The Dew Settled on the Grass*; ¶ the rock *My Son Peter* (in collaboration with BAUR); ¶ the blues *Who is Whistling Here*; ¶ the charleston *Parents*, ¶ the waltz *The Sea is Writing a Blue Letter* and others.

His orchestral compositions are well known too; most of them have been recorded by the orchestra of Karel Vlach. They include *Trampolina, Greetings to the Orchestra, Pepper and Salt, The Warsaw Boogie* and others.

Furthermore Hála has composed music to films: *There will be a Circus, A Visit from the Skies, An Easy Life, My Friend the Liar, Two from Another World* and *A Holiday with Minka*; for television films *The Lost Review, Life Without Music or Quiet-Quiet, Prague Without Glasses*, as well as to short films, animated cartoons, puppet and advertisement films.

He is also co-author of music to theatrical plays, for instance *Lemonade Joe* (also to the film of the same name), *Circus Orion, Nasreddin, Eileen is Pleased, Let Susanne Sing, I Am in Love, One Man Like Another* (BERTOLD BRECHT) and others. He also arranged music to KURT WEILL's *Beggars' Opera*.

With JIŘÍ BAŽANT and JIŘÍ MALÁSEK he composed music to the first Czechoslovak film musical *Old Hop Pickers*.

HANÁK, Mirko
[born Slavkov, 4 September 1891]

Hanák graduated from the School for Organists in Brno. Later he studied violin at the Cracow Conservatory.

For many years he was conductor at the Ostrava Theatre.

His creative work comprises several successful operettas: *A Pink Talisman, An Ingenious Cobbler, The Master's Chambermaid, The Queen's Necklace, The Deck of Love, The Village Maid, Love is Blind, Let Youth Have Its Fling, Miss Mannequin, Courting in the Mountains, Hetty, Radegast* and *The Main Role*.

He is also the author of the ballet *Fantaska* (1929),

a *Fantastic Suite* for string quartet (1929), a *Ballad about Radhošť* for tenor, mixed choir and orchestra (1949), *The Beskid Suite* for choir and orchestra to texts of Wallachian songs (1951), a song cycle *New Intrigues* to texts by FRAN SMĚJA in the Silesian dialect (1953), *Romance* and *Humoresque* for violoncello and piano (1961), a symphonic rhapsody *Slavkov 1805* (1961), *The Wallachian Sinfonietta* (1962) as well as masses, songs and choirs.

HANOUSEK, Karel

[born Brno, 14 August 1902]

Hanousek graduated from the violin class of the Brno Conservatory and was active for twenty years in the Brno Radio Orchestra, for a short time acting as concert-master of the former Symphonic Orchestra of the Brno district. He was as well the first violinist of the State Philharmonic in Brno. After the Second World War he completed his theoretical study of music at the Brno University. He became head of the violin department at the Advanced Pedagogic School of Music in Ostrava.

He has composed a number of compositions for violin and orchestra (*Capriccietto-Valse Caprice, Lights and Shadows, Rondo, Burlesque, Scherzo Capriccioso*), several arrangements and paraphrases, male choirs, as for intance *That's Work Singing* set to words by JOSEF HORA, and others.

HANOUSEK, Vladimír

[born Przemyśl, 2 May 1907]

After completing the secondary school, Hanousek matriculated at the Prague Conservatory where he studied violin and composition, completing his studies at the Master School as a pupil of KAREL HOFFMANN and JOSEF SUK.

He was a member of the PRAGUE PIANO TRIO and the first violinist of the NEW QUARTET. He is artistic adviser of the chamber music ensemble of the FILM SYMPHONY ORCHESTRA and of the PRAGUE CHAMBER ORCHESTRA.

His creative work includes the following compositions: *Aria* and *Passacaglia* for violin and string orchestra, *Tragic Sinfonietta* for full orchestra, *Cantata* for recitation, solos, mixed choir and full orchestra to texts of the Indian poets SHIVANANDA and VIVEKANANDA, *To Silent Heroes*, a *Divertimento* for violin, viola and violoncello, a *Quartetto Abbandonato*, a cantata *Prague* for solos and mixed choir to words by FRANTIŠEK HALAS, as well as two female choirs *The Moon* and a *Woman*, *Maestoso-prologue* for symphonic orchestra, *Heroic Oratorium* for solos, recitative, mixed and recitative choir and full orchestra, and a ballet pantomime *The Death of a Pierrot* (1964).

HANUŠ, Jan

[born Prague, 2 May 1915]

MERITED ARTIST, LAUREATE OF THE STATE PRIZE

Hanuš studied composition with OTAKAR JEREMIÁŠ and conducting at the Prague Conservatory under PAVEL DĚDEČEK.

He was active in organizational work in the Society for Contemporary Music THE PRESENT TIME and for some time occupied the post of editor-in-chief of music at the State Publishing House of Literature, Music and Art. He has participated in the ideological and organizational activity of the Guild of Czechoslovak Composers and of the Prague Spring Music Festival.

He is how managing director of the Publishing House of the Guild of Czechoslovak Composers PANTON.

Hanuš is a versatile artist. His creative work has reached extensive proportions, embracing all genres of music. In the first phase of his creative activity, the bulk of his work consisted of smaller forms and chamber music. In the course of time, he deepened his creative power to achieve larger forms, especially in the field of orchestral and choral works.

Stage Works

His first opera-rhapsody *The Flames*, op. 14 [libretto by the author and JAROSLAV POKORNÝ] (1942—44, première in Pilsen 1956), is imbued with war-time problems.

His second opera *The Servant of Two Masters*, according to CARLO GOLDONI, op. 42 (1958, première in Pilsen 1959), evoked a response in Germany [premières at Duisburg 1960, Düsseldorf 1961, Altenburg 1963 and in Dresden 1965].

In 1963, Hanuš completed the opera *Prometheus' Torch*, op. 54 [to the libretto by JAROSLAV POKORNÝ], in which the antique myth is confronted with modern science fiction (première in Prague 1965).

He has composed two ballets: *Salt is Worth More Than Gold*, according to a fairy-tale by BOŽENA NĚMCOVÁ, op. 28 (1953, produced for the first time in Olomouc, 1954) and the dance-drama *Othello*, according to the tragedy by WILLIAM SHAKESPEARE, op. 36 (1956, première in Prague 1959, at Rostock, Zwickau, Dessau, Erfurt and Karlsruhe 1962 and at Altenburg 1965).

Chamber Music

Amongst his many chamber music compositions are to be mentioned: *Fantasy* for string quartet, op. 6 (1939), *Preludietto* and *Allegro Appassionato* for violin and piano, op. 7 (1939), *Sonata Rhapsodia* for violoncello and piano, op. 9 (1941), *Serenata* for nonet, op. 30 (1953), *Sonatina* for viola and piano, op. 37 (1956), suita dramatica *Meditation* for string quartet, op. 46, based on AISCHYLOS'

Prometheus (1959) [this work was awarded in the artistic jubilee competition in 1960] and *Suita Domestica* for wind quintet, op. 57 (1964),

Orchestral Works

One of his earliest works was the orchestral *Rondo Capriccioso*, based on ČELAKOVSKÝ's poem "The Bird Fair", op. 3 (1939).

Hanuš has composed four symphonies:

the *first Symphony* in E for alto solo and orchestra, op. 12 (1942);

the *second Symphony* in G for orchestra, op. 26 (1951),

the *third Symphony* in D minor for orchestra, op. 38 (1957) and

the *fourth Symphony*, op. 49 (1960).

Appended to these symphonies was the *Concert Symphony* in C minor for organ, harp, timpani and string orchestra, op. 31 (1954).

His other symphonic and orchestral works contain: sinfonietta *The Eulogy* for soprano solo and orchestra, op. 16 (1945), the symphonic fantasy *Peter and Lucia*, basing on a play by ROMAIN ROLLAND, op. 35 (1955) and *Overture* for orchestra, op. 53 (1961).

Instrumental Works

Into the first era of his creative activity belongs the piano cycle *Meditations*, op. 5 (1938—39). After the war followed *The Suite*, inspired by MÁNES' paintings, op. 22 (1947) and the *Preludia* for piano, op. 23 (1949); for organ he composed the *Suita Lirica*, op. 39 (1957).

Vocal Works

Voices: *Two Psalms* for baritone solo, orchestra and organ, op. 11 (1941) and *Sonnets*, set to texts of renaissance poets, for lower voice and piano, op. 48 (1960).

Songs: *Winter Songs*, op. 15 (1945), which show a return to a more intimate atmosphere after the war, and a cycle of songs *The Wooden Christ*, with piano accompaniment, op. 40 (1957).

Marching and military songs: both were composed when the war ended—*To the Army*, op. 19 (1945) and the *Song of the Partisans* personify his glorification of his country's liberation.

Female choir: a cycle *To Love*, set to words by J. V. SLÁDEK, op. 4 (1938).

Male choirs: his first compositions belonged to his parents—*To My Father*, set to a poem by J. V. SLÁDEK, op. 1 (1936) and *My Mother*, based on a deep poem by OTAKAR BŘEZINA, op. 10 (1941). Recently, he composed *Antique Chants*, set to words by VÁCLAV RENČ (according to SOPHOCLES' Antigona), op. 56 (1964).

Children choirs: *Czech Year* on folk texts from K. J. ERBEN, with small orchestra, op. 24 [*Spring* (1949), *Summer* (1950), *Autumn* (1951) and *Winter* (1952)]; a cycle of choirs for children, op. 41 (*Songs* about a Ball, about a Bear, about a Scooter and others) and op. 43 *I Tell a Fairy-tale*; then a choir for three voices *A Merry Day*, op. 50 (1961) and a children's choir with piano *Mummy*, set to verses by JAROSLAV SEIFERT, op. 55 (1963—64).

Mixed choirs: *Destitute Love*, op. 34 (1954) and *The Land which We Come From*, op. 52 (1961).

Cantatas: *The Country Speaks*, op. 8 (1940) calls to mind events under German oppression (1940) and *The Song of Hope*, op. 21, when the German yoke was thrown off (1945—48).

Masses: The first mass—*Missa* in D flat (*Pentecosta*), op. 13 (1942); the second mass—*Missa* in G major (*Pastoralis*), op. 25 (1949); the third mass—*Missa* in D minor (*Paschalis*), op. 33 (1954) and the fourth mass—*Tantum Ergo*, op. 44 (1959).

●

For his opera *Prometheus' Torch* he was awarded the First Prize in the artistic jubilee competition 1965.

HARAŠTA, Milan

[born Brno, 16 September 1919, died Brno 29 August 1946]

After completing the secondary school, Harašta entered the composition class of VÁCLAV KAPRÁL at the
Brno Conservatory, from which he graduated in 1942
with his graduation work, a *Symphony* for full orchestra.
Then he taught music at the music school at Líšeň
(suburb of Brno); he was also active as a conductor and
from 1940 to 1942 as a critic. During the German occupation he was sent as a labourer to the Brno Engineering Works. Eventually he became secretary and teacher
at the music school of the Philharmonic Society, the
Brno BESEDA.

In addition to the *Symphony* (referred to above) he is
the author of a *String Quartet* (1940), a cycle of small
piano compositions *Sonnets* (1940—41, 1944—45), *Po-
loniny Dances* for full orchestra (1941—42), *Cocktail
Jests* (1942) for full orchestra, *Symphony* No. 2 [chamber
symphony with obligato solo violin] (1942—43), a *Sonatina* for violin and piano (1942), the opera *Nikola
Šuhaj*, according to IVAN OLBRACHT's novel *Nikola
Šuhaj—the Highwayman* (1941—43), a *Suite* for orchestra
(1944), *Male choirs* (1945), *Symphony No. 3* (a fragment,
1943—44) and others.

The operas *The Wolves* (according to ROMAIN ROLLAND)
and *General Adamov* (after B. LAVRENCHEV), the symphonic poem *To the Woman*, the cantata *Blood Does not Flow
In Vain*, in memory of GUERNICA, were left in a sketch
form.

He wrote theoretical treatises on music entitled *What
I Must Know About Musical Art* (A Short History of the
Development of Music, 1945) and *Chapters from Music
and About Music* (How Ears Learnt to Listen, 1944—45).

HAVELKA, Svatopluk
[born Vrbice, 2 May 1925]

LAUREATE OF THE STATE PRIZE

Havelka is a pupil of K. B. JIRÁK in composition.

Symphonic Works

His expressive creative vigour is manifested in his *Symphony* in B minor (1956), then in his monumental cantata *Praise of Light* to verses of the *Sonata of Horizontal Life* by S. K. NEUMANN (1960, State prize in 1961) and *Heptameron*—the poem about nature and love for four solo voices, reciter and orchestra to poems by S. K. NEUMANN, JIŘÍ WOLKER, GUILLAUME APOLLINAIRE and VÍTĚZSLAV NEZVAL (1963, awarded by the Guild of Czechoslovak Composers 1964).

Of similar character are his compositions *A Wallachian March* and the *Wedding at Suchá Hora* for symphony orchestra.

Orchestral Compositions

Havelka acquired compositional experience while collaborating with the popular Ostrava Variety ensemble NOTA. His variety compositions, dance music and arrangements of folk songs have placed him in the ranks of Czech composers of programme music.

His compositions for variety orchestra comprised *The Path Leading to My Sweetheart*, *Verbunk* (a folk dance), *Verbunk of May First*, the valse *This Evening Everything Ends*, songs to words by ANEŽKA GORLOVÁ for three girls' voices (*What a Sonny*, *My Mother Dear*, *Listen to Me*, *Nannette!*, *I Shall Embroider a Kerchief*, and others).

Havelka is as well the author of the music to *Exercises with a Rifle* and *Fencing Exercises with a Bayonet* for the First Spartakiad (1955).

Vocal Works

Havelka's vocal works, which attract attention, are

the cantata *Spring* for solos, mixed choir, children's choir and orchestra (1949), two symphonic *Pastorals* (1948, 1951) and four musical dramatic *Suites* for solo, voice-band and chamber orchestra.

His variety songs include the following: *We Walk and Walk About, Kitty, To Fields, Boys, A Farmer's Song, A Sunflower, Little Spruces in May, An Evening Song, A Song About Secrecy, A Song About Jack.*

Havelka is at present working on a poem depicting the beauty and power of nature.

Scenic and Film Music

He composes scenic music and music to films (*Yearning, September Nights*). For his music to the film *That Cat!* he was awarded the principal prize in the competition for the best musical work in the field of Czechoslovak film production 1963.

HERTL, František
[born Zbuch, 18 April 1906]

Hertl graduated from the instrumental section of Prague Conservatory (doublebass). He studied conducting under VÁCLAV TALICH and composition under OTAKAR ŠÍN and later under JAROSLAV ŘÍDKÝ. He was first doublebass player at the National Theatre in Ljubljana (and simultaneously pedagogue at the musical institution Glasbena Matica), then in the Czech Philharmonic in Prague and in the Symphonic Orchestra of the Czechoslovak Radio. He had many performances as a soloist.

In 1936—50 he was doublebass player and artistic chief of the Czech Nonet; to both these activities he returned in 1964.

In 1950 he founded the PRAGUE CHAMBER ORCHESTRA WITHOUT CONDUCTOR. In 1951—61 he was artistic chief and principal conductor of the Brno Variety Radio Orchestra.

At present, Hertl is active as pedagogue at the Prague Conservatory and at the Academy of Musical Arts (doublebass, chamber music).

Instrumental Works

His activity as an orchestral artist, chamber music interpreter and conductor has influenced his creative compositional work in the direction of instrumental music. He composed a *Sonata* for doublebass and piano (1947), a *Concerto Polka* for doublebass and orchestra (1949), a *Concerto* for doublebass and orchestra (1955) and a *Suite* for doublebass and piano (1964).

Of Hertl's other works the following have attracted particular attention: a *Sonatina* for flute and piano (1946), a *Dramatic Overture* for full orchestra (1948), *Scherzo* for full orchestra (1949), a *Tarantella* for flute and orchestra (1952), *a Czech Dance* for violin and orchestra (1952), *Small Pieces* for oboe and orchestra (1953), a *Sinfonietta* for oboe and orchestra (1956), *Sonata* for violoncello and piano (1958) and the orchestral *Tarantella* (1962).

Various Compositions

He has written as well several marches, suites, arrangements and programmes of folk songs, variety programme compositions and others. His *March of the Builders* and a *Signature Tune* were awarded in the artistic jubilee competition in 1960.

Writings

Hertl has written an instructive book *School for the Doublebass* (1961).

HIPMAN, Silvester

[born Čáslav, 23 July 1893]

Hipman studied law at Charles University. In his native town he acquired a basic education in music as a pupil of the bandmaster OTTO ULLMANN and the choirmaster JOSEF MALÝ, himself a pupil of Antonín Dvořák. In Prague he studied piano under ADOLF MIKEŠ, composition under OTAKAR ŠÍN and instrumentation under JAROSLAV ŘÍDKÝ.

He was active as a music critic. In the years 1925—44 he was secretary of the music section of the Artistic Union. In 1937—38 he organized the first and second European Festivals of chamber music in Trenčanské Teplice.

Orchestral Works

His orchestral work includes a four-movement *Symphony* in B flat major, celebrating the liberation of Czechoslovakia in 1945, the funereal march *Slavín*, *Menuets from F. L. Věk*, *Valse Scenes*, four short pieces for small orchestra *From a Children's World* and two symphonic pictures *The Sea and Palms* and *The Vosges Square*. In 1960 he composed the symphonic suite *In Bohemia* (arranged also for doublebass and piano).

Chamber and Instrumental Music

Hipman has devoted himself to writing for chamber music groups as is evidenced by his three *String Quartets*, four *Intermezzos* for piano quartet, *The Čáslav Suite* for wind quintet, *Kladno Variations* for flute, two violins and viola, *Říčany Trio* for two violins and clarinet, a *Violin Sonata* and a *Violin Sonatina*. In 1962 he composed a *Concerto da Camera* for clarinet and strings and an *Introduction* and *Capriccio* for flute and strings.

He has also written for solo instruments: *Five Pieces* for violin and piano, *Three Pieces* for violoncello and piano, *Five Pieces* for flute and piano, and others. In addition he has composed five *Concert Polkas*, ten *Concert Etudes* and a *Scherzo*.

Vocal Works

In the vocal field he is the author of several cycles of female choirs and following cycles: *French Ballads*, *Three Songs from Pushkin*, *The Most Beautiful River*, *Two Songs* with piano accompaniment (string quartet), a *Fisherman's Lullaby*, a *May Song*, and others.

International Prizes

In 1956, Hipman was awarded the second prize in the International competition of the French radio and television for his *Rondo* for piano and orchestra (première in Cannes 1957).

HIRNER, Teodor
[born Smolenice, 20 April 1910]

After completing the study of organ at the Music and Dramatic Academy and at the Pedagogic Institute in Bratislava, Hirner was active as a military bandmaster. On his return to civilian life he joined The Army Artistic Ensemble Vít Nejedlý in Prague; at the same time he studied musical science at Charles University and composition under JAROSLAV ŘÍDKÝ.

From Prague he went to the Košice Radio (as a chief of musical broadcasting) and later to the Radio in Bratislava, becoming as well the secretary of the Slovak Guild of Composers. At present he is director of the Košice Conservatory.

Hirner's creative work shows the strong influence of the folklore of Eastern Slovakia to which he repeatedly returns in various arrangements: *Songs from my Home*, for solos, choir and orchestra (1949), *Into Karička*, for solos, choir and small orchestra (1952), *Wedding Dances from Lower Branisko* (1952), *Christmas of the Kysuca Tinker Apprentices* (1959), *A Small Overture from Šariš* (1960).

He selected folk songs from Western Slovakia into a montage for solos, choir and orchestra, called *In the wide Fields of Smolenice.*

He wrote several cantatas (*From Danube to the Pines of the Tatra Mountains, Greetings to Moscow*) and several chamber music and orchestral compositions, in which folklore links up with romantic elements [*The String Quartet* (1954), a *Serenade* for string orchestra (1958) and a *Suite* for strings, winds, harp and celesta (1959), a *Wind Quintet* (1960) and a *Carpathian Overture* (1961)].

From his recent works we note a cycle of piano compositions *Immagini* (1964) and a poem *Dukla* for full orchestra (1964), dedicated to the twentieth anniversary of the Slovak National Uprising.

HLAVÁČ, Miroslav

[born Protivín, 23 October 1923]

Hlaváč graduated from the Technical University. He lived in Eastern Slovakia and Southern Bohemia (where he was born), with deep impressions that strengthened his interest in music. While in Pilsen, he studied composition under BOŘIVOJ MIKODA and in Prague the same under JAROSLAV ŘÍDKÝ and KLEMENT SLAVICKÝ.

Stage Works

He composed a one-act ballet *The Sorcerer's Apprentice,* according to the ballad by J. W. GOETHE (1962, première in Pilsen 1963).

Chamber Music

Among others we have to mention *Pastoral Sonatina* for flute and piano (1945), *Pastorale* (1945), *Pastorale lydico* (1947), *Balladic Sonata* for violoncello and piano (1952), three canonical compositions for string quartet or for string orchestra *Slovak Inventions* (1953, 1955), *String Quartet* (1955) and a fable *About a Little Dog, Cat and Moon* for chamber orchestra with a narrator (1958) and three rhythmic inventions for strings *Arytmikon* (1961).

Orchestral and Instrumental Works

For orchestra Hlaváč composed *The Evening Suite* (1950), *A Spring Overture* (1954), *A Fantastic Rondo* (1955), *A Love Legend* (1956), *Rhapsody* (1957), a *Symphony* (1960, awarded in the artistic jubilee competition in 1960) and *Elegikon*, three compositions for winds, piano and percussion instruments (1964).

Then he wrote a *Piano Sonata* (1946), piano variations on a Czech folk song in the classic style entitled *Portraits* (1954), a *Violoncello Concerto* (1953) and *The Birds' Prelude* for piano for four hands (1960).

Vocal Works

His compositions in this field include the song-cycles *Lyrikon* (1943), *Your Sixteen Years* (1944), *Castles in the Air* (1947), *Songs of Old China* (1948) and *In the Meadows* (1954). Furthermore a *Lyric Prelude* for soprano, flute and harp [or for violin, viola and harp] (1962).

His choral works are represented by *East Slovak Folk Songs* (1949) and *Songs About Little Animals* for children's choir and piano (1956).

HLOBIL, Emil

[born Veselí, 11 October 1901]

MERITED TEACHER

Hlobil spent his youth at Přerov, where he was taught harmony by the composer JOSEF ČAPKA DRAHLOVSKÝ; later he studied composition at the Prague Conservatory under JAROSLAV KŘIČKA and at the Master School under JOSEF SUK.

From 1941, Hlobil taught composition and musical theory at the Prague Conservatory; at present, he is teaching composition at the Academy of Musical Arts in Prague.

For a number of years he was chairman of the Czech Music Fund.

Hlobil was influenced by the style of his teacher SUK and at the same time absorbed much from the work of JANÁČEK. Very early he acquired an individual compositional technique characterized by conciseness of thought, pregnant expression and a rapid musical flow, as well as a keen sense for inner tension of voices and for proportionality in structure.

The center of gravity of Hlobil's creative work lies in orchestra and chamber music.

Stage Works

In 1962 Hlobil completed his three-act opera *Anna Karenina*, according to the novel by L. N. TOLSTOY.

Orchestral Works

His symphonies are closely interwoven with life itself.

The *First Symphony*, op. 31 (1949) expresses a zest for life;

the *Second Symphony*, entitled *The Day of Victory*, op. 58 (1951) depicts the impressions of May 9th, 1945 (the liberation of Prague by the Soviet Army);

the *Third Symphony*, op. 53 (1957) is concerned with the

inner life of the contemporary man; his *Fourth Symphony*, op. 58, was composed in 1959.

The suffering of the people during the German occupation is reflected in the extensive symphonic composition for full orchestra *The Commemoration of the Martyrs*, op. 25 (1944—45). The poetry that the composer sees in the young people around him is expressed in the symphonic picture for full orchestra *The Song of the Youth*, op. 22 (1943—44).

In the symphonic suites *Summer in the Giant Mountains*, op. 33 (1950) and *Spring in the Gardens of Prague*, op. 35 (1953) Hlobil depicts the beauty of his native country. Both works were awarded the prize of the City of Prague in 1961.

From his other orchestral compositions we may mention: the suite *Week-end* for small orchestra, op. 6 (1933), *Divertimento* for small orchestra, op. 17 (1935), *Sinfonietta*, op. 19 (1939), *Three Moravian Dances*, op. 32 (1949), *Folk Merry-making* for small orchestra, op. 34 (1950), *A Wallachian Village*, op. 39 (1952), *The Serenade* for small orchestra, outstanding for its genuine gracefulness, op. 49 (1955); his symphonic picture *Labour Day* (1960) was awarded second prize in the artistic jubilee competition in 1960; further *Concerto per archi*, op. 62 (1963) and *Concerto filarmonico*, op. 66 (1964).

Instrumental and Chamber Music

Instrumental concertos held an important role in Hlobil's compositional development, as is evidenced by the *Violin Concerto* with orchestra, op. 47 (1955), *Rhapsody* for clarinet with orchestra, op. 51 (1955), *Concerto* for accordion with orchestra, op. 54 (1956), and *Concerto* for organ, strings and timpani, op. 61 (1963), the basic thematic material of which is the tonal sequel B-A-C-H.

His chamber music comprises a *String Quintet*, op. 1 (1925), *String Quartet* No. 1, op. 5 (1931), *Sonatina* for violin and piano, op. 13 (1934), *String Quartet* No. 2, op. 15 (1936), a piano *Trio*, op. 18 (1938), a wind

Quintet, op. 20 (1940), a *Sonata* for French horn and piano, op. 21 (1942, reworked in 1948), *Quartet* for harpsichord, violin, viola and violoncello, op. 23 (1943), *Spring Impromptu* for violoncello and piano, op. 24 (1944), a *Nonet*, op. 27 (1946), *Serenade* for string quartet, op. 41 (1952), *String Quartet* No. 3, op. 50 (1955), a *Wind Octet*, op. 52 (1956), a *Sonata* for two pianos, op. 55 (1958), a *Sonata* for violin and piano, op. 57 (1959), *Aria e toccata* for organ, op. 46 (1963), *Quartet* for flute, oboe, clarinet and bassoon, op. 64 (1964) and *Aria e Rondo* for oboe and harp, op. 65 (1964).

Vocal Works

Hlobil has done relatively little in the field of vocal music. He wrote community songs, several choirs, *Three Songs*, op. 8 (1933), a cycle of mixed choir *My Home*, set to words by JAROSLAV SEIFERT, op. 48 (1955) and the cantata *On the Gift of Coal* for bass, mixed choir and orchestra, to words by FRANTIŠEK BRANISLAV, op. 42 (1952).

Writings

He wrote a book about his teacher *Josef Suk* and a manual *The Theory of Musical Forms*.

HOLOUBEK, Ladislav

[born Prague, 13 August 1913]

Holder of the decoration FOR OUTSTANDING WORK and of the distinction FOR RECONSTRUCTION SERVICES

Holoubek lived since his boyhood in Slovakia. He divides his interests between conducting and composition. He prepared himself for both these fields at the Bratislava Music and Dramatic Academy under JOZEF VINCOUREK and ALEXANDER MOYZES, studying piano as well under ERNEST KRIŽAN. He continued the study of composition at the Master School of the Prague Conservatory under VÍTĚZSLAV NOVÁK.

His first post was accompanist at the opera of the Slovak National Theatre in Bratislava; then he became conductor of the opera and after the liberation its deputy-chief. For a short time he was chief-conductor of the Military Artistic Ensemble and chief of the opera in Košice. At present he is again conductor of the Bratislava Opera.

He is known as an eminent conductor not only at home but abroad as well and has done outstanding work in his productions of new Slovak operas, such as *Krútňava, The Resurrection* and others.

Stage Works

By the end of the thirties, Holoubek had begun to devote himself intensively to operatic creative work and had written five operas: *Stella* (1937—38, première in Bratislava 1939; in a revised version Košice 1957); *Dawn* (1939—40, première in Bratislava 1941); *Longing* (1944, première in Bratislava 1944); *The Family* (1956 to 1960, première in Bratislava 1960, the latter possessing rich artistic merit) and a two-act opera *Professor Mamlock*, to own libretto, according to the drama by FRIEDRICH WOLF (1964).

Orchestral Works

Significant compositions of his orchestral creative work are *The Overture* for full orchestra, op. 5 (1933), *The Symphony*, op. 19 (1946, reworked in 1949), *The Sinfonietta*, op. 36 (1950) and *Ten Variations* on the composer's own theme for full orchestra, op. 37 (1950).

Chamber Music

Among his early compositions are *Sonata* No. 1 for piano (1930), *Sonata* for violin and piano in E minor (1932), *String Quartet* No. 1 (1935), a *Wind Quintet*

(1938), *String Quartet* No. 2 (1946), *Sonata* for piano No. 2 (1947), *String Quartet* No. 3 [dodecafonic] (1964). In these works he has adjusted himself to the stimuli of contemporary music while his pronounced lyrical expressiveness has freed itself of constructivism and the supremacy of the harmonic element.

Vocal Works

Voices: He has written a number of notable song cycles as the ballad for soprano and orchestra *The Dead Woman*, op. 6 (1933), *Songs about a Woman* for tenor and orchestra, op. 7 (1933), *Songs About Mother* for alto and piano, op. 13 (1936), *Youth* for coloratura soprano and piano, op. 29 (1935—44).

At the beginning of the fifties Holoubek again began to write non-operatic compositions, such as the cycles of songs *To the People* (1951) and *Daughter of Mine* (1953) both for soprano and piano (or orchestra).

Cantatas: the momentous *Moonlit Night* for soprano, male choir and orchestra, op. 48 (1951).

Various

Holoubek has also written music to several films [full-length film *The Dam* (1947)] and to radio and stage plays.

HOLUB, Josef

[born Holice, 23 February 1902]

Holub is a prominent Czech violinist and chamber music player; he was a pupil of RUDOLF REISSIG in Brno and of OTAKAR ŠEVČÍK in Vienna and in Prague and completed also a course of interpretation, organized by CARL FLESCH in Berlin. Composition he studied under LEOŠ JANÁČEK at the Brno branch of the Master School of the Prague Conservatory and later also privately with Vítězslav Novák. He is at present professor of violin at the Brno Conservatory.

In the compositional work he unites virtuosic romantic traits with those of impressionism.

He has composed four violin *Concertos* (1923—24, 1931, 1954—55 and 1964), a one-movement *String Quartet* (1924), fourteen compositions for violin with piano accompaniment (*A Spring Composition—Ecstasy—Tarantella—A Ballad—Introduction and Scherzo—An Idyll—Intermezzo—A Melody—Dance of the Dragon-flies*), smaller compositions for flute and trumpet, two orchestral suites and others.

HORKÝ, Karel

[born Štěměchy, 4 September 1909]

Horký first studied composition privately with Vladimír Polívka and later with Pavel Haas, completing his courses of study under Jaroslav Křička at the Master School of the Prague Conservatory. He was active as a professor at the Brno Conservatory, where he is now its director.

Stage Works

He has distinguished himself as a musical dramatist by his operas *Jan Hus* (1944—49, première in Brno 1950, rewritten 1956-57, première in Brno 1957), *Captain Šárovec* (1951—52, première in Brno 1953) and the ballets *The Conch* (1939—40, première in Brno 1945) and *King Ječmínek* (1949—50, première in Brno 1951).

Instrumental Works

Of Horký's other compositions we may list a *String Quartet* (1938), the symphonic poem *Klythia* (1942), a *Violin Sonata* (1943), a *Suite* for wind quintet (1943), the *Romantic Sinfonietta* (1944), *Concerto* for violoncello (1953), two *String Quartets* (1954 and 1955), *Concerto* for violin (1955), *Sonatina* for oboe and piano (1958), *Nonet* (1958), *Quintet* for two violins, viola, violoncello and clarinet (1960), *Sonatina* for doublebass and piano (1961) and a cantata *The Czech Dream* (1961—62).

Vocal Works

Songs and choirs [such as *The Czech Dream,* a cantata for mixed choir and orchestra set to words of Josef Kainar (1961)] make a complete picture of the character of the composer and his work.

HRADIL, František M.

[born Vsetín, 8 December 1898]

Hradil acquired the rudiments of a musical education from his father ANTONÍN HRADIL who was one of the first graduates of the Janáček School for Organists in Brno. He completed his musical education at the Brno branch of the Master School of the Prague Conservatory under LEOŠ JANÁČEK.

Hradil has had a permanent effect on the life of the city of Ostrava and the Ostrava region, where he has been active for almost forty years as choirmaster, organizer of musical activity, pedagogue, composer, writer and critic. From 1954 he was regional cultural inspector in Ostrava and from 1956 he has held the post of director of the Advanced Pedagogic School of Music in Prague.

Orchestral Works

The Beskid Mountains were the inspirational source for his symphonic poem *Beyond the Ostravice*, based on a poem by PETR BEZRUČ (1922), and *Symphonic Rhapsody* (1930).

Intrumental Compositions

The piano sonatina *Greetings to a Soviet Man—Victor over the Univers* (1961) is, for the time being, Hradil's latest work in instrumental music.

Vocal Works

They are to a considerable part based on poems of PETR BEZRUČ.

Female choirs: *Praise to the Native Land* (1958) and *The Surf* (1960).

Male choirs: *Silesian Hymns* (1924), *Tošonovice* (1924), *Who Will Take My Place* (1926), *The Song of the Beskid Mountains* (1927), *Below the Beskid Mountains* (1928), *Three Colours* (1929), *Brotherhood* (1931), *Ostrava* (1934), a *Tribute to Ostrava* (1935), *Green Grass* (1936), *God Speed!* (1938), an *Old Time Country Lassie* (1941) and then a *Worker's Hand* (1958).

Children choirs: *Flowers in Bloom* (1955), *Singing Blossoms* (1958) and the *Sweet Smell of Home* (1960).

Mixed choirs: *Three Musicians* (1926) and *Vatra* (1960).

Cantatas: His creative work has been influenced by LEOŠ JANÁČEK, as is to be seen from his first choirs and chamber cantata *Poluška* for soprano, alto, tenor and chamber orchestra (1925). JIŘÍ WOLKER influenced him by his poem *Ballad in the Eyes of a Stoker*, composed by Hradil as a cantata (1932). After an interval of many years he continued in this direction by a four-part cantata *A Song of Peace* for solos and orchestra, set to a poem by VÍTĚZSLAV NEZVAL (1950). Further he composed a symphonic melodrama *The Hero*, set to a poem by BORIS LICHAREV (1953), which pays tribute to the immortal memory of JULIUS FUČÍK. In close affinity is the pioneer cantata *The Children of the Sun* for solos, children and youth choirs and orchestra (1960).

Various compositions

Hradil has written as well, a number of compositions for children and arrangements of folk songs.

Writings

The themes of the poet PETR BEZRUČ and Ostrava region itself have also imbued Hradil's musical literary works: *Petr Bezruč and the Czech Musical Creative Art* (1937, second edition 1947), *Music and Song in the Land of Janáček* (1940).

His understanding of choral works led Hradil to compile a bibliography of Czech and Slovak literature since 1822 up to the present (awarded in the artistic jubilee competition in 1960) and a treatise on choral creative work of prominent Czech composers.

For teachers of music schools he has written a handbook *The Basic School of Music* (1958).

HRUŠKA, Jaromír Ludvík

[born Písek, 6 January 1910]

Hruška comes from an outstanding musical family. His father, Jaromír Hruška (1880—1954), graduated from the Prague Conservatory as a pupil of ANTONÍN DVOŘÁK and in the years 1901—53 distinguished himself as a leader in the field of music at Písek. His grandfather, František Hruška (1847—1889), played the second violin in the orchestra of the Provisional Theatre in Prague under BEDŘICH SMETANA; later he became a theatre conductor and finally master of the choir at Mladá Boleslav.

Hruška studied law at Charles University and simultaneously composition at the Prague Conservatory under RUDOLF KAREL, conducting under METOD DOLEŽIL and organ under ANTONÍN ELŠLÉGR. He continued his study of composition as a pupil of JAROSLAV ŘÍDKÝ and KAREL JANEČEK, completing it at the Academy of Musical Arts under PAVEL BOŘKOVEC. Prior to his present position at the Czechoslovak Radio (in the musical archives) Hruška worked in the military administration.

Orchestral and Chamber Music

Hruška composed two *Sonatas* for piano, two *Sonatas* for violin and piano, a *Sonata* for clarinet and piano (1948), two *String Quartets* (1945 and 1955), a *Wind Quintet* (1950), a *Sonata* for viola and piano (1958), a *Suite* for chamber orchestra (1962) and four compositions for clarinet and piano (1964).

In this field he has written a *Sinfonietta* for strings (1951) and a *Prelude* for full orchestra (1953).

Vocal Works

He wrote songs with piano accompaniment [*The Ballad of a Beautiful Death* (1937)], a cycle of songs set to words by JAROSLAV SEIFERT (1944), a cycle of songs to verses by RABINDRANÁTH TAGORE (1945), a cycle of children's songs entitled *Lillian's Little Songs* (1945) and several male choirs.

HRUŠOVSKÝ, Ivan

[born Bratislava, 23 February 1927]

In composition he was pupil of ALEXANDER MOYZES, under whom he completed his course of study at the Bratislava Conservatory and at the High School of Musical Arts. At the same time he was awarded a degree of Doctor of Philosophy by the Komenský University.

Hrušovský divides his interests between composition and musicological activity. He is lecturer at the High

School of Musical Arts, where he teaches musical theoretical subjects; in addition, he is dramaturgist for opera of the Slovak National Theatre.

His compositional beginnings are marked by neo-romantic and impressionistic principles and show the influence of his teacher. Recently his work has achieved an individual character while its dominating trait continues to lie in an inclination to lyricism and in a sovereign technique.

Orchestral Music

Of his orchestral works the *Suite Pastorale* (1955), a *Concerto* for piano and orchestra (1958), a symphonic picture *The Tatra Poem* (1960) and a *Symphony* for two string orchestras, piano and percussion instruments (1962) are of outstanding quality.

To the twentieth anniversary of Slovak national uprising he composed an orchestral *Passacaglia eroica* (1964).

Hrušovský is the author of a number of chamber music compositions.

Vocal Works

Hrušovský's bend towards lyricism is most pronounced in his vocal compositions such as the song cycle for soprano and piano *The Red Poppy* (1959) and in the significant parts of the cantata trilogy *Against Death* [Hiroshima—A White Birch Tree—Marching Past (1961—62)].

To the twentieth anniversary of the liberation of the Czechoslovak Socialist Republic he composed a cantata *A Dream About a Man* (1964).

Arrangements

He devotes himself as well to making arrangements of folk songs [the small cantata *Below Kriváň*, *Two Slovak Dance Fantasies*], and to film and scenic music.

Writings

Of his scientific works, the article on musical classicism in *The History of Slovak Music* (1957) is particularly significant. The same is true of his *Introduction to the Study of the Theory of Harmony* (1960) and of this extensive monograph *Slovak Music* (1963), *The Slovak Music in Profiles and Analyses* (1964) and *Antonín Dvořák* (1964).

Due to his critical and analytical studies Hrušovský ranks among the foremost Slovak musical critics.

HUDEC, Jiří

[born Brno, 31 August 1923]

Hudec graduated from the organ division of the Brno Conservatory and studied composition at the Janáček Academy of Musical Arts.

In the years 1943—45 he was accompanist and conductor at the Czech Folk Theatre and in 1945—53 of the State Opera, both in Brno. He is chief conductor of the Brno Variety Radio Orchestra.

Together with JAN TĚŠÍK he is a member of a piano duo.

In 1955, with the Variety Radio Orchestra, he appeared with great success at the exposition "Ten Years of the People's Democratic Czechoslovakia" in Moscow; he went, together with JAN TĚŠÍK, to Moscow again in 1960 to participate with a satirical montage at the exhibition "Fifteen Years of the People's Democratic Czechoslovakia". He has appeared as well as conductor in Budapest, Lodź, Berlin and Leipzig.

For the radio he has produced several classic and modern operettas and has cooperated as composer and arranger with the Brno Variety Radio Orchestra ever since its inception.

His compositions include *Capriccio* (1949) and *Rhapso-*

dy for piano and orchestra (1949), *Ballet Scenes* for orchestra (1950), a *Comedy Overture* (1951), *Three Czech Dances* (1953) and *Aquarelles* (1953), smaller variety and dance compositions, satirical songs, compositions for piano duo and similarly.

He has written ten operettas, two of which are the well-known *Everybody to His Hobby* and *Marianne Smiles*.

He has also written music to popular-scientific films *Attention-Gas*, *Autonomous Movements of Plants*, and to the two-part film *The Brno Fair 1959*.

HŮLA, Zdeněk
[born St. Anton in Tyrol, 12 May 1901]
MERITED TEACHER

Hůla was a pupil of VÍTĚZSLAV NOVÁK and later of JAROSLAV ŘÍDKÝ (composition). At the Master School of the Prague Conservatory he resumed his studies under VÍTĚZSLAV NOVÁK. At present, he is professor of harmony, contrapunct and composition at the Prague Conservatory.

His compositional work dates back to the beginnings of the twenties. At first he composed popular music: the operetta *The Gentleman* and small orchestral compositions such as *The Little Soldier*, *The Idyll*, *Furiant* (a Czech folk dance), *The Slav Capriccio*, *In the Slovak Countryside*.

Later, his work consisted of more ambitious compositions such as the ballet *Blue Blossom* (1935—37, première in Prague 1937), *Passacaglia* and *Fugue* for full orchestra (1940) and four *Fairy-tale Moods* according to K. J. ERBEN for wind quintet (1941). For the radio he arranged a montage of *National Songs* from the Klatovy and Domažlice regions (1944).

Hůla is outstanding as a theoretician and pedagogue

and is the author of an eminent work *The Science of Harmony* (1956) and the two volume *Science of Counterpoint* (the first volume appeared in 1958, the second in 1965).

He is also co-author of *The Textbook for distance-schooling of leaders of Choral Ensembles of Folk Art* (1954).

For participants of Television Conservatory (1963 to 1964) he wrote a treatise *Melody—the Foundation of Music* and *The Mystery of Harmony*.

HURNÍK, Ilja
[born Poruba, 25 November 1922]

Hurník attended the secondary school in Ostrava and Prague and simultaneously studied piano with VILÉM KURZ, professor at the Master School of the Prague Conservatory and later under ILONA ŠTĚPÁNOVÁ at the Academy of Musical Arts.

As a pianist Hurník has excelled above all in the interpretation of French impressionists and of LEOŠ JANÁČEK. He undertook a number of concert tours abroad and his reproductive achievements have been recorded on gramophone records.

He is at present soloist for the State Philharmonic in Ostrava.

He studied composition under F. M. HRADIL and JAROSLAV ŘÍDKÝ and was the last pupil of VÍTĚZSLAV NOVÁK.

Orchestral, Instrumental and Chamber Works

Hurník began to compose early in childhood; his first piano composition *The First Melodies* (1931) was published in 1933. For piano he has also composed *Motifs from Childhood* (1935), *Summer Sonatina* (1937),

Two Toccatas (1941), *Preludes* (1943) and a *Sonatina* in C major (1952). For flute he composed a *Concerto* (1953). To piano he returned in 1963, when he composed *Home Music* for four hands.

Out of his recent works we quote the orchestral composition *The Cyclops* (1963).

In the field of chamber music the following compositions came into being: *String Quartet* with polka themes (1949), a suite *Four Seasons of the Year* (1952), *Piano Quintet* (1953), *Sonata da camera* (1953). His *Concerto* for oboe, piano and string orchestra and *Piano Trio* (1953) were awarded in the artistic jubilee competition in 1960.

Further we may quote a *Ballet* for nine instruments (1954), *Esercizii* for flute, oboe, clarinet and bassoon (1958), a *String Quartet* with baritone solo to the text of the Song of Songs (1961), *Les Moments Musicaux* for eleven wind instruments, in which the composer makes use in an individual manner of certain traits of punctuallism (1962), *Chamber Music* for strings (1962) and a suite for twenty instruments entitled *The Musicians*, set to verses by FRANTIŠEK BRANISLAV (1962).

Film Music

For his music to the film *The Liberated Palette* he was awarded the prize in the competition for the best musical composition for Czechoslovak film production in 1963.

Vocal Works

Songs: Of Hurník's vocal creative work, mention should be made of the song cycles *The Flowers* (1941), *A Girls' Song* (1942), *Silesian Songs* (1946), the choral cycles *Choirs about Mother* (1955) and *Sulamit* (1963).

Cantatas: Up to the present, Hurník's finest work have been those compositions finding inspiration in Silesian folklore, as the cantata *Maryka* (1948, reworked 1955) and the ballet *Ondráš* (1950, see lower).

In 1959, Hurník completed an extensive oratorio *Noah* for solos, choir and orchestra.

Songs for children: Hurník's compositions *The Fairy-tale About the Princess Little Frog* and *About the Big Sugarbeet* grew out of the composer's spiritual affinity to the world of children. This is true as well of his many songs and choirs for children, such as the *Sun-Warmed Field Boundary* and *Little Songs* (1958).

Various

He is also the author of attractive feuilletons and apocryphas from the history of music *The Trumpeters from Jericho*.

For the Third Spartakiad (1965) he composed music to exercises *In the Sun*.

International Prizes

His ballet *Ondráš* (libretto J. REY, 1950, première in Ostrava 1951) was awarded a silver medal in the competition at the Festival of the World Federation of Youth in Warsaw.

HURT, Jaroslav
[born Prague, 25 April 1914]
Holder of the decoration FOR OUTSTANDING WORK

Artistic manager of Hurt's variety collective made an intensive study of violin and of bass-bugle horn at the Military School of Music where he also began experimenting with composition. He completed his musical studies at the Prague Conservatory in the violin class of BEDŘICH VOLDÁN.

From 1940 to 1960 he was a member of the orchestra of the National Theatre in Prague and in 1960 the title of Merited Member of the National Theatre was conferred upon him.

Orchestral Works

Recently Hurt has written a number of orchestral compositions as for instance *The May Overture* for full orchestra, the suite *Youth*, *Overture* in D major, a rhapsody *Light and Shadow*, and symphonic suites *The Indonesian Motif* and an *Episode*.

Light Music

His light music and dance compositions amply fulfilled the requirements demanded in the respective fields. They include the operettas *Curtain Up*, *A Family War* and *A Reporter in Love* and compositions for ¶ variety programmes *After the Ball*, *Aladin's Lamp*, *The Devil of a Fellow*, *The Watch on the River Bug*, *A Ballet Scene*, *Lights in the Harbour*, *Recollections of Cracow*, ¶ the valses *Edelweiss*, *A Dream* and *A Neighbourly Dance* (a slow folk dance) and ¶ modern dances *A Melody*, *Tell Me a Fairy Tale*, *Forget-me-nots* and *The Journey for a Fairy-tale*.

Vocal Music

Hurt devotes particular attention to our young people and to their vanguard—the pioneers. This is evidenced by his cantatas *The Song of Youth*, *For Peace and Our No!*, by his songs on the building up of the country, such as *Everyone Sings With Us*, *To Young Miners*, *We Want to Live in Peace*, *A Better World*, *To the Worker Sportsman*, *A March of New Sportsmen*, by the pioneer and youth songs *On the March*, *A Kite Flies to the Sky*, *Little Pioneers*, *Hallo Pioneer!*, *The Lady-bird*, *The Rangers*, *The Youth Song*, *The Farmer's Song* and others.

Hurt has concerned himself as well with political songs (*I Sing for Youth*, *It is So*, *Old Man*). His song *The World has Changed* received a special award in the artistic jubilee competition in 1960. His small cantata *For Peace* received honourable mention.

Small études and ten *Concerto études* for accordion are Hurt's contributions to the instructive and concerto literature for this instrument.

HURT

HYBLER, Jindřich

[born Semily, 31 December 1891]

Hybler studied organ at the Prague Conservatory and composition at its Master School under J. B. FOERSTER. As an external student he also studied musical science at Charles University.

He was active as musical pedagogue, as an instrumentalist (viola) in various symphonic orchestras, choirmaster and conductor and as an editor and organizer.

Instrumental Compositions

He has composed a *Duo* for violin and piano (1929), three *Duos* for violin and violoncello [the first in 1956 (diploma in the international competition of composers at Vercelli, 1957), the second in 1958 and the third in 1959], three *String Quartets* (1927, 1958, the third with recitative and soprano solo in 1961).

Vocal Works

In his creative work, Hybler has devoted himself primarily to vocal music:

Voices—*In the Frost-Bound Land* for soprano, violin, clarinet, French horn and bassoon (1939), *Stars Above Home* for soprano, violin, clarinet, French horn (1955) [diploma in the international competition of composers at Vercelli 1957].

Male choirs—*The Tree of Freedom*, set to words by F. X. ŠALDA (arranged also for mixed choir), *To My Brothers the Czechs*, to words by JAROSLAW IWASKIEWICZ, *A Song on My Native Land*, to words by FRANTIŠEK NECHVÁTAL, *One to the Other* to words by JAN NOHA (1939).

Cantatas—he has composed four cantatas: *The Song of the Land* (1928), *Slovakia has Arisen* (1930), *Sierra Ventana* (1933) and *The Cheb Rhapsody* (1962).

Hybler's other vocal works include the vocal symphony *Mountains and People*, set to poems by ANTAL STAŠEK, IVAN OLBRACHT and S. K. NEUMANN for solos, recitative, choir and orchestra (1957) and several melodramas.

ILLÍN, Evžen,
[born Podunajské Biskupice, 2 November 1924]

Illín studied composition at the Prague Conservatory under EMIL HLOBIL and at the Academy of Musical Arts under JAROSLAV ŘÍDKÝ and ALOIS HÁBA.

Chamber Music

He composed a wind *Quintet* (1949), a *Children's Suite* for wind quintet (1952), *Divertimento* for winds, harp and percussion instruments (1952), *Trio* concertante for flute, clarinet and viola (1955) and two *String Quartets* (1958 and 1960).

Orchestral Music

He has written a *Scherzo* for full orchestra (1947), a *Symphony* (1950), *Fantasy* for viola and orchestra (1951), *Rhymes* for children's choir and orchestra (two series: 1951 and 1952), *Rhapsody* for flute and orchestra (1954), *Concertino* for violin and orchestra (1956) and *Concerto* for orchestra (1957).

Scenic Music

Illín has written a new score for the play of JIŘÍ VOS-KOVEC and JAN WERICH *The Executioner and a Madman*, as well as scenic music to a number of plays for the National Theatre in Prague [CARLO GOLDONI: *Panic on the Lagoon*, PETER KARVAŠ: *The Midnight Mass* and *Antigona and Those Others*, VÍTĚZSLAV NEZVAL: *Lovers from the Kiosk*].

Film Music

In this field Illín composed musical accompaniment to the full-length films *Death in the Saddle*, *The Fifth Division*, *People Live Everywhere*, *Rabbits in High Grass*, *Tarzan's Death*, *The Star Goes South*, *Unusual Class*, *White Lady*, and to television film *The Lost Revue*.

●

Arrangements and montages of folk songs and variety
and dance compositions complete the characterization
of Illín's personality as a composer.

IŠTVAN, Miloslav

[born Olomouc, 2 September 1928]

Ištvan studied composition under JAROSLAV KVAPIL
at the Janáček Academy of Musical Arts, where he also
completed his post-graduate studies. He is senior lecturer
in the section of composition at the same Academy.

His creative activity up to the present has passed
through three stages: (1) The years 1948—53 represented the period of a quest for compositional methods based
on principles of socialist realism; (2) the years 1953—58
showed a striving for a balance between a socialist
content and contemporary expression; (3) since 1958
he has pursued consciously and consistently a modal
way in his musical thinking and recently as well in the
serial compositional technique.

Orchestral Works

The Czechoslovak Suite for orchestra (1951), Concerto
Symphony for piano and orchestra (1958, received a special award in the artistic jubilee competition in 1960)
and a Ballad About the South [three symphonic frescoes
suggested by a song of LEWIS ALLAN and expressing
the oppressive atmosphere of racial segregation in the
American South and a protest against it (1960)].

Chamber Music

His first period is testified by his Concerto for French
horn, piano and strings (1949), Rondo for viola and piano
(1950), Trio for clarinet, violoncello and piano (1950);
in his second stage he composed Sonata for clarinet and
piano (1954), Suite for French horn and piano (1955),

Winter Suite for strings and piano (1956), *Sonata* for violin and piano (1956); his third stage is represented by *Trio* for violin, violoncello and piano (1958), *Concertino* for violin and chamber orchestra (1961), *Rhapsody* for violoncello and piano (1961), *Dodecameron,* twelve compositions for twelve players (1962—64) and *String Quartet* (1963).

Instrumental Works

His inner strife for a balance of expression is shown in his *First Sonata* for piano (1954), *Impromptu* for piano (1956), *Second Sonata* for piano (1959) and *The Lidice Odyssey* for piano (1963).

Cantatas

The cantata *The War Incendiaries Shall Not Pass* (1952) shows his endeavour to find a way for his conception of socialist realism.

Various Compositions

In addition to chamber music and symphonic works Ištvan has devoted himself to compositions for Folk Art Ensembles (*A Little Song of Joy, Harvest Song, The Winter Song* and *Fountain Song*) and to scenic music (*The Bagpiper of Strakonice, Vojcek, Frolics with the Devil, Bajaja* and others).

For his *String Quartet* he was awarded the State Prize in the artistic jubilee competition 1965.

JANEČEK, Karel

[born Czenstochowa, Poland, 20 February 1903]

Janeček is doctor of sciences of art. After completing the secondary school he matriculated at the Prague Conservatory as a student of composition under JAROSLAV

KŘIČKA and graduated from the Master School under VÍTĚZSLAV NOVÁK.

He became a teacher at the City School of Music in Pilsen and subsequently professor in composition at the Prague Conservatory. In 1946 he transferred to the Academy of Musical Arts.

During the period between the two World Wars Janeček proved to be a composer with a vigorous modern orientation, not permitting himself to be lured by the destructive tendencies in the artistic events of those years. He was protected from such by-paths by his judicious critical sense and by his respect for perfect compositional work acquired in the Novák school. His is a penetrating spirit, not satisfied with mere creative impulses, but demanding a clear understanding of the ideas and results of the compositional process. His music is a synthesis of his broad knowledge of contemporary and older music and of a thorough conception of its substance.

Orchestral Works

His creative work in the field od symphonic music is represented by an *Overture* (his graduation work), op. 3 (1926—27), *First Symphony*, op. 17 (1935—40), *Variations*, inspired by the tragedy of Lidice, op. 23 (1942, reworked for full orchestra 1944—46), the symphonic triptych *Lenin*, op. 29 (1953), *Second Symphony*, op. 30 (1954—55), an overture *A Legend About Prague*, op. 32 (1956) and by a *Fantasy* for orchestra, op. 39 (1962—63).

Chamber and Instrumental Music

His chamber music includes *String Quartet* No. 1, op. 1 (1924), a *Divertimento* for eight instruments (1925—26), *String Quartet* No. 2, op. 4 (1927), *Trio* for violin, viola and violoncello, op. 9 (1930), *Trio* for flute, clarinet and bassoon, op. 10 (1931), *String Quartet* No. 3, op. 15 (1934), *Duo* for violin and viola, op. 19 (1938), *Children Trio* for piano, violin and violoncello (1940), *Divertimento* for oboe, clarinet and bassoon, op. 24 (1943), a *Small Symposion* for wind instruments, op. 34 (1959), *Duo* for violin and violoncello, op. 37 (1960) and a *Chamber Overture* for nonet (to the life-drama of Giordano Bruno), op. 38 (1960).

Janeček's compositions for organ include *The Prelude, Chorale and Fughetta*, op. 28 (1952), *The Prelude, Chorale and Toccata*, op. 31 (1958) and *Partita*, op. 40 (1963, instrumented 1964).

Janeček composed a large number of piano compositions; mention should be made of the following: *Concerto Etudes*, op. 12 (1931), *Fantasy and Capriccio*, op. 13 (1933), *Introduction and Fugue*, op. 22 (1942) and a *Sonata*, op. 25 (1944). Several smaller and larger piano compositions and instructive works for four hands complete this survey.

He wrote as well a *Violin Sonata*, op. 21 (1940) and a *Violoncello Sonata*, op. 33 (1958).

Vocal Works

To Czech vocal music he contributed the cycles of male choirs *Autumn 1930* (set to texts by GÉRARD NERVAL, F. HALAS, J. HORA), op. 7 (1930), *A Song of Anguish* (to a poem by F. HALAS), op. 20a (1939), *Czech Psalms* (to poems by JOSEF HORA), op. 20b (1939), *To the Dead and to the Living* (to poems by F. HALAS), op. 26 (1951), *Cosmic Songs* (set to verses by F. HRUBÍN) op. 34 (1959) and *The Epitaphs*, op. 35 (1959).

Three children choirs *From the People*, op. 27a (1951), *The Silver Forest* (set to verses by F. HALAS), op. 27b (1951) and *The Joy and the Work* (to verses by F. L. ČELAKOVSKÝ), op. 27c (1952).

Mixed choir *Lights and Shadows* (a cycle of madrigals, set to words by JEAN COCTEAU and JAROSLAV SEIFERT), op. 16 (1934).

Writings

Janeček is a prominent music theoretician and has written many articles and several books: *The Basis of Modern Harmony* (1942—49), *Musical Forms* (1955) and *Melodics* (1956), firmly establishing himself as a foremost authority in the field of music theory. His work *An Analytical Introduction to Harmony* received a special award in the artistic jubilee competition in 1960; it was published in 1963 under the title *Harmony by Analysis*.

JANKOVEC, Jaroslav

[born Malenice, 26 April 1896—died Prague, 6 September 1961]

Jankovec studied composition at the Prague Conservatory under JAROSLAV KŘIČKA. He was a popular operetta conductor at the Theatre na Fidlovačce in Prague-Nusle.

Many of his songs had already been published during his studies.

Stage Works

Jankovec composed music to numerous variety performances and programmes and his operettas *Love of Her Highness, The Cuckoo, The Brandejs Dragoons* and the musical comedy *Asleep in a Pyramid*, were successful.

His other stage works of note include

the operettas *Sounding the Retreat, The Heart in the Reeds, Greener and Greener, On Saint Ann's Day, Little Lois, A Squadron on Parade, The Sparrow, Countess Lucky's Honeymoon, A Girl from the Harbour, In That Backyard of Ours, The World Knows of Us, A Gypsy Princess, A Heart for a Million, A Peasant Princess, Water Flows Against the Current, Spring Will Come, Don't Forget, Children of the Vltava River, Marguerite, A Tobacco Captain, The Queen of*

Hops, The World is Round and *The Steamboat "Lord Mayor Dittrich"*;

the musical comedies: *That's How Kmoch Lived and Played for Us, Charlotte and the Robbers* (in cooperation with JAROSLAV KŘIČKA);

the revues: *Just One Night, His Majesty in Bathing Costume, A Pound of Happiness, Loving Without End, Hiker's Lovemaking.*

Film Music

Jankovec composed as well music to the films *Pepina Rejholcova, How to Make a Million* and *Lojzička* (Lois), in collaboration with ERNO KOŠŤÁL.

His compositions are enriched by folk melodics, very often of a pronouncedly Prague character.

JAROCH, Jiří

[born Smilkov, 23 September 1920]

After completing the secondary school he entered the Prague Conservatory, where he studied composition under JAROSLAV ŘÍDKÝ. After graduation he joined the orchestra of the Smetana Theatre in Prague, continuing his study of composition at the Academy of Musical Arts, again in the class of JAROSLAV ŘÍDKÝ.

At present he is dramaturgist of musical programmes at the Czechoslovak Radio. Jaroch's creative work has not up to the present been very extensive but each new work has been an unmistakable contribution to Czechoslovak music.

Chamber Music

He composed a *Burlesque* for violin and piano (1946), *String Quartet* (1949—50) and a poetic suite *The Wallachian Christmas* (1951). In 1952 he wrote *A Children's*

Suite for nonet, in which he succeeded in finding a spontaneous expression for musical presentation of themes pertaining to the world of children.

His most recent composition is a *Nonet* (1963).

Orchestral Works

Following his *Overture* (1946, his graduation work), he composed an orchestral *Scherzo* (1947) a humorous *Burlesque* for orchestra (1951), a *Symphonic Dance* (1953), a *Funeral Fantasy* (1954) and an orchestral suite *Shakuntala* (1957). His *First Symphony* (1954—56) testifies the maturing of Jaroch's compositional style.

The Second Symphony for chamber orchestra represents, for the time being, a high point in his creative work (in 1960 this *Symphony* was awarded a special prize in the artistic jubilee competition).

His symphonic poem *The Old Man and the Sea* (1961) expresses in a suggestive manner the basic idea of the well-known novel by ERNEST HEMINGWAY.

Recently, Jaroch composed a tarantella for full orchestra *Summer Festival* (1964).

JEREMIÁŠ, Otakar

[born Písek, 17 October 1892—died Prague, 5 March 1962]

NATIONAL ARTIST,
holder of the ORDER OF THE REPUBLIC

Jeremiáš was a prominent personality in Czech music, due to his many-sided activity in both the sphere of creative work and in the field of reproductive music.

He studied organ (JOSEF KLIČKA) and violoncello (JAN BURIAN). In composition he was a pupil of the exacting school of VÍTĚZSLAV NOVÁK, but it was Bedřich Smetana, Richard Wagner, J. B. Foerster and Otakar Ostrčil who decisively influenced his compositional development.

For years, he was director of music school at České Budějovice. He has made an outstanding contribution to Czechoslovak musical life as leading conductor of the Symphony Orchestra of the Prague Radio, which he developed and built up to an international standard.

After the Second World War, he was named chief of opera of the National Theatre and was elected the first chairman of the Guild of Czechoslovak Composers.

Stage Works

He made a significant contribution to Czech musical culture by his operas and orchestral works.

Jeremiáš composed two operas: *The Brothers Karamazov*, according to F. M. DOSTOIEVSKY (1922—27, première in Prague 1928) and *Eulenspiegel*, according to a novel fresco Till Ullenspiegel by CHARLES COSTER (1940—44 première in Prague 1949, newly studied Pilsen—arrangement Jan Hanuš).

Orchestral Works

The *First Symphony* (1910—11) and the *Second Symphony* (1914—15), the symphonic *Spring Overture* (1912) and *Fantasy* for full orchestra with two mixed choirs (1915) are works of lasting importance.

Closely attached to these compositions is the melodrama with orchestra on *Charles the Fourth* set to words by JAN NERUDA (1917).

Chamber Music

The Munich dictate prompted Jeremiáš to write *The Fantasy on Old Czech Chorals* for nonet (1938).

Vocal Works

His choral compositions show his deep understanding of inner values. Amongst them are the extensive *Medynia Glogowska* (1922), *An Injury on the Street*, with mixed choir (1924) and a full-length work *On the Eve of a New Day* (1933).

The marching song *Steadily Forward!*, set to words by JAN NERUDA (1918) was written in the best tradition of Czech national music. As a fighter for progress, Jeremiáš gave expression to his attitude in his male choirs *Ostrava* (1920) and *You and I* (1927) to words by PETR BEZRUČ. In these compositions he presented the passionate yearning of the working class for freedom in a suggestive musical expressive form.

His cantata *The Song of the Native Land* (1941), set to an elegy by JOSEF HORA, is one of the greatest artistic monuments of the people's resistance during the German occupation.

The popularly arranged folk songs (three potpourris for children's choir, solos and orchestra from the years 1934, 1935 and 1941—42), then instrumental and chamber compositions, as well as considerable scenic and film music complete the picture of Jeremiáš' musical personality.

Writings

He has written a popular book *Practical Suggestions for Instrumentation of Symphonic Orchestras* (1942) and *Practical Suggestions for Conducting* (1943), in which he discusses the basic problems of these two branches of music in a concise and intelligible form.

JEŽEK, Jaroslav

[born Prague, 25 September 1906—died New York 1 January 1942]

Ježek graduated from the piano section of the Prague Conservatory in the class of ALBÍN ŠÍMA and from the composition section in the class of K. B. JIRÁK, attending as well lectures by ALOIS HÁBA and continuing his study of composition at the Master School under Josef Suk.

Ježek was an intimate collaborator of Jiří Voskovec and Jan Werich, the founders of the Prague satirical Liberated Theatre and was during the years 1928—38 the conductor of this theatre; he composed music to their revues (*The Première Skafander, Court Is Adjourned, Fata morgana, The Island Dynamite, North Against South, Don Juan and Company, Golem, Caesar, Robin the Brigand, The World Behind Bars, The Donkey and the Shadow, A Straw Hat, The Executioner and the Madman, Keep Smiling, Panoptikum, The Ballad of Rags, Heaven on Earth, Back and Front, Heavy Barbara* and *Out of Place*).

Shortly before the occupation of Czechoslovakia he had to leave his country and emigrated to New York, where he became choirmaster of the Czechoslovak Choral Ensemble.

Symphonic and Chamber Compositions

Ježek was not, however, solely a composer of dance and light music but a talented writer as well of symphonic and chamber compositions, imbued with jazz rhythm and intricate tonal forms. This is particularly evident in his *Concerto* for piano and orchestra (1927), *Fantasy* for piano and orchestra (1930), *Concerto* for violin and brass band (1930), *Bagatelles* for piano (1933) and a *Symphonic Poem* (1936).

His chamber music creative work is especially versatile. It includes a *Suite* for the quarter-tone piano (1927), a *Sonatina* (1928), a *Small Suite* for piano (1928), a *Wind Quartet* for flute, two clarinets and bassoon, a *Serenade*, (1929), a *Wind Quintet* (1931), two *String Quartets* (1932 and 1941), a *Capriccio* for piano (1932), a *Sonata* for violin and piano (1933, presented at the International Festival of Music in Florence, 1936), a *Piano Etude* (1933), a *Duo* for two violins (1934), *Rhapsody* (1938), *Toccata* (1939), *Grand Valse* brillante (1939) and *Sonata* for piano (1941).

Film Music

Most of Ježek's film music was a result of his cooperation with JIŘÍ VOSKOVEC and JAN WERICH (*Powder and
Petrol, Money or Life, Heigh-Ho!, The World Belongs to Us*).

His marching songs such as the *March of the Neutrals*
from the revue North Against South, the *March of the
Hundred-Percent Men* from Golem, the marching song
Against the Wind from the revue Panoptikum, the marching song *Heigh-Ho!* from the film of the same name and
others were an inspiration to the people during the
German occupation and became a source of optimism
and a weapon of progress.

JINDRA, Alfons

[born Čechovice, 28 July 1908]

Jindra (in civilian life Alfons Langer) comes from
a musical family. He studied violin under W. DEGGELAAR
at the Hague and under BEDŘICH VOLDÁN in Prague.

For several years he made many tours with his ten-
piece orchestra, appearing in Austria, Switzerland,
England, Netherlands, Germany, Norway and Sweden.

At first he arranged dance music of various composers,
including JAROSLAV JEŽEK (under the name Allan).

Since his return to Czechoslovakia in 1939 he has
devoted himself to composing dance music and those
compositions, that have gained popularity, include
¶ the slow foxtrots: *The Clock Sleeps, Don't Leave Me, A
Few Recollections, Your Steps Sound, Today is not a Weekday,
Your Home is Asleep, Thank You, Little Song*; ¶ the foxtrots: *I Shall Say it With a Dance, Catch the Beetle* and
Come to See Us this Evening; ¶ the waltz *The Rose in the
Window*; ¶ the charleston *Love on Wheels* and others.

Many of them, after the Second World War, were
among the most frequently played dance songs in

England (*Song of Yesterday*, *Treading on a Cloud*, *You, Oh You!*, *While You Are Sleeping* and others).

Of Jindra's instrumental compositions for variety programmes, mention should be made of *On Four Strings*, *Magic Strings*, *The Wasp's Nest*, *Nocturne*, *Bolero*, *Capricious Violin*, the valse concerto *Prague Balls*, *Lento* for trombone as well as the popular *Bucolic Poem*, *Violin Novellette*, *Elegy* and *Legend*.

JINDŘICH, Jindřich

[born Klenčí, 5 March 1876]

NATIONAL ARTIST,
MERITED ARTIST and Holder of the ORDER OF WORK

Jindřich graduated from the Teachers' Training Institute at Soběslav. He studied music at first with his father and later piano with KAREL HOFFMEISTER and composition with VÍTĚZSLAV NOVÁK.

As a pianist he appeared with prominent Czech singers —EMMY DESTIN, KAREL BURIAN and EMIL BURIAN.

All his life Jindřich found particular delight in Chod folklore research and specifically in the Chod folk song. His *Chod Song-Book*, consisting of nine volumes, known as *The Golden Book of the Chod Region*, contains over fourteen hundred melodies and over four thousand texts. Crowning the results of a life-long piece of work is the ethnographic publication *The Chod Region* and the *Chod Dictionary*. At Domažlice he built up *The Jindřich Ethnographic Museum*.

The *Chod folk* songs constitute the basis of his compositional creative work. He not only collected and registered these songs assiduously but arranged them as well for solo voice and piano or for various choral combinations. His published works include, all with piano accompaniment, 12 *Chod Songs*, 30 *Czech National Songs* and Dances of the Domažlice Region, 15 Folk Songs and Dances of the Domažlice Region, 32 Chod Songs, 50 Chod Songs and Dances, a Treasury of the Chod People (102 songs), The Burian Album (36 Czech, Moravian and Slovak Songs of Moravian Slovakia), 33 Moravian Folk Songs, 6 Czechoslovak Songs and others.

His work as choirmaster prompted him to write arrangements for various choral combinations (four series of the Chod songs for male, female and mixed choirs, Two Czechoslovak Folk Songs for four women's voices, and others).

It is understandable that Jindřich's profound knowledge of folk melody found expression as well in his original choral creative work;

male choirs: Saint Wenceslas set to words by J. V. SLÁDEK, Three Male Choirs (The Ploughman's Song—My First of May—The Bluebell), The Choral set to words by J. V. SLÁDEK, You Bluish Forests, Bright Days Will Again Return, Three Melancholy Male Choirs, The Song of Victory, Four Theer's Male Choirs, The Battle of Domažlice;

mixed choirs: A Czech Song, The Spring Song, Quiet Remembrances, To the Czech Song, The Magic of a Summer Day;

female choirs: Three Female Choirs with piano, Eight Female Choirs and others. His Bulačina to words by J. S. BAAR has became very popular.

Jindřich has also written a number of song cycles dedicated to prominent Czech poets (such as In Memory of Neruda, In Memory of Vrchlický, Heyduk's Songs, The Songs of Sova, Kvapil's Songs, Sládek's Songs, Theer's Songs, Wolker's Songs).

Should we supplement this portrait by the numerous songs for school youth and piano compositions such as Characteristic Variations, Chod Dances from the region of the Dog-Heads (for piano, for two and four hands, instrumented as well for full orchestra), Moments of Happiness and others and orchestral compositions and the melodramas *The Dove* and *The Chod Region*, we stand before the inspiring work of a great man, artist and patriot.

JIRÁK, Karel Boleslav

[born Prague, 28 January 1891]

Jirák studied law and musical science at Charles University and simultaneously privately composition with VÍTĚZSLAV NOVÁK; he continued his study of composition in Vienna under J. B. FOERSTER.

He was choirmaster of the Prague City Theatre at Vinohrady, theatre conductor in Hamburg, Brno and Ostrava, choirmaster of the choral ensemble HLAHOL in Prague, professor of composition at the Conservatory and chief of the music department of the Czechoslovak Radio.

From 1947, he was professor of music theory and composition at the Music Faculty of the Roosevelt College in Chicago and from 1949 chief of the section of music theory and composition at the same college.

As a conductor of symphonic orchestras he was a devoted interpreter of contemporary music. Due to his conscientious dramaturgical work on radio programmes he has done much to educate the radio public to a finer appreciation of music and has popularized many outstanding compositions.

He was, as a composer, one of the representatives of a new musical expression after the First World War. During the German occupation of Czechoslovakia he consciously drew on older sources of Czech music. This was reflected most expressively in his *Three Poetic Polkas* for piano (1944), dedicated to the memory of Bedřich Smetana.

After 1947 Jirák returned to un uncompromising modern form of expression which he started to assert in his piano-cycle *At the Dividing Line* (1923).

Recently, he has been making experiments in the twelve-tone technique.

Stage Works

The one-act opera *A Woman and God* (Appolonius of Tyana) to the libretto by Jiří Karásek (1911—13, première in Brno 1928).

Orchestral Works

He composed five symphonies (The First 1915—16, Second 1923, Third 1929—37, Fourth 1945 and Fifth 1949). Then an *Overture* to a Shakespearean Comedy (1921), symphonic *Variations* (1940), the overture *Youth* (1940—41), a *Rhapsody* for violin and orchestra (1942), *Sinfonietta* for small orchestra (1944, an orchestral version of a nonet), and a symphonic *Scherzo* for brass or symphonic orchestra (1957).

Chamber and Instrumental Music

The field of chamber music is represented by *String Quartet* No. 1 (1915), *String Sextet* with alto solo to words of Chinese poetry (1916—17), *Violoncello Sonata* (1918), nocturne *Night Music* for violin and small orchestra (1918), *Violin Sonata* (1920), *Divertimento* for violin, viola and violoncello (1925), *Viola Sonata* (1925), *Piano Sonata* No. 1 (1926), *String Quartet* No. 2 (1927, awarded a State prize), *Flute Sonata* (1927) *Wind Quintet* (1928), *Serenade* for string orchestra (1939), *String Quartet* No. 3 (1940), *Serenade* for wind instruments (1944), *Violin Sonatina* (1946), *Clarinet Sonata* (1947), *String Quartet* No. 4 (1949), *Piano Sonata* No. 2 (1950), *String Quartet* No. 5 (1951), *Horn Sonata* (1952), *Oboe Sonata* (1953), *Trio* for wind instruments (1956), *Concertino* for violin and small orchestra (1957), *String Quartet* No. 6 (1958) and *String Quartet* No. 7 (1960).

Amongst many others a *Suite in an Old Style* for piano (1920), *Five Preludes and Fugues* for organ (1957) and smaller piano and instrumental compositions.

Vocal Works

Jirák's vocal music includes the song-cycles *The Lyrical Intermezzo* (1913), *The Tragi-comedy* (1913—14), *Meditations* (1915), *Fleeting Happiness* (1915—17), *Thirteen Simple Songs* to texts from the collection Des Knaben Wunderhorn (1917), *Three Songs of Home* (1919), *Psalm XXIII* (1919), *Evening and the Soul* (1921), *The Awakening* (1925), *The Rainbow* (1925—26), *Reconciliation* (1935—37), *The Sweetest Voice* (1942—45), *Charitable Flowers* (1943), *The Year* (1944), *Five Patriotic Songs* (1945), *Songs of Solitude* (1945—46), *Three Songs* (1947—48), *Requiem* (1951—52) and the *Wells of Home* (1960) .

Critic

As a critic (1910—30) Jirák had an individual approach to questions of musical creative work, education, social problems pertaining to musical life as well as to organizational questions.

Writings

His pedagogic activity at the Prague Conservatory prompted him to write *The Study of Musical Forms* (1924). After the war he published *The Keyboard Harmony* (1950).

JIRÁSEK, Ivo

[born Prague, 16 July 1920]

Jirásek studied composition privately at first with OTAKAR ŠÍN. After completing the secondary school he matriculated at the Prague Conservatory where he studied composition under ALOIS HÁBA, JAROSLAV ŘÍDKÝ, MIROSLAV KREJČÍ and OTAKAR ŠÍN. He supplemented his studies privately with OTAKAR JEREMIÁŠ. Similarly, he first studied conducting privately with ZDENĚK CHALABALA and subsequently at the Prague Conservatory in the class of PAVEL DĚDEČEK.

For a number of years Jirásek was active as conductor at the theatre at Opava and as pedagogue at the Ostrava Conservatory of Music. At present he is secretary of the Ostrava branch of the Guild of Czechoslovak Composers.

Stage Works

He composed an opera *Mister Johannes*, set to a play of the same name by ALOIS JIRÁSEK, libretto by JIŘÍ ŠRÁMEK (1951—52, première at Opava 1956). In 1961 he completed an opera *Dawn on the Waters* to a libretto by JIŘÍ PROCHÁZKA (première in Pilsen 1963). Among the recent dramatic works of Czechoslovak composers belongs *The Bear*, according to the comedy by ANTON P. CHEKHOV (première in Prague 1965).

Orchestral Works

Noteworthy are: *Ciaccona* for full orchestra (1944), *Symphony Concertante* for violin and orchestra (1957) and a *Small Suite* for orchestra (1962).

Chamber Music

Sonata in G for violin and piano (1945), a *Wind Quintet* with percussion instruments, set to verses by JOSEF KAINAR (1962) and *Four Studies* for string quartet (1963).

Vocal Works

Jirásek has a predilection for vocal music:

Women's voices—duet *The Zodiac*, set to words by VÍTĚZSLAV NEZVAL (1944) and *Lullabies* to folk texts for female voice (1950).

Songs—*Silesian Songs* (1958), a cycle of songs *My Native Land* for male voice and small orchestra to words by ANDREJ PLAVKA (1960) and several songs for youth.

Male choirs—*The Promised Land* (1943).

Children's choir—*Rhymes* for children (1962).

Cantatas—*A Ballad from a Hospital* to text by JIŘÍ WOLKER (1946) and *Love*, set to a text by KAREL BEDNÁŘ (1960).

JIRKO, Ivan

[born Prague, 7 October 1926]

He is the son of the poet and writer Miloš Jirko and was a pupil of KAREL JANEČEK and PAVEL BOŘKOVEC. Parallel to his work, as a physician, he participates actively in Prague musical life as a critic and composer.

Among his first compositions are cycles of song miniatures such as *The Bestiary* and *Songs* set to folk poetry (1945—46), a *Wind Quintet* (1947), a *Quartetino* (1948) and the *First Piano Concerto* (1949); in this concerto he endeavours to achieve a popular musical expression, characteristic in his subsequent compositions: a cantata *The Most Beautiful Land* (1950—51), a *Serenade* for small orchestra (1951) and the *Festival Overture* (1951).

He has found his inspirational source for these compositions and for his numerous community songs in the new life of his native land and of its people. After these works, a pause ensues in his creative activity but further compositions demonstrate his attempt to arrive at an individual expression reflecting the pulsation and problems of today. They include a *Violoncello Sonata* (1954), *First String Quartet* in D minor (1954), a *Clarinet Concerto* (1955), a *Piano Sonata* (1956), successful even abroad, and *Third Piano Concerto* in G major (1958, awarded in the artistic jubilee competition in 1960). His *Sonata* for violin and piano received honourable mention in the same competition.

His latest works, noted for their strongly emotional effectiveness, include a cycle of songs for baritone and orchestra *The Day* (1959—62), the *Second Symphony, The Year 1945* (1960—62), a symphonic *Fantasy* set to Shakespeare's drama Macbeth (1962) and the second *String Quartet* (1962).

Recently, he has finished an opera *The Twelfth Night* on his own libretto, according to Shakespeare's comedy of the same name (1965).

Jirko is as well the author of a number of aesthetic studies dealing particularly with the modern trend, contemporary problems and with the social function of art. He has written a study *Beauty and Harmony in the work of W. A. Mozart* which attracted attention both at home and abroad.

JONÁK, Zdeněk

[born Prague, 25 February 1917]

Jonák studied composition at the Prague Conservatory and its Master School under JAROSLAV ŘÍDKÝ. His creative work embraces the most varied genres.

Chamber Music

In this field Jonák composed *String Quartet* in C sharp minor (1941), *String Quartet* in E minor (1947), *Sonata* for violoncello and piano (1954), *Divertimento* (1959), *Chamber Symphony* (1962) and *Wind Quintet* (1964).

Orchestral and Instrumental Music

He has composed as well several *Suites* (the suite *At the Circus* was awarded the second prize in the jubilee competition of the Guild of Czechoslovak Composers and the Czech Music Fund in 1956).

Of his larger works, on the first place is the *Overture* for symphonic orchestra, then a *Passacaglia* for piano, the *Serenade* for violin, violoncello and orchestra, *Romance* for clarinet and orchestra and *Concerto* for wind orchestra (1963).

He also wrote the musical comedy *Confusion about Lydia* and a number of compositions of popular and light music character, as an *Evening Stroll*, the march *Fall In!*, the gallop *In the Morning before Eight* and others.

Various

His creative work for voice is extensive as well. In addition, he writes scenic and film music. His last work is an *Instructive Composition* for piano (1964).

JUCHELKA, Miroslav

[born Velká Polom, 22 March 1922]

Juchelka studied composition at the Prague Conservatory as a pupil of EMIL HLOBIL and JAROSLAV ŘÍDKÝ and graduated from the piano class of the Master School under ALBÍN ŠÍMA.

In Ostrava, together with ZBYNĚK PŘECECHTĚL and SVATOPLUK HAVELKA, he organized a creative group which endeavoured to maintain a high standard in variety and dance music in the ensemble NOTA (The Note). At present he is music producer at the Czechoslovak Radio in Prague and chairman of the committee on popular music at the Guild of Czechoslovak Composers.

Instrumental and Orchestral Music

Juchelka has devoted his attention to other genres and forms as testified to by his *Fantasy* for symphonic orchestra (1947), *Concertino* for accordion with orchestra (1955), *Sonata* for clarinet and piano (1958), a *Concert Valse* for piano and full orchestra (1958), the suite *Scenes from a Holiday* (1958), a *Spring Overture* for symphonic orchestra (1959), *Burlesque* for piano and orchestra (1960), a *Suite* on motifs of the Lach folk dances for nonet (1960), four compositions for harp and string orchestra (1961), *The Czech Carnival*, suite for symphonic orchestra, choir and solos (1962), *Scherzo* for chamber orchestra (1963), *Humoresque* for oboe and chamber orchestra (1964), and lyric compositions for various instruments.

Vocal Works

Vocal music is represented in Juchelka's creative work by his cycles of songs *The Late Blossoms* (1949), *From the Neighbourhood of Těšín* (1950) and *Over Hills and Dales* (1951), by songs for youth ensembles (*The Song Knows No Frontiers* received the third prize in the competition at the Festival of the World Federation of Youth in Helsinki 1962), by military songs and arrangements of folk songs.

Juchelka wrote as well a medley of folk songs from Moravian Slovakia for symphonic orchestra *The Land Sings* (1962).

Dance Music

Convincing evidence of the high standard of his compositions can be seen in *The Whirl Dance*, *Trnka* (on the basis of a choreographical folk dance *Trnka*), *The Rožnov Trnka*, *The Cooperative Worker's Trnka*, *Verbunk* (Recruiting, a folk dance), *The Silesian March*, *An Old-Time Dance*, *The Brigand's Dance*, *In the Whirl of the Dance*, *In Rhythm*, *The Czech Polka*, *Coquetting Polka*, *The Variety Gallop*, *The Round Dance*, *The Rožnov Valse*, *Romantic Valse*, *Poetic Polka*, *The Mazurka*, *The Highlander's Dance*, *Country Folk Polka*, *The Miner's Polka*, *Lach Polka* for brass band, a valse for trombone and variety orchestra *The Toast*, *An Optimistic March*, *The Grand March* for the Spartakiad (third prize in 1954) and others.

Various

He is the author of scenic music and musical accompaniments to the films *Blue Monday* and *The Poppy Cake*. In 1963 he completed the musical accompaniment to the programme of the Folk Art Ensemble "*The Liberated Song*" for the third Spartakiad in 1965.

JURIST, Rudolf

[born Prague, 15 November 1880—died Prague 9 April 1964]

Jurist was one of the most popular writers of songs and author of various cabaret montages and revues during the period between the two World Wars. He collaborated with the Prague cabarets The Red Seven, Humour, The Lantern, Halo Cabaret and with the theatres Rokoko, Adria and Arena and in 1938—39 was managing director of the Prague Variété and in 1940—51 dramaturgist of the theatre Na Fidlovačce.

The songs that he wrote or was co-author of include *The Radecký March, The Lane of Youth, Today's Merry Carnival, We Live Only Once* and others.

Jurist wrote songs as well for plays of E. E. KISCH (*Tonka the Gallows, A Journalist's Sensation, The Affair of Colonel Redl*), for revues and cabaret montages, mostly in collaboration with KAREL HAŠLER, KAREL TOBIS and others.

He was one of the authors of first Czech talking films (*The Hollywood Revue, Fidlovačka, Little Girl, Don't Say No, The Affair of Colonel Redl, A Thousand for One Night, Anita in Paradise, From the World of Forest Solitudes*) and the author of radio cabaret programmes and revues.

In addition, he wrote the operetta *An Attack on Prague* and was co-author of the operettas *The Slovak Princess* and *In That Backyard of Ours*.

JUROVSKÝ, Šimon

[born Ulmanka, 8 February 1912—died Prague, 8 November 1963]

Holder of the decoration FOR OUTSTANDING WORK

Jurovský began to study music after completing the Teachers' Training Institute. He studied composition and conducting at the Music and Dramatic Academy in

Bratislava in the class of ALEXANDER MOYZES and JOZEF VINCOUREK. Later, he continued in his studies by JOSEPH MARX in Vienna.

From 1940 to 1951 he was active in the music department of the Bratislava Radio. Thereafter he filled progressively several posts in Slovak cultural life: he was in charge of the music division at the Ministry of Education and Culture, chief secretary of the Slovak section of the Guild of Czechoslovak Composers, artistic director of the Slovak Folk Art Ensemble, artistic manager of the National Opera in Bratislava and chairman of the West Slovak branch of the Guild of Slovak Composers.

During his studies Jurovský turned his attention mainly to chamber music compositions. In this genre he asserted his inclination to a melodically pronounced expressive media growing out of neoromanticism and impressionism. His graduation work, a *Quartet* for wind instruments (1936), testifies to his well developed sense for chamber music and tone colour quality.

Stage Works

He composed the opera *Daughters of Abel* (1961) and a full-length ballet *The Song of Chivalry* (1960, première in Bratislava 1960).

Orchestral Works

The *Pastoral Suite* for small orchestra (1939), a symphonic overture *A New Morning* (1948), a symphonic poem *The Journey Begun* (1948), a symphonic scherzo *A Joyous Competition* (1949); his first *Peace Symphony* (1950) represents an important milestone in his development; then followed his *Second Symphony*, with organ (1962), intended to give a picture of the contemporary man.

Chamber and Instrumental Music

The *Serenade* for string orchestra (1940) and the string quartet *Melodies and Dialogues* (1944) are characteristic and are his most frequently played chamber compositions. In later years he composed a *Concerto* for violoncello and orchestra (1955) and a *Concertino* for piano and string orchestra (1962).

Jurovský composed two suites, the *Piano* (1960) and a virtuosic *Concert dance* for piano (1960) from the music to his ballet The Song of Chivalry.

Vocal Works

During the war he occupied himself intensively with the arrangement of folk songs. He composed several song-cycles, as *The Geranium* (1943) and then, after the war, *Songs of a New Life* (1954), *Song of Peace* (1955) and the cantata *The Murmur of the Native Mountain* (1959), which was given a special award in the artistic jubilee competition 1960.

Film Music

In the fifties, he devoted himself to film and scenic music and wrote arrangements for ensembles, as is shown by the full-length film *The Unploughed Field* (the group responsible for its production was awarded the State Prize in 1953), by the documentary film *Master Paul of Levoča*, *The House at the Crossroads* and the co-production film *The Umbrella of Saint Peter*.

•

For his whole-life creative work, especially with respect to his second *Symphony*, he was awarded the prize *J. L. Bella in memoriam* (1964).

KABELÁČ, Miloslav

[born Prague, 1 August 1908]

LAUREATE OF THE STATE PRIZE

Kabeláč matriculated at the Prague Conservatory in 1928; he was a student of composition by K. B. JIRÁK and of conducting by Pavel Dědeček. After graduating from the composition class, he studied piano at the Master School under Vilém Kurz.

From 1932 he was active at the Czechoslovak Radio in Prague and simultaneously had a considerable experience as conductor. From 1958 to 1962 he was professor of composition at the Prague Conservatory.

Orchestral Works

At the beginning of his career as composer, Kabeláč wrote *Sinfonietta* (1931) and *Fantasy* No. 1 for piano and orchestra (1934).

Symphonies:

No. 1 in D major for strings and percussion instruments, op. 11 (1942),

No. 2 in C major for full orchestra, op. 15 (1944—46); this symphony brought the composer an international renown;

No. 3 in F major for organ, brasses and timpani, op. 33 (1948—57);

No. 4 for chamber orchestra, op. 36 (1957—58);

No. 5 (Dramatic) for soprano and orchestra, op. 41 (1959—60) and

No. 6 (Concertante) for clarinet and orchestra, op. 44 (1961—62), in which the composer reached a climax in his artistic work.

Then followed the second *Overture*, op. 17 (1947), *The Mystery of Time*, passacaglia for full orchestra, op. 31 (1957). To the four hundred anniversary of Shakespeare's birth Kabeláč composed *Hamlet's Improvisations* for full orchestra, op. 46 (1962—63); his recent work are nine miniatures *Reflection*, op. 49 (1964).

Of Kabeláč's incidental music, mention should be made of the music to *Electra* of Sophocles op. 28 (1956), written also as an orchestral suite, and to the *Master of Nine Songs* by the Chinese poet Kuo-Mojo, op. 34 (1957) [written also as an orchestral suite] and three melodramas.

Chamber Music

In this field of his creative efforts should be mentioned *The Wind Sextet*, op. 8 (1940), *Sonatina* for oboe and piano, op. 24 (1955), *Ballata* for violin and piano, op. 27 (1956) and *Suite* for saxophone and piano, op. 39 (1959).

Instrumental Works

Among them the noteworthy are *Eight Preludes* for piano, op. 30 (1955—56), *Fantasy* for organ, op. 32 (1957), piano cycle *Motifs*, op. 38 (1959), *Small Suite* for piano for four hands, op. 42 (1960) and four *Preludes* for organ, op. 49 (1963).

Vocal Works

The first of a number of small intimate works is *The Small Cantata* for solos and chamber orchestra, op. 4 (1937), followed by the cantata *Don't Retreat!* for mixed choir, op. 7 (1939), which has a simple, yet effective melody, a forceful rhythm and uninterrupted gradation, reflecting the historical events of the year 1939.

During the German occupation he wrote *Male Choirs* set to words by Jiří WOLKER, op. 10 (1942).

After the war he composed a small cantata *Graceful*, to folk text for mixed choir and orchestra, op. 40 (1959) and a cycle of twenty children choirs with piano *We Are Singing*, to words by Lydie MACHÁČKOVÁ, op. 43 (1961) and five songs without words *Far Away Echoes* for alto and piano, op. 47 (1963).

Inspired by the world of children and by the vigour and the directness of expression of folk poetry, he has written numerous compositions in the small form. They include *Rhymes for Children*, op. 16 (1947) and op. 23 (1955), *The Blue Sky*, op. 19 (1950), *Moravian Lullabies*, op. 20 (1951), *The Merry Feast Songs* and *The Merry Songs of Love* (two suites of *Moravian Songs* of 1951—52), *Love Songs*, op. 25 (1955), *Six Lullabies*, op. 29 (1956), *To Nature*, op. 35 (1958), *The Huntsmans' Songs*, op. 37

KABELÁČ

(1958—59) and a cycle of children's choirs *We Sing*, op.43 (1961).

Recently, he has finished *The Mystery of Silence* (Eufemias Mysterion) for soprano and chamber ensemble of twenty members (1965).

Writings

Lately he devotes himself to the theory and practice of electronic music and wrote *The Composer in the Sound Laboratory* (1964).

For his *Hamlet's Improvisations* he was awarded the STATE PRIZE 1965.

KAFENDA, Frico (Friedrich)

[born Mošovce, 2 November 1883—died 3 September 1963 in Bratislava]

Holder of the ORDER OF WORK

Kafenda was a prominent piano virtuoso and pedagogue; he acquired his artistic education at the Leipzig Conservatory where he studied piano (ROBERT TEICHMÜLLER), composition (STEPHAN KREHL and HEINRICH ZOELLNER) and conducting (ARTUR NIKISCH). At the same time he attended lectures on musical sciences at the Leipzig University (HERMANN KRETZSCHMAR, HUGO RIEMANN).

He was active as choirmaster and bandmaster at Zwickau, Tilsit, at the Opernschule des Westens in Berlin, at Bielitz, Colmar and had a school for accompanists at Dresden.

After the First World War he returned to Slovakia where he became professor of piano and from 1922 director of the Music School in Bratislava, the present Conservatory. He was a member of the well-known Bratislava TRIO. In recognition of his meritorious pedagogic work he was appointed assistant professor at the High School of Musical Arts.

As a composer, Kafenda was influenced by the Leipzig school of late romanticism. His interests were centered on instrumental chamber music and song lyricism [a *Piano Suite* in an ancient style (1904), *Sonata* for violoncello and piano (1905), *Four Songs* for high voice and piano (1913), a *String Quartet* in G major (1916) and a *Sonata* for violin and piano (1918)].

About the year 1950, after a pause of more than thirty years, Kafenda began to compose again, taking up with the cultivated and precise musical expressive media of his younger years. The chamber music genre is again in the forefront while choral compositions represent a novel aspect in his creative work.

He has written several cycles of songs such as *Three Songs* for male voice and piano (1961), *Three Miniature Songs* for high voice and piano (1961), *Four Songs* for male voice and piano (1961), *Three Male Choirs*, set to texts and tunes of Slovak folk poetry (1949), *A Song of Peace* for mixed choir and piano, the male choirs *Windows Into the Past* (1952), *Three Piano Compositions* (1954), *Three Male Choirs* (1955) and *Variations and Fugue* on the composer's own theme for piano (1958).

KALABIS, Viktor

[born Červený Kostelec, 27 February 1923]

Kalabis belongs to the foremost representatives of young Czech composers. He graduated from the Prague Conservatory in the composition class of EMIL HLOBIL. At the same time he attended lectures on musical science at the Charles University. After graduation from the Conservatory, he continued his study of composition at the Academy of Musical Arts under JAROSLAV ŘÍDKÝ.

At present, he is music manager at the Czechoslovak Radio in Prague.

Kalabis' creative work can be divided into three periods: (1) The first one (to 1950) is marked by a considerable technical maturity; (2) at a further stage (to 1956) Kalabis has created a number of works characterized by his efforts to achieve a more intensive and profound content, where the technical aspect refuses to be technique for technique's sake; (3) a subsequent stage is evident by his symphonical compositions.

Orchestral and Chamber Works

The *Overture* for full orchestra, belonging into his first period (1950), *Concerto* for piano and orchestra of the second period (1955) and works of the third stage: *First Symphony* for full orchestra, representing a meditation on life, its riches, beauty and difficulties (1957), *Concerto* for violin and orchestra (1959, awarded in the artistic jubilee competition in 1960), and the *Second Symphony* (Sinfonia pacis) for full orchestra, an important work for its contents and character of musical expression (1961); further symphonic *Frescoes* for organ (1963) and *Variations* for full orchestra to his own theme (1964).

First *String Quartet* (1949), *Concerto* for chamber orchestra (1950), violoncello *Concerto* (1951), *Divertimento* for wind quintet (1952), *Suite* for oboe and piano (1953) and a *Classical Nonet* (1956). His *Chamber Music* for strings (1962—63) is marked by individual formation of musical material and tempestuous expression.

Instrumental Works

In the early period of development his maturity was shown by two piano *Sonatas* (1948 and 1949). The last stage is represented in the instrumental field by his six two-part *Canonical Inventions* for harpsichord (1962).

Vocal Works

Noteworthy is his cycle of songs for tenor and soprano *The Bird's Wedding*, set to folk poetry (1949). He is also the author of many favourite children's songs.

•

For his *Sinfonia pacis*, chamber music for strings and the *Second String Quartet* he was awarded the First Prize in the artistic jubilee competition 1965.

KALACH, Josef

[born Lukohořany, 18 May 1901]

Kalach studied composition privately with Pavel Dědeček. He was a military musician, a bandmaster and a member of various musical ensembles. In 1943 to 1954 he played viola in the Film Symphonic Orchestra in Prague.

Stage Works

He composed three operettas: *Love is a Strange Herb*, *It's Not My Fault* and *What We Are Like*.

Instrumental Music

Amongst his compositions are a *Serenade* for strings, a dance suite *In the Glow of Light, a Variety Suite*, a suite *In Summer*, six concert valses (*The Magic of the Evening, Children of Nature, Rose Blossoms, In the Storm of Life, At the Close of Summer* and a *Summer Day*), the *Concert Polonaise* and *Tarantella* for full orchestra, and music to three short films (*The Green Valley, Water Calls, Hydraulic Presses*), five solo compositions for alto-saxophone with piano accompaniment (*Almacks Valse, Foxterrier, The Cat's Grotesque, Serenade*, and fantasy on the *Song I Dreamed of You, My Lassie*); then *The Old with the Young* for bassoon and oboe and *The Bear on Ice* and *The Sweet-toothed Bear* for bassoon.

Vocal Works

Songs *A Wandering Singer* set to words by JAROSLAV KVAPIL, *Three Comrades* to words of the Chinese poet LI Po and the cycle *Three Songs* to words of VÍTĚZSLAV HÁLEK.

Various

He has written numerous marches, including *The Barrier of Peace* (awarded first prize in Army competition), *At a Victorious Pace*, *Under the Star of Peace*, *Freely Ahead!*, *Always in Tempo*, *Merrily We Start* and the *Festive March* (awarded the second prize in the competition for the best march of Spartakiad in 1955).

He has written many compositions for dance music; ¶ polkas: *Polka and Jump-Dance*, *To the Native Village*, *As Brothers* and many others; ¶ the gallop *The Flat Track and Flight to the Moon*; ¶ valses: considerable popularity has won *The Silver Wedding* and *Beyond the Pond*; ¶ folk dance: *Neighbourly* and *As At Home*; ¶ tangos: *Ramoncita*, *Pepita*, *Clarita*, *Isabel*, *The Rose from Argentina* and *Southern Blossoms*.

Quite recently, the composer has written *Tomorrow is Ours*, *Paraphrases on Polish Folksongs*, the *Jump Dance* and the *March to our Friends*, all potpourris of well-known songs for community singing.

KALAŠ, Julius

[born Prague, 8 August 1902]

MERITED ARTIST

Kalaš studied law at Charles University and music (composition) at the Prague Conservatory, in the classes of J. B. FOERSTER and JAROSLAV KŘIČKA, and at the

Master School under JOSEF SUK. He completed his study with a *Symphony* in C minor (The Domažlice Symphony).

Since 1948 he has been active at the Film Section of the Academy of Musical Arts as professor in the field of music and sound in films.

He has wide organizational experiences in the trade union and ideological organizations of artists; he was the first chairman of the Czech Music Fund, held office in the Authors' Association for Protection of Rights on Musical Works, in the Czechoslovak Theatrical and Literary Agency and at the Academy of Musical Arts.

Stage Works

His opera *The Unconquered,* to a libretto by M. L. KRATOCHVÍL (1960, première in Prague 1961), received a special award in the artistic jubilee competition in 1960.

Kalaš has enriched the Czech operetta repertoire by following works: *Love Knows No Frontiers* (1934), *The White Lady* (1941), *The Comedian* (1943), *The Wallachian Bride* (1953), *Holiday with an Angel* (1954) and the *Miller's Wife from Granada* (1954).

He is as well the author of musical comedies: *Scottish Mummy* (1961) and the *Teacher of Dance* (1962).

Orchestral Works

Of his symphonic compositions we note a *Serenade* in A major for string orchestra (1944), a *Concerto* for violoncello and orchestra (1949), a *Concerto* for viola and orchestra (1950—51), a *Fantasy* for violoncello and orchestra (1952), a symphonic poem *The Nightingale and the Rose* for flute and orchestra, according to a fairy-tale by OSCAR WILDE (1956), and a symphonic picture *Drums of Peace* (1959), for which he was awarded in the artistic jubilee competition in 1960.

Chamber Music

His chamber music compositions include a *String*

Quintet in A major with two violoncellos (1924), *Quartet-tino* (1928), a *String Quartet* in F minor (1939, awarded the first prize of the Czech Musical Society 1941), a *Sonata* in A major for violin and piano (1962), *Serenade* for piano trio (1963) and an *Arabesque* for oboe and harp (1963).

Vocal Works

To complete the picture of Kalaš' work, mention should be made of a number of his programme compositions, choirs and cantatas, as *The Juggler* (1939), *On and On* (1951), the *Polka Sounds* (1952) and a *Song of the Czech Land* (1962), a mixed choir with orchestra.

Kalaš was active as composer and pianist in the ensemble THE TEACHERS OF GOTHAM, with which he achieved great success not only at home but also abroad. The expressive traits of his musical humour manifested themselves particularly in his compositions for this ensemble. Out of more than one hundred and fifty compositions, great popularity was achieved in its time by *The Ballad about an Axle with Four Double Cranks*, *Otoman and the Nymph of the Woods*, *Fudjiyama*, *The Congress of Ghosts*, parodies on the pseudo-art of that time such as *Hawai Stripped of its Glamour*, *Recipe for a Hiker's Song* and others.

Popular Music

Kalaš' musical humour was demonstrated as well in a number of popular compositions: *A Czech Dance*, *A Spanish Dance*, four *Wallachian Dances* and *Tarantellas*. One of his latest popular compositions is the *Cuckoo Mambo* and a *Serenade* for trumpet from the film A Man of No Importance.

Film Music

Kalaš is one of the first Czech composers who worked in the sound films from their very beginning (1930). In his present pedagogic activity he can apply the experience he gained as a composer for many films (for inst. *People on a Floe, We in Gotham, Catacombs, From Czech Mills, Revolt in the Village, The Emperor and the Baker, Man of No Importance, Between Earth and Heaven, The King of Kings).*

Writings

He wrote for his lectures scripta *The Development of Music and of other Arts.*

KÁLIK, Václav

[born Opava, 18 October 1891—died Prague, 18 November 1951]

Kálik studied at the Philosophical Faculty of Charles University. In composition he was a pupil of JAROSLAV NOVOTNÝ, VÍTĚZSLAV NOVÁK and JOSEF SUK, under whom he graduated from the Master School. His teacher for piano was ADOLF MIKEŠ but his multiple interests led him to the study of violin, singing and conducting (Dresden, Rome).

He directed several choirs and appeared as concert pianist and conductor.

Stage Works

In his operatic works Kálik endeavoured to free himself of all extraneous elements. He composed two one-act operas *A Spring Morning*, to his own libretto (1933, première in Olomouc 1943), and *Love's Wonder*, to his own libretto, according to a theme of JULIUS ZEYER from *Tuskany Legends* (1942—43, première at Liberec 1950), as well as an opera consisting of five scenes entitled *Consecration of Youth*, to his own libretto, according to a subject of JIŘÍ MAHEN (1946—48; the reworking of the opera was not completed).

　　　　　　　　　　　　　　KÁLIK

Orchestral Works

Kálik's orchestral compositions are imbued with an individual polyphonic thinking. They include *Fantasy* (1915), symphonic poem *The Sea* (1924), two symphonies [the first, *Peace Symphony* (1927), and the second (1943)], *Prelude* (1931) and a symphonic triptych *Venezia* (1932) for a string orchestra.

Chamber Music

His chamber music is represented by the song-cycles *Intermezzo* for tenor, violin and piano (1913), *Evil Love* for soprano, violin and piano (1919), *The Return* for soprano and piano (1916), a *Piano Suite* (1915) and a *Violin Sonata* (1919).

Vocal Works

In his creative work he was a lyric who achieved an ecstatic expression particularly in his choirs. These choirs, tied in with the Smetana—Foerster school, include

male choirs: *Four Nocturnes* (1912), *Four Choirs* (1912—16), the cycle *My Country* (1916), *Return to the Fatherland* (1917), the cycles *A Summer Day* (1919), *The Apostrophe* (1920), *Grief Assuaged* (1933), *From the Native Country* (1936), *Prague Pictures* (1948—50) and *The Heart* (1951);

female choirs: *The Return* (1916), *Her Country* (1917), *An Autumn Day* (1925), three *Jolly Choirs*, *A Small Requiem* (1946), *The World of Children* (1949), *The Guardian Angel —Mother* (1950), *Spring* (1950);

mixed choirs: *After Father* (1934), *A Spring Day* (1935), *Home* (1939), *Thunder and the Violin* (1939), *Song of the Night of Liberation* (1946), *The Rapids* (1946) and *September* (1946).

Various

Kálik has as well arranged folk songs and folk dance music and wrote a work on the art of composing a fugue and made numerous contributions to music periodicals.

KAPR, Jan

[born Prague, 12 March 1914]

LAUREATE OF THE STATE PRIZE,
MERITED ARTIST,
LAUREATE OF THE STALIN PRIZE for music

Kapr studied at the Prague Conservatory under JAROSLAV ŘÍDKÝ and at the Master School under JAROSLAV KŘIČKA.

He was active at the Czechoslovak Radio as music producer, later as music critic and editor-in-chief in the field of music publishing. Since 1961 he is assistant professor in composition at the Janáček Academy of Musical Arts.

Compositions, written during his studies (a *String Quartet*, *Fantasy* for viola and piano and *Concerto* for piano and orchestra), drew attention to his talent.

Stage Works

In 1962, he finished the opera *Musicians' Fairy-tale.*

Orchestral Works

Kapr has written the exuberant symphonic scherzo *Marathon* (1939), which was followed by his first step to symphonical creative work *Sinfonietta* for small orchestra (1940). The centre of gravity of his orchestral compositions are his six *Symphonies*: the first was composed in 1943, the second in 1946, the third, for small orchestra, in 1946, the fourth in 1957 (second version in 1958), the fifth, *Olympic* (1959) [awarded the second degree prize in the artistic jubilee competition in 1960] and the sixth in 1960 (new version in 1964).

The post-war period of Kapr's creative work is marked by his efforts to attain a perspicuity of the expressive media while maintaining the contemporaneity of the musical idiom. His works in this period were the rhapsody *Harvested* (1950), symphonic picture *Tomorrow* (1953), which is a musical glimpse into the future, the orchestral

Suite (1955—56) and the *Summer Prelude* (1957); further-more, he has composed a *Concertino* for viola and wind orchestra (1964, also with piano).

Chamber Music

First of all were his five *String Quartets*: No. 1, compos-ed during his studies (1937), No. 2 (1941), No. 3 (1955), No. 4 (1957) and No. 5 (1961). His other works in this field were the *Nonet* (1943), *Fantasy* for violin and piano (1958, with instrumentation for orchestra in 1960), *Variations* for flute and string orchestra (1958) and *Four Moods for Nonet* (1959).

Recently, he has written his sixth *String Quartet* with a baritone solo.

Instrumental Works

He composed two *Piano Concertos* with orchestra, the first in 1938 and the second in 1953 (this one was award-ed the third prize in the artistic jubilee competition in 1955), and three *Sonatas* for piano, the first in 1945, the second in 1947 and the third in 1958. Then four *Piano Compositions* (1946), piano cycle *Home* (1953—55), *Violin Concerto* with orchestra (1955) and *Variations* for piano on a theme by JAROSLAV KŘIČKA (1961).

Vocal Works

His extensive work, based mainly on folk song motives, is shown in following compositions:

Songs—four *Song Cycles* set on folk poetry (1938—39), a cycle of songs for mezzosoprano and piano *The Lost Songs* (1943), a cycle of songs for tenor and piano *The Crystal* (1944), a cycle of songs for soprano and piano *The Awakened Land* (1946), a cycle of songs *The Avowal* (1952), *Love Songs* for baritone and piano or small orchestra (1954) and songs for mezzosoprano and piano *The Child* (1961).

Female choir—a cycle with piano *Gay Natural Science* (1938).

Male choirs—*Ondráš* (1944) and *On One's Own Land* (1944), *The New Spring* (1949) and *The May Day and the Native Land* (1950).

Children choir—with piano (or orchestra) *Play for Happiness* (1956).

Mixed choir—*Dreams and Plans* (1960).

Cantatas—*A Song to the Native Land*, set to poem by JOSEF HORA (1950), and *In the Soviet Land*, set to words by VÍTĚZSLAV NEZVAL, for baritone and choir or orchestra (1950, awarded the prize of the City of Prague 1950).

In addition, his creative work includes a wide range of scenic, radio and film music.

Prizes

For the film *New Czechoslovakia* (1951), to which Kapr composed music, he received the STALIN PRIZE for music.

His piano cycle *Home* (1953—55) was awarded second prize in the competition of the fifth World Festival of Youth in Warsaw (1955).

For his sixth *String Quartet* (composed in 1964) he was awarded a PRIZE in the artistic jubilee competition 1965.

KAPRÁL, Václav

[born Určice, 26 March 1889—died Brno, 6 April 1947]

Kaprál graduated from the Janáček School for Organists in Brno. He studied piano in Prague under ADOLF MIKEŠ and in Paris with ALFRED CORTOT and composition under VÍTĚZSLAV NOVÁK.

In cooperation with LUDVÍK KUNDERA, professor of the Conservatory in Brno, he appeared as a concert artist in works for two pianos.

He was in great demand as a teacher of piano and

composition. In 1936 he was appointed professor of composition at the Brno Conservatory and at the same time was elected vice-chairman of the Czech section of the International Society for Contemporary Music.

After the liberation of Czechoslovakia he became a chairman of the Syndicate of Czechoslovak Composers.

He directed his creative activity almost exclusively to instrumental compositions. Kaprál's compositional expression grew out of the influence of LEOŠ JANÁČEK and VÍTĚZSLAV NOVÁK, temporarily of CLAUDE DEBUSSY and RICHARD STRAUSS, but gradually assumed an individual character, effective for its ardent lyricism, touching melancholy and deep sadness.

Orchestral Works and Church Music

The orchestral *Wedding March* (1923), *Two Little Idylls* for string orchestra (1931) and the *Czech* (or Svatobořice) *Mass* with mixed choir (1943), which bore the mark of personal persecution during the Second World War.

Chamber Music

String Quartet No. 1 (1925), *String Quartet* No. 2 (1927, awarded a State prize) and *The Ballad* for violoncello and piano (Kaprál's last composition, written in 1946).

Instrumental Works

Piano *Sonata* No. 1 (1912), the concerto étude *Nocturne* (1915), *The Spring Lullabies* (1916—17), *Suita romantica* (1918), piano *Sonata* No. 2 (1921), the experimental *Miniatures* (1922), piano *Sonata* No. 3 (1924), piano *Con duolo* for left hand (1926), piano *Sonatina* No. 1 (1930), an instructive cycle *Lyrica* (1930), a lofty *Fantasy* for piano (1934), piano *Sonatina* No. 2 (1936), the *Fourth Piano Sonata*, gloomily and defiantly reacting to the national misfortune (1939), and piano *Sonatina* No. 3 (1943).

Vocal Works

Kaprál's creative work in the field of song is represented by the following compositions: *Nocturnetta* (1911), *Two Simple Motifs* (1913), *Three Songs* (1918), *For Her* (1927), *The Song of Autumn*, with string quartet (1929), *Lullabies* to words of Slovak folk poetry with small orchestra (1932, performed at the Festival of the International Society for Contemporary Music in Barcelona, 1936), *Melancholy Songs* (1935—36), and a cycle of duets *Gracious Flowers* for soprano and alto with piano (1942).

Of his numeral choral compositions reference should be made to the male choir *A Spring Evening* (1931) and male duet with tenor solo *The Pilgrimage to Saint Anthony* (1936).

Writings

In his literary work, he commented on musical life in Brno and contributed greatly to an elaborate revision of current didactical and performative compositions for piano.

KAPRÁLOVÁ, Vítězslava

[born Brno, 24 January 1915—died Montpellier, France, 16 June 1940]

She was daughter of the composer Václav Kaprál. Her pronounced compositional talent was moulded by Vilém Petrželka at the Brno Conservatory, by Vítězslav Novák at the Master School of the Prague Conservatory and by Bohuslav Martinů in Paris. In addition to studying composition she devoted herself simultaneously to the study of conducting, her teacher and advisor being Zdeněk Chalabala of the Brno Conservatory, Václav Talich at the Master School of the Prague Conservatory and Charles Munch at the Ecole Normale de Musique in Paris.

Her creative aptitude is particularly demonstrated by

the following compositions: *Concerto* for piano and orchestra, op. 7 (1934—35, her graduation work at the Brno Conservatory), a *String Quartet*, op. 8 (1936), *Three Pieces* for piano, op. 9 (1935—36), a cycle of intimate songs *An Apple From One's Lap*, to words by JAROSLAV SEIFERT, op. 10 (1936), *A Military Sinfonietta*, op. 11 (1937, her graduation work at the Master School, performed by the composer at the International Festival for Contemporary Music in London 1938), a cycle of songs *Forever*, op. 12 (1936—37), *April Preludes* for piano, op. 13 (1937), a song *Adieu and the Kerchief*, to words by VÍTĚZSLAV NEZVAL, op. 14 (1937, her last composition from the period of her studies in Prague, instrumented in Paris 1938), *Variations on the chimes of the Church of Saint-Etienne du Mont* for piano, op. 16 (1938), *Suita Rustica* with citation of Czech folk songs for symphonic orchestra op. 19 (1938), *Partita* for string orchestra and piano, op. 20 (1939), a cycle of songs *Sung to a Distance*, op. 22 (1939), a *Christmas Prelude* for two flutes, two oboes, French horn, trumpet, piano, harp, eight violins and three violoncellos (1939) and *Two Dances* for piano, op. 23 (1940).

KARAS, Rudolf

[born Bucharest, 27 October 1930]

Karas graduated from the violin and composition section of the Prague Conservatory. He was pupil of FRANTIŠEK PÍCHA (composition).

Up to the present he has composed a *Sinfonietta* for strings (his graduation work, written in 1950—51), a *Violin Concerto*, op. 5 (1952), two *String quartets* op. 3 and 6 (1949, 1953) an *Eastern Suite* op. 7 (1954), a *Symphony* op. 10 (1959), a *Concerto* for flute and orchestra, op. 11 (1959—60), music to puppet films, variety compositions and dance songs.

KARAS

In 1962 he completed *Three Czech Dances* for orchestra, *Roumanian Dances* and a symphonic sketch *The Orient*.

He is a violinist with the Film Symphonic Orchestra in Prague.

KARDOŠ, Dezider

[born Nadlice, 23 December 1914]

LAUREATE OF STATE PRIZES,
holder of the CZECHOSLOVAK PEACE PRIZE,
MERITED ARTIST

Kardoš contributed to the development of contemporary Slovak music particularly in the field of symphonic creative work. As a composer he matured under the guidance of ALEXANDER MOYZES at the Music and Dramatic Academy in Bratislava and under VÍTĚZSLAV NOVÁK at the Master School of the Prague Conservatory. At the University in Bratislava he completed the study of musicology.

After his studies he spent several years in Eastern Slovakia where he was active at the Radio at Prešov and after liberation in Košice. His work in this region gave him the opportunity to acquaint himself thoroughly with its folklore, the music of which is unusually pure and original.

In 1951 Kardoš came to Bratislava where he became chief of the folk music section at the Radio and later managing director of the Slovak Philharmonic.

He is chairman of the section of composition at the Slovak Guild of Composers. Recently he has accepted an appointment as teacher of composition at the High School of Musical Arts.

Orchestral Works and Cantatas

During the war Kardoš prepared himself for a new activity with concentrated interest in symphonic and cantata creative work, imbued with an expressive patriotic feeling, and composed his *First Symphony*, op. 10 (1942).

Enlightened by the work of modern symphonic composers like BÉLA BARTÓK, ARTHUR HONEGGER and D. D. SHOSTAKOVICH, Kardoš attains an ever increasing mastery in the handling of tone grouping of modern orchestra. His work becomes more profound from the point of view of its subject and assumes the role of interpreter of socialist humanism, out of which stems its pathos and optimism.

In this period he composed *The Peace Cantata* (1951), which was awarded the Czechoslovak Peace Prize, and the cantata *Greeting to a Great Country*, op. 25 (1953), which received the State Prize 1954.

In the same vein was written the *Eastern Slovak Overture*, op. 22 (1951); this was followed by the programme Second Symphony *On the Native Land*, op. 28 (1955, the State Prize 1956), the virtuosic *Concerto* for orchestra, op. 30 (1957), the emotionally profound and condensed *Heroic Ballad* for string orchestra, op. 32 (1959) [awarded the second prize in the artistic jubilee competition 1960], the philosophically and compositionally mature *Third Smyphony*, op. 33 (1961) and the *Fourth Symphony Piccola*, op. 34 (1962).

After the Fourth Symphony he wrote a *Concert* for strings, op. 35 (1963), awarded the prize J. L. Bella (1964). In the same year he composed *The Fifth Symphony* for full orchestra, op. 37.

Instrumental and Chamber Music

Kardoš had acquired a definite form of musical expression even in his early compositions. *His Songs of Love*, op. 2 (1935), the *Piano Suite*, op. 5 (1937), as well as the *Quintet* for wind instruments, op. 6 (1938) are in their expressive media works conceived in a modern spirit. A certain reorientation took place in his compositional creative work under the influence of Eastern

Slovak folklore. Similarly to Vítězslav Novák and Béla Bartók he ascertains new qualities of expression in its tonal and rhythmic characteristics.

Vocal Works

His first attempt to cope with these qualities resulted in two collections of arrangements for voice and piano [*Eastern Slovak Songs* No. I., op. 9 (1939) and No. II., op. 17 (1948)].

In this field his creative development matured in the male choir *One-handed*, op. 36a (1963) and in *Two Songs from Eastern Slovakia* (arranged for female and mixed choir), op. 36b (1964).

Various

Parallel to symphonic creative work, Kardoš devoted himself to film music (*A Rainbow Over Slovakia*), to arrangements of folk songs and dances for ensembles and to compositions for children and youth.

In the field of instructive music he has composed *Piano Compositions for Youth*, op. 27 (1956), in which, in a more exacting form, he ties in with Bartók influenced *Bagatelles*, op. 18 (1948) and composes as well an instructive cycle of simple and delightful children's songs entitled *Let's Help the Nightingale*, op. 31a (1959).

International Prizes

The cantata *Greetings to a Great Country* was awarded second prize at the Fifth Festival of Youth in Warsaw (1955).

KAREL, Rudolf

[born Pilsen, 9 November 1880—died in the Germen concentration camp at Terezín, 6 March 1945]

Karel began to study law but his love of music led him to the Prague Conservatory (1901) where he studied composition under KAREL KNITTL and KAREL STECKER. The most important period of his studies was the time, less than a year, he spent in the composition class of ANTONÍN DVOŘÁK.

In 1904 Karel completed his studies, his graduation work being small piano and chamber music compositions and two parts from his orchestral suite which he conducted himself.

He then lived in Prague, visiting Dalmatia and Bulgaria from time to time for reasons of health and for purposes of study. He taught music theory. From 1914 to 1920 he lived in Russia, first at Orenburg and Taganrog and later at Rostov and in Irkutsk, as teacher of piano, violin, composition, counterpoint and instrumentation, appearing also as conductor.

After his return home, he was appointed professor of composition at the Prague Conservatory in 1923.

During the Nazi occupation of Czechoslovakia he took an active part in one of the national resistance groups and in March 1943 was arrested by Gestapo. He was later sent to Terezín where, shortly before the liberation of Czechoslovakia, he met his death.

Karel's work was influenced by the tradition of the founders of Czech national music, particularly by the work of ANTONÍN DVOŘÁK. He followed up this tradition, developing it further in the spirit of the new musical intonations of the twentieth century. He was particularly skillful in the use of the variation form, with a predilection for polyphonic elaboration.

Stage Works

His musical dramatic works include the lyrical comedy from Bohemian life entitled *Ilsa's Heart* (1906—09, première in Prague 1924), the merry musical fairy-tale of life and death *Godmother Death* (1928—32, première at Brno 1933) and *Three Hairs of the All-Wise Grandfather* (1944—45 in a draft, instrumented by ZBYNĚK VOSTŘÁK, première in Prague 1948).

Orchestral Works

Karel's orchestral work comprises the Symphony in E flat minor *Renaissance* (1910—11), the Symphony in D major *Spring* (1935—38); two further symphonies (F minor of 1904 and D major of 1917) have been lost.

His other orchestral works include the four-movement *Suite* (1903—04), a *Comedy Overture* (1904—05), a symphonic epopee from an artist's life called *The Ideals* (1906—09), *Four Slavonic Dance Moods* (1912), a *Concerto* for violin and orchestra (1914, newly instrumented in 1924 when the composition was divided into two works, namely *The Symphony* for violin and orchestra and *Capriccio* for violin and orchestra), the symphonic poem *The Demon* (1918—20) and *The Revolutionary Overture* (1938—41).

Chamber Music

Karel's chamber music includes three *String quartets* (1902—03, 1907—13, 1935—36), a *Piano Trio* in G minor (1903—04), a *Sonata* in D minor for violin and piano (1912—one of his finest compositions) and *The Nonet* (a draft from 1945, instrumented by FRANTIŠEK HERTL).

Instrumental Works

For piano Karel composed *Notturno* (1906—07), *Tema con variazioni* (1910), a *Sonata* in C minor (1910), and a *Burlesque* (1913).

Vocal Works

Karel's vocal creative work is represented by the symphony for solos, choir and orchestra *The Resurrection* (1923—27), *The Lovely Ballad for Children* for soprano, choir and orchestra (1928—30), the male choir *Zborov* (1922), a number of songs and song-cycles, as *In the Light of the Hellenic Sun* (1921), *Only Love* (1933) and *Love* (1934).

KAŠLÍK, Václav

[born Poličná, 28 September 1917]

MERITED ARTIST and LAUREATE OF THE STATE PRIZE

Kašlík graduated from the Prague Conservatory where he was a pupil of RUDOLF KAREL and from the Master School in conducting which he studied under VÁCLAV TALICH. At present he is chief opera manager of the National Theatre in Prague.

His creative work has been greatly influenced by the folklore of his native Wallachian region and he has achieved considerable success in the field of musical drama.

Stage Works

In 1940 he composed a full-length ballet *Don Juan* for organ, two pianos, string quartet and percussion instruments (première at the theatre of E. F. Burian in 1941, Czechoslovak Television 1959, Amsterdam, Haag and Rotterdam 1964). Later he reinstrumented this work for symphonic orchestra (première in Prague 1946, Magdeburg 1958). In both versions the ballet was successfully produced in Czechoslovakia as well as abroad in the theatre and television.

During the Second World War Kašlík composed radio (television) opera, on a theme pertaining to active resistance against the foreign occupation of his country, entitled *The Brigands' Ballad* (1942—43, première in Prague 1948, reworked in 1962—63 into a full-length opera).

His opera *The Stations of the Cross*, imbued with the form of folk passions and partisan themes (1943—45) and the dramatic cantata *Morana* (1944), a folk requiem for the victims of the subjugation of his country, date from the same period. He has also created a full-length ballet *Jánošík* (1950, première in Prague 1953) successfully produced at Czechoslovak and foreign theatres as well as at television.

In 1959 Kašlík completed the ballet triptych *The Prague Carnival* (*Golem—Dore—Magician Rye*).

His television opera *Krakatit*, set to theme by KAREL ČAPEK, in which he used electrophonic and electronic musical media (1960, première in 1961 at the Ostrava Theatre and at Czechoslovak Television), achieved unusual success.

Orchestral Works

He is also the author of a three movement *Village Symphony* (1954) and *Folk Nocturnes* for solo instruments and small orchestra (1956—57). In 1956 he was awarded the State Prize of the first degree for his music for the First Czechoslovak Spartakiad, entitled *A New Shift on Duty*.

Film Music

In addition he composed a number of songs and musical accompaniments to films, including a full-length film *Julius Fučík*.

Stage Producing

In his work as stage producer Kašlík had the courage of an experimentalist and endeavoured to arrive at as great as possible intelligibility of the musical dramatic form on the operatic stage, in the film, television and at Laterna Magica. This is true of his production of the opera *Julietta* by BOHUSLAV MARTINŮ at the Prague National Theatre, of the musical arrangement and conducting of OFFENBACH's *Tales of Hoffmann* for Laterna Magica, of the fairy-tale opera *Rusalka* (The Nymph) by ANTONÍN DVOŘÁK at the National Theatre in Prague and of the film of the same name, and of his staging of operas by LEOŠ JANÁČEK.

KAVKA, Arnošt
[born Prague, 4 March 1917]

Kavka studied law at Charles University in Prague. During his secondary school studies he had already founded a jazz orchestra and was a member of the jazz orchestra GRAMOKLUB. During the Second World War he joined the orchestra of KAREL VLACH as a singer and since 1940 he has devoted himself as well to compositional activity.

His first song *I Whisper Into Your Ear* is still popular. His other compositions include ¶ the slow foxtrots *Jerry, The Comrade Little Song, Pale-blue Fountains, A Pilgrim, A Bunch of Violets, Why I Love Him* (awarded the third prize in the Czechoslovak Television competition in 1962), ¶ the foxtrots *Our Grandmama, A Song About Applause, One for All, Song About Hair, Song and Laughter, Love and Gas, The Seventh Day in the Week, That's the Way it Goes, What One Would Not Do for Love, Saturday, The Lost Umbrella, Let's Go to the Moon, On the Fifth Floor,* ¶ the fox-polka *Olinka,* ¶ the comedy foxtrot *I Am Not a Satellite,* ¶ the valses *Even Songs Grow Old, Lovers,* ¶ the waltz *My Secret Wish,* ¶ the beguine *Lights and Shadows,* ¶ the twist *Fashion* and others.

Kavka has composed a notable cycle of fables about animals called *The Fables in Dance Rhythm* (published in 1957).

KINCL, Antonín
[born Velké Opatovice, 15 March 1898]

Kincl graduated from the Brno Conservatory where he was a pupil of of JAROSLAV KVAPIL, VILÉM PETRŽELKA and FRANTIŠEK NEUMANN. He continued his studies in Prague under JAROSLAV KŘIČKA and VÁCLAV TALICH. He was a violinist at the Brno Theatre, later choirmaster and accompanist and since 1921 conductor of the operetta.

After leaving Brno he was active as conductor at Prague theatres (Arena, Rokoko, Vinohrady Theatre, The Grand Operetta and the Karlín Operetta), at the East Bohemian Theatre, at the orchestra of the Luhačovice Spa and at the Moravian Philharmonic at Olomouc. In Prague Kincl conducted a whole series of significant operetta premières, among which was LEHÁR's *Giuditta*.

In his creative work, Kincl was influenced by Bohemian, Moravian and Slovak folklore as testified to by his popular medleys *Dance—Dance, Marina, Play for Me* for solos, choir and full orchestra, *The Blue-Eyed Girl, In that Little Orchard of Ours, Play That Song of Mine, Saturday is Coming*.

He wrote a number of operettas (*Czarina's Aide-de-camp, Traces on the Heart*, a *Sweet Adventure, Marinarella*), operettas for amateurs and music to the revue *From Brno to Brno*.

In the field of light music he wrote the compositions *Miriam, A Spanish Dance, Spring, Valse Caprice* for violin and orchestra, *Scherzino* for oboe and orchestra.

The battle songs of the people of North Korea inspired him to write the composition *The Korean Suites*.

Kincl has arranged and instrumented the revolutionary songs of the Soviet people for brass band.

He has also composed the cantata *From the Village* to a text by ALOIS JIRÁSEK and a *Concerto* for trombone and orchestra. His *Furiant* (a folk dance) and the *Jump Dance* were awarded third prize in a competiton set up by the French television.

KLEGA, Miroslav

[born Ostrava, 6 March 1926]

Klega graduated from he composition section of the Bratislava Conservatory where he was a pupil of EUGEN SUCHOŇ and JÁN CIKKER. At present he is teaching composition at the Conservatory in Ostrava. His early creative work is marked by enthusiastic experimentation as evidenced by his *Songs* for alto and eight instruments to words by JEAN COCTEAU (1946), a *String Quartet* (1948) and the *Burlesque Overture* (1948).

Klega surmounted this stage by his efforts for a synthesis of contemporary, firmly forged elements of expression while at the same time inclining to the works of the classics as well as those of NIKOLAI RIMSKY-KORSAKOV and MAURICE RAVEL. In substance the melodic line of his compositions today is traditionally tonal.

This period of the composer's creative activity gave rise to such compositions as the *Suite-Bagatelle* for piano (1948), five *Madrigals* for male choir set to the early works of VIKTOR DYK (1949), a *Small Funereal Scene* for violoncello and orchestra (1949), a *Dance Suite* for full orchestra (1950), a grand march *Sokol* (gymnastic organization "Falcon", 1952), *Brigands' Ideas* for piano (1953), symphonic variations *The Black Earth* (1954), *Night Festivities* for full orchestra (1956), *Two Songs* for bass and piano (1958), a *Nocturne* for piano (1958), a *Symphony* (1959), a *Concertino* in C for four string instruments (1961), a *Pantomime* and a *Suite* for orchestra (1962).

In 1961 he newly elaborated the opera *Medont, The King of Epirus* by JOSEF MYSLIVEČEK (1737—1781).

In addition to the works referred to, Klega has written music to numerous short films and radio plays and many incidental compositions.

KLÍMA, Alois
[born Klatovy, 21 December 1905]
MERITED ARTIST

At the age of four he began to play violin and when he reached the age of seven, he appeared in public. After completing the secondary school he matriculated at the Prague Conservatory where he devoted himself to the study of composition under Jaroslav Křička and Jaroslav Řídký, and conducting under Metod Doležil and Pavel Dědeček.

After completing his studies he was, for a short time, a member of the Symphonic Orchestra of the City of Prague. In 1936 he was appointed conductor of the radio orchestra in Košice. Since then radio has become the principal field of his activity. He has acquired broad experience with the radio at Ostrava, Brno and finally in Prague where he became conductor and music manager. Since 1950 Klíma has been chief of the Symphonic Orchestra of the Czechoslovak Radio in Prague. With this ensemble as well as by himself as guest conductor, he has represented successfully Czech interpretative art on concert tours abroad.

Klíma has been active as well as a pedagogue at the Prague Conservatory and at the Academy of Musical Arts.

His first public recognition as composer came to him with his graduation work, an *Overture* for orchestra (1935). After his studies he wrote his *String Quartet* (1936) and a year later two compositions for piano (*Intermezzo* and *Variations*) came into being. Within the chamber music field he wrote a *Terzettino* for oboe, clarinet and bassoon. By the end of the thirties he had written a number of compositions most of which (particularly his songs) were lost during the war years. The best known and most popular of Klímas work is *The Polonaise* for orchestra.

A substantial part of his creative work is directly concerned with his radio activity. He has composed music to radio plays, arranged folk songs (*Four Songs from Těšín, Three Children's Choirs* with orchestra, *Carols*), instrumented compositions of Ferdinand Laub, Otakar Ševčík, Franz Schubert and others.

KLUSÁK, Jan

[born Prague, 18 April 1934]

After completing the secondary school, Klusák
studied composition at the Musical section of the Academy of Musical Arts as a pupil of JAROSLAV ŘÍDKÝ and
PAVEL BOŘKOVEC.

His noteworthy works include *Music to the Fountain* for
wind quintet (1954), a *Concertino* for flute and strings
(1955), *Partita* for strings (1955), the first *String Quartet*
(1955—56), three *Symphonies* (1956, 1959, 1960), *Three
Etudes* for piano (1956—57), *Concerto grosso* for wind
quintet and strings (1957), *Four Small Voice Exercises* set
to texts by FRANZ KAFKA (1960), *Pictures* for twelve
wind instruments (1960), *Concertino* for eight instruments
(1960) and *Black Madrigals* to words by FRANTIŠEK
HALAS (1961).

His *Inventions* form a special combination of five compositions: the *first* for chamber orchestra (1961), which
received an award at the Third Bienale of Young
Artists in Paris, 1963; the *second* for chamber orchestra
(1962); the *third* (multiserial) for strings (1962), performed also in Darmstadt; the *fourth* for orchestra, inspired
by the novel *Den* of FRANZ KAFKA (1964) and the *fifth*,
Chess-playing, for wind quintet (1965).

Furthermore, he composed the *Variations* set to
a theme by GUSTAV MAHLER for orchestra (1960—62),
the second *String Quartet* (1962), *Four Fragments* from the
Divine Comedy by DANTE ALIGHIERI for alto and piano
(1962), a *Monoinvention* for solo violoncello (1962),
Risposte per violino solo (1963), *Two Czech Dances* (dodeca-
fonic polka and neighbourly) for wind orchestra (1964),
Three pieces for organ (1964), *Seven Male Choirs* set to
words by VLADIMÍR HOLAN (1964) and *Sonata* for violin
and string instruments (1964—65).

He composed as well an opera-seria *The Trial*,
according to a novel by FRANZ KAFKA.

In his creative work Klusák consciously ties in with

neo-classicism and with the musical idioms of the masters of the twentieth century [SCHÖNBERG's Viennese School, IGOR STRAVINSKY, ARTHUR HONEGGER, BOHUSLAV MARTINŮ]. His musical speech develops from the grotesque by way of irony and depression to the expression of health, energy and equipoise.

KOHOUT, Josef

[born Vienna, 29 October 1895—died Brno, 12 January 1958]

Kohout graduated from the instrumental section (French horn) of the Viennese Academy of Music. After the First World War he was a member of the orchestra of the National Theatre at Brno, studying at the same time composition at the Conservatory under JAN KUNC and VILÉM PETRŽELKA and conducting under FRANTIŠEK NEUMANN.

In 1928 he was appointed professor of the French horn at the Brno Conservatory and from 1947 to his death taught at the Janáček Academy of Musical Arts. His pedagogic results were outstanding.

Instrumental Compositions

He devoted his creative activity to the French horn for which he wrote *Seven Compositions* with piano (1926), a *Ballad and Pastorale* with piano (1948), *Concertino* with piano (1947—48, instrumented in 1952).

In his creative work Kohout demonstrated his sense for a pure chamber music quality and a poised effectiveness of sound while taking advantage of the specialities of different instruments. He wrote arrangements and cadences for concertos for French horn (HAYDEN, MOZART, STICH-FUNTO, RŮŽIČKA-ROSETTI, ŠKROUP and others.

He enriched Czech music by a *Sonata* (1923—24),

233   **KOHOUT**

two *Sonatinas* (1926, 1931) and a *Small Suite* for piano (1932) as well as a *Concert Suite* (1937), *Variations* on a Czech folk song Fly Little Bird (1944—45) and *Miniatures* for wind quintet (1946—47), the latter marked by a freshness of expression.

Vocal Works

Kohout's vocal music includes *One World* for mezzo-soprano and chamber orchestra (1924), the cycles *Lovers* (1925) and *Four Songs* set to words of old Chinese poetry for higher voice and wind quintet (1932) and *Two Songs* for alto with piano (1943). He composed many male and children choirs.

Writings

He is also the author of *The Method and Didactics of French Horn Technique* and *The History and Literature of the French Horn*.

KOHOUTEK, Ctirad

[born Zábřeh, 18 March 1929]

After completing a special course at the Brno Conservatory of Music, Kohoutek finished his study of composition under JAROSLAV KVAPIL at the Janáček Academy of Musical Arts. He is senior lecturer at the section of composition, music theory and conducting at the Janáček Academy of Musical Arts.

He found his original inspiration in folk songs, influenced as he was by his long collaboration with the Úlehla Moravian Dance and Song Ensemble. Several arrangements of folk songs, songs set to words of folk poetry and four pictures of scenic montage *The Brigands' Ballad* (1950) testify to this inclination.

His subsequent cooperation with the ensembles of the Czechoslovak Union of Youth in Brno—Joy and JULIUS

Fučík—inspired him to write young people's songs on the building up of a new life in his country and compositions for musical variety programmes.

He attracted attention by his compositional talent particularly by his *Sonatina* for oboe and piano (1950) and by his cantata *On Behalf of All Children* (1952).

Among Kohoutek's other compositions are the following: symphonic poems *Munich* (1953) and *February 1948* (1954), male choirs *The Ballad of Buchenwald* (1956), *Paris* (1956), *Two Balladic Songs* for soprano and piano (1956), *Three Characteristic Compositions* for piano (1956), a *Sonata* for piano (1957), a *Suite* for viola and piano (1957) and *Suite* for wind quintet (1958).

His *Festival Overture* for orchestra (1956) achieved considerable success and was awarded the second prize and Silver Medal in the international competition of composers at the Sixth Festival of Youth in Moscow 1957.

Kohoutek's compositional development is marked by a gradual but direct path from the period of folklore and romantic music to an effort for a contemporary, realistic musical expression. Up to the present, these efforts have become most evident in his *Concerto* for violin and orchestra (1958), in his *String Quartet* (1959) and *Sinfonietta* for full orchestra (1963).

In 1962 he wrote his three-movement symphony *The Great Turning Point* which he dedicated to the fifteenth anniversary of the liberation of Czechoslovakia and to the fortieth anniversary of the founding of the Communist Party in Czechoslovakia.

Recently he has composed three female choirs *For Life* (1960), *The Ballads of the Uprising* (two cantatas to words by JARMILA URBÁNKOVÁ: the first—*Spring* and the second—*Little Red Apples*, 1960), then *Symphonic Dances* (1961), melodrama with orchestra *The Fifth Element*, set to words by OLDŘICH MIKULÁŠEK (1962) and scenic music (to the play *The Stubborn Woman* by J. K. TYL and to the television version of the play

Gazdina Roba by GABRIELA PREISSOVÁ), as well as a one-movement *Rhapsodia eroica per organo* (1963).

In his book *Modern Compositional Theories of Western European Music* (1962, second edition 1965) Kohoutek presented a survey of the problems of contemporary musical creative work.

KOLMAN, Peter

[born Bratislava, 29 May 1937]

Kolman is one of the highly talented young Slovak composers. At the Bratislava Conservatory he was a student of composition under ANDREJ OČENÁŠ and of conducting under KORNEL SCHIMPL. He graduated from the composition section of the High School of Musical Arts under JÁN CIKKER. At present he is editor of symphonic music at the Bratislava Radio.

His early compositions bear the imprint of the influence particularly of PAUL HINDEMITH and SERGEY PROKOFIEV; they are symphonic poem *Romeo and Juliet* (1956), the *String Trio* (1957) and *Pensive Music* (1958); through expressionism in his *Violin Concerto* (1960) they aim at serial expression [*Three Piano Pieces in Memory of Arnold Schoenberg* (1960), *Two Parts* for flute, clarinet, violin and piano (1960), *Partecipazioni per dodici stromenti* (1962), *Four Orchestral Pieces* (1963)].

To the twentieth anniversary of the Slovak national uprising he composed "*Monumento per 6,000.000*" for full orchestra (1964).

He has also written a cantata *My Native Land* (1961) and several noteworthy compositions for the radio, television and stage (ARTHUR ADAMOV: *The Spring of the Year 71*; GEORG BÜCHNER: *Wozzeck*).

KONVALINKA, Karel

[born Rosice, 21 December 1885]

Konvalinka studied composition under JAROSLAV KŘIČKA and K. B. JIRÁK. The distinctive quality of Moravian cultural life gave his compositional activity an individual character.

Vocal Works

The great part of Konvalinka's creative work is dedicated to vocal music with male choral compositions holding a predominant position, as for instance:

Male choirs: *The Slovak Ballad*, op. 11b (1923), *Songs of the Mountains* op. 27 (1927—29), *A Christmas Ballad*, op. 28a (1930), the ballad *Steva* op. 28b (1935), the cycles *My Land*, op. 45 (1939—41), *The Resuscitated Land*, op. 57 (1953), *Songs of Life*, op. 59 (1954—55), the choirs *Medynia Glogowska* and the *Ballad About the Partisan Girl Nasťa*, op. 60 (1958), *The Highlands*, from op. 62-1 (1959), *In the Land of Childhood*, op. 62-2 (1960), *The Pit*, op. 64-1 (1962), *Czech Lindens*, op. 64-2 (1962) and *A Letter from Active Service*, op. 64-3 (1962).

Equally significant are his female choirs: the cycle *Moments*, op. 5 (1921), *From the Depths*, op. 15 (1923), *Eternal Spring*, op. 22 (1927), *The Voice of Home*, op. 46 (1941—42) and *Seven Female Choirs*, op. 61 (1959) as well as the choir *The Fountain is My Land*, op. 65-1 (1962).

Of particular note are his song-cycles *From Home*, op. 6 (1921), *About Love*, op. 7 (1921), *Smile of Life*, op. 32 (1930—33), *A Tree in Bloom*, op. 47 (1941), *Songs About the Native Land*, op. 58 (1954—55), *Four Female Duets* with piano, op. 40 (1957) and *Love* for two female voices and piano, set to words of folk poetry, op. 63 (1961).

Arrangements

His arrangements of folk songs: *Moravian Songs* (1918), *Moravian Folk Ballads*, op. 16 (1923), *Mountaineers' Songs*, op. 29 (1932).

237 **KONVALINKA K.**

Chamber Music

In addition to vocal compositions Konvalinka has written as well piano compositions, a *Divertimento* for flute, clarinet, French horn, trumpet and bassoon, op. 23 (1928), a *Serenade* for two clarinets, trumpet and bassoon, op. 25 (1929) and several orchestral works.

Writings

He was also active in the literary field and has written numerous articles, reviews and publications (*Preparation for Choral Singing on the Basis of the Canon, Imitation* and *Counterpoint*) which were of a pioneering significance for musical education.

KONVALINKA, Miloš

[born Nové Město in Moravia, 3 January 1919]

He is the son of the composer Karel Konvalinka; he studied composition privately under VÁCLAV KAPRÁL and at the Brno Conservatory in the class of JAROSLAV KVAPIL. He is active as conductor at the Olomouc Radio Station.

In his creative work he endeavours to arrive at an individual and, from the point of view of motivation, an expressive and dramatically vigorous musical expression.

After completing his studies (his graduation work, *The Spring Symphony*, dates from 1941—43) he concentrated on chamber music and vocal compositions: *Fantasy* for piano, *Two Compositions* for violin and piano (*Con dolore, Con amore*), a cycle of songs *An Old Viola* for voice and piano, *Variations* for oboe and piano, a male choir *Faith Alone* (all from 1944).

Within the last few years Konvalinka has resumed his compositional activity and has written *Two Dumkas* for piano, a cycle of songs for tenor and orchestra *The Con-*

fession and a melodrama on the theme of the tragic strike of the north Moravian stone-cutters at Frývaldov 1931 (all in 1954), a cantata *The Beloved Country* (1955), a *Symphonic Poem* for violin and orchestra (1956) and a cycle of songs for higher voice with orchestra *The Earth From Which We Come* (1960).

Konvalinka devotes himself as well to the composition of scenic music for the Olomouc Theatre. From his music to HIKMET's play *Joseph and his Brethren* (1956) he has composed a concert suite. In addition, he has made an arrangement of folk songs from the mountainous region entitled *Mountaineers' Songs*.

KOPELENT, Marek

[born Prague, 28 April 1932]

Kopelent graduated from the Academy of Musical Arts where he was a pupil in composition of JAROSLAV ŘÍDKÝ.

At present, he is editor for contemporary music at the State Publishing House of Music.

His most extensive compositions are:

Chamber Music

Two *String Quartets* (1954—55), a *Small Dance Suite* (1955), *Preludes* for three flutes (1958), *Three Movements* for string orchestra (1958), *Small Pantomimes* for wind quintet (1961), a *Trio* for flute, clarinet and bassoon (1962) and a *Trio* for flute, bass clarinet and piano (1962).

Recently, he has composed *The Reflections* for flute, violin, viola and violoncello, his third *String Quartet* (1963) and *The Music for Five* for oboe, clarinet, bassoon, viola and piano, in serial technique (1964).

Orchestral Works

Overture for orchestra (1954) and *Overture* for full orchestra (1960).

Vocal Works

Two song cycles *Embittered Songs* for baritone (1956), *Monologues* for alto (1957—58), *Miniature Songs* for baritone and piano, set to words of old Japanese poetry (1961) and the cantata *The Blue Bird* for alto, recitative, choir and orchestra (1957—62). Furthermore the cantata *Bread and Birds* for alto, reciter, mixed choir and orchestra, set to words by JAN SKÁCEL (1962) and a fresco for mixed choir and flute *The Mother* (1964).

Music for Radio

Since 1960, Kopelent has been making intensive use of the results achieved in the course of world music development. This is demonstrated, for instance, in his radio chamber music composition *Nenie* with flute [in memory of Hana Hlavsová], for eight wind instruments, piano, percussion instruments and nine women's voices (1960). He wrote for the radio considerable scenic music (*Hamlet, the Glass Doll*), accompaniments to verses (*Edison, the Wonderful Magician*) and improvizations.

KORBAŘ, Leopold
[born Vienna, 7 June 1917]

Korbař studied the rudiments of composition under JAROSLAV ŘÍDKÝ during his University studies. Since 1939 he was active in the orchestra of KAREL VLACH. He is now an editor for dance music in the Publishing House of the Guild of Czechoslovak Composers PANTON.

His first song *The Way to the West* was followed by dance music, much of which has become popular. Korbař's creative work, giving a picture of life around us, include ¶ the foxtrots *Hm-Hm, Seven League Boots, Old Masks, What Your Heart Commands, What Was Adam to Do, Streetcar Driver in Love, Sour Grapes, A Smile Dearer Than Gold, The Unkindly Telephone, Come to Us to Prague, The Musical Clock, Excursion Day, I Was Lonely, Because I Love You*, and *The First Walk*; ¶ the slow foxtrots *A Souvenir, Au Revoir, Love Makes the World Beautiful, Your Picture, The Fluttering Scarf, Golden Rain, Parting, Yesterday and Today, Love and Peace*; ¶ the slow rock *Thousands of Faces*; ¶ the calypso *A Fairy-Tale, About a Painter*; ¶ a cowboy's song *A Wide Prairie* and ¶ the march song *Golden Prague*.

KOŘÍNEK, Miloš
[born Brno, 29 January 1925]

Kořínek acquired his education in composition under ALEXANDER MOYZES at the Bratislava Conservatory, from which he graduated also in conducting (KORNEL SCHIMPL), as well as at the High School of Musical Arts.

Since 1950, he has taught at Bratislava Conservatory and lately as well at the Faculty of Philosophy at the Comenius University, where he lectures on theory and composition.

Stage Works

His most successful work is the children's opera *How the Egg Went on a Tramp* (première in Bratislava in 1960), which was awarded in the Artistic Jubilee Competition in 1960.

Orchestral Compositions

Of these should be mentioned a *Concerto* for accordion and orchestra (1957) and the *Grande Overture* (1959).

Chamber Music

Kořínek is a prolific composer, in particular of expressive chamber music compositions. These include a *String Quartet* in E flat major (1951), *Four Compositions* for violoncello and piano (1961), a *Trio* for two oboes and English horn (1962), and his compositions for young people for whom he has written a number of valuable works stressing execution, such as the cycle of ten piano compositions *Ferenc' Summer* (1957), *Nine Compositions* for four violins (1957), nine sonatinas for wind instruments with piano accompaniment *The Sonatinas of Joyous Youth* (1960) and a *Divertimento for Strings* (1962).

Writings

His pedagogic activity brought him the impulse to the writing of the book *Study of Harmony*, conceived in a modern spirit.

KORTE, Oldřich F.

[born Šala on Váh, 26 April 1926]

Korte graduated from the section of composition at the Prague Conservatory in the class of FRANTIŠEK PÍCHA. He is pianist and music manager of the experimental scene LATERNA MAGICA in Prague.

Korte's earliest compositions are marked by his searching efforts to evolve various methods for the handling of musical material. These include the piano suite *Iniuria*, the ballet *Orbis*, an instructive cycle *Excursion*, *In Praise of Death* for the octave flute and chimes, and the piano variations *The Drinker's Metamorphosis*.

His later creative work is characterized by its well-developed expression, detailed thematic elaboration, richly differentiated harmony and a sense for the structure in musical form.

Korte's compositional talent was distinctly evident in his atonal *Sinfonietta* for full orchestra (his graduation work of 1945—47), which evoked considerable response at its première in 1949.

Up to the present, Korte's most successful work is his *Sonata* for piano (1951—53), which achieved the distinction of being a much sought after-repertoire composition for pianists at home and abroad; in its original form, as a one-movement fantasy, it was awarded the first Special Prize in the Busoni International Competition of Composers in Bolzano (1956), where it was played by the Laureate of the Warsaw Chopin Competition Maurizio Pollini.

In 1958 Korte completed a symphonic drama *The Story of Flutes*, in which he took his position in favour of the romantic ideal of beauty of form and of a dramatically graded content.

His latest composition for the time being is a *Concerto grosso* for strings, trumpets and piano.

KOŠŤÁL, Arnošt

[born Prague, 18 January 1920]

Košťál is son of the composer ERNO KOŠŤÁL. He studied composition at the Prague Conservatory where he was a pupil of RUDOLF KAREL, OTAKAR ŠÍN and KAREL JANEČEK. As his graduation work he composed *Sinfonietta* for full orchestra (1944). He has been a lecturer on musical subjects at the Academy of Musical Arts and co-founder of the Folk Art Ensemble of the Prague Conservatory.

At present he is dramaturgist of the Czechoslovak State Ensemble of Songs and Dances for which he has created stylizations of folk songs and dances for choir, solo voices and instrumental ensembles. He has written numerous community songs, scenic and film scores and music for performances of the Folk Art Ensemble at the First, Second and Third Spartakiad.

Lately Košťál has cooperated with the Czechoslovak Radio and the State Publishing House of Music on arrangements and publications of folk songs. In 1963 he completed a full-length ballet *The Fountain of Love* on a theme by Jan Reimoser.

KOŠŤÁL, Erno

[born Prague, 26 November 1889.—died Prague 26 January 1957]

Košťál graduated from the organ section of the Prague Conservatory. Before the First World War he was active in Žitomir and in Kursk in Russia as a pedagogue and conductor; during the First World War he lived in Italy and in Albania.

He has written many instrumental compositions and dance music and marches. His orchestral suites, particularly the two Albanian, one Italian and one Russian, assured his popularity.

He is author of following works:

choral works: oratorio *Ecce Homo*; singspiel: *Marjanka, Mother of the Regiment*; one-act plays (with songs): *Annie, You've Got to Go About It Round About, Behind that Little Barn of Ours*; operettas: *What is Love, Children of the American West, Soldiers-Pampered Children, The Waterman of Miller's Journeyman Švejnoha, My Golden Little Girl*; music to films: first Czech sound film *Tonka-the Gallows* (E. E. Kisch, première 1930), *For the Native Soil, The Dog-Heads, Karel Havlíček Borovský, Because of Love, A Lark's Song, Erotikon, Louise* (with Jaroslav Jankovec), *Schwanda the Bag-piper, People at the Foot of the Mountains, Marriage under a Microscope* and *Beware—the Place is Haunted*.

KOVAŘÍČEK, František

[born Litětiny, 17 May 1924]

Kovaříček studied composition at the Prague Conservatory in the class of EMIL HLOBIL. He continued his
studies at the Academy of Musical Arts under JAROSLAV
ŘÍDKÝ, graduating in 1952. His graduation work was an
Overture for orchestra.

Of his compositions up to the present we can cite his
Little Songs, set to folk poetry (1951), *Four Pieces* for violin
and piano (1954), a *Suite* for orchestra (1955), a cycle
of songs called the *Golden Wave of June* (1957), to verses
by MIROSLAV FLORIÁN, a *Sonata* for violoncello and
piano (1958), a *Serenade* for nonet (1959), a *Divertimento*
for strings (1960), a *Larghetto* for clarinet and piano (1963),
Three Songs for tenor, set to words by JOSEF KAINAR
(1963) and *Concerto* for clarinet and orchestra (1964).

KOWALSKI, Július

[born Ostrava, 24 February 1912]

He studied composition and conducting at the Prague
Conservatory under RUDOLF KAREL, ALOIS HÁBA and
PAVEL DĚDEČEK, continuing his studies at the Master
School under JOSEF SUK and VÁCLAV TALICH and in
Vienna with CLEMENS KRAUSS. After the liberation of
Czechoslovakia he associated himself with musical life in
Slovakia. At present he is active as director of the
People's School of Arts in Bratislava.

His early compositional work showed the influence
of the European avantgarde and of ALOIS HÁBA (*Four Piano
Pieces*, *Fantasy* in the quarter-tone system) but his later
work was largely influenced by the late romantic tradition.

Of his postwar creative work mention should be made

particularly of a small cantata *A Tribute to Bratislava* for solos, choir and orchestra (1953), the first *Concerto for violin and chamber orchestra* (1955), a song cycle *On Freedom* for baritone and piano (1956), *The Comedy Overture* (1957), two chamber *Symphonies* (1958 and 1962), an overture *The Uprising* (1959), a *Poem* for violoncello and piano (1959) and of several chamber music compositions, with particular stress on a *Quartet* for flute, violin, viola and piano and the second *String Quartet*.

Kowalski's most significant creative work was his chamber opera *A Chinese Lantern Festival* (1962, première at the Czechoslovak Television in Bratislava in 1962, at Meiningen [German Democratic Republic] 1964).

As a pedagogue Kowalski has written extensively for children and youth. Of importance is his children's opera *Tales at the Spinning Wheel* (The Golden-haired Beauty, 1954, première at Ústí on Labe). His song-cycle *The Zodiac*, for voice and piano, respectively for chamber ensemble, has achieved equal popularity. His cycles *From the World of Toys* and *Five Small Capricious Compositions* are designed for young pianists. For violinists Kowalski has written a suite *Let's Play*, a *Youth Concertino* for violin and piano, *Scenes from Tales* for string quartet and a small overture *Happy Youth* for strings and piano.

KOZDERKA, Ladislav

[born Brno, 2 March 1913]

Kozderka studied piano under VÁCLAV KAPRÁL. It was not until he was twenty that he decided to study composition, graduating from the Brno Conservatory as a pupil of VILÉM PETRŽELKA.

He has devoted himself to dance and light music and appeared as a pianist in Prague with the orchestra of Dolfi Langer, at one time managing his own orchestra.

Since 1942 he has been active at the Brno Radio. As a co-founder of the Brno Radio Variety Orchestra he has written tens of compositions for it.

The following dance music achieved considerable popularity: ¶ the polkas: *Bohdalov Polka*; ¶ the slow foxtrots: *A Pleasant Chat, I am Waiting for Your Letter, Those Eyes that Opened*; ¶ the foxtrots: *The Cinema Phantom, Happiness Waits for No One, Moon in Wine, The Crossroads, On the Slide*; ¶ the valse: *The Breeze Said*; ¶ the tango: *When Day Ends*; ¶ the rumbas: *Greetings from Afar, The Chatterers*.

His ¶ foxtrots for accordion *The Early Bird* and *Rhythm With an Accordion* are constantly played and are a particular success.

His other dance music includes ¶ a foxtrot for xylophone: *Singing Sticks*; ¶ a foxtrot for piano: *The Frolicking Keyboard*; ¶ a foxtrot for two pianos: *Between You and Me*; ¶ a foxtrot for two trombones: *Our Friendship*; ¶ a foxtrot for four trombones: *To a New Day*; ¶ a waltz and foxtrot for four trombones: *Cantilena* and *Rhythm*; two *Rhythms* for four trombones and small orchestra; ¶ a slow folk waltz *Neighbourly* for two trumpets, ¶ a *Rapid valse* for accordion; ¶ a polka for contrabassoon *Out-of-Breath* and a ¶ polka for ocarina and contrabassoon: *A Strange Friendship*; ¶ the intermezzo *At the School of Music* belongs as well among Kozderka's popular compositions.

Furthermore he composed music to ¶ the animated cartoon: *A Brick to a Brick*; ¶ to cabaret programmes: *An Invitation with the Devil, A Little Song in Attack, The Heat on Ice, Mister Plašmuška at the Harvest*, music to ¶ the fairy-tale: *Concerning Lost Time*, music to ¶ the radio play *Friends of Miss Veronica*, music to ¶ the montages: *The Song of Life* and *Love Grief* and *Millions*.

He is also the author of a number of songs for children, medleys of children's and folk songs and of several suites, as *Pictures from the Highlands, In an Old Style, In a Newer Style* and *Greetings to Luhačovice*.

He has arranged as well many Negro songs and has collaborated with many young composers, singers and musical ensembles.

KOŽELUHA, Lubomír

[born Brno, 1 September 1918]

Koželuha graduated from the Teachers' Training Institute in Brno. In composition he was a pupil of VILÉM PETRŽELKA at the Brno Conservatory. He also studied musical education at the Brno University. He is a teacher of musical education and is active as choirmaster.

Stage Works

Koželuha has composed a one-act opera *The Betrayed Country* to a libretto by JAROSLAV ZATLOUKAL (1956).

Chamber Music

He has written a *Sonata* for violoncello and piano (1943), a *Suite* for viola and piano (1957) and a *Wind Quintet* (1962).

Orchestral Works

He started with *Grande Overture* (1944) and wrote then *At Games* (1950), *A Chain Dance* (1951), *A Slovak Dance* (1951), a *Suite* (1952), a march *To the Victors of Work* (1956) and the rhapsody *Orlík* (1962).

Instrumental Works

He wrote a *Small Suite* for piano (1939), *Variations* on folk songs for piano (1942), *Four Compositions* for piano (1947) and *To Children* for piano (for beginners, 1962).

Vocal Works

Voices: *Songs* set to words of folk poetry for higher voice with piano accompaniment (1942), *Three Songs* for baritone and orchestra *Hail to Spring!* (1943), three songs for baritone and orchestra *For a New Life* (1949), *Folk Songs from Moravia* for solos, choir and orchestra (1950), *Pioneer Songs* (1950), three songs for higher voice and orchestra *To One's Own Children* (1958) and *Love Songs* for higher voice with piano accompaniment (1959).

Female choirs: *Mother* (1957), *Lullaby* (1960).

Male choirs: *The Victorious* (1950), *The ninth of May* (1952), two male choirs *We Shall Not Forget* (1958), *To the Working People* (1962), *Alone, You Are Naught* (1962).

Children choirs: *Lullaby* (1960), *Counting-Out Rhymes* with piano accompaniment (1962).

Mixed choirs: *Four Slovak Folk Songs* (1948), *The Victory Songs* for choir and orchestra (1949), *Three Slovak Folk Songs* (1950), *Modra* (1951), *Songs of Slovak Youth* for mixed choir and piano accompaniment (1957), *Communism Shall Win* (1961), *Moravian Slovakia* (1962).

Cantatas: *The Liberated Land* for baritone, choir and orchestra (1960).

In addition, Koželuha makes also arrangements of folk songs.

KRATOCHVÍL, JIŘÍ

[born Prague, 17 August 1924]

Kratochvíl graduated from the instrumental section of the Prague Conservatory (MILAN KOSTOHRYZ' clarinet class). He continued his studies at the Academy of Musical Arts under VLADIMÍR ŘÍHA (clarinet) and MILAN KOSTOHRYZ (chamber music). In addition, he studied musical science and aesthetics at Charles University and composition privately with VLADIMÍR POLÍVKA.

From 1951 he has been teaching the history and literature of wind instruments at the Academy of Musical
Arts (scripts 1960) and since 1961 clarinet playing at the
Prague Conservatory. From 1958 Kratochvíl has been
secretary of the section of concert artists of the Guild of
Czechoslovak Composers. He appears on concert platforms as a clarinetist.

In composition his attention is mainly directed to the
field of chamber music for wind instruments.

Amongst others he has composed three *Symphonies*,
a symphonic *Prelude*, a *Sinfonietta* for wind instruments
and doublebasses (given an award in the competition
of the Czechoslovak Radio in 1947); further a cantata
Ostrava, a *Quintet* for clarinet and strings, *Small Serenade*
for oboe, clarinet and bassoon, *Trio* for clarinet, French
horn and bassoon, *Suite* for solo clarinet, *Small Suite* for
clarinet and piano (instructive, published by the State
Publishing House of Music in Prague 1962), a *Suite* for
French horn and piano, *Short Funereal Music* for three
basset-horns, *Nocturnes* for female choirs and compositions for piano. At present he is working on a clarinet
concerto.

He has written cadences for the clarinet concertos of
J. V. STAMIC, Š. V. KALOUS, J. A. KOŽELUH and F. A.
ROSETTI. Furthermore he has revised *The Clarinet
Concerto* by F. B. KRAMÁŘ, op. 36.

The State Publishing House of Music has published
his *School for the Clarinet* (first edition 1961, second 1963).

KRAUTGARTNER, Karel

[born Mikulov, 20 July 1922]

After completing the secondary school Krautgartner
studied clarinet at a music school at Brno and as ex-
ternist at the Conservatory under STANISLAV KRTIČKA.

In Brno he also founded a dance orchestra. Later he appeared as saxophonist in the orchestra of KAREL VLACH in Prague.

In 1955 he set up a dance quintet, then a septet which he later enlarged into a nonet and was one of the founders of the ensemble of modern dance music "STUDIO 5". In January 1960 he was named conductor of the Czechoslovak Radio Dance Orchestra.

He is the author of considerable dance music and noteworthy arrangements which have forged a new path in contemporary Czech dance music.

His creative work includes ¶ the foxtrots *Saving Means Having, The First Turn, Rena, The Southern Cross, Hot Pie*; ¶ the fox-polka *The Devil Knows Why*, ¶ the slow foxtrot *The Shy Gardener*, ¶ the dance fantasy *Neons*; then a *Student's Suite* and *Concertino* in C minor for clarinet.

He has also composed music to documentary and short films, appears as concert saxophonist and lecturer on jazz and modern dance music. He has written a booklet on the instrumentation of dance and jazz orchestra (1961) and was active as a pedagoguc at the People's Conservatory in Prague.

KREJČÍ, Iša

[born Prague, 10 July 1904]

MERITED ARTIST and LAUREATE OF THE STATE PRIZE

Son of the founder of Czech scientific psychology František Krejčí; studied at the Prague Conservatory piano under ALBÍN ŠÍMA and composition under K. B. JIRÁK and at the Master School under VÍTĚZSLAV NOVÁK. Besides composition he studied conducting at the Conservatory under VÁCLAV TALICH and musicology at Charles University.

During the period when OSCAR NEDBAL was active at

the Bratislava Opera, Krejčí was accompanist and conductor there, later becoming music manager at the Prague Radio; then, for thirteen years, he managed the opera in Olomouc. At present, he is dramaturgist of the opera at the National Theatre in Prague and conductor of the opera at České Budějovice.

He ranks among the foremost contemporary Czech composers. The *Divertimento-cassazione* for flute, clarinet, trumpet and bassoon (his graduation work at the Conservatory, 1925) attracted considerable attention at its première due to its neoclassical orientation and brought him his first acclaim.

Stage Works

Krejčí's representative work is the opera *The Uprising in Ephesus* (1943—44, première in Prague 1946), composed to a libretto by JOSEF BACHTÍK according to SHAKESPEARES's *Comedy of Errors*.

Out of intention to set into music The Darkness, written by ALOIS JIRÁSEK, he composed *Four Pictures* (1944—45).

During the years 1958—59 and in 1962 he reworked his scenic cantata *Antigona*, according to SOPHOCLES (1932, the television inscenation in 1964).

Orchestral Works

Krejčí composed three *Symphonies*, significant for their effectiveness of thought: the first from 1947—50, the second from 1956—57 and the third from 1961—63 (the last one was awarded a prize by the Czech Music Fund 1964).

Amongst his other symphonic works are *Sinfonietta* (1929), *Twenty Variations* for orchestra set to a theme in the style of national songs (1946—47), a *Serenade* for full orchestra (1949). One of his most outstanding compositions are fourteen orchestral *Variations* to the folk song *Good Night, My Beloved* (1951—52), a nenia on his late wife.

Instrumental and Chamber Music

The first *String Quartet* (1928), *Trio* for oboe, clarinet and bassoon (1935). *Trio* for clarinet, double-bass and piano (1936), *Nonet* (1937), *Concertino concertante* for violoncello and piano (1939) and three *Scherzinos*, written originally for flute but later arranged for piano (1945), then second (1953) and the third (1960) *String Quartet*.

Vocal Works

After his graduation he composed *Songs*, set to words by VÍTĚZSLAV NEZVAL (including a small ballet to a theme of NEZVAL's *Pantomime*). A tragically sturdy intonation is characteristic for his *Small Funereal Music* (1933), for alto with accompaniment of viola, to which was added the middle section of a cycle of poems *Old Women* by FRANTIŠEK HALAS (1936). In the cycle *Five Songs*, set to texts by JAN AMOS KOMENSKÝ [Comenius] (1938), Krejčí achieved a remarkable tension and impressiveness, while in contrast his four *Madrigals*, set to texts by K. H. MÁCHA (1936), have a meditative character.

Krejčí arranged as well two montages of folk songs for the radio: *From the Land of the Bag-pipers* (1939) and *Carols Sung at Christmas Time* (1940).

KREJČÍ, Miroslav

[born Rychnov on Kněžna, 4 November 1891—died Prague, 29 December 1964]

His mother noted his first little compositions when he was four years old. He studied composition privately with VÍTĚZSLAV NOVÁK. First, he became secondary school teacher and since 1943 was professor of composition at the Prague Conservatory (until 1953, when he retired).

In his inclination to imitative polyphony and by the structure of his harmony, he shows himself a faithful disciple of his teacher, though in certain aspects of his works he approaches J. B. FOERSTER.

He was very prolific and his work exceeds one hundred works, touching practically every field and genre.

Stage Works

The operas: *The Summer*, according to FRÁŇA ŠRÁMEK, op. 41 (1937), première in Prague 1940, national prize 1941) and *The Last Captain*, libretto by E. KLENOVÁ, set to the novel Brotherhood by ALOIS JIRÁSEK, op. 62 (1944, première Prague 1948).

Orchestral Works

Among his orchestral compositions are first of all three *Symphonies*: *first* in G, op. 70 (1944—46), *second* in D, op. 90 (1952—54), *third* received second prize in the jubilee competitions of the Guild of Czechoslovak Composers (1955).

His other works in this field are a symphonic poem *King Lávra*, op. 6 (1917), *Life and Time* for string orchestra and French horn, op. 23 (1927), a *Viola Concerto* op. 72 (1947), a *Clarinet Concerto* op. 76 (1949), a *Violin Concerto* op. 96 (1953) and a number of other orchestral compositions. These include two series of *Czech Dances*, op. 75 (1948) and op. 95 (1952), a *Dance Suite*, op. 84 (1950), *Four Compositions on pictures by Max Švabinský*, op. 104 (1954) and *Spring in My Fatherland*, op. 106 (1955).

Chamber Music

Krejčí's chamber music is extremely extensive and includes numerous *String Quartets* (for instance *The Chant To My Native Land* with alto solo, based on a poem by JOSEF HORA, op. 50, 1941), quintets for various combinations of instruments, trios, a large number chamber music works for two to ten instruments, many sonatas for various instruments and piano and organ compositions.

Vocal Works

In the vocal field he wrote cycles of songs *To My Darling*, set to a poem by JOSEF HORA, op. 14 (1925), *Songs About a Baby*, op. 28a (1927—29), *Songs for a Baby*, op. 28b (1929), *Autumn Songs* and *Spring Songs*, op. 67 (1945), *The Book of Proverbs*, op. 65 (1942—52), *Three Songs*, set to poems by RABINDRANÁTH TAGORE, op. 85 (1951) and *Strophes of Love*, on texts by STIEPAN SHCHIPA-CHEV, op. 107 (1956).

In addition, Krejčí has written the choirs *Hellada*, op. 8a (1919) and *Summer Festivals*, op. 40 (1936) as well as numerous marches, songs for community singing, popular music and harmonized folk songs.

Of his cantatas, *The Wedding Song*, op. 20 (1926), *The Death of Christ*, op. 46 (1937—40) and a *Better Love*, op. 102 (1954) deserve special mention.

Various compositions

His *Funereal Music* for brass band received an award in the artistic jubilee competition in 1960.

KRESÁNEK, Jozef

[born Čičmany, 20 December 1913]

Holder of the decoration FOR OUTSTANDING WORK

Kresánek studied composition at the Prague Conservatory under RUDOLF KAREL and at the Master School under VÍTĚZSLAV NOVÁK. Simultaneously he studied the science of music at Charles University. After graduation he was a teacher at the Teachers' Training Institute at Prešov, member of the staff of the musical section of Slovenská Matice (Slovak Cultural Association) and since 1944 a lecturer at the Faculty of Philosophy at Bratislava University; in 1952 he was appointed senior lecturer and in 1963 professor. At present he holds the post of director of the Institute of Musical Science of the Slovak Academy of Sciences.

His compositional creative work was influenced partly by Vítězslav Novák and Josef Suk and partly by Igor Stravinsky and Sergei Prokofiev, as well as by Slovak folk song. His compositional work, which is not extensive, is devoted mainly to the field of chamber music and is a significant contribution to the so-called "new folklorism" in Slovak music.

Chamber Music

Of his chamber music works, reference should be made in particular to his *String Quartet* (1935), two piano *Suites* (1936 and 1938), a piano *Trio* (1939), which ranks among his finest compositions, two *Suites* for violin and piano (1947 and 1951) and a *Brigands' Ballad* for piano.

Orchestral Compositions

For orchestra he wrote two *Suites* (1951—61, 1953) and a *Prelude and Toccata* (1957). He is also the author of the cantata *Ho, Away!* (1937).

Writings

Kresánek is the leading personality in Slovak musicology. By his book *The Slovak Folk Song from the Standpoint of Music* he laid the foundation for scientific research in the field of Slovak folklore (1951). In a substantial measure he contributed as well to research in the history of Slovak music (*The Rise of National Music in the Nineteenth Century* in the *History of Slovak Music*, 1957).

His studies on problems concerning the social function of music, musical thinking and aesthetics of contemporary music (*Social Function of Music*, 1961) and a *Monograph on Eugen Suchoň* (1961) belong to his most original works in this field.

KŘIČKA, Jaroslav

[born Kelč, 27 August 1882]

MERITED ARTIST

Křička comes from a schoolmaster musical family. He graduated in composition from the Prague Conservatory, where he was a pupil of KAREL STECKER, and then continued his studies in Berlin.

He was active as a pedagogue in Jekatierinoslav (Dniepropetrovsk) in Russia, where he also organized symphonic concerts. After his return to Prague he became choirmaster of the Vinohrady Hlahol, later of the Prague HLAHOL and of the Choir of Czech Philharmonic. In these ensembles he launched a concert activity of a pioneering significance as regards programme and interpretation.

As professor of composition at the Prague Conservatory and at its Master School Křička trained a whole generation of Czechoslovak composers.

Křička is a master of humour and wit in music as well as of a melodious lyricism. His prolific compositional work founds its roots in the folk song, in the heritage of the Czech classic, in the stimuli of the neo-Russian school and in that of VÍTĚZSLAV NOVÁK.

Stage Works

Křička expressed his sense for the musical-dramatic in his opera *Hypolita*, according to the novel by MAURICE HEWLETT (1910—1916, première in Prague 1917), which was followed by the comic opera *The White Gentleman* (or Today Ghosts Have a Difficult Time), according to a theme by OSCAR WILDE (1927—29, première in Brno 1929, reworked in 1930, produced in Breslau 1931), a fairy-tale with dances *King Lavra* to the satirical poem by KAREL HAVLÍČEK BOROVSKÝ (1936—37, worked over in 1938—39, première in Prague 1940), the Christmas opera *The Czech Christmas Manger*, according to Czech folk Christmas plays and carols

(1936—37, première in Prague 1949), the folk romance *Jáchym and Juliana* after B. BENEŠ BUCHLOVAN (1947—48, première in Opava 1951), the comic opera *The Cradle*, according to ALOIS JIRÁSEK (1950, première in Opava 1951) and the Rococo buffa *The Serenade*, according to ALOIS JIRÁSEK's "Zahořany Hunt" (première in Pilsen 1950).

The following musical-dramatic works were intended for youth: the children's opera from the life of Wallachian children *Ogari* (Lads) to the text by JOZEF KALDA (1918, première in Nové Město in Moravia 1919), an opera for small and grown-up children *It Turned Out Well* or *The Plump Great Grandfather*, then *Robbers and Detectives* to a libretto by JOSEF ČAPEK (1932, première in Prague 1932), two small operas for children's theatre *A Little Letter Atravelling* and *Matěj Kopecký's Puppets Come to Life* and *The Fairy-tale about the Twelve Months*.

Due to his outstanding aptitude for a folk musical expression, Křička became a pioneer in the effort for the regeneration of Czech musical comedy and operetta.

In this genre he composed several works: *The Czech Paganini* (Slavík and Chopin), *A Quiet House*, *The Polka Wins*, *Good Soldier Schweik*, *Circus Humberto* and others.

The television comedy *A Pair of Trousers*, scenic and film music, numerous choirs and dance compositions (The popular *Estadrata Polka* and *The Maršov Grandmother's Valse* from the opera *Ogari*) round off Křička's compositional work.

Orchestral Works

Křička's symphonic works demonstrate his complete understanding of the orchestra and of colourful instrumentation: *Symphony* in D minor *Spring* (1905—06, reworked 1942), a symphonic poem *Faith* (1907), *A Children's Suite* (1907), *Idyllic Scherzo* (1908), an overture *A Blue Bird*, to the fairy-tale by MAURICE MAETERLINCK (1911), a symphonic composition *Adventus* (1920—21), an overture *Matěj Kopecký* (1928), *The Upland Suite*

(1935), *Sinfonietta* for string orchestra and timpani (1940—41), overture *Majales* (1942), a violin *Concerto* (1944) and others.

Chamber Music

Chamber music instrumental works belong to Křička's most significant creative expression: first *String Quartet* (1907), *Caprice* (1907), a *Small Suite* for two violins and piano (1907), *Intimate Compositions* (1910—11), *The Lyrical Suite* for piano (1919), a piano trio *At Home* (1923—24), a *Sonata* in E minor for violin and piano (1925), a *Sonatina* in C major for two violins (1926—27), later for violin and viola, second *String Quartet* (1938—39), a *Concertino* for violin, wind quintet and piano (1940), *Partita* for solo violin (1941), third *String Quartet—Wallachian* (1949), *Divertimento* for wind quintet (1950), a flute *Sonatina* (1951), a *Concertino* for French horn and string quartet or orchestra (1951), a *Sonatina* in G for violin and piano (1962), and others.

Instrumental Compositions

Křička has written also piano compositions for children, which include: *The Puppet Suite*, *A Circus in Five Tones* (published by Schott in 1936), *A Children's Lunapark*, *Lullabies* and others.

Songs

In the field of children's songs he has become a Czech classic. A sparkling musical humour permeates his *Songs and Marches* for Czechoslovak Youth, *New Songs and Marches* for Czechoslovak Youth as well as song-cycles: *To Children*, *Little George's Songs*, *Dana's Little Songs* and *Nursery Rhymes*, *Mickie's Little Songs*, *The March of Little Animals*, *Little Animals of the Woods*, *Nursery Rhyme Songs for Boys and Little Girls*, *Rhymes for Little Singers*, *Flower Riddles*, *Amidst Drops of Rain*, *Blue Sky*, *Little Daniel's Ditties*, *The Alphabet*, *Pebbles of Love* for little voices and others.

His cycles of songs have a witty musical character and an ardency of expression. These include *First Yearnings* (1903—05), *Northern Lights* (1909—10), *Of Love and Death* (1910), *Farewell Songs* (1916), the popular *Three Fables* (1912—1917) and *Infant Spring* (1919), *An Album of the Old School* (1922), *Cosmic Songs* (1927), *Shouting Songs* (1952 and 1956), *Our Božena Němcová* (1954), *Boys' Songs* (1955), *Old-Fashioned Songs* (1956), *Sunny Songs* (1957) and others.

The cycle of children's songs *Of Little Trains* and *Little Machines* to texts by JAN ČAREK was awarded in the artistic jubilee competition in 1960.

Choral Works

Amongst them are masses and requiems, as *Missa brevis*, *Missa cantabilis*, *Requiem in memoriam fratris*, *The Wallachian Morning Mass* and *The Šumava Pastoral Mass*.

Cantatas

This is another important field to which Křička has devoted himself with full artistic fervour: *Temptation in the Desert* (1921—22), the ballad *Jenny, the Thief* (1927), *Tyrolian Elegies* (1930), *A Eulogy to Woman* (1933), *Student Recollections* (1934), *Moravian Cantata* (1935—36), *The Golden Spinning-wheel* (1943).

His cantata *To Prague* was awarded in the artistic jubilee competition in 1960.

Writings

Křička has written as well a brief survey of the development of Russian secular music in the nineteenth century, entitled *Russian Music* (1922); a popular introduction into the world of music *What Are C major and C minor?* (1931) and an essay *Music and the Films* (1943).

KŘIVINKA, Gustav

[born Doubravice on Svitava, 24 April 1928]

Křivinka studied violin at the Brno Conservatory under FRANTIŠEK KUDLÁČEK and later composition under VÁCLAV KAPRÁL and VILÉM PETRŽELKA. He completed his study of composition under JAROSLAV KVAPIL at the Janáček Academy of Musical Arts; his graduation work was *The String Quartet* (1954).

He has directed a number of ensembles of Folk Art and as composer has cooperated with ensembles of the Czechoslovak Union of Youth—Joy and JULIUS FUČÍK.

He was secretary of the Brno branch of the Guild of Czechoslovak Composers. Recently, he has been active as television music manager.

Orchestral Works

His symphonic creative work is represented by his two *Symphonies* (first in 1951, second in 1955); further he has written two *Concertos grosso* [the first for piano and string orchestra (1950) and the second for string quartet and orchestra (1963)] and symphonic poem *The forty-first* (1958).

Chamber Music

Cassation for four wind instruments (1949), and the first *Violin Concerto* (1949—50).

Instrumental Works

His *Sonata* for solo violin (1960) was awarded in the artistic jubilee competition in 1960.

Vocal Works

Songs: *The Grasscutter's Songs* for two voices with piano (1949), *Echoes of Russian Songs* for soprano, alto and female choir with piano (1950), a cycle of songs *Life, Be Greeted!* for baritone and piano (1952) and the duet *The Ashen Dove*, set to poems by OLDŘICH MIKULÁŠEK for soprano, alto and piano (1962).

Choirs: His mourning choir *In Memory of a Comrade*, for female and male choirs (1959), received an honourable mention in the artistic jubilee competition in 1960.

Children choirs: *The Christmas Suite* for choir and orchestra, according to a television film of the same name (1962), *Nursery Rhymes* for solos, children choir and orchestra, set to texts of FRANTIŠEK HRUBÍN (1963) and *Children Alphabet* for solos, children choir and orchestra, according to JOSEF LADA (1963).

Cantatas: "*Twenty-five thousand*" for soprano, alto, strings and timpani (1961), a small cantata *Our Life* for mixed choir and orchestra (1962) and the oratorio *Butterflies Do Not Live Here*, to poems of Jewish children who died in the concentration camp at Terezín, for soprano, baritone, children choir and orchestra (1960 to 1962).

Film Music

Křivinka has written numerous scenic and film compositions of which the most successful was the music to the film *The School for Fathers* (the film collective was awarded the State Prize in 1958).

Various

He is also the author of a number of compositions for the Brno Radio Orchestra of Folk Instruments and for the Brno Radio Variety Orchestra as well as of jazz music.

Recently, he wrote a musical (jazz) comedy for children *Beware of Fifin* (1964).

Křivinka is a staunch and consistent propagator of the new socialist art growing out of national roots.

●

For his cantatas "*25.000*" and *Butterflies Do Not Live Here* he was awarded a prize in the artistic jubilee competition 1965.

KŘÍŽEK, Zdeněk

[born Prague, 26 September 1927]

Křížek graduated from the section of composition at the Prague Conservatory where he was a pupil of FRANTIŠEK PÍCHA and FRANTIŠEK BROŽ. He is the music instructor of the Army Artistic Ensemble Vít Nejedlý.

His work includes following compositions: *Sonata* for violin and piano (1955), *Burlesque* for piano (1955), a *Romance* for violin and orchestra (1958), an orchestral *Capricious Valse* (1954), *Three Czech Dances* (1957), a *Lyric Intermezzo* (1960), a *Short Variety Overture* (1961), a suite *A May Sunday* (1961), a dance picture *The Slovak Ballad* (1961) and a *Black and White Nocturno* for piano with orchestra (1964).

For the stage he has written two ballets a *Ballad About a Sailor* (1960) to a libretto by LUBOŠ OGOUN according to a poem of the same name by JIŘÍ WOLKER (première in Pilsen 1961) and the *Hypnotist* to a libretto by JIŘINA MLÍKOVSKÁ (1962, première Prague 1963).

Recently, he has composed music to *Fairy-tales* of the Television Merry-go-round for a puppet serial.

He has also written a *Concerto* for trumpet and orchestra (1957), which was widely acclaimed both at home and abroad.

In addition, he is the author of a number of compositions and arrangements of folk songs and dances for the Army Artistic Ensemble Vít Nejedlý.

KROMBHOLC, Jaroslav

[born Prague, 30 January 1918]

MERITED ARTIST and LAUREATE OF THE STATE PRIZE

Krombholc studied composition at the Prague Conservatory under OTAKAR ŠÍN, at the Master School under VÍTĚZSLAV NOVÁK and conducting under PAVEL

DĚDEČEK, OTAKAR OSTRČIL and VÁCLAV TALICH. He has demonstrated his outstanding compositional talent in three orchestral *Suites* (1934, 1937, 1939), in a *Sonatina* for piano (1935), two *String Quartets* (1936 and 1938), *Suite* for piano (1937), a violoncello *Sonata* (1939), three pastoral *Intermezzos* (1940), a clarinet *Sonata* (1941), a *Symphony* (1942), *Songs of Parting* for higher voice and piano (1943), a *String Sextet* (1944), a viola *Sonata* (1944 to 1945) and a *Partita* for piano (1945).

From the year 1945 Krombholc has given up compositional work in order to be able to devote himself completely to conducting. He is chief conductor of the opera of the National Theatre in Prague.

KROTIL, Zdeněk

[born Horní Mokropsy, 9 June 1926]

After completing the secondary school, Krotil began to study architecture. He was simultaneously a pianist in various dance orchestras and has devoted himself to compositions and arrangements of dance music.

He is the editor for orchestral edition of dance music at the Publishing House of the Guild of Czechoslovak Composers PANTON.

His best known compositions include ¶ the foxtrots *The Most Beautiful Conductress*, *A Spring Breeze*, *In Unison*, *A Good Idea*; ¶ the slow foxtrots *Played For Us*, *The Place of My Childhood*, *Snow-flakes*, *Autumn Rivers*; ¶ the valses *This Time* and *Dance the Mambo*; ¶ passo doble *Isabella*; ¶ the polka *Všenory Polka*; ¶ the rapid polka *The Merry-go-round*; ¶ the habanera *The Madrid Nights*, *Twist-twist-twist*, *Small Dance Suite*, *A Sad Trumpet*.

Recently, Krotil has composed for brass bands, endeavouring to introduce into this field modern elements of composition and instrumentation.

He lectures on dance music and on arrangements of music for dance orchestras. His book *Arrangements for a Modern Dance Orchestra* (1960, second edition 1963) explains the principles and method of writing arrangements of dance music.

KUBÍN, Rudolf
[born Ostrava, 10 January 1909]
<small>LAUREATE OF THE STATE PRIZE,</small>
holder of the ORDER OF WORK

Kubín belongs among the foremost Czech composers. He was trained in the school of ALOIS HÁBA and his creative work is imbued with social themes of the people of Ostrava.

He was very active in his native region as a contributor of music to radio, as director of Ostrava Conservatory and as chairman of the Ostrava branch of the Guild of Czechoslovak Composers.

Stage Works

He is the author of the first Czech radio opera *A Summer Night* (1930—31, première the Prague Radio in 1931), *Our Swaggerers* (1946, première in Ostrava 1949) and *Men of the Glades* (1951, première in Ostrava 1954), an opera set to Wallachian folk songs; all demonstrate his endeavours to create a new type of folk opera.

Kubín has composed as well a one-act dramatic pantomime *The Intruder* (1931), a ballet *A Fairytale About a Millionaire who Stole the Sun* (1955) and several operettas (plays with songs and dances): *Three Musketeers* (1930), *A Bridegroom from the Prairie* (1930), *A Cavalier* (1932), *The Circus of Life* (1933), *The Rustic Count* (1946), *The Rails of Youth* (1948—49) and *Heva from the Beskids*

(1955—57); his operetta *A Lass from the Colony* (a miners' suburb), set in mining surroundings (1942, reworked 1955) achieved exceptional popularity.

Orchestral and Instrumental Works

His *Sinfonietta* for full orchestra and organ (1936) is his most effective work from the period prior to the Second World War; it was inspired by the suggestive verses *I* by PETR BEZRUČ. The same year he composed the *Overture* to the unfinished opera The Song of Coal. His later orchestral compositions were the *Miners' Suite*, *Maryčka Magdónova*, set to a poem by PETR BEZRUČ (1950) and *In the Beskid Mountains* (1953).

His compositional work up to the present attained a climax in his monumental cycle of five symphonic poems *Ostrava* (1951), in which he expressed his enthusiasm at the liberation of Ostrava by the Red Army and pictured the social exploitation of the past (Maryčka Magdónova), the vigorous post-war efforts to build-up new conditions of life (Ostrava), the beauty of his native land and the indomitable strength of its people (In the Beskid Mountains) and finally the great perspectives of future Ostrava—the steel heart of the Republic; this work was awarded a State Prize (1952).

In an untraditional manner Kubín handled the subject and the form of the instrumental *Concerto for trombone* (1936), *Concerto for violin* (1940), *Concerto for clarinet* (1941), *Concerto for accordion* with small orchestra (1950) and *Concerto for violoncello* (1961).

He composed a *Sinfonia concertante* for four French horns and strings (1937), a *Moravian Rhapsody* (1942) and a *Suite* for chamber orchestra (1945).

Vocal Music

Songs: Kubín has created significant works based on mining themes. The song *Ostrava*, set to words by PETR BEZRUČ, for baritone with piano accompaniment (1932) expresses the hard lot of the Ostrava miner in a capitalistic society. This is closely connected with his medley of Silesian, Lach and Wallachian folk songs. *The Recruits* for vocal octet with accompaniment by nine instruments and accordion (1936) and a cycle of Wallachian folk songs *Little Songs of Trojanov* (two parts, 1956 and 1958) are depicting the life in his native region. His *Songs of Polish Miners* (1957) and *Songs of English Miners* (1958), both for baritone and alto with orchestra accompaniment, attracted considerable attention.

Successful was also his cycle of songs *It's Worth-while to Live*, set to words by E. F. BURIAN (1958).

His community song *I Am a Miner and Who is More* became very popular in all coal mining regions; it is now the signature tune of the Ostrava Radio Station.

Children choir *Tears and Smiles* with small orchestra or with four hand piano (1936) shows his understanding for small children.

Mixed choir *From a Silesian Village* with orchestra (1935) pictures the life in mountaineous regions.

Cantatas: Kubín has written several cantatas of noteworthy value. His native region is depicted in *About Nature and Love*, set to Wallachian text and tunes for solo voices and small orchestra (1935), in a Wallachian cantata *At the Fountain* (1936) and in a Wallachian pastorale *The Shepherd* (1937).

Shocked by a mining catastrophy at Petřvald (1937) he composed the miners' cantata *The Pit Progress*.

Various

He composed many instrumental, chamber music and orchestral compositions, scenic music and musical accompaniments to films, songs and choirs, as well as marches and dance music.

KUČERA, Václav

[born Prague, 29 April 1929]

After completing the secondary school, Kučera studied at Charles University; first musical education and then musical science and aesthetics. In 1951 he was granted a scholarship for the study of musical science and composition at the Moscow Conservatory, where he was a pupil of J. V. SHEBALIN.

After his return he became editor of symphonic music, then editor-in-chief of foreign music at the Czechoslovak Radio in Prague and later scientific secretary of the Cabinet for the study of contemporary music at the Guild of Czechoslovak Composers. Since the foundation of the Institute for Musicology at the Czechoslovak Academy of Sciences (in February 1962) he has been in charge of the section for musical aesthetics. At present he occupies the post of scientific secretary of the Institute.

Compositions

His compositional work includes a sonata for violin and piano *The Distant Home* (1955), a song cycle *Songs of the Earth* for baritone and piano set to words of S. K. NEUMANN (1955), a full-length dance drama with Jánošík theme *The Brigand's Fire* (1956—58), a one-act ballet *A Festival Fairy-tale* (1959), a cycle of children's choirs with accompaniment by a wind quintet *Shine on, Oh Sun!* (1960), musical choreographic scenes *The Revolution Victorious* (1961), *A Joyous Day* (1961), the *Dramatas* for nine instruments (1961), a *Symphony* (1962), a four-movement cycle for violin, piano and timpani *Protests*, inspired by the struggle of Negroes for freedom and civil rights in the American South (1963).

Recently, he has composed a *Slovak Dance Suite* for symphonic orchestra, a stereophonic concertino *Modern Rat-catcher* for flute and two chamber orchestras (1964) and *Genesis*, a one-movement duo for flute and harp (1965, première Warsaw 1965).

Writings

In his diploma work Kučera studied Leoš Janáček's relationship to Moravian folk music culture (1956, in Russian). He also wrote a number of monographs of composers (Prokofief, Scriabin, Dallapiccola, Stravinsky, Bartók, Kabalevsky) and elaborated a selection of letters, documents and memoirs of contemporaries on M. P. Mussorgsky (called *Music of Life*, 1959). In his book *Talent, Mastership, World Conception* (1962) he gave a concise picture of the birth and development of Soviet music, supplemented by his *Microencyclopedia of Soviet Musicians and Musical Institutions*; further he has written a study *The Artistic Picture in Music* (1965).

As a critic he devotes himself mainly to problems of contemporary music in Czechoslovakia and abroad.

KUNC, Jan

[born Doubravice, 27 March 1883]

After graduation from the Janáček School for Organists, Kunc studied composition at the Prague Conservatory under Karel Stecker and Karel Knittl and privately with Vítězslav Novák.

He was a teacher at an elementary school in Brno, but at the same time taught singing at secondary schools and reading of scores and instrumentation at the School for Organists.

He considerably affected the musical life in Brno and in Moravia as a result of his articles on music in newspapers, in The Musical Review and other periodicals.

He was the first biographer of Leoš Janáček.

Kunc was active as well as accompanist and reciter. During the season of 1918—19 he was accompanist and from 1919 conductor at the Prague National Theatre. As of 1919—20 he became secretary and professor of composition at the Brno Conservatory and later its administrator and director. Due to his exemplary organizational and pedagogic work he built up the Brno Conservatory into an outstanding institution. During the occupation of Czechoslovakia, his undaunted character and courage were noteworthy. After the liberation he became professor in composition and dean at the Janáček Academy of Musical Arts; at the same time he lectured at the Faculty of Pedagogy at the Brno University (up to the end of the school year 1951—52).

For his constructive activity at the Conservatory he was awarded The Prize of Liberation of the City of Brno.

Compositions

A survey of his compositional activity, where we find the influence of KŘÍŽKOVSKÝ, JANÁČEK and NOVÁK, shows the following picture:

Instrumental and orchestral compositions (including chamber music works)—*Piano Sonata*, op. 1 (1903), *Piano Trio*, op. 3 (1905); even prior to Janáček, he set to music the socially outspoken poem by PETR BEZRUČ *Seventy Thousand*, op. 8 (1907); then he composed the socially conceived choir *Ostrava*, op. 11 (1912) and the symphonic poem *The Song of Youth*, op. 12 (1915—16). A climax was reached in his work by the ballad for alto and orchestra entitled *Catty Stood at the Danube*, op. 14 (1918—19).

In his work Kunc has closely associated himself with the folk song as is evidenced by his *Chronicle* for piano, op. 23 (twenty variations on Slovak folk song, 1926).

Songs: *Molinburg Songs*, op. 6 (1905), *Moravian Slovak Folk Songs*, op. 18 (1922—23), *Thirty Five Folk Songs of Moravian Slovakia* for three-four voice female choir (1960) and others.

Dances: *Czech Dances* (1947), *Folk Dances of Líšeň* [the suburb of Brno] (1950) and *Children's Dances of Líšeň* (1954).

His unfinished symphonic poem *Life of a Worker* and

KUNC

the opera *The Lady from the Seashore*, at which he is now working, indicate the path Kunc has taken in order to be able to consummate his ideological intentions and compositional technique.

A number of song cycles, choirs, piano miniatures and several scenic compositions complete a characterization of Kunc's personality as a composer.

KUPKA, Karel

[born Rychvald, 19 June 1927]

Kupka studied music at the Ostrava Music School under F. M. HRADIL, violin at the Prague Conservatory and composition at the Conservatory in Brno under JAROSLAV KVAPIL and VILÉM PETRŽELKA. Since 1951 he has been assistant conductor at the Ostrava Theatre.

Stage Works

Kupka has devoted himself intensively to musical-dramatic work as witnessed by his stage works:

Operas: one-act opera *The Joker*, according to PLAUTUS (1955), *Lysistrata* according to ARISTOPHANES (1957, second version 1958), *When Roses Dance*, according to the play by PETROV (1961, première in Ostrava 1962), *The Death of Socrates*, on his own libretto, according to the play by GUILHERM FIGUEIREDE (1963) and an opera for Television *My Love*, according to the theme of MARIE DŮRASOVÁ (1963).

Ballets: *The Death of Jánošík* (1950), *Florella* (1959, première in Ostrava 1960), and *Cassandra* to a libretto by GÜNTHER RÜCKER (1963).

Chamber Music

He composed three *String Quartets* (1956, 1958, 1960), *Partita* for strings (1957), *A Suite in the Baroque Style* for

271

chamber orchestra (1957) and *Sinfonietta* for chamber orchestra (1961).

Orchestral Works

Double Concerto for two orchestras and organ (1944), an orchestral overture *The Nature* (1953), a symphonic picture *The Shafts* (1955), a suite *Picassiada* for full orchestra [on PICASSO's drawings to the *Metamorphoses* by OVIDIUS] (1958), *An Ode on a Joyous Tomorrow* for full orchestra (1959), *Piano Concerto* (first in 1951, second in 1961) and a *Sinfonietta* for full orchestra (1962).

Vocal Works

He has written a cantata *The Native Land* for mixed choir and orchestra (1953) and a cantata on the new *Metallurgical Works Klement Gottwald* for solos, mixed choir and orchestra to words by JAROSLAV NOHAVICA (1959).

KUPKOVIČ, Ladislav

[born Bratislava, 17 March 1936]

Kupkovič graduated from the violin section of the High School of Musical Arts in Bratislava. He is a member of Slovak Philharmonic; he devotes himself at the same time to conducting as a manager of the ensemble for new music, founded by him under the name THE MUSIC OF TODAY.

He is an autodidact in composition and belongs to the most active elements of his generation in Slovakia. He composes in the intentions of the postserial European avantgarde. Several of his compositions were performed at international festivals (Warsaw, Vienna, Venezia).

The most important of his compositions are *Dialogues* for flute and bassoon (1961), the impression of the picture painted by MIKULÁš MEDEK *"Flesh of the Cross"* (1962),

Answers without Questions for three flutes and tamtam (1962), a *Sketch* for six players (1962) and *Décoltage* [the second impression for chambre ensemble] (1964).

Kupkovič composes as well the film and scenic music.

KVAPIL, Jaroslav

[born Fryšták, 21 April 1892—died Brno, 18 February 1958]

MERITED ARTIST

Kvapil studied at the Janáček's School for Organists in Brno. His musical education was completed at the Leipzig Conservatory under MAX REGER, HANS SITT and ROBERT TEICHMÜLLER.

He played a significant role in the development of musical life in Brno and in Moravia as a pianist, choirmaster of the Philharmonic Society Beseda in Brno, with which he presented cantatas by Czech and foreign authors, and as composer and pedagogue. At the Brno Conservatory and at the Janáček's Academy of Musical Arts he trained many composers.

Symphonic and chamber music is the core of his extensive creative work, supplemented by his vocal compositions, written in an individual manner.

Stage Works

He wrote a three-act opera *The Fairy-tale of May*, to a libretto by FRANTIŠEK KOŽÍK and BOHUMÍR POLÁCH, according to the novel of the same name by VILÉM MRŠTÍK (1940—43, première in Prague 1950, reworked in 1955, première in Brno 1955).

Orchestral Works

His best works came into being in close connection with the life of the nation. This is shown in his symphonies: *First Symphony* (1913—14, performed in Brno

1929), *Second Symphony* (1921, performed in Brno 1922), *Third Symphony* (1936—37, performed in Brno 1937)and *Fourth Symphony* called *Victorious* (1943, performed in Brno 1945).

His symphonic and orchestral works which deserve to be mentioned: *Violin Concerto* with orchestra (1927—28); during the German occupation he created the symphonic variations *From Anxious Times* (1939), then a *Jubilee* (Slavonic) *Overture* (1944), a symphonic poem *Dawn* (1948), a *Violin Concerto* with orchestra (1952) and a *Piano Concerto* with orchestra (1954).

Chamber Music and Instrumental Works

Piano Trio (1912), *String Quartet* No. 1 (1914), *Piano Quintet* (1914—15), *Wind Quintet* (1925), *String Quartet* No. 2 (1926), *Variations* on his own theme for trumpet with piano (1929), *Suite* for trombone with piano (1930), *String Quartet* No. 3 (1931), *Intimate Pictures* for violin with piano (1934), *String Quartet* No. 4 (1935), *Wind Quintet* No. 2 (1935), *Burlesque* for chamber orchestra (1935), *Pastoral Suite* for clarinet and piano (1944), *Nonet* (1944), *Burlesque* for flute (1944), *Quartet* for flute, violin, viola and violoncello (1948), *Duo* for violin and viola (1949), *String Quartet* No. 5 (1949), *String Quartet* No. 6 (1951), *Oboe Concerto* (1951) and *Suite* for viola with piano (1955).

Spring Violin Sonata No. 1 with piano (1910), *Piano Sonata* (1910—12), *Violoncello Sonata* (1913), *Violin Sonata* No. 2 with piano (1914), piano cycle *In the Valley of Lament and Grief* (1922), *Piano Sonata* No. 2 (1925), *Violin Sonata* with organ (1931), *Organ Fantasy* in E minor (1935), *Violin Sonata* No. 3 with piano (1937), *Violin Sonatina* (1941), *Fantasy* (1942), *Piano Sonata* No. 3 (1946), *Piano Fantasy* in the form of variations (1952), *Sonatina* for piano (1956).

Vocal Works

Kvapil composed many songs (*The Spring Night* (1920)

set to a poem by OTAKAR BŘEZINA), choirs, cantatas (*A Song on Time That Is Passing*, set to words by ANDRÉ SUARÈS, 1924; in his oratorio *The Lion's Heart* (1930—31) Kvapil solemnized the building-up of the Czechoslovak State; *Italian Cantata* set to words by MILAN KUNDERA, 1950).

KYRAL, Vilém

[born Parník, 16 August 1909—died Prague, 26 September 1961]

Kyral acquired a basic musical education at a school of music at Pardubice; then he studied composition at the Prague Conservatory under OTAKAR ŠÍN.

He taught singing at a secondary school at Česká Třebová, was active in the cultural section of the Trade Unions and in the Army, occupied the position of instructor of youth music ensembles and was the programme editor of band music at the Radio.

In his creative work he tied up with the popular tradition established by FRANTIŠEK KMOCH (1848—1912) in the field of Czech folk music. He composed ¶ mazurkas *Marietta and Miluška, The Vinohrady Polka* and *The Grandmother's Polka*; ¶ the valses *Autumn Blossoms, A Spring Fairy-Tale* and *Gay Musicians*; ¶ the marches *In the Glare of the Davy Lamp, Strahov 1948, Merrily Forward, The Sport March*, two funereal marches and others. His ¶ polka *Brigade Workers' Polka* has become very popular.

From his more extensive compositions we mention ¶ the dance suite *In Three-Four Rhythm*, ¶ the suite *From the Native Region, Grand Overture, Kraslice Overture* and *The Festival March*.

A Potpourri of the *Melodies of Vilém Kyral* was published in 1960.

LANGER, Adolf

[born Rejchartice, 11 June 1910]

Langer studied law in Prague and simultaneously music at the German Academy of Music from which he graduated as an instrumentalist. He then appeared in various ensembles and later led a dance and light music orchestra. After the Second World War he supplemented his studies in composition under JAROSLAV ŘÍDKÝ.

He is active as composer, pedagogue and translator. As composer he has turned his attention to dance and light music: *On a Rocking Horse*, *A Dance of Machines*, *Clarinets in Love*, *Syncopation*, *Light Fingers*, *Clarinets in Mood*, *The Joker*; the gallop *The Artists*, the mazurka *May I Have this Dance*. Langer's work ties with folk tradition as witness his *Loquacious Polka*, *The Grandfather's Valse*, *Gladly Do I Return*; the variety valse *The Lusty One*, *The March of Motorists*, *Remembrance*.

His newer compositions include: *Every Day Is a Première*, *It's Always My Fault*, *The Rose and the Words*, *It's Easy to Sing*; the chanson *When Sport, then Sport*, the jazz song *Dixieland in the Cosmos*; the march *The Gay Holidaymakers* and others.

His pedagogic publications are significant as well, as for instance *A Modern School for the Piano-Accordion*, *Scales and Chords*, *The Chords of the Scale*, *Variations for Accordion* and an *Instructive Aid for Self-taught Accordionists*.

He has arranged numerous dance and variety compositions for piano-accordion. For children he has revised an instructive book *The Young Virtuoso and Musical Cards*, and has written as well a *School for the Mouth Harmonica* (with E. MACH) and an information booklet about a two- and four-stop mouth harmonica. Furthermore he has elaborated a theoretical treatise on whole-tone clavichord from the point of view of the technique and composition.

Langer has translated into German a number of Czech musical methods, prefaces, analyses and others, as well as numerous songs for World Festivals of Youth. Under the pseudonym MARTIN TRENK, he has translated into German the texts of the most popular Czech dance songs, thus contributing to the propagation of Czech dance music abroad.

LENSKÝ, Ctibor

[born Bratislava, 2 March 1908]

In addition to his work as an attorney, he was one of the first composers in Slovakia to devote himself to the writing of dance music. He is one of the creators of the "Slovak tango". His most successful compositions include ¶ the tangos *Why Don't You Love Me a Little* and *It Was Not by Accident*; ¶ the foxtrot *An Early Evening in Autumn* and ¶ the chanson *The Red Tulip*.

LEOPOLD, Bohuslav

[born Škrdlovice, 6 September 1888—died Prague 12 May 1956]

Leopold studied violin under JOSEF BLOCH during his service in the military band in Budapest, later under F. S. TOPIČ in Lwow and ŠTĚPÁN SUCHÝ in Prague.

On his return to civilian life, he was concertmaster with various orchestras and during the First World War was concertmaster and conductor of the Exposition Orchestra in Budapest. After the war he joined the Šak Philharmonic in Prague. Later he appeared abroad with his own musical ensemble and spent considerable time in Alexandria.

After his return home he devoted himself to composition and to the publishing of music, founding and managing the Filmton Publications; in 1928 he reorganized it into Continental Publications and published compositions of Czech and world classics and of popular composers in the most varied arrangements.

His fantasies set to folk songs (*The Voices of Nations*) brought him world popularity. He revised and arranged compositions as well for foreign publishers.

He himself wrote much dance music, marches, intermezzos and potpourris. His last works include ¶ the marches *Festival, The Line-Up, Company of Honour, Horymír, On the Alert, Attention!, The Start*; ¶ the valses *Ex Libris, Three Graces, Greetings from Teplice*; ¶ the grande valse *Memorial and Panorama*, ¶ the polkas *Playful Clarinets, Daffodil, We Learn by Living, The Polka Leads, Cross Your Heart, When I See You, Maisie, The May Polka, The Gay Polka, Capricious Polka.*

He also wrote the ballet scene *The Woman of Haná* (1952), a *Comedy Overture* (1952), a suite *Festive Music* (divertimento) for 13 brass and percussion instruments (1955), a *Czech Rhapsody* for full orchestra (1955), a *Ballet Suite* (1955) and a concerto composition *Greetings to the Fatherland* (1956) for trombone and orchestra.

He is as well the author of music to JAROSLAV KVAPIL's play *Princess Dandelion*, a *Concerto* for double-bass and orchestra (1952) and of several compositions for solo instruments.

He has written and published *Practical Instrumentation Tables* (1947).

LETŇAN, Julius
[born Krokava, 14 December 1914]

Letňan has had a commercial education but during his studies in Prague he attended classes at the Conservatory of Music, completing later his study of organ at the Bratislava Conservatory.

Initially he held a post as clerk in a bank but in 1949 became administrative director of the Slovak Philharmonic and soon thereafter director of the Slovak Music Fund. At present he is a secretary of the Guild of Slovak Composers and an external teacher at the Slovak Conservatory.

In his compositional work he inclines to vocal and smaller instrumental and instructive genres. His important compositions include a *Sonata* for piano (1954), a small cantata *This Native Land of Ours* (1955) and *Four Patriotic Choirs* (1959).

For children he has composed *Songs About the Váh River* (1961) and a cycle of small orchestral compositions *Miraculous Music* (1962).

He is as well author of numerous folk song arrangements for folklore ensembles and of compositions for physical culture festivals.

LÍDL, Václav
[born Brno, 5 November 1922]

Lídl studied composition at the Prague Conservatory under JAROSLAV KVAPIL.

He has composed music to more than sixty films (*The Czech Carp, Our Primeval Forests, Moravian Gothic, the Przemyslids at Znojmo, The Waves—Language of the Sea, The Law of the Bees, Lada's Swaggerers, The Unextinguished Earth, One Moment—I Shall Put You Through, Attention—the Fox is Calling, Rays and Mirrors, Doubleton Re, Before Spring Came, An Episode of a Night* and *Watercure*), as well as to animated cartoons (the series *Three Men, Anatol, The Struggle for Oil, When I Find a Rose* and *Alice in the Wonderland*) and to full-length films (*The Case Has Not Yet Ended, The Circle* and *The Fear*).

Some of his music to the films has received prizes and awards at film festivals.

In addition, he has composed two *String Quartets*, a *Divertimento* for flute, clarinet and bassoon, a *Romantic Sonata* for violin and piano, *Ten Preludes* for piano, *Children's Choirs* accompanied by piano or small orchestra, an *Overture* for large orchestra, a *Concertino* for clarinet and jazz orchestra and a four-movement *Symphony*.

He composed also several compositions for different types of variety orchestra.

LIESKOVSKÝ, Andrej
[born Hlohovec, 22 November 1913]

Lieskovský is one of the successful authors of Slovak dance music. He studied music privately at first and later at the High School of Pedagogy in Bratislava. He is editor at the Czechoslovak Radio there.

His successful compositions have been written in the folk style, and include ¶ the polkas *The Wiser Gives Way*, *I Know Nothing More Beautiful*, *Don't Be Angry With Me*, *My Dear* and others; he has written as well ¶ popular dance music in more modern style such as *I Shall Kiss You Good Night*; ¶ the rumbas *My Husband and Don Juan*; ¶ the beguine *At the Square* and others.

In addition he composes music for brass bands (*The Myjava Polka*) and for accordion.

LIŠKA, Zdeněk
[born Smečno, 16 March 1922]

Liška ranks among the well-known Czech composers of musical accompaniments to films. He evidences an unusual sense for musical characterization of individuals, situations, humour and parody. The success of his music is due to a considerable degree to his aptitude for the characteristic use of sound media. He writes music to full-length, short and puppet films, to the travel films of HANZELKA and ZIKMUND and for the polyecrans and LATERNA MAGICA.

Recently he has composed music to the full-length films *An Invention of Destruction*, *The Higher Principle*, *A Song About a Gray Pigeon*, *Baron Munchhausen*, *Green Horizons*, *On the Rope*, *Three Golden Hairs of the All-Wise Grandfather*, *Man From the First Century*, *The Midnight Mass* and *Trio Angelos*, *Marketa Lazarová*, *Tales about Children*, *So Near to Heaven*, *Museum of Wonder*, *The Accused*, *The King of Comics*, as well as to numerous short popular-scientific films.

He is the author of music to a serial of twelve short and puppet films *Mister Prokouk at the Office—On a Brigade —Filming—Tempted—An Inventor—A Friend of Animals— In the Country—A Detective—An Acrobat—In Outer Space— An Aeronaut—A Contestant*.

For his music to the film *Death Calls Itself Engelchen* he received a prize in the competition for the best musical work to Czechoslovak full-length films in 1963.

LUCKÝ, Štěpán

[born Žilina, 20 January 1919]

Lucký graduated from the Master School at the Prague Conservatory, section of composition, headed by JAROSLAV ŘÍDKÝ, as well as from the Institute for musicology at Charles University. In addition he studied piano under ALBÍN ŠÍMA and quarter-tone composition under ALOIS HÁBA.

He was active as a music critic, was musical director at the Central Office for Music and Arts and manager of transmissions of Czechoslovak Television. At the musical section of the Academy of Musical Arts, he lectured on television production of operas.

Stage Works

Lucký composed one-act opera *The Midnight Surprise* (1959, première in Prague 1959).

Orchestral Music

In the field of symphonic music, he has created following works up to the present: *The Symphonic Prologue* (1939), the symphonic poem *Mors Imperator* (1940—41), a *Concerto* for violoncello and orchestra (1946), a *Concerto* for piano and orchestra (1947) and the *Orlice Suite* for string orchestra (1951).

Chamber Music

In the sphere of chamber music he has composed: a *Sonata* for piano (1940), a *Sonatina* for piano (1945), *Three Etudes* for quarter-tone piano (1946), a *Divertimento* for three trombones and strings (1946), a *Wind Quintet* (1946), a *Sonata brevis* for violin and piano (1947), *Instructive simple compositions* for string ensembles (1951) and little compositions for children.

Vocal Music

Lucký's vocal music is represented by song-cycles *Nostalgia* (1939—40), *Parting* (1940) and *The Unfinished Songs* (1945), the song *The Beloved One on Guard* (1952) and numerous songs and choirs for children.

Film Music

Lucký is also composer of numerous scenic works for radio plays, the theatre and television. In addition to many compositions to short films he wrote music to the following full-length films: *It's Not Always Cloudy*, *For a Joyous Life*, *One of the Relay Race*, *Unusual Summers*, *The Wedding Hasn't Taken Place Yet*, *After Night Comes Day*,

Jurášek, The Black Flag, The Mystery of Writing, The First and The Last, 105 % Alibi, End of the Journey, Express to Ostrava, The Torches, Birds of Passage, The Cock Frightens Death, Sunday on a Weekday, For Whom Havana Dances, Football and *The Chap*, totally on the Shelf.

LUDVÍK, Emil

[born Prague, 16 August 1917]

Ludvík studied musical science at Charles University in Prague and belongs to the generation which, after the Second World War, tied in with the Czech jazz tradition of E. F. BURIAN, JAROSLAV JEŽEK and of the orchestra of the Gramoklub. In 1939 he organized a students' jazz orchestra.

His compositions, which are an inseparable part of basic Czech jazz repertoire, date from this period; they include *The Congress of Dancers*, ¶ the blues *Tears on Cushions*, ¶ the foxtrot *The Rhythm* and others.

Since the liberation of Czechoslovakia in 1945 he has devoted himself almost exclusively to writing music to the films. His film music up to the present includes more than three hundred scientific-popular films, animated cartoons, medium footage and puppet films and many full-length films, among them the following: *Academician Burian, The Goalkeeper Lives in Our Street, When Photographs Came to Life, When the Film Began to Speak, How to Get to the Spectators, The Czechoslovak Postage Stamp, Materials of Tomorrow, The Mountains Belong to the Courageous, With Play to Work, Karel Svolinský, Where We Look for Joy, A Course for Men, The Shadow, A Course for Women, Little Causes, Little Bobeš, Little Bobeš in Town, A Little Dream, Beyond the Skies, The Right Course, Below Freezing Point, Holidays in the Skies, Crude Oil for Us, The Form and the Purpose, In Deep Waters, The Model Cinema of Jaroslav*

283   **LUDVÍK**

Hašek, From the Life of a Trout, Fossilized Motion and Life in Motion, Into Every Corner of the World.

Ludvík also composed music to many television films and to a number of television scenes, to the variety scenes *A Match for Jacob*, to the theatrical fairy-tale *Come and Make the Princess Smile*, to the comedy by JOSEF KAINAR *The Late Nasredin* and others.

As a musicologist he has collaborated with ANNA HOSTOMSKÁ in writing a guidebook to operatic creative work entitled *The Opera* (the 6th edition in 1965).

MACÁK, Bohumil
[born Prague, 1 January 1927]
LAUREATE OF THE STATE PRIZE

Macák studied organ at the Prague Conservatory under JAN BEDŘICH KRAJS and composition under EMIL HLOBIL and ZDENĚK HŮLA. He was music editor and editor-in-chief of the Central House of the Czechoslovak Army and music editor for the State Publishing House of Music. At present he is the editor of the Publishing House of the Guild of Czechoslovak Composers PANTON.

His activity with dance orchestras and the Ensembles of Folk Art has left an imprint on his creative work. He has written about two hundred arrangements of folk and concert songs for these Ensembles and has also made arrangements of compositions for the accordion (BRAHMS, DVOŘÁK, CHOPIN valses, *An Album of Selected Compositions* of EDVARD GRIEG, *An Album of Old Czech Masters* and others).

In his own original creative work he has directed his attention to music for gymnastic exercises, to songs with youth themes and to dance music. For the First Spartakiad he composed music to the exercises of the Sokols (State Prize 1956); for the second Spartakiad he wrote the signature theme and music to the exercises *Youth-Beauty-Strength*.

Several of his songs have received awards in various competitions.

MACH, Sláva **(Pravoslav)**
[born Kladno, 18 November 1902]

Mach, a well-known composer of popular and dance music, studied flute and piano at the Prague Conservatory. Later he studied composition as a private pupil of ALOIS HÁBA.

He was accompanist, theatrical bandmaster, editor for the publishing house Melantrich and a member of the musical staff of the former gramophone firm ESTA in Prague.

In 1925—45 he composed a number of operettas (*The Desert Blossom, Apolenka Valse, We Have Caught a Salmon, From Czech Breweries, The Princess of Abyssinia, Olden Times, The Spirit of Uncle Jacob, Mrs. Mathilda's Pancakes, Superfluous, Under the Oak, The Vagabond's Heart*) and much dance and incidental music for musical revues.

His *Revolutionary Prague Suite* for orchestra (1945) and the four-part musical poem *The Ancient Czech Legends* for orchestra (1946) date from the period of his studies under ALOIS HÁBA. Mach also composed the ballet *Dawn* (1949), a children's opera *The Friend* (1950), music to the films *The Wife Suspects Something* and *Adam and Eve*, a *Small Dance Suite* (1959), several successful marches such as *The Gay Sailor, The Sport March, There Is Strength in Slavonic Nations, The March of the Victors, Fall In!* and others.

MÁCHA, Otmar

[born Ostrava, 2 October 1922]

Mácha studied composition at the Prague Conservatory and at its Master School under JAROSLAV ŘÍDKÝ. He was the chief dramaturgist for musical programmes at the Czechoslovak Radio in Prague.

Stage Works

He wrote a one-act comic opera called *Entrapped Faithlessness*, based on texts of Czech farces from the beginning of the seventeenth century (1956—57, première in Prague 1958). Recently Mácha has finished the opera *Lake Ukereve* to a text by VLADISLAV VANČURA.

Orchestral Works

His *Symphonic Intermezzos* (1958) and the symphonic poem *Night and Hope* (1959) were awarded in the artistic jubilee competition in 1960. Further we have to note his *Overture, Symphony, Slovak Rhapsody* and *Dances of the Moravian Frontiers* in folk tones, as well as *Variations* for symphonic orchestra, set to theme of JAN RYCHLÍK (1964).

Chamber Music

Chamber music and songs were the stepping stones of his compositional growth. Following the *String Quartet* (1943) and the *Sonata* for violoncello and piano (1944) it was particularly the inventionally fresh *Sonata* for violin and piano (1948) which attracted considerable attention.

Vocal Works

He has written numerous song-cycles, as *Bachelor's Songs*, set to words by FRÁŇA ŠRÁMEK (1945), children's rhymes and adages *The Wild Thyme* (1946), *Songs* to texts of Ukrainian folk poetry (1947), *Songs of Men* (1947),

Letters of Karel Burian (1947), *Fairy-tales* set to prose of
BOŽENA NĚMCOVÁ (1949) and *Folk Ballads* for soprano,
tenor and piano (or orchestra) (1949). Mácha has also
contributed *Children's Choirs* to texts by FRANTIŠEK HALAS
and FRANTIŠEK HRUBÍN (1956) in the field of vocal music.

In 1965 he finished the cantata *About Conscience* to
text by F. X. ŠALDA.

Prizes

For his opera *Lake Ukereve* he was awarded the FIRST
PRIZE in the artistic jubilee competition 1965.

MACOUREK, Karel

[born Báňská Hodruša, 11 April 1923]

Macourck graduated from the section of conducting
at the Prague Conservatory. He studied composition at
Ostrava under JOSEF SCHREIBER and in Prague under
KAREL JANEČEK and VÍTĚZSLAV NOVÁK.

During his studies in Prague he was already active as
pianist, singer, conductor and composer at the Theatre
of Satire. His subsequent activity included that of an
accompanist and chorus-master at the National Theatre,
choirmaster and conductor of the Czechoslovak State
Ensemble of Songs and Dances and the managing editor
of light and dance music at the Czechoslovak Radio.

At present he is a radio dramaturgist and appears as
conductor of light and dance music (for many years
he has been artistic manager of the Ensemble Julius
Fučík).

He has written music to all the comedies performed
by the Theatre of Satire (*The Tin Circus, A Special Edition, Ferda-Matches-Europe, Action Ajbis* and others).

He is author of the dance tragedy *Electra of Our Days*

(1946, première in Prague 1947), of the musical-dance transcription of the folk commentary *The Shopkeeper's Suite* (1946, première at Ústí on Labe 1950), of the cantatas *Glorious Communist Party* set to words by PAVEL KOHOUT (1949) and *About the Czechoslovak Army* to words by KAREL ŠIKTANC (1951), of a cycle of songs to words by PAVEL KOHOUT entitled *Longings* (1955), two *String quartets* (1948 and 1949), the orchestral *Slovak Suite* (1955, awarded the second prize at the Festival of the World Federation of Youth in Warsaw 1955), a *Small Lyrical Suite* (1956), *Three Pieces* for symphonic orchestra (1962), *Love Songs* for saxophone and symphonic orchestra (1963), choirs, scenic music, musical accompaniment to films and to radio plays and musical montages.

Macourek wrote as well ¶ the musical comedies *The Colonel Wants to Sleep*, *Hallo*, *Freddie*, *The Assumption of Colonel Heilig*, *Eternally Young Story* and *Tobacconist John*, ¶ the radio musicale *The Escape of Mister MacKinley*, music to the children's ¶ fairy-tale revue *Strange Adventures of Mister Pimpipun*, to the revue *Golden Prague* (première in Berlin 1958) and to the first Czechoslovak ¶ television musical on theme of the story *Reformation of Jim Valentin by* O'HENRY (1964).

In addition to these compositions Macourek has written many ¶ political and community songs for the Ensemble Julius Fučík; they include *The Smiling Land*, *A Letter to Prague*, *The Song of Pursuit Pilots*, *A Song about the First Satelite*, *A Greeting to the Station at the North Pole*, *Millions on the March*, *Cuba si*, *Let's Try it Otherwise*, *Only People Are Like That* and ¶ the small cantatas *The Country of Peace* and a *Song About Prague*.

Macourek's popular dance music includes ¶ the foxtrots *The Singing Tree*, *A Great Invention*, *Little Train No. 5* and *Clap-Clap*; ¶ the slow foxtrots *The Return Journey*, *The Boy and the Stars*, *A Little Different*, *I Love You*, *When They Play the Charleston*; ¶ the twist *The Curse*; ¶ the bossa-nova *Orion* and others.

He has made a number of arrangements of folk songs.

MACUDZINSKI, Rudolf

[born Opatia, 29 April 1907]

Macudzinski studied composition at the Brno Conservatory (for a short time as a pupil of LEOŠ JANÁČEK). He is a prominent Slovak pianist and piano pedagogue and senior lecturer at the Bratislava High School of Musical Arts. In addition to his intense concert activity, he has devoted himself as well to composition. His compositional interests are many-sided.

He has composed the opera *Monte Christo*, to the libretto by ŠTEFÁN HOZA, according to the novel by ALEXANDER DUMAS (1944—1949), followed up by the symphonic poem *Edmond Dantes* (1949) and *Variazioni Olimpiche* for piano and orchestra (1960).

For chamber music he has written a *Sextet* for wind instruments and piano (1934), *Variations and Fugue* on a theme by P. I. TCHAIKOVSKY for piano trio (1953), a *Slovak Sonata* for violin and piano (1956) and a *Suite* for violoncello and piano (1957).

His creative work for solo piano and two pianos is also relatively extensive. It includes *Five Characteristic Variations* (1934), a *Small Fantasy* (1946), a *Sonatina Monotematica* (1956) and *Pictures from an Exposition "In the Footsteps of Captain Nálepka"* (1959).

He is as well the author of several cycles of songs, small cantatas, arrangements of folk songs, various instructive and performing compositions for young pianists (*Scale Exercises* I., II., *From the Life of the Pioneers*).

MALÁSEK, Jiří

[born Brno, 7 August 1927]

Malásek has been a pianist in the foremost dance and jazz orchestras in Prague and Brno. He also appeared as soloist with the orchestra of Dalibor Brázda. At present he is music dramaturgist at the Czechoslovak Television and a member of the well-known piano duo JIŘÍ MALÁSEK—JIŘÍ BAŽANT.

In his musical creative work he devotes himself to film and scenic music. Mostly in cooperation with JIŘÍ BAŽANT he wrote over sixty music accompaniments to films as *The Defect Is Not In Your Receiver*, *How People Have Captured Motion*, *Noise is the Enemy*, *Where Are We to Play*, *A Castle for Little Barbara*.

He is as well the author of music to the popular television serial stories *The Blahovič Family* and *Three Men in a Cottage*, to the television musical comedy *A Three Minute Chat*, to musical comedies *Lights of the Metropolis* and *The Beautiful Unknown*, of popular songs *I Met a Painter*, *The Cyclist*, *Youth*, *A Song About Jasmine*.

With JIŘÍ BAŽANT and VLASTIMIL HÁLA he composed music for the first Czechoslovak film musical *The Old Hop Pickers*.

MALINA, Jaroslav

[born Hořice, 4 July 1912]

Malina was professor of mathematics at a secondary school in Prague. He studied musical theory under ZDENĚK HŮLA and passed the examinations as a musical pedagogue.

During his university studies in Prague he was a member of the student dance orchestra SMILING BOYS of which he became later the conductor. At that time (1933) he wrote ¶ the rumba *The Pyramid* (played in the Austrian film *The Orient-Express*), ¶ the tangos *Marcella*, *The Beautiful Unknown*, *I Have a Red Rose for You* and others.

In 1938 he founded a dance orchestra with which he recorded many gramophone records and numerous radio programmes. He composed songs for radio revues of which ¶ the slow foxtrot *Devote Yourselves to History* and ¶ the tanganilla *The Song of Man*, ¶ the rumba *Unfaithful Rosita*, ¶ numerous valses and polkas (the popular *Old Czech Music, The Raspberry is Red, The Little Gardener*) have attracted particular attention.

Furthermore he has composed a suite *Pictures of the Countryside*, a cycle of dances *From the Native Region*, an overture *Life in the Menagerie*, a grande valse *Summer Carnival*, the musical comedies *Marriage with Allan* and *Two Steps to Paradise*, an operetta *Summer Holiday*, music to the full-length cabarets *Mister Victorin Fell Asleep, A Vain Marks-woman* and *The Circus Folk* (according to EDUARD BASS), and songs to SCRIBE's comedy *Women's Weapons*.

He has also written *The Exhibition March*, music to the revue *Laugh With Us*, the chansons *My Umbrella and I, An Advertisement, Quiet Please, Tomorrow This Time*.

MALOVEC, Jozef
[born Hurbanovo, 24 March 1933]

Malovec studied composition at the High School of Musical Arts under ALEXANDER MOYZES and at the Academy of Musical Arts under JAROSLAV ŘÍDKÝ and VLADIMÍR SOMMER. At present he is active as musical advisor at the Czechoslovak Radio in Bratislava.

His creative work up to the present has been relatively inextensive but has indicated a significant talent, developing as it has to a more highly concentrated instrumental expression. In contradistinction to his graduation work *The Overture* for orchestra (1957) his later compositions (particularly *Two Parts* for orchestra, 1962) show a tendency towards the dodecaphonic style. His other works include a *Scherzo* for orchestra, two piano *Sonatinas*, a *Cassation* for wind quintet, a *Small chamber music* (1964), music to films, to radio and stage plays. Occassionally he composes music to dance songs as well.

MARAT, Zdeněk

[born Prague, 15 February 1931]

After completion of the secondary school he became editor of the cultural section of the Czechoslovak News Agency. He graduated from the department of composition and conducting of the Prague Conservatory under EMIL HLOBIL and BOHUMIL ŠPIDRA.

During his studies he was conductor of youth ensembles and led a dance orchestra. His first dance music and chansons date from this period (the slow foxtrot *Confessions* and the popular foxtrot *A Vain Tulip*).

After completion of his studies he became editor of musical programmes at the Czechoslovak Radio in Prague and conductor of the String Dance Orchestra. At present he is artistic chief and conductor of the dance orchestra of the Prague Cultural Centre and also collaborates with the dramatic section of the National Theatre in Prague as conductor.

Marat has composed numerous songs for community singing and much dance music, as *May Is Ours*, *My Love*, *Smoke of Home*, *Once During the Night*; ¶ the foxtrots: *A Good Counsel*, *She Called Me Francis*, *Not Yet*, *Hallo Moon*, *Does He Love or Does He Not*, *When Rivers Flow Backwards*, *A Song about a Cockleshell* (which won the television competition), *Songs for Tomorrow*, *The New Year Valse*; ¶ the musical comedy *The Six Wives of Viktor Jandeček*, music to several short films, radio plays and cabarets.

MARTINČEK, Dušan

[born Prešov, 19 June 1936]

A member of the young generation of composers, Martinček at first concentrated on the study of piano at the Bratislava Conservatory under ANNA KAFEN- DOVÁ. He broadened his study of composition after private instruction by JÁN CIKKER and JÁN ZIMMER at the High School of Musical Arts, graduating in composition (JÁN CIKKER) and in piano (RUDOLF MACUDZINSKI).

He is active as assistant at the Pedagogical Institute at Trnava where he lectures on music theory.

Martinček's creative work draws markedly on impulses stimulated by piano which he endeavours to present in a new, unconventional manner. His models are the great personalities of modern piano composition such as A. N. SCRIABIN, S. V. RACHMANINOV, BÉLA BARTÓK and D. D. SHOSTAKOVICH.

He creates mostly for piano, the element of virtuosity being dominated by seeking for new colour and harmonic possibilities: *Rhapsody* for piano and orchestra, *Six Etudes*, *Three Preludes* and *Fugues*, *Poem*, *Two Dances in Bulgarian Rhythm*, *Two Romantic Preludes in memory of A. N. Scriabin* and a concert rhapsody *Negrea*.

Noteworthy are *The Dialogues* in the form of variations for piano and orchestra (1961) and *Simple Overture* (1963).

Martinček has also written a number of chamber music compositions as *Passionato* for viola and piano, *Capriccio* for string quartet and *Forgotten Songs* for baritone and piano.

MARTINŮ, Bohuslav

[born Polička, 8 December 1890—died Liestal, Switzerland, 28 August 1959]

Martinů studied violin at the Prague Conservatory under STĚPÁN SUCHÝ and JINDŘICH BASTAŘ and composition under KAREL STECKER and ONDŘEJ HORNÍK. In

1922, as a violinist of the Czech Philharmonic, he entered the Master School as a pupil of JOSEF SUK.

From the year 1923 he lived in Paris where he studied with ALBERT ROUSSEL.

By tenacious application, he soon made there a position and a name for himself. In 1935, with several of his contemporaries, he formed a composers' group known as ÉCOLE DE PARIS. In 1941, he left France and Europe, remaining throughout the war years in the United States, returning in 1953 to Europe, where he lived alternately in Italy, France and Switzerland.

Martinů ranks among the world-known Czech composers. His creative work is extensive and, similarly to Antonín Dvořák, embraces all fields of music. The French school clarified his sense for tone quality which, with sovereign skill, he blended with expressive Czech musical inspiration.

His path to compositional mastery was accompanied by an ever firmer attachment to the Czech milieu, to Czech intonations and Czech themes. It is an undeniable fact that his artistic selfconfidence found constant sustenance in the simplicity of the enchanted world of the Czech folk song and poetry, imbued with the fragrance of his native land. Striking indeed was his creative reaction to the tragic fate of his native country.

Stage Works

At the very beginning of Martinů's operatic creative work, a courage in experimentation is met with, boldly using new media of stage technique.

This is true of his comic opera *The Soldier and the Dancer*, set to a libretto by J. L. BUDÍN [Jan Löwenbach] (1927, première in Brno, 1928) and his further three operas to librettos by G. RIBEMONT-DESSAIGNES: *Les larmes du couteau* (Tears of a Knife, 1928), *La semaine de bonté* (A Week of Goodness, 1929, unfinished) and *Three Wishes and Vicissitudes of Life* (1929).

The cycle of three plays, *The Miracles of Our Lady*,

set to libretto of H. GHEON (1934, première in Brno 1935), *The Suburban Theatre*, an opera buffa to composer's own libretto (dialogues LEO STRAUSS, 1936, première in Brno 1936) and *Juliette or The Key to Dreams*, to the composer's own libretto, according to a play by G. NEVEUX (1937, première in Prague 1938) represent the climax of Martinů's prewar work.

In the last years of his life, it is the sprightly opera *Mirandolina*, according to CARLO GOLDONI (1953—55, première in Prague 1959), *The Greek Passion*, set to a theme by NICOS KAZANZAKIS (1958, première in Zürich 1961, Brno 1962) and *Ariadna*, according to the play by G. NEVEUX (1958, première in Gelsenkirchen 1961, Brno 1962), which represent the high point in Martinů's operatic creative activity.

His radio and television operas are works of pioneering importance for Czech music: *The Voice of the Forest*, to a libretto by VÍTĚZSLAV NEZVAL (1935, première Czechoslovak Radio 1935), *A Comedy on a Bridge*, according to a play by V. K. KLICPERA (1935, première Czechoslovak Radio in Prague, 1937), *The Marriage*, according to N. V. GOGOL (1952, television première in New York, 1953, in Prague 1960) and *What Men Live By*, according to L. N. TOLSTOY (1952, première in New York 1953, Plzeň 1964).

Martinů's ballet compositions were to a certain extent preparatory to his operatic work. However, it was his later ballet which acquired a particular significance, namely the *The Chap-book* with songs to texts of folk poetry (1932, première in Prague 1933) and *The Judgment of Paris* (1935).

Orchestral Works

Martinů composed six *Symphonies*: the *first* (1942), first performance in Boston 1942, the *second* (1943), first performance in Cleveland 1943, the *third* (1944), first performance in Boston 1945, the *fourth* (1945), first performance in Philadeplphia 1945, the *fifth* (1946), first performance in Prague 1947, and the *sixth* entitled *Symphonical Fantasies* (1953), first performance in Boston 1955.

Martinů has written six *Piano Concertos*: the *first* (1925), first performance in Prague 1925, the *second* (1934), first performance in Prague 1934, the *third* (1948), first performance in Dallas 1949, the *fourth* called *Incantations* (1955—56), first performance in Prague 1957 and the *fifth* (1957) and *Fantasia concertante* (1957). Of his unusually numerous orchestral works the following are of special importance (in chronological sequence): *La Bagarre* (Tumult) composed in Paris (1926), *Violoncello Concerto* No. 1 (1930), *Sinfonia concertante* No. 1 (1932), *The Double Concerto* for two string orchestras, piano and timpani (1938), *Sinfonietta giocosa* for piano and chamber orchestra (1940), *Violin Concerto* (1943), *Concerto* for two pianos and orchestra (1943) and the profoundly contemplative orchestral memorial to *Lidice* (1943), *Violoncello Concerto* No. 2 (1944), *Sinfonia concertante* No. 2 (1949), *Sinfonietta La Jolla* for chamber orchestra and piano (1950), *Oboe Concerto* with orchestra (1955), *Frescos of Pieva della Francesca* (1955), *Parables* (1958) and *Trois Estampes* [Three Prints] (1958).

Chamber Music and Instrumental Works

Similarly Martinů's chamber music creative work can be indicated only in a selection: *String Quartet* No. 1 (1918), *String Trio* No. 1 (1923), *Nonet* No. 1 (1924), *String Quartet* No. 2 (1925), *String Quintet* (1927), *String Quartet* No. 3 (1929), *Violin Sonata* No. 1 (1929), *Sonatina* for two violins and piano (1930), *Piano Trio* No. 1 (1930), *Serenade* No. 1, sextet (1932), *Serenade* No. 2 for two violins and viola (1932), *Violin Sonata* No. 2 (1931), *Serenade* No. 3, septet (1932), *Sonata* for two violins and piano (1932), *Piano Quintet* No. 1 (1933), *String Trio* No. 2 (1934), *String Quartet* No. 4 (1937), *Violin Sonatina* (1937), *String Quartet* No. 5 (1938), *Nonet* No. 2 (1939), *Violoncello Sonata* No. 1 (1939) and No. 2 (1941), *Piano*

Quartet (1942), *Violin Sonata* No. 3 (1944), *Piano Quintet* No. 2 (1944), *Sonata* for flute and piano (1945), *String Quartet* No. 6 (1946) and No. 7 (1947), *Piano Trio* No. 3 (1950), *Serenade* No. 4 for violin, viola, violoncello and two pianos (1951), *Violoncello Sonata* No. 3 (1952), *Sonata* for viola and piano (1955), *Sonatina* for clarinet and piano (1956) and *Sonatina* for trumpet and piano (1956).

Martinů's creative work for piano is extensive as well and includes the cycle *The Puppets* (from his youth), *Three Czech Dances* (1926), the cycle of seven *Czech dances Borová* (1929), *Fantasy* for two pianos (1929), *Preludes* (1929), *Fantasy and Toccata* (1940), *Polkas and Etudes* (1945), *Three Czech Dances* for two pianos (1949) and *Sonata* (1954).

Vocal Works

Vocal compositions are represented by large oratorios and cantatas, as well as by smaller vocal forms.

V o i c e s : a cycle of compositions for solos, mixed and children's choir and orchestra *The Bouquet,* set to words of folk poetry (1937), duet *The Opening of Wells,* set to Moravian folk poetry (1955) and *The Legend of the Smoke from the Potato-tops* (1957);

S o n g s : Eight songs set to words of Moravian folk poetry *New Chap-book* (1942), further *Little Songs for one Page* (1943) and *Little Songs for Two Pages* (1944).

M a l e choirs: *The Prophecy of Isaiah* for male choir and instrumental ensemble (1939) and *Brigands' Songs* for male choir to words of folk poetry (1956).

C a n t a t a s : *Dandelion Romance* (1957) and *Mikeš from the Mountains* (1959);

M a d r i g a l s : *Madrigal* No. 1 for female voices (1939), No. 2 for mixed voices (1948) and No. 3 for five voices (1959), all set to words of Moravian folk poetry.

O r a t o r i o : *Gilgamesh,* according to an ancient Babylonian epos (1955).

Film Music

Martinů composed as well music to VLADISLAV VANČURA's film *Faithless Marijka*, according to the novel by IVAN OLBRACHT.

MÁSLO, Jindřich
[born Čistá, 11 April 1875—died Prague, 22 June 1964]

Máslo studied composition under BOHUMIL WENDLER and VÍTĚZSLAV NOVÁK. He was active as a teacher in Prague and was simultaneously the choirmaster of the Prague choral societies LUMÍR and HLAHOL. It was he who initiated and organized printing of music in Prague.

He composed a number of orchestral works, among them the following: *The Symphony* in A minor (1905—06), a four-movement suite *From Our Village* (1907), a *Dance Suite* (1937), a *Festive March* and a *March of the Victors* (1946), a *Violin Concerto* in A major (1951), *Piano Concerto* in D minor (1952), a *Serenade* for string orchestra (1953), four polkas, five miniatures, *A Small Suite* and others.

His chamber music work includes two *String quartets* (1903 and 1915), *Trio* in D major for piano, violin and violoncello (1916), a *Duo* for oboe and bassoon (1938), a cycle of piano compositions *In a Bright Light* and *At Dusk* and compositions for violoncello with piano or orchestra (*Humoresque*, *Lullaby*, *Elegy*, *Serenade*, *Allegretto*, *Barcarola*).

Máslo composed as well the music to the children's Christmas play of K. V. RAIS *In a Lone Cottage* (1922), a one-act opera *Children of the Mountains* (1932—33), four songs *To the Memory of K. H. Mácha* with piano or orchestral accompaniment (1935) and several male and female choirs.

He rearranged and extended the *Ferdinand Bayer*

School for Piano (1919) and wrote a number of instructive piano compositions of which *Remembrances from Childhood Years* were published in 1917 in Germany as well. For beginning violinists he wrote three books of instructive compositions called *Encouragement* (1920). He also gained recognition as a music arranger.

MAŠTALÍŘ, Jaroslav
[born Karviná, 1 May 1906]

Maštalíř studied composition under K. B. JIRÁK and VÍTĚZSLAV NOVÁK and conducting under PAVEL DĚDEČEK and VÁCLAV TALICH.

He was chief of the archives of the Prague Conservatory and at present is active there as a pedagogue. He is an excellent piano accompanist.

His creative work embraces practically every field of music.

Stage Works and Melodramas

He composed a ballet entitled *Sasha* (1948) and two melodramas to words by MIROSLAV HALLER— *A Picture in a Tin Pitcher* (1960) and *Weeping Snowdrops* (1961).

Orchestral Works and Chamber Music

He has written orchestral *Variations* No. 1 (1931), *Symphony* No. 1 (1932), *Piano Concerto* (1932), *Concertino* for harp with orchestra (1933), *Violin Concerto* (1934), *Piano Concerto* (1934), *Toccata* for organ with orchestra (1934), orchestral *Variations* No. 2 (1935), *Concerto* for French horn and orchestra (1936), *Concerto* for two French horns and orchestra (1936), *Symphony* No. 2

MAŠTALÍŘ

(1936), *Scherzo* for orchestra (1936), orchestral *Variations* No. 3 and 4 (both 1937), *Concertino* for oboe and orchestra (1937), *Symphony* No. 3 (1940), *Concertino elegiaco* for clarinet and orchestra (1950), *Fantasy* for trombone with orchestra (1952), two *Concertos* for accordion with orchestra (1956 and 1958), symphonic picture for full orchestra and organ *Vita brevis, ars longa* (1961), *Serenade* for a Young Bassoon Player, for bassoon with orchestra (1962) and *Nocturne* for French horn and orchestra (1962).

String Quartet No. 1 (1931), *Violoncello Sonata* (1931), *Wind Quintet* No. 1 (1933), *Nonet* (1935), *Suite* for string quartet and organ (1935), *String Quartet* No. 2 (1935), *Serenade* for eight French horns (1937), *Wind Quintet* No. 2 (1941), *Concerto* per il cembalo con accompagnamento d'orchestra da camera (1942), *Concertino* pastorale per il organo con accompagnamento d'orchestra d'archi (1942), *Wind Quintet* No. 3 (1943), *Quintet* for French horn and string quartet (1944), *Violin Sonata* No. 1 (1946), *String Trio* (1946), *Violin Sonata* No. 2 (1953), three *Compositions* for bassoon and piano (1955), *Sonatina classica* for violin and piano (1957), *Prelude and Rondo* for harp and strings (1957), *Ballad* for tuba and piano (1958), *Capriccio* for viola and piano (1958), *Concertino* for violin and viola with piano (1958), *Small Overture for Youth* for small orchestra (1959), *Variation Fantasy* on a Moravian Christmas Song (1960), *Concertino* for double-bass and piano (1961), *Variations* for themes of GIOACHINO ROSSINI (1962), *Fugue* for bassoon and piano (1962), *Quartet* for double-basses (1962) and *Variations* for double-bass and piano (1963).

Vocal Works

Maštalíř did considerable work in the field of vocal music as proved by his many cycles of songs, choirs and arrangements of folk songs, as *Five Slovak Songs* (1962) and *Seven Slovak Songs* for violoncello and string orchestra (1963).

Arrangements and Instrumentations

He is the author of a suite from Henry PURCELL's opera *King Arthur*, two *Scarlattinas* for string orchestra and instrumentations of classical concertos, as J. F. GALLAY: *Concerto* for French horn; KAREL STAMIC: *Concerto* for viola and orchestra; JOHANN CHRISTIAN BACH: *Concerto* in C minor for violoncello and orchestra; ANTONIO VIVALDI: *Concerto* in a minor for violin and orchestra and *Concerto* for four violins with orchestra.

MATĚJ, Josef

[born Brušperk, 19 February 1922]

Matěj studied organ under J. B. KRAJS and composition under EMIL HLOBIL and ZDENĚK HŮLA at the Prague Conservatory. At the Academy of Musical Arts he continued his study of composition under JAROSLAV ŘÍDKÝ.

His compositional development has to a considerable extent been influenced by his extensive work as an instrumentalist. This is evidenced by such compositions as *Two Concertos* for trombone, a *Sonata* for oboe and chamber orchestra, *Bagatelles* for oboe, a *Concertino* for trumpet and several compositions for brass bands.

Other works by Matěj include a cantata *The Choral Song* for full orchestra, solos and chorus, *Jewish Folk Poetry* for chamber choir (1964), nine symphonic dances, two serenades for chamber orchestra, two symphonies and numerous compositions in the field of popular music.

His *Second Symphony* (1959—60) was inspired by the novel of FRANZ WERFEL, Forty Days, and received an award in the artistic jubilee competition in 1960. In 1961 Matěj completed his *Viola Concerto*, in 1962 a *Concerto* for violin and orchestra, *Intermezzos* for flute and piano, the *Kazak Intermezzo* for string orchestra, piano and percussion instruments, an extensive *Informatorium* for wind instruments (1964) and *Concerto* for cornet and chamber orchestra (1964).

In his compositions Josef Matěj strives for a convincing melodic and individual expression based on folk music of his native Lach region in Moravia.

●

For his *Concerto* for violin and orchestra he was awarded a PRIZE in the artistic jubilee competition 1965.

MATUŠKA, Janko
[born Liptovský Hrádok, 25 October 1897—died Bratislava, 16 August 1959]
MERITED ARTIST, LAUREATE OF THE STATE PRIZE

After graduation from the Bratislava Music and Dramatic Academy where he studied piano under ERNEST KRIŽAN and FRICO KAFENDA, he held a post at the radio, first in Košice and later in Bratislava, where he was active as pianist and music manager.

Matuška was conductor of the ensemble TATRAN, a group which devoted itself to the interpretation of Slovak folk songs and he arranged many of them for this ensemble.

Slovak folklore became the inspirational source for his numerous orchestral compositions. Matuška's optimism, good humour and understanding of the atmosphere of folk legends as well as his almost childlike conception of life around us found expression in his suites *Joy to Children* and *In a Slovak Cottage* and in piano compositions for youth such as *A Devil in the Chimney*, *The Musical Clock*, *Humoresque*, *The Hare and the Gamekeeper* and others.

His cycles of songs and choirs for children are equally attractive melodically and include *Hviezdoslav to the Youth*, *Spring*, *A Tree in Full Blossom*.

Matuška's concert valses have gained great popularity due to their frequent recordings on the radio (*Forest Flowers, The Ice Queen*) as is true as well of his characteristic compositions (*At a Chinese Clockmaker*), intermezzos (*The Dance of Nymphs*) and of his suites (*From Our Mountains*).

His most momentous works are melodramas based on social poems by Slovak poets (*Zuzanka Hraškovie* set to words by P. O. HVIEZDOSLAV, *The Orphans* to a text by LUDMILA PODJAVORINSKÁ).

MATYS, Jiří

[born Bakov, 27 October 1927]

Matys acquired his musical education at the Brno Conservatory where he graduated from the organ class of FRANTIŠEK MICHÁLEK. In composition he graduated from the class of JAROSLAV KVAPIL at the Janáček Academy of Musical Arts. He became a lecturer at the Janáček Academy and later headmaster of a music school in Brno.

Orchestral Works

In the orchestral field he composed a *Symphony*, op. 11 (1951) and *Morning Music* for string orchestra, trumpets and percussion instruments, op. 33 (1961—62).

Melodramas: a symphonic picture *To those Fallen in May 1945* to words by JAN ALDA, op. 7 (1949), *The Lyrical Melodrama*, set to words by JOSEF KAINAR, op. 22 (1957) and *Variations on Death* for string quartet, French horn and recitation of poems by MILAN KUNDERA, op. 27 (1959).

Chamber Music and Instrumental Works

In his compositional work he has devoted himself primarily to chamber music. This orientation is demonstrated by following compositions: *Sonata* for French horn and piano, op. 2 (1948), *Fantasy* for string orchestra, op. 4 (1949), *Quartet* with flute, op. 5 (1949), *Partita* for violin, viola and piano, op. 6 (1949), *Wind Quintet*, op. 10 (1951), *Sonata* for viola and piano, op. 16 (1954), five *Impromptus* for violin and piano, op. 18 (1955), *String Quartet*, No. 1, op. 21 (1957), suite for wind quintet *The Children's Ballet*, op. 26 (1959), *String Quartet* No. 2, op. 31 (1960) and *String Quartet* No. 3 (1963).

A *Quartet* for four violins, op. 29a (1960), *Inventions* for three violins, op. 29b (1960), *Dance Suite* for piano and ballet for pupils of the People's School of Art, op. 30 (1960), a piano suite *Pictures of Winter*, op. 36 (1962) and *Sonata* for violin and piano (1964) have an instructive character.

He composed several cycles of compositions for piano, as *Sonata*, op. 9 (1950), *Small Preludes*, op. 20 (1956), *The Lyrical Suite*, op. 32 (1961), *Sonatina*, op. 34 (1962) and *Sonata* for solo viola (1963).

Vocal Music

Matys' vocal creative work is prolific. It includes five cycles of chamber music songs, several choral cycles, a large number of songs for children, youth and military ensembles and numerous arrangements of folk songs.

Cantatas: *My Love* for full orchestra, mixed choir and baritone solo, set to words by Jiří Havel, op. 12 (1950) and a chamber music cantata *The Bells of Velice* for mixed choir, soprano and organ to a folk text, op. 17 (1954).

MEIER, Jaroslav
[born Hronov, 7 December 1923]

Meier studied composition with F. F. Finke, Alexander Moyzes and organ with B. A. Wiedermann, A. Nowakowski and E. Riegler-Skalický.

As an organist he has appeared on the concert stage and on the radio, where he was on the staff of the department of music. At present he is dramaturgist of musical programmes at the Bratislava television.

As a composer he has made a name for himself mainly in chamber music and songs and in music to radio, television and theatrical plays and scenes.

His most noteworthy compositions include the song-cycles *Night Songs* for mezzosoprano and piano, *Strophes of Love* for baritone and piano, *Six Songs* from the collection of ŠTEFAN ŽÁRY, *Such a Fragrance* for soprano, baritone, choir and small orchestra.

Meier has written as well a number of compositions for organ, including a *Concerto for Organ* and a small cantata for baritone, choir and orchestra *The Resurrection*.

MIHULE, Jiří

[born Prague, 22 July 1907]

Mihule studied oboe and composition (K. B. JIRÁK) at the Prague Conservatory and was oboist in the orchestra of the Liberec Theatre. At present he is musical editor of the Theatrical and Literary Agency in Prague.

His compositions include such works as *The Orava Fantasy* for violin and piano (1928), a *String Quartet* (1937), a *Wind Quintet* (1945), *Children's Songs* for middle voice and nonet to words by MILOSLAV BUREŠ (1950), a *Ballad* for clarinet and piano (1955), a *Concerto* for clarinet and orchestra (1953) and others.

He has enriched literature for the oboe by his pastoral poem *Spring in Bohemia* (with chamber orchestra, 1948), three *Concertos* (1952, 1954, 1956) and a *Sonata* (with octet, 1953).

His orchestral creative work includes an *Overture* (1940), *The Middle Ages Suite* (1941), an overture *Joyous Greetings* (1954), a popular variety suite *The Capricious Summer* (1955), *May Suite* for full orchestra (1957), musical pictures *A Summer Afternoon in the Park* (1958), *A Greeting from the Cosmos* (1962) and *On Old Town Corner* (1963).

To a libretto by MILOSLAV BUREŠ he composed a full-length ballet *The Bluish Land* (1949, première in Liberec 1950).

He has written as well a number of dance compositions and incidental music to various plays.

MIKODA, Bořivoj
[born Počátky, 20 July 1904]

Mikoda studied composition at first under OTAKAR JEREMIÁŠ, later he graduated from the composition section of the Master School of the Prague Conservatory as a pupil of VÍTĚZSLAV NOVÁK and from the section of conducting in the class of PAVEL DĚDEČEK. At Charles University the degree of doctor of pedagogical sciences was conferred upon him.

Mikoda was professor of musical subjects at Teachers' Training Institutes, lecturer at the Pedagogical Faculty of Charles University (taught at the Pilsen branch of this Faculty) and assistant professor of music education at the Higher Pedagogical School at Pilsen. At present he is active at the Pilsen Pedagogical Institute. He is secretary of the Pilsen branch of the Guild of Czechoslovak Composers.

Orchestral Works

Mikoda's work is comprised in four *symphonies* (C minor 1943—44, E minor 1956—57, one-movement symphony in C major 1959, D minor 1962), a *Serenade* in G major for small orchestra (1958) and an *Overture* in C major for full orchestra (1962).

Chamber Music

His chamber music is represented by a *Suite in an Old*

Style for violin and piano, a *Piano Trio* in C minor, *Sonata* for viola and piano, a one-movement *Trio* for oboe, clarinet and bassoon, *Sonata* for flute and piano with soprano solo, a piano *Sonata* and two *Suites* for solo viola, solo violoncello and solo violin, a one-movement *String Quartet* (1944), *Duo* for violin and viola, *Duo* for violin, *Piano Sonatina* , *Legends* for viola and piano, *Sonata* for violin and piano, *Wind Quintet*, *Nonet* (1948). His piano compositions include *Songs of the Native Country*, *Lyrical Compositions*, *Impromptus* and *Lullabies*.

Vocal Music

In the field of song he composed the following: the song-cycles *Your Voice* to words by JOSEF HORA (1934), *Four Songs* for alto to his own texts (1937), *The Necklace* to words by RABINDRANÁTH TAGORE (1937), *The Face* to words by FRANTIŠEK HALAS (1941), *Spring* to words of old Chinese poetry (1942), *The Landscapes* (1943), *The Fleeting Hinds* to words by VLADIMÍR ŠTUCHL and *Three Songs* set to words by A. S. PUSHKIN.

Mikoda's choral creative work includes a cycle of male choirs *Simple Flowers* and children's and mixed choirs, and a cantata for middle male voice and string orchestra *I Believe in Peace* (1950).

Writings

He is also the author of *Intonation Studies* (Etudes) in the first position and of *Etudes in All Keys* for violin.

In his music scientific publications he occupied himself with the choral creative work of JOSEF SUK and VÍTĚZSLAV NOVÁK and with theoretical and pedagogical subjects. He has also written a book *Composers of Pilsen in the Contemporary Development of Musical Creative Work* (published 1956).

•

Fantasy for string quintet (1956) was awarded a diploma in the International Competition of Composers in Vercelli.

MIKULA, Zdenko

[born Vyhne, 27 November 1916]

Mikula studied at the Bratislava Conservatory as a pupil of EUGEN SUCHOŇ in composition and of KORNEL SCHIMPL in conducting. He was active as a military bandmaster and as conductor of the Military Artistic Ensemble. At present he is secretary of the Slovak Guild of Composers and is active as well as a pedagogue at the Conservatory and at the High School of Musical Arts in Bratislava.

In his compositions he is particularly concerned with song and choral creative work. In these fields he has composed a number of works exacting both technically and from the point of view of expression. Noteworthy are the mixed choir *To the People* (1957), the male choir *Homeland of Mine* (1960) and the mixed choir *Today* (1960, this cycle exists as well in an arrangement for male choir and tenor solo).

He has also written several songs and small cantatas for solos, choir and orchestra: *A Song on Nálepka* (a Slovak hero of the Second World War), *A Song of a River*, *A Song On the Fatherland*, *A Song On Lenin*.

Of his orchestral popular compositions, the well-known are *A Slovak Folk Dance*, *A Bulgarian Dance* and the overture *Tatra Nights*.

His arrangements of folk songs have achieved even greater popularity, particularly the montage *Oriešany Merry-making* for solos, choir and orchestra (eventually for brass-band). He arranged for choir singing *The Meadow-Games* and the cycle *A Falcon's Flight*.

MLEJNEK, Vilém Prokop

[born Prague, 19 February 1906]

After completing the secondary school, Mlejnek matriculated at the Prague Conservatory. There he

studied piano under ALBÍN ŠÍMA, violoncello under JAN
BURIÁN and JULIUS JUNK and composition under JARO-
SLAV KŘIČKA nad OTAKAR ŠÍN. He studied in Paris as
well in order to complete the musical training he had
received at the Prague Conservatory. Upon his return
to Prague he continued his study of the violoncello at
the Master School of the Conservatory, adding to it conducting.

Mlejnek was a member of the Czech Philharmonic,
conductor at different theatres and the first bass da gam-
ba player in the chamber ensemble PRO ARTE ANTIOUA.

He has directed his creative activity to scenic music
and has composed a great deal of scenic music for radio
and several Czechoslovak theatres.

Of his other work, we may mention the cycle of songs
Through Life for alto and piano (1924), the opera *The
Romanticists*, according to EDMOND ROSTAND (1924, première in Strasbourg 1925), a *Fantasy* for violin and
piano (1930), a *String Sextet* (1930), a symphonic poem
Satanela (1931), three children's operas—*The Goat
Dereza* (1946), *The Mysterious Itinerant Player* (1950) and
The Fairy-tale About Two Needles (1955); further cycles
of children's songs, songs and mixed choirs with orchestra, the opera *How the Double-bass Came to Heaven* (1960,
première in Brno 1960) and two wind *Quintets* (1959 and
1962).

As a publicist, he occupies himself with old Czech and
Oriental music.

MODR, Antonín

[born Strašice, 17 May 1898]

Modr studied at the Prague Conservatory violin
under RUDOLF REISSIG and composition under JAROSLAV
KŘIČKA and J. B. FOERSTER and at the Master School
composition under JOSEF SUK.

First he served as violinist in the Czech Philharmonic, then in the orchestra of the National Theatre in Prague and the Symphonic Orchestra of the Czechoslovak Radio. Later he taught the lute, guitar and old violas at the Prague Conservatory, lecturing as well on music theory.

He was the founder of the chamber music ensemble of old violas, PRO ARTE ANTIOUA.

Orchestral and Chamber Music

His compositions include *String Quartet* No. 1 (1922), *Sinfonietta* (1924), the orchestral *Suite* (1925), *String Quartet* No. 2 (1926), an *Overture* (1929), a *Symphony* (1934), *Two Ballet Suites* (1938), *Variations* on his own theme for full orchestra (1939), *String Quartet* No. 3 (1940), a *Concerto* for violin and orchestra (1954), a *Concerto* for viola and orchestra (1955), an orchestral *Suite* (1956), a *Serenade* for strings (1957), a *Concerto* for trumpet and orchestra (1957), a *String Quartet* No. 4 (1959) and a *Symphony* (1962).

Instrumental Compositions

Amongst them are a *Small Piano Suite* (1938) and *From the Organ Sketch-book* (1944—45) with seventy-five preludes for organ and a number of compositions with organ accompaniment.

Montages, Arrangements

In addition to these compositions, Modr wrote eleven scenic works and two music montages for radio. He made also arrangements of Czech, Slovak, Russian, Ukrainian, Hungarian, Roumanian and Italian folk songs.

Light Music

His work in the field of light music is prolific as well and mention may be made of seven *Festival Marches*, of *Three Neighbourlies* (Czech folk dance) and of *Five Polkas* for full orchestra.

Instructive Works

For instructional purposes Modr has written *A School of Playing Scales on Guitar*, *A School of Playing Chords on Guitar* and eight *Etudes* for bassoon with piano.

His theoretical writings deal with musical instruments, harmony, counterpoint, musical forms and general information and instruction about music.

Writings

His book *Musical Instruments* has gone into five editions (in 1959 it appeared in Russian language in Moscow).

MÓRY, Ján
[born Banská Bystrica, 10 July 1892]

Móry studied originally law but soon concentrated his attention on composition. His success not only at home but abroad as well was achieved by his operettas *Torrero*, *The White Dove*, *A Winter Tale*, *Miss Widow*, *The Midshipman*, *La Vallière*, by his orchestral paraphrases on Slovak folk songs *Slovak Pastoral Dances*, the dance suites *Under Kriváň*, *The Carpathian March*, the Slovak suite *In the Shadow of the Mountains* and by his compositions for chamber music (*Deux poèmes* for violin and piano) and for dance orchestra and brass band.

His exacting efforts in the field of song compositions are testified by an extensive cycle set to words by RABINDRANÁTH TAGORE and by choir arrangements of folk songs.

MOYZES, Alexander
[born Kláštor pod Znievom, 4 September 1906]

MERITED ARTIST, LAUREATE OF THE STATE PRIZE

Moyzes was the first composer to lay down the foundations of contemporary Slovak music by his creative work (particularly symphonic) as well as by his pedagogic and public activity.

His father, MIKULÁŠ MOYZES, a noted composer of the older generation, early began to give him a musical education. When, in 1925, Alexander Moyzes matriculated at the Prague Conservatory, he had already considerable experience in composition (the choirs *Santa Helena*, *Instead of a Wreath*), so that as early as 1928 he graduated in composition (OTAKAR ŠÍN and RUDOLF KAREL), in conducting (OTAKAR OSTRČIL) and organ (B. A. WIEDERMANN). His graduation work, the *Symphony* in D major, was the first symphony in Slovak music and its première in 1929 became the symbol of the emergence of a new generation.

In 1928 Moyzes became professor of composition at the Music and Dramatic Academy in Bratislava which, however, did not prevent him from perfecting his study of composition at the Master School under VÍTĚZSLAV NOVÁK (he graduated in 1930). Now he is professor of composition at the Musical Faculty of the High School of Musical Arts in Bratislava.

Moyzes' artistic programme was formulated on the basis of the progressive ideas of the Czech and Slovak artistic vanguard. He aimed at doing away with the provincialism in Slovak music and at creating works which by their new, unconventional grasp of the idea of nationality would have broader European influence. He fought for this programme not only as a composer but as a publicist as well and attracted to it young pupils, only a little younger than he himself (LADISLAV HOLOUBEK, DEZIDER KARDOŠ, ANDREJ OČENÁŠ, ŠIMON JUROVSKÝ, TIBOR FREŠO).

At the beginning of the thirties Moyzes experimented with songs *Colours on the Palette*, op. 5 (1928), with *West Pocket Suite* for violin and piano, op. 7 (1928), with *Divertimento*, op. 11 (1930), *Jazz Sonata* for two pianos, op. 14-I (1932) and *The Fox Etude*, op. 14-II (1935).

His sinfonia cantata *The Dismantling*, op. 12 (1930) is

a penetrating cry against the pauperization of man at the time of the world economic crisis. It indicates that the composer views the problem of the struggle for a new musical expression in close relationship with the struggle for social progress.

The first stage of Moyzes' creative work is rounded off by the splendid *Wind Quintet*, op. 17 (1933) which after the Thirteenth Festival of the International Society for Contemporary Music in Prague was played in Europe, calling attention to the birth of a new compositional school.

With his overture *Jánošík's Lads*, op. 21 (1934), which like the dramatic overture *Nikola Šuhaj*, op. 22 (1934) has a strong social character, Moyzes demonstrates his attachment to folklore. This is even more strikingly evident in his orchestral suite *Down the River Váh*, op. 26 (1936), a eulogy of his native country, as well as in the montage of folk songs *Sing, Play and Dance*, op. 33 (1938), which became the prototype of this genre in Slovak music.

During the war, Moyzes practically remained silent, the only important work of that period being *The Poetic Suite*, op. 35 (1940), written in the neoclassic style. He devoted himself intensively to rewriting his earlier compositions, in particular the *Sonata* in E minor for piano (1942) which came into being by the reworking of his *Seven Piano Compositions* of 1928.

After the liberation, Moyzes stands again in the forefront of the struggle for progressive Slovak music. His *Fourth Symphony* in E flat major, op. 38 (1947) is autobiographical, depicting the struggle of the tragic years of the war. Prior to it, he wrote a cycle of arrangements for choir of Slovak folk songs entitled *Whose Organ Is Playing*, op. 37 (1947) which became a classical model in the same manner as those of BÉLA BARTÓK and ZOLTÁN KODÁLY.

Moyzes himself followed this up by writing the first programme for the Slovak Folk Art Ensemble (1949), a group with which much of the folklore creative work of Slovak composers is linked up. On the basis of this music, Moyzes wrote the popular symphonic suite *Dances of the Hron Country*, op. 43 (1950), *The February Symphonic Poem*, op. 48 (1952) which, similarly to the *Sixth Symphony*, op. 43 (1951), endeavours to depict the pathos and optimism of the revolutionary years.

After a prolonged pause Moyzes wrote his *Seventh Symphony*, op. 50 (1955), a work of profound tragedy and catharsis representing a climax in his symphonic work (awarded the State Prize).

In the compositions, written during the latest stage of his creative activity, Moyzes' style attains even greater definiteness of form. The *Concerto* for violin and orchestra, op. 53 (1958) and particularly the song-cyle *In Autumn*, op. 56 (1960) are characteristic of the high level of his compositional mastery. It was at this time that he re-worked his earlier cantata *The Dismantling* into *The Balladic Cantata*; in this version the work was given an award in the artistic jubilee competition in 1960.

In recent time, Moyzes composed *Two Songs* for soprano and orchestra, set to words by JÁN SMREK (1963), a cycle of songs *The Morning Dew* for mezzo-soprano and orchestra, to the poetry of VOJTĚCH MI-HÁLIK (1963) and a *Sonatina giocosa* for chamber orchestra (1963).

MÓŽI, Aladár

[born Bratislava, 21 May 1923]

Móži is active mainly as a violin virtuoso and peda-gogue, this characterizing as well the nature of his compositional creative work. He studied at the Brati-slava Conservatory under TIBOR GAŠPAREK and at the Hochschule für Musik in Vienna under WOLFGANG SCHNEIDERHAN.

As a soloist, concert-master of the Symphonic

Orchestra of the Bratislava Radio and first violinist of the Bratislava Quartet he ranks among prominent Czechoslovak violinists, often giving concerts abroad.

In his compositions he is oriented mainly to chamber music and instructive works for violin. He has written two *Concertinos* for violin and piano, a *Concertino* for violin and orchestra, *Epigrams* for children's voice and string quartet, as well as several compositions stressing execution for violin (*Trifles*), viola, string trio and others.

He is the author of transcriptions of piano compositions (BÉLA BARTÓK, *Slovak Folk Songs* from the cycle For Children, DEZIDER KARDOŠ, *The Bagatelles*).

MÓŽI, Július

[born Berlin, 27 March 1908]

Móži studied violin originally with his father, then at the Budapest Academy and finally under GUSTAV NÁHLOVSKÝ at the Music and Dramatic Academy in Bratislava.

He was active as musical pedagogue, as member of the Bratislava Radio Orchestra and the Slovak Philharmonic. Since 1952 he has been chief conductor of the Slovak Folk Art Ensemble with which he has undertaken numerous tours of European countries as well as overseas.

In addition to occasional violin compositions and compositions of the light music genre, as well as for string orchestras, his creative work consists mainly of arrangements, paraphrases, variations and fantasies set to Slovak, Hungarian and Roumanian folk songs and dances (*The Slovak Rhapsody, The Roumanian Fantasy Doina, A Wallachian Dance, A Highland Dance, A Gypsy Dance*).

NEČAS, Jaromír

[born Kyjov, 21 February 1922]

After completing the secondary school, Nečas matriculated at the Brno Conservatory as a pupil of composition in the class of JAROSLAV KVAPIL.

He is editor at the Czechoslovak Radio in Brno in the field of small musical forms and the folk song.

He has composed a *Concertino* for viola and orchestra (his graduation work), a cycle of songs *Spring in Two* for alto and piano, to words by JAROSLAV SEIFERT, a piano suite *The Sun Dial*, *Three Hamlet Motifs* for trumpet and piano, a symphonic dance *Girl's Games in Kopanice*, music to a radio cycle of literary broadcasts *A Year in the Village*, scenic music to the play *Captain Šárovec* and others.

Nečas is predominantly interested in dance music and chansons which include ¶ a twist *Black and White*, ¶ a foxtrot *Where is the Truth*, ¶ a grotesque foxtrot *A Cat Creeps Through the Hole*, ¶ a polka *A Model Song about a Mask and a Tuba* (heligon), ¶ a slow foxtrot *Love in the Snow*, ¶ a rumba *A Song about a Camera*, ¶ a charleston *A Song of the Week* from the year 2061, ¶ a waltz *A Song about a Chrysanthemum*; furthermore ¶ the chansons: *Man of Many Faces*, *Unfaithful*, *A Song about Different People*, *A Peaceful Sky*, *Mind Your World-order!*, *Light and Shadow*, a *Declaration of Love*, and ¶ satirical songs: *Gossipers and Lard* and a *Widow*.

Nečas is as well an arranger of folk songs.

NEJEDLÝ, Vít

[born Prague, 22 June 1912—died Dukla, 1 January 1945]

Son of the Czech musicologist ZDENĚK NEJEDLÝ (1878—1962), completed the study of musical science at Charles University. In composition he was a pupil of OTAKAR JEREMIÁŠ.

Early in his career, during his studies, he joined the working class movement, embarking on an intensive artistic and cultural programme. He soon excelled as a music critic and at the same time was choirmaster of the Prague choral society LUKEŠ. After taking his doctor's degree he became accompanist and conductor at the Olomouc Theatre.

After the occupation of Czechoslovakia in 1939 he emigrated to the Soviet Union where he was active at the Moscow Radio as editor of Czech music programmes for transmission to foreign countries. Simultaneously he studied conducting at the Moscow Conservatory under L. M. GINSBURG. Temporarily he was active as well at several Soviet theatres.

Finally he joined the Czechoslovak Military Unit where he built up an artistic group modelled on the Alexandrov's Ensemble of the Red Banner. In creating the Army Artistic Ensemble he laid the foundation for artistic work in the Czechoslovak Army under battle conditions. Within the Army Artistic Ensemble he became composer, conductor and organizer.

Nejedlý is known above all as the author of the march *Victory Shall Be Ours* (1941), military lyrical songs, *The Oath of a Woman of the Ukraine* for mezzosoprano and symphonic orchestra (1942), a cantata to a text by FRANTIŠEK NEČÁSEK *To You—The Red Army* (1943, in honour of the 25th anniversary of the birth of the Red Army) and others.

Of Nejedlý's other compositions, written during his stay in the Soviet Union, mention should be made of his *Fantasy* for piano, op. 16 (1940), *Dramatic Overture*, op. 17 (1940) and *Concertino* for nonet, op. 18 (1940).

Of his earlier compositions the following attracted attention:

Stage Works

Nejedlý demonstrated his musical dramatic talent in his opera *The Weavers* to a theme by GERHART HAUPT-

MANN (1938, completed by JAN HANUŠ, première in Pilsen 1961) and in the melodrama *The Dying*, set to poem by JIŘÍ WOLKER, op. 6 (1933) and in scenic music.

Orchestral Works

Three *symphonies* (first in 1931, second *Poverty and Death*, in 1934, third—*Spanish* in 1937—38, dedicated to the Spanish defenders of democracy and freedom), *Overture to* VERHAEREN's *Dawn*, op. 5 (1932), a symphonic composition *Commemoration* (1933), a symphonic march *Deploy the Ranks* (1934), and *Sinfonietta*, op. 13 (1937).

Chamber Music

Two *Compositions* for wind quintet, op. 8a (1934), two *Compositions* for nonet, op. 8b (1934), a *Small Suite* for violin and piano, op. 11 (1935, performed at the International Festival for Contemporary Music in Paris 1937), a *String Quartet*, op. 12 (1937).

Vocal Works

A cycle of songs set to texts of old Chinese poetry *The Black Tower*, op. 4 (1932), three passages from the epos by VLADIMIR MAJAKOVSKY *"150,000,000"* for male choir, op. 9 (1935), a cantata set to the poem *The Day* by JAN NOHA, op. 10 (1935) and arrangements of folk songs, and songs for community singing (the one-time popular *March of the United Workers' Front* and *Ukraine, My Ukraine*).

NÉMETH-ŠAMORÍNSKY, Štefan
[born Šamorín, 29 September 1896]

He studied piano, organ and composition at the Budapest Academy of Music and in the Master Class of the Vienna Music Academy under FRANZ SCHMIDT.

He was active as a teacher of piano at the City School

of Music in Bratislava, simultaneously as the Cathedral organist and later as professor of organ at the Bratislava Conservatory. At present he is senior lecturer of the piano and chamber music at the High School of Musical Arts.

He was also an outstanding soloist and choirmaster of the choral ensemble SPEVOKOL BÉLA BARTÓK (for a certain period he was BARTÓK's pupil and even later maintained contact with his teacher).

In his compositional activity Németh-Šamorínsky originally concentrated mainly on the chamber music genre [compositions for piano, the cycle of songs *The Chinese Flute* (1940), *Songs* to words by E. ADY, (1942)]. Later his interest was focused on various arrangements of Slovak and Hungarian folk songs, according to the example set by BARTÓK, as well as on ambitiously conceived chamber music and orchestral compositions. The influence of late-romanticism is blended with newer stylization stimuli and with folkloristic elements.

His best chamber works include the *First String Quartet* in G minor (1948), a *Sonata* for piano (1955), a *Piano Quintet* (1957) and a *Sonata* for violin and piano (1962).

His finest orchestral works are a *Concerto* for piano and orchestra (1958), a *Concerto* for organ and orchestra (1958) and the symphonic poem *Birches* (1961).

For young people he writes as well compositions with the main accent on execution.

NEUMANN, Věroslav

[born Citoliby, 27 May 1931]

Neumann studied composition at the Academy of Musical Arts under JAROSLAV ŘÍDKÝ. He first drew attention to his compositional work by military songs and songs on the building-up of the country, songs considerably popular among young people and in the

Army. His work received awards in numerous competitions and the song *Nations Have Sworn* was awarded a bronze medal in the competition at the Festival of Youth in Warsaw 1955.

Neumann's systematic compositional creative work in the field of community songs resulted from his experiences as artistic chief of the Artistic Ensemble of the Ministry of Interior and from his function as choirmaster. This type of work aroused his interest and stimulated him, resulting in many small cantatas, choirs, chamber music songs, scenic music, small orchestral compositions and arrangements of folk songs.

In the field of more extensive works he has composed, up to the present, *The Peace Symphony* for full orchestra and mixed choir (his graduation work at the Academy of Musical Arts, 1954), particularly interesting for its choral finale. His other larger works include scenic pictures *People Among Us* (1956), two cycles for mixed choir *Czech Poems* (1958), a *Concerto* for piano and orchestra (1959), a cycle of children's duets *The Green Years* (1961) and three symphonic pictures for baritone and full orchestra *Panorama of Prague* (1962). His mixed choir *The Miners' Ballad*, the march song *We Sing For the Lads* and the variety song *The Old Double-bass* were awarded in the artistic jubilee competition in 1960.

Recently, he has written a cycle of songs for soprano and piano *Lonely*, set to words of old Chinese poetry (1964).

He composed music for the Third Spartakiad (1965).

NIKODEM, Bedřich

[born Vienna, 12 August 1909]

Nikodem is one of the popular composers of Czech dance music. Among his best known tramp songs are *Swing High—Swing Low*, *Ever Merrily*, *Your Little Mouth*,

The Song of White Plains, A Hut of Mine, In Canoe so Alone, The Hermit, Never More, Our Camp Fire, The Day Is Dawning, My Camp, See You Again; from his dance songs attained popularity *It is, It is So, The Daisy, The Sunday Train, It's Grand to be Alive, The Rain Has Stopped, Daggers Drawn with Accords, The Day after Tomorrow in the Evening, A Boat Out of Bark, Little Barbara, This Contrabass Beat or not Beat*.

His pioneer songs include *An Excursion, The Storks, Hooray the Holidays, Black and Yellow and White Children.*

His foxtrot *Two Little Blue Balloons* enjoyed particular popularity and won the first prize in the competition "In Quest of a Song for a Weekday" (1958). The same is true of his song *A Small Tent Have I*, which was acclaimed in the television programme "Songs for Tomorrow 1962". His songs from the play *Tartuffe* was awarded in the artistic jubilee competition in 1960.

Nikodem has also composed a full-length operetta and several feature programmes of music for various groups and ensembles. He has collaborated with the Theatre of OLDŘICH NOVÝ and with the theatres ROKOKO and ALHAMBRA.

At present he is editor for light and dance music at the State Publishing House of Music.

NOVÁČEK, Blahoslav Emanuel

[born Prague, 2 January 1911]

Nováček studied piano privately with KAREL HEŘMAN and composition at the Prague Conservatory in the class of ALOIS HÁBA. He was pianist and conductor of dance orchestras and of several theatre orchestras.

He has written a *Duo* for violin and violoncello, a *Concert Fantasy* for piano and orchestra, two *Rhapsodies* for orchestra, the music for six full-length and eight short films, seven musical comedies, music to several radio plays and variety programmes and about two hundred dance songs, of which the best known are *Only for this Day*, *Don't Wait*, *I should Like So Much to Get Married*, *The Girl in Blue*, *The Sunflower*, *I Am Fond of Life*, *What For?*, *The Sparrows on the Roof*, *Sing It Already*, *Blue Morning*, *The White Little Ball*, *Two In a Fog*, *September Thirteen* and others.

As a composer he also collaborated with E. F. BURIAN.

NOVÁK, Jan

[born Nová Říše, 8 April 1921]

After completing the secondary school, Novák entered the class of composition under VILÉM PETRŽELKA at the Brno Conservatory. After graduation from the Conservatory he continued the study of composition under PAVEL BOŘKOVEC at the Prague Academy of Musical Arts, then with AARON COPLAND in Tanglewood and with BOHUSLAV MARTINŮ in New York.

His creative work includes *Toccata chromatica* for piano (1946), *Carmina Sulamitis* for mezzosoprano and orchestra (1947), *Variations and Fugue* for two pianos on a theme of BOHUSLAV MARTINŮ (1948, later instrumented), a *Concerto* for oboe (1953), a *Concerto* for two pianos and orchestra (1954), a ballet ballad *The Spectre's Bride*, according to K. J. ERBEN (1954, première in Pilsen 1955), *Passer Catulli* for bass and nonet (1954), *Ballet* for nonet (1955), *The Song of Záviš* for tenor and orchestra (1957), *Concertino* for wind quintet (1958), *Carmina Horati* for middle voice and piano (1959), a four-part suite for brass band *Musica Caesariana* (1960), *Sonata brevis* (1960) and *Inventions* for hapsichord (1960).

Recently, he has composed a *Capriccio* for violoncello and orchestra (produced as a ballet in Pilsen 1963)

Dulces Cantilenae in odaria Magistri Campani for soprano
and violoncello, *Ioci Vernales* and *Toccata georgiana* for
organ (1962).

He is as well the author of much scenic and film
music. His *Proverbial Polkas* are of a variety nature.

With his wife, ELIŠKA NOVÁKOVÁ, he makes concert
appearances on programmes for two pianos.

NOVÁK, Jiří F.

[born Litoměřice, 15 August 1913]

From his childhood he occupied himself with music.
He graduated from the Prague Conservatory as pianist,
studying in the piano class of ALBÍN ŠÍMA, continuing at
the Master School where he was a pupil of JAN HEŘMAN.
Simultaneously he studied composition, at first privately
and later with JAROSLAV ŘÍDKÝ at the Academy of
Musical Arts.

He is active as a pedagogue at the Prague Conservatory.

Stage Works

His compositional work includes the comic opera
It's Not I, according to JAN NERUDA (composed during
his years of study at the Academy of Musical Arts),
the opera *Vojnarka*, according to the drama by ALOIS
JIRÁSEK to a libretto by MILAN MACKŮ (1958—60) and
a melodramatic fairy-tale *About the Golden-haired Beauty*,
to a text by BOŽENA NĚMCOVÁ, for flute (piccolo), clarinet,
French horn and six harps (1955).

His significant works during recent years are following
melodramas: *How a Jackal Duped a Tiger*, to a text
of an Indian fairy-tale fable (1961), *A Story of Female
Cunning, A Story of a Rogue from Cairo* and *A Story of a Rogue from Damascus*, to texts of oriental fairy-tales (1961),

Of a Grateful Pheasant, to a text of a Korean fairy-tale (1962), *Since When is a Keyhole Black* or *A Diplomat and the Devil*, to a text by FERENC MÓRY (1962), *A Night Guest*, *A Christmas Romance* and a *Romance about King Ječmínek*, set to a poem by VÍTĚZSLAV NEZVAL (1962), *From Mother's Fairy-tales*, to a text of an unknown author (1962) and *The Village Ležáky* set to words by MIROSLAV HELLER (1963).

Orchestral Works

Concerto for organ and orchestra (1952), *Serenade* for eleven wind instruments (1954) and a one-movement *Concertino* for xylophone and orchestra (1957).

Chamber Music

Rondo for contra-bass tuba (1951), *Quintet* for string quartet and French horn (1952), *Sonata* for violin and piano (1954), *Serenade* for string orchestra (1960), *Sonata* for oboe and piano (1961), *Scenes* for bassoon and piano (1962) and *Passacaglia* and *Fugue* for two clarinets and bass clarinet (1964).

As an instrumental composition is to be noted a *Concerto Fantasy* for piano (1961).

Vocal Music

Voices: *Our Lives* for baritone, accompanied by piano or symphonic orchestra, *Steps of Peace* for bass with piano accompaniment and *Two Airs* for baritone, piano, viola and tympanum, set to words by NICOLÁS GUILLÉN (1964).

Songs: *The Land of Peace* for tenor (soprano) with accompaniment by symphonic orchestra (piano), written on the occasion of the fifteenth anniversary of the liberation of Czechoslovakia, and a cycle of songs *Wild Thyme* for mezzosoprano and piano (1962);

Male choir: *A May Greeting*;

Mixed choir: *Keep Waving, Flag of Ours, Keep Waving!*

Cantatas: *Thank You, Prague*, to words by Vasil Švec (his graduation work at the Academy of Musical Arts, 1951), *With Head High* and *The Old Town Hall* (1961).

NOVÁK, Milan

[born Trahovice, 12 August 1927]

Novák comes of a musical family and acquired his all-round musical education at the Bratislava Conservatory where he studied piano (Frico Kafenda), conducting (Kornel Schimpl) and composition (Alexander Moyzes). He studied conducting as well with Václav Talich.

His extensive creative work has had an important effect particularly on the development of the Slovak operetta, political songs, folkloristic arrangements and music to films.

Stage Works

Novák is the author of two successful operettas, the story taken from contemporary life (*A Full Field of Love* and *It is not an Ordinary Day*).

Chamber Music

An individual characteristic field in Novák's creative work is his meticulous chamber music (*Sonatina for clarinet* and piano, *Sonatina for violoncello* and piano).

Vocal Music

Novák has been the conductor and artistic leader of the Military Artistic Ensemble since its inception and has written for it numerous political songs, small cantatas, musical-dramatic montages, dance scenes and folkloristic arrangements (*The Unconquerable Eagle's Nest, Gay Military Service, Direction-Prague, Soldiers' Teasings,*

Lezginka, Four Songs Against War, Communists Up To Victory, Greetings to the Soviet Union).

He has written as well many folkloristic montages and dance scenes for the ensembles Lúčnica, Technik, The Slovak Folk Art Ensemble and the Dukla Ukrainian Folk Ensemble (*The Goral Tavern, Vintage Time, Winter Games, Parting, Dawn Over Dukla*).

He wrote as well choral compositions (female choir *Love Sonatina*) and delightful songs for children (*Round, Round the Circle; Should All the Children in the World*).

Film Music

He has composed considerable film and scenic music, the most important of which arc thc films *Forty Four* and *Captain Dlabač*.

NOVOSAD, Lubomír

[born Hlučín, 9 October 1922]

Novosad graduated from composition section of the Brno Conservatory as a pupil of JAROSLAV KVAPIL. He has been a pianist in dance orchestras and at present is music manager at the Brno Radio.

As pianist, composer and music arranger, he has oriented himself towards popular symphonic and jazz music. His compositions include a *Wind Quintet* (1948), *Dramatic Overture* for full orchestra (his graduation work in 1948), *Sonata* for oboe and piano (1948), *Rondo and Variations* for trumpet (1949), *Three Songs of the Old China* for voices and piano (1949), *A Revolutionary March* (1950), *Silesian Dances* No. 1 and No. 2 (1951) and *Pioneer Songs* (1955).

He is the author of much dance music and jazz compositions, of which a few are: *A Greeting to the Beloved, A Glass Toy*, ¶ the foxtrots: *The Prettiest Rose, Protocol No. 13*,

A Snow-man, A Restless Night, In the Old Manner, Chips for Luck, A Girl with a Ball, and *I Start With a Foxtrot* and ¶ the waltz *The Star on the Cornice.*

He has also written a *Fantasy* for trombone and full orchestra, an *Impromptu, Contrasts, Romance in Rhythm, Aperitif, Three at the Piano* and the variety *Episode* and *Legend.*

OBORNÝ, Václav

[born Radvanice, 24 September 1915]

Oborný studied composition under JAROSLAV KVAPIL. At present he is a teacher at the Pedagogic Institute in Brno and a member of the Brno quartet.

His symphonic compositions *Song of the Native Land,* op. 3 (1950), *Sinfonietta,* op. 12 (1956) and *The Pits,* op. 13 (1957) were inspired by miners and the lives they lead.

Oborný has composed musical pictures of his native region in his male choir *I, Ostrava,* op. 4 (1951), the cantata *The City of Lights,* op. 5 (1951), the song *My Wife,* op. 7 (1953), *Ondráš Rhapsody* for symphonic orchestra, op. 9 (1954), *Mountaineer's Songs,* op. 10 (1955), the song *This Is My Land,* op. 11 (1956) and *A Poem on the Land of the Mountains* for a string orchestra, harp and percussion instruments, op. 15 (1959), the male choir *The Old Village,* op. 20 (1963) and *The Skies,* songs for higher voice and piano, op. 24 (1964).

His other works include four *String Quartets* (1948, 1953, 1958, 1962), the piano trio *From the Dreary Years,* op. 2 (1949), and *The Balladic Quartettino,* op. 6 (1952).

OBROVSKÁ, Jana

[born Prague, 13 September 1930]

Obrovská studied composition at the Prague Conservatory under MIROSLAV KREJČÍ and EMIL HLOBIL. Her graduation work was a *Piano Concerto* (1955).

Her orchestral compositions include *The Bulgarian Rhapsody* (1956), *Toccata, Interlude and Fugue* for string orchestra (1961), a symphonic poem *In Memory of Hiroshima* (1962), and *Scherzino* for brass band (1962). She followed up her graduation work with the second *Piano Concerto* (1960).

Obrovská's chamber music is represented by a *Sextet for Wind* instruments (1955), *Autumn Preludes* for violin and piano (1957) and a *Sonata* for violin and piano (1963).

As far as vocal creative work is concerned she has confined herself for the time being to a cycle *Five Songs* to words of folk poetry for middle voice and piano (1955).

Her works have been played in the German Democratic Republic.

OČENÁŠ, Andrej

[born Selce, 8 January 1911]

Holder of the ORDER OF WORK

Očenáš is a prominent representative of contemporary Slovak music. Initially he was a teacher, studying simultaneously composition at the Bratislava Music and Dramatic Academy under ALEXANDER MOYZES and conducting under JOZEF VINCOUREK. After graduation from the Academy he was a pupil of VÍTĚZSLAV NOVÁK at the Master School in Prague.

Since 1939 he has been active at the Bratislava Radio and from 1945 has taught choir conducting at the Conservatory. In 1950 he became director of that institution (where he taught simultaneously composition). Since 1954 he has been programme secretary of the Guild of Slovak Composers and in 1956—62 was director of musical programmes of the Czechoslovak Radio in Bratislava.

Since 1962 he has devoted himself to composition and to pedagogic activity and is now first secretary of the Guild of Slovak Composers.

Očenáš grew up in a milieu where musical folklore had preserved its primary vital function, so that his attitude to the folk song and dance is direct and authentic.

Stage Works

Before the war, he wrote his first ballet pantomime *At the Brigands' Ball* (1941); in 1957 he returned to this theme in his *Highland Songs* (première 1964 in Banská Bystrica).

Orchestral Works

His noteworthy works include the cycle of *Three Songs* for soprano and orchestra (1938) and the orchestral suite *Legends of the Native Land* (1943), which represents a realistic picture of the composer's homeland. His endeavour to compose monumental symphonic poems reached its climax in the trilogy *The Resurrection* (1946, second version 1953) and in the cycle of symphonic poems *To My People* (1947). It was followed by a *Concerto* for violoncello and orchestra (1952). One of the most outstanding of Očenáš's works is a cycle of symphonic poems *Ruralia Slovacca* (Parting with Youth, 1957), which is of an autobiographical nature.

Compositions dating from the most recent period include the symphonic tetralogy *The Monuments of Glory* for tenor solo, children's choir, mixed choir and orchestra (1961), in which the composer depicts the key moments in the struggle of his people for freedom during the Second World War.

Instrumental and Chamber Music

Among other compositions should be mentioned his first string quartet *Pictures of the Soul* (1941), emotionally rich and original in tone, the second *Piano Suite* (1938), a cycle of poetic piano pictures *A New Spring* (1954), a suite *Youthfulness* (1956), *Piano Concerto* (1959), *Organ Pastels* (1961), *Concertino* for flute and piano (1961—62) and *Concertino Rustico* for cimbalom, strings and piano (1963).

Vocal Works

Among the first of his works was the scenic cantata *Margarita and Besná* (1939); there he attempted to arrive at a stylization of folklore elements in a large balladic compositions.

During the war Očenáš devoted himself to compose cantatas: *Song of the Green Mountains* (1943), and a cycle of four cantatas *The Prophesies* set to verses of the classic of Slovak poetry P. O. HVIEZDOSLAV.

Of his relatively large choral music, the cycle of love songs *Marina* (1957) is particularly well known; further he composed a *Song About the Communist Party in Slovakia* (1959), which was followed by a cycle of male choirs set to poems by JÁN KOSTRA *About Life* (1964), a cycle of songs set to words by PAVOL KOYŠA *As the Stars are Falling* (1963—64) and *Children Choirs* to words by F. CITOVSKÝ (1964).

Arrangements

Of Očenáš' numerous folkloristic arrangements the full-length medley of songs *A Year in the Village* (1948) and *The Oravian Pastorale* (1961) attained great popularity.

Prizes

For his tetralogy *The Monuments of Glory* he was awarded the STATE PRIZE in the artistic jubilee competition 1965.

OČENÁŠ

PÁDIVÝ, Karol

[born Cerekev, 10 September 1908—died Trenčín, 25 September 1965]

Pádivý was at first active in military music and as a member of the orchestra in Sibiu. Later he graduated from the conducting section on the Bratislava Conservatory. In the years 1951—62 he was a member of the music branch of the Central Institution for Culture.

He is one of the most successful composers of music for brass band, for which he has written many arrangements as well as compositions of his own; these include the following: *The March of Textile Workers*, a valse *On the Bank of the Orava River*, *The Vajnory Polka*, *Around Suča*, *Suča Czardases*, *A Slovak Dance*.

He has composed also several popular symphonic compositions—*Three Roumanian Dances*, *Two Slovak Dances*, *A Melancholy Valse*.

In addition he has published several manuals on method for brass bands: *Methodics of Wind Instrument Playing*, a *School for Choir Singing* and *Instrumentation for Brass Bands* (together with JINDŘICH PRAVEČEK).

PÁLENÍČEK, Josef

[born Travnik in Jugoslavia, 19 July 1914]

Páleníček was a pupil of OTAKAR ŠÍN and VÍTĚZSLAV NOVÁK. He achieved first success with his composition for violin and piano entitled *Prelude and Caprice* (1935) and with his *Piano Sonata* (1936), which received favorable reception. He continued in his studies at the Paris Ecole Normale de Musique in 1936-37, where he wrote his orchestral *Concertino* under the guidance of ALBERT ROUSSEL.

Since 1962, he is professor of piano and chamber music at the Academy of Musical Arts (previously soloist of the

Czech Philharmonic in Prague and of the Moravian Philharmonic in Olomouc) and devotes himself not only to concert activity as pianist (solist and member of chamber music ensembles) but is a composer as well.

Orchestral Works

He composed a *Concerto* for saxophone and orchestra (1944), a *Concerto* for flute and orchestra (1955) and a full-length oratorio *A Poem About Man* for solos, mixed choirs and full orchestra (1958); the transformation of man from idealism to materialism is the fundamental philosophical conception that characterizes this work.

In his efforts to create a new musical style, he has used folk chorals as well in this work.

Chamber Works

A *Sonata* for clarinet and piano (1936), *Choral Variations* for violoncello and piano (1942), a *Suite* for clarinet and piano (1943), a *String Quartet* (1954), a *Concertino da camera* in D major for clarinet (1957), a *Suita Piccola* for violin and piano (1958), a *suite* for saxophone and piano *Masks* (1959).

Instructive Compositions

For the piano Páleníček wrote *The Piano Sketch-Book* (1939) and numerous instructive compositions, the most popular of which are the *Fairy-tales* (1943) and three *Concertos* with orchestra (1939, 1952 and 1961, of which the third piano *Concerto* is intended for young pianists).

Vocal Works

Songs for soprano and piano, set to Chinese poetry (1947), *Songs* for baritone and piano to Chinese poetry (1947), a cycle of male choirs *The Snowed-over Footprints* (1958) and a small cantata for children's choir and instrumental ensemble *Abacus*.

PÁLKA, Dušan

[born Liptovský Mikuláš, 1 October 1909]

Pálka graduated from the Faculty of Law. He studied composition privately with Jaroslav Křička.

He ranks among the successful composers of dance music; some of his songs have achieved success abroad. His song *Tell Me, My Dear!*, written to words by Andrej Plavka, composed when he was only fifteen years old, has become so popular that it has acquired a folk song character.

He composed as well the first Slovak ¶ tango *Don't Tell Anyone, My Dear!* It was followed by the tangos *With Tears in My Eyes* and *I Shall Come Once More*.

Recently, the following of his dance music has become popular: ¶ the valses *By Mere Chance* and *Ten Meadow Flowers*; ¶ the valse chanson *Lovers' Bench* (third prize in the competition of the Czechoslovak Radio and Television for the best chanson and dance song in 1957); ¶ the tangos: *Why Are We to Part?*, *In the Tatra Mountains* and *We Dance the Tango*; ¶ the calypso *The Little Drummer*; ¶ the rumba *Learn It From Me*; ¶ the foxtrot *The Rococo Doll*; ¶ the blues *City at Night*; ¶ the chachas: *That Big-Eyed Girl* and *Whom does that Child Take After*, ¶ lipsi *Good Day*, and ¶ the slow-fox *Monsieur Gaugin*.

He has written ¶ a foxtrot *A Cluster of Children* (second prize in the competition of the Guild of Slovak Composers in 1961), composed in particular for children.

PALKOVSKÝ, Oldřich

[born Brušperk, 24 February 1907]

After graduating from the Teachers' Training Institute, Palkovský studied composition at the Brno Conservatory under Vilém Petrželka, completing his study at the Master School of the Prague Conservatory under JOSEF SUK.

At present, he teaches theoretical subjects at the Kroměříž branch of the Brno Conservatory.

Orchestral Works

He has composed six *Symphonies*: No. 1, op. 8 (1933 to 1934), No. 2, op. 10 (1939), No. 3, op. 14 (1944), No. 4, op. 19 (1947), No. 5, op. 28 (1956—57) and No. 6 (1962).

Amongst his other orchestral compositions we should note *Concerto for cimbalom* and small orchestra, op. 24 (1952—53), *Scherzo capriccioso* for full orchestra, op. 25 (1953), *Moravian Suite* for full orchestra, op. 26 (1954 to 1955), *Moravian Dances* for orchestra, op. 27 (1956), *Concerto for flute* and orchestra (1959), *Concerto for oboe* and orchestra (1961), and *Concerto for accordion* and orchestra (1961).

Chamber Music and Instrumental Works

He composed five *String Quartets*: No. 1, op. 4 (1931), No. 2, op. 6 (1933), No. 3, op. 9 (1937), No. 4, op. 29 (1957) and No. 5 (1962).

Besides that noteworthy are *Piano Trio*, op. 11 (1940), *Concertino* for wind instruments, op. 16 (1945), *Wind Quintet* No. 1, op. 21 (1949), *Quartet* for flute, violin, viola and violoncello, op. 22 (1950), *Variations* for cimbalom and piano on a Slovak theme (1955), *Wind Quintet* No. 2 (1958), *Variations* and *Fugue* for cimbalom, string orchestra and timpani (1959), *Sonata* for French horn and piano, op. 38 (1963) and *Chamber Music* for eight instruments, op. 39 (1964).

Amongst his instrumental compositions are to be noted:

Violin Sonata, op. 12 (1942), *Violin Sonatina*, op. 13 (1943), *Viola Sonata*, op. 15 (1944), *Violoncello Sonata*, op. 17 (1946), *Clarinet Sonata*, op. 20 (1947) and *Pictures from the Countryside* for piano (1950), which were in-

PALKOVSKÝ

334

fluenced by his activity of many years in the Wallachian and Moravian Slovak regions.

In addition, Palkovský has written a number of compositions for variety programmes as well as instructive works.

PALOUČEK, Alois

[born Prague, 15 April 1931]

After completing the secondary school Palouček studied composition under JAROSLAV ŘÍDKÝ at the Academy of Musical Arts. He was active in the Czechoslovak radio, in the Ensemble Julius Fučík and in the Army Artistic Ensemble Vít Nejedlý.

Light Music

Palouček ranks among the foremost authors of Czech light music. He composed about three hundred songs which include:

Songs: *A Sunny Day*, the pioneer song *Boys and Girls Onward*, dance songs for children *A Perfect Daddy*, *Grandmother Tramway*, *The Puppy*, chansons *From Here to Eternity*, *The Romance of Hašek's Mug*, *The Song of Hooligan's Heart*, *The Unconfessed Confession*;

Dance music *Ungrateful Friend*, *It Feels Lonely*, *Such Snow Doesn't Fall Anymore*, *The May Valse*, *Waiting*, *My Pal* and the march song *When the Day Rises in the Morning*.

The song *The Morning Meeting* received a special award in the artistic jubilee competition in 1960.

For the Ensemble Julius Fučík, Palouček wrote music to dance for girls *The Goose-Herdesses*, the dance grotesque *Mushroom-Pickers* and *Odzemek* (a folk dance).

For the Army Artistic Ensemble Vít Nejedlý he composed the military songs *The First Outing*, *A Little Song to Keep in Step*, *Oh, that Civilian*, *A City a Hundred Times Cursed*, *Be Welcome Soldier*; songs on topical themes such as

Africa Accuses and *Fusilero*; and music to *The Dance of the Astronauts* and to the miners' dance *At the Height of the Coal Bed*.

Film Music

Palouček has written as well music to the medium-footage films *The New Shift*, *The Slapy Dam* and *The May Song*, music to two film grotesques *The Night Full of Snowmen* and *Football Boots*.

Scenic Music

J. K. TYL: *Fidlovačka* (Cobbler's Feast), VOJTĚCH CACH: *My Aunt, Your Aunt*; V. K. KLICPERA: *The Liar and His Kin*, STIEPAN SHCHIPACHOV: *Strophes of Love* and music to the revue *Soldier Maclíček* by MIROSLAV MRÁZ.

Various

Other fields of Palouček's creative work are represented by the cantatas *The Rose and Blood* (1955) and *The Oath of the Warsaw Treaty's Regiment* (1959), a symphonic suite *In Love With You* (1956), a *Serenade* for strings (1957), music to the pantomime *The Bump* (1959 to 1960, première in Prague 1960), the orchestral *Overture* (1963) and the television musicale *Once a House Stood in Blumenstrasse* (1963).

PARÍK, Ivan

[born Bratislava, 17 August 1936]

Parík studied initially with ALEXANDER ALBRECHT, then composition at the Bratislava Conservatory under ANDREJ OČENÁŠ and conducting under KORNEL SCHIMPL. Subsequently he became a pupil of ALEXANDER MOYZES in the composition class of the High School of Musical Arts.

He is active as a musical dramaturgist at the Bratislava Television.

Parík is one of the most talented composers of his generation. In his efforts to arrive at a contemporary and unconventional expression, he achieved the most telling results in chamber music: *Music for Four String Instruments* (1958), *Two Songs* set to Japanese poetry for mezzo-soprano, violin, clarinet, xylophone and gong (1960), *Three Pieces* for piano (1961), four compositions for violoncello and piano *The Song About A Tall Tree* (1962), a *Sonata* for flute (1962).

Of Parík's orchestral compositions mention should be made of his *Overture* for orchestra (1962), his graduation work.

PARMA, Eduard

[born Prague, 22 April 1929]

Parma took an active part in numerous musical ensembles during his secondary school studies. He studied composition privately with ZDENĚK HŮLA. Since 1961 he is the band-leader of a dance and variety orchestra.

His creative work includes ¶ the foxtrots: *We are Nine, When the Rain Drips Behind My Collar, On the Green, I have Somebody, My Laddie Sleeps, Seven Wonders of the World, In Seventh Heaven, An Ordinary Adventure, A Restless Fellow, A Handsome Antagonist, An Excursion on a Motorcycle* and *I Don't Want Any Other*; ¶ the slow foxtrots: *What Can I Say, Tomorrow for the First Time* and *All Over the World*; ¶ the waltz *This Evening*; ¶ the slow rock *The Magic Whistle* nad ¶ the twists *Far Under the Stars* and *I Envy You to Everyone*.

His foxtrot *A Sad Confectioner* and slow foxtrot *The Girl Named Pygmalion* received both second prize in the competition "In Quest of a Song for a Weekday".

Parma has also written compositions for solo instru-

337

ments as for instance the fantasy *The Path to the Stars* for alto-saxophone, ¶ the slow foxtrot *A Foggy Day* for trumpet, the fantasy *The Dreamer* for trombone, ¶ the foxtrot *Camilla* for alto-saxophone and *Summer Impromptu* for trumpet.

PAUER, Jiří

[born Libušín, 22 February 1919]

LAUREATE OF THE STATE PRIZE, MERITED ARTIST

Pauer studied composition under OTAKAR ŠÍN, ALOIS HÁBA and PAVEL BOŘKOVEC. He ranks among the foremost of contemporary Czech composers.

Pauer's organizational activity is extensive. He was active in the former Musical and Artistic Central Office, in the Ministry of Education and Culture and in the Czechoslovak Radio. At present, he is artistic director of the Czech Philharmonic Orchestra and president of the Czechoslovak Performing Rights Society (OSA). At the same time he is the first secretary of the Guild of Czechoslovak Composers and artistic director of the Opera of the National Theatre in Prague.

Stage Works

For stage performances he composed two one-act operas *The Talkative Snail* (1949—50, première in Prague 1958, Wittenberg 1965) and *Little Red Riding Hood* (1958—59, première in Olomouc 1960).

His full-length opera *Zuzana Vojířová* (1954—57, première in Prague 1958) met with a warm response by large audiences and was awarded the State Prize in 1961.

Orchestral Works

Happy impressions of post-war life in Czechoslovakia permeate his *Youth Suite* for orchestra (1951), the symphonic march *Heroes of Work* (1951) and the orchestral *Scherzo* (1951), as well as the *Rhapsody* for full orchestra (1953), a *Children's Suite* for chamber orchestra (1953), a *Concerto* for oboe and orchestra(1954), a *Concerto* for French horn and orchestra (1957), a *Concerto* for bassoon and orchestra and a *Symphony* for full orchestra (1962 to 1964).

Chamber Music and Instrumental Works

Capriccio for oboe or flute, clarinet or bassoon and piano (1952), *Sonata* for violin and piano (1953), a *Sonata* for violoncello and piano (1954). His *String Quartet* (1959) was awarded the second degree prize in the artistic jubilee competition in 1960. In 1960 he composed a *Wind Quintet* and a *Divertimento* for nonet, in 1963 a piano *Trio*.

Considerable interest was aroused by Pauer's instrumental compositions, above all by his *Suite* for harp (1947) and *Divertimento* for three clarinets (1948—49); recently, he has written *Monologues* for solo clarinet (1964).

Instructive Works

His instructive compositions are very popular: for piano *My Notebook* (1942), *A Happy Journey* (1950) and *We Play for Pleasure* (1957); for violin and piano *Ten on One String* (1958).

Vocal Works

He has written several successful songs for youth ensembles, as *We Build a New World*, *The Miners' Song*, *The Pioneers' Song*, *The Agricultural Song* and others.

An outstanding supplement to the picture of Pauer's compositional personality are his *Children's Lullabies* (1941), a cycle of songs *The Snowed-in Road* (1942), two male choirs in folk character *The Hen* and *Parting* (1944), four *Female choirs* (1945) a potpourri of folk songs for children's choir and orchestra *Singing* (1948), *Children's*

Choirs (1951), the nursery rhyme choirs *The Cricket Violinist* and a *Surly Fellow* for septet (piano) and voice (revised in 1957), a cycle of songs for voice and piano *Fables*, set to words by IGNAC KRASICKI, translated by ERICH SOJKA (1959) and a cycle of children songs and rhymes *Kaleidoscope*.

His two-part dramatic cantata *I Call You, People!* for soprano, tenor, baritone, mixed choir and orchestra to words by JOSEF NOVÁK and VÍTĚZSLAV NEZVAL (1952) expresses a universal yearning for peace.

PEČKE, Karel
[born Prague, 14 September 1890]

Pečke was originally a violinist, member of the Czech Philharmonic in Prague and conductor of the City Theatre at Pilsen. Later he was active in the Prague revue The Red Seven (as band-master and composer of chansons), at the Arena, Variété, Grand Operetta and at the Czech Folk Theatre at Brno.

After the Second World War he became artistic chief of the theatre Urania in Prague, conductor of the Poděbrady Spa Orchestra and music-editor of the Theatrical and Literary Agency Dilia.

Stage Works

His centre of interest was light music. He composed the musical comedy *Helen's Return* (1917, première in Prague 1918), the one-act piece *The Sinner* (1920, première in Prague 1920), the burlesque operetta *Foxtrot Molly*, the revue operetta *What Every Woman Must Have*, *Napoleon's Trumpeter* (in collaboration with M. SMATEK) and *Madeleine* (with B. NIKODEM). Scenic music to the play *Frigidil* by J. NOVÁK and the farce with songs *The Crime of the Brothers Lumière* conclude his stage creative work.

Orchestral Compositions

His orchestral compositions include the lyrical sketch *The Forest*, a concerto valse *Playful Youth*, a dance improvisation *A Melody of Yearning*, the csardás paraphrase *Puszta* (for solo violin and orchestra) and *The Poděbrady Serenade*.

Chamber Music

Pečke has also written chamber music as is evidenced by the *Impromptu and Legend* for violin, harp and violoncello (1913).

Dance Music and Songs

The composer's path led from the chansons to song--dance forms which included ¶ the tangos *Pepita, You Have Taught Me to Lie, The Mimoses, Kiss Me More, I Want to Love You, Don't Complain*; ¶ the valses: *The Dream of Love, A Woman's Love, My Little Dog, Snow on the Plains, The Blue Garden*; ¶ the foxtrot: *Young Men, Not Yet, My Girl*; ¶ the polka *A Headstrong Girl*; ¶ the marches *Present Arms, That Sparta of Ours*.

¶ The march songs: *A White Road, The Song of Spring, That Beautiful Land of Ours, When the Trumpet Calls, Long Live Ostrava* and above all, the world-known march *The Artists* (in collaboration with M. SMATEK) and the one-time popular song *The Field Poppies*.

PEK, Albert

[born Poděbrady, 21 October 1893]

MERITED TEACHER

Pek studied in the composition class of VÍTĚZSLAV NOVÁK. After completing his studies at the Prague Conservatory he became a teacher at Prague secondary schools, was choirmaster of the Vinohrady choral society Hlahol and conductor of the Vinohrady Opera. In 1920 he assumed the post of director of the City School of Music at Znojmo.

In addition to his pedagogic and organizational activity he was an untiring collector of folk songs, studied various folk instruments, founded a bagpipers' ensemble, directed the Znojmo Philharmonic and was choirmaster of the choral association Vítězslav Novák.

In 1940 he joined the Prague Radio where he was director of the ethnographic division. For the radio programme Songs of Home he wrote tens of broadcasts. In 1953 he was appointed teacher of folk instruments at the Prague Conservatory.

Stage Works

Pek's musical dramatic forms are represented by the operas *Tintagil's Death* (an opera for puppets, 1920), *A Red Letter* (1925—31), *The Dancer from Šemacha* (1939), the opera *Love*, the opera trilogy *Arabesque, Humoresque* and *Idyll*, children's operas *Three Hellers, The Waterlily Queen* and *A Golden Thread*, the ballet *I Relate a Fairy tale* (1935, première at Znojmo 1935) and arrangements of folk plays.

Folk Song Adaptations

Pek's creative work bears the mark of the influence of the folk song and folk dance evidenced by his compositions for cimbalom (16 études, two concertos, numerous arrangements of folk songs of Moravian Slovakia), a suite and a concerto for accordion, two suites for bagpipe with accompaniment by string orchestra, marches, dances, songs and arrangements of folk songs for bagpiper ensembles, a Sonatina and a Suite for flute à bec, *Highlander's dances, Russian dances* and two *Spanish dances* for full orchestra, *Tartar Melodies*, a *Serenade on Spanish Motifs*, a *Christmas Prelude* and *Carol* for string orchestra, *The Jugoslav Rhapsody* and *From South Bohemia* for string quartet, *The String Quartet* in A minor on Russian motif and a large number of arrangements of Czech, Moravian, Armenian, Jugoslav, White Russian, Polish and Kizilbash folk songs.

Among his choral works are the cantata *Pastoral Christmas Songs* for solos, choir and orchestra (using the pastorals of the Czoks, a cantor's family, dating from 1758) and orchestral pictures from the literal hymnals *Christmas* and improvisations on a Gothic theme for orchestra and organ *Flos Florum*.

Film Music

Pek is the author of successful accompaniments to short films (*Old-Age Beauty*, *A Warsaw Summer*, *The Art of Etching*, *Karlštejn*, *Masters of Lithography*, *The Art of Woodcutting*, *Iranian Miniatures*, *A Baroque Suite*, *Arts and Crafts*, *Istanbul*, *Where Flies a Stork*, *Ferhat*, *The Mystery of the Hettites*, *The Valley of Wonders* and *A New Home*).

PELIKÁN, Miroslav

[born Prague, 20 February 1922]

After completing the secondary school, he graduated from the composition section of the Prague Conservatory as a pupil of EMIL HLOBIL and took as well the state examination in piano. For several years he was a teacher at a school of music; at present he devotes himself exclusively to composition.

Prior to his matriculation at the Conservatory he had already composed a *Suite* for flute and piano (1943) which attracted the attention of musical circles. In the course of his studies his expressive compositional talent was evidenced in his *Four Capricious Compositions* for piano (1946), first *Sonatina* for violin and piano (1948), a cycle of songs set to folk love poetry carrying the title

343

Love of Simple Hearts (1948) and the *String Quartet* (1950, his graduation work).

Pelikán's other creative work includes *Two Czech Dances—Polka* and *Furiant* for piano (orchestra, 1954), *Toccata* for piano (1955), *Suite* for French horn and piano (1955), a *Symphony* (1958), a cycle of female choirs *Home* (1960), an orchestral scherzo *A Day of Joy* (1962), *Capricious Miniatures* for wind quintet (1962), a *Merry Overture* for small orchestra (1962) and the second *Sonatina* for violin and piano (1963).

He is as well the author of a *Festive March*, the march *The Variety Show Begins*, *The March of Our Weekdays*, and of other orchestral compositions such as *Tarantella*, *The Jump Dance*, *An Idyllic Polka* and a *Lyric Intermezzo*, of songs for youth ensembles, choirs, many arrangements of folk songs and instructive compositions for violin and piano.

PEŘINA, Hubert

[born Přerov, 25 December 1890—died Prague, 29 December 1964]

Peřina graduated from the higher economic school and became a teacher at economic schools. During his pedagogical work at Třebíč, he studied piano at the Brno Conservatory (1920—28). In 1945 he graduated from the section of composition at the Prague Conservatory and its Master School.

He has composed several symphonic compositions as an *Overture*, a *Concertino* for piano and orchestra, a *Symphony*, a *Piano Concerto*; a cantata *The Winter Ballad*; three *String Quartets*, a *Wind Quintet*, a *Trio* for wind instruments, *Sonatas* and *Sonatinas* for piano, clarinet, French horn, bassoon; song-cycles, *Instructive Compositions* for piano and a *Medley* for children's choir, flute and string trio.

PETR, Zdeněk

[born Kopřivnice, 21 September 1919]

Petr studied architecture and later philosophy. After the universities were closed down during the German occupation, he was active as editor, arranger and administrative clerk at the Dvorský Publishing Company for light and dance music in Prague.

After the Second World War he continued the study of musical science and aesthetics at the Faculty of Philosophy of Charles University.

In 1949 he joined the staff of the Czechoslovak Radio in Prague where he was first editor of light music broadcasts, later of popular and operetta music and finally of symphonic, chamber and vocal music programmes.

At the Radio he founded and for several years directed a full dance orchestra and a variety ensemble with a choir, collaborated in cabarets, variety shows and particularly in the popular programmes MUSIC FOR JOY. He introduced a new type of popularizing broadcast MUSIC, OUR FRIEND. At present he is in charge of small musical genres at the State Publishing House of Music.

His successful compositions include songs from the musical comedy *A Hundred Ducats for Juan* and *The Song for Christine* which attained world-wide popularity.

For the film *Emperor's Baker* and *Baker's Emperor* he composed the main song which became very popular with the broad public. His other successful songs include: *Tomorrow, Good Night, The First Swallow, When the River Sings, Then I Don't Know, Beware of Jealousy, The Red Automobile Aero* and *One Woman Loves You.*

Petr arranged the music from the comedy Finian's Rainbow *A Magic Pot* for the orchestra of Karel Vlach and has also written music to the play *The Comedian* by the contemporary English dramatist JOHN OSBORNE for the National Theatre in Prague and songs for the satirical review *Beware! A Kind Dog.*

Recently he has written the march song *A Bluish*

Day for the Festival of Youth in Helsinki (1962) and a cycle of songs and chansons entitled *Prague Songs*.

He is active in the organizational work in the section for composition of the Guild of Czechoslovak Composers.

PETRŽELKA, Vilém
[born Brno, 10 August 1889]
MERITED ARTIST,
holder of the decoration FOR OUTSTANDING WORK

Petrželka is a pupil of LEOŠ JANÁČEK and VÍTĚZSLAV NOVÁK and ranks among the most outstanding contemporary Moravian composers and pedagogues. As professor of composition of many years standing at the Brno Conservatory and later at the Janáček Academy of Musical Arts he has trained several generations of composers.

Tenaciously, he fought his way clear of the influence of his teachers nor did he succumb to the fashionable trends of the twenties and thirties but with forethought found an individual musical expression imbued with the earthly fragrance of his native Moravia.

Stage Works

The fundamental dramatic idea of his three-act opera *The Miner Paul* (1935—38) is the struggle of the working man against capitalism.

Orchestral Works

Petrželka's orchestral work includes a three-part musical poem *The Eternal Return* (1922—23), a *Suite* for small orchestra (1924—25), the three-part symphonic drama *Sailor Nicholas* (1929), *The Dramatic Overture* (1932), *Partita* for string orchestra (1934), a one-movement *Sinfonietta* (1941) and a *Pastoral Sinfonietta*

(1951—52). The one-movement *Concerto* for violin with orchestra (1943) and the *Symphony* for full orchestra (1956) complete Petrželka's symphonic work in a characteristic manner.

Instrumental and Chamber Music

Petrželka achieved great success as well in this field. We refer to the *Sonata* in C minor for piano (1908), *Songs of Poetry and Prose* for piano (1917), a *Sonata* for solo violoncello (1930), a *Sonata* for violin and piano (1933), the *Piano Trio* (1936—37), *Four Impromptus* for violin and piano (1939—40), five *String Quartets*, *Divertimento* for wind quintet (1941), a *Serenade* for nonet (1946) and others.

Vocal Works

His cycles of male choir *Life* (1914), *The Resurrection* (1917), song-cycles *The Elements* (1917), *Solitude of the Soul* (1919), the cantata *A Prayer to the Sun* (1921), *The Path* (1924), *Relay Race* (1926—27) and *Views of Nature* (1933) represent one evolutionary whole of an austere philosophical and artistic conception.

His male choir *The Alarm* (1939) is simultaneously an expression of desperation written on the occasion of the Munich Pact, as well as a call for revenge. His male choir *This is My Land* (1940) had a revolutionary impact upon his students during the war. In the male choir *For Peace* (1949) the artist speaks as a defender of freedom for the happy future on this earth.

At the end of 1962 Petrželka completed his male choir *The Spring Song* to words by FRANTIŠEK BRANISLAV.

●

In a significant manner Petrželka has also made his place as a musical critic. He is honorary chairman of the Brno branch of the Guild of Czechoslovak Composers.

PÍCHA, František

[born Řípec, 3 October 1893—died Prague, 10 October 1964]

Pícha received his musical education at first under BOHUSLAV and OTAKAR JEREMIÁŠ at České Budějovice. After the First World War, he studied composition at the Prague Conservatory under J. B. FOERSTER, JAROSLAV KŘIČKA and JOSEF SUK and was one of the first graduates of the Master School of SUK.

He became a pedagogue and this intensified his interest in the folk art of his native Southern Bohemia, which inevitably led to an extensive activity as collector. In 1938 he became professor of composition at the Prague Conservatory.

Orchestral Works

His orchestral music includes: a symphonic poem *The Pilgrim's Night Songs,* op. 7 (1924), a *Suite* for orchestra and gong, op. 18 (1932), a symphonic allegro *The Challenge,* op. 19 (1933), a dramatic overture *Stiepan-chikovo,* op. 20 (1931), *Two Festive Marches,* op. 26 (1938) a symphony for string orchestra *Christmas,* op. 30 (1941), a symphonic scherzo *Song of Courage,* op. 32 (1946), *Two Suites* for small orchestra, op. 34 (1953) and op. 39 [*Children's World*] (1962—63); *The Violin Concerto* in D major, op. 36 (1960) concludes, for the time being, his symphonic work.

Chamber Music

String Quartet No. 1, op. 6 (1923), *Violin Sonata* No. 1, op. 9 (1925), *Trio quasi una fantasia,* op. 21 (1934), *Violin Sonata* No. 2 op. 23 (1935), *Prelude* and *Scherzo* for piano, op. 29 (1936), *String Quartet* No. 2, op. 30 (1943) and *Wind Quintet,* op. 31 (1944).

Vocal Works

The major part of his compositional work consists of vocal music. He has a special affinity for vocal music and song since he has the faculty of handling the human voice with great sensitiveness and a thorough grasp of choral compositions. He has written a number of song cycles: *In later Years*, op. 1 (1925), *Night Voices* op. 3 (1926), *I'll Return Again*, op. 5 (1926), *The Revolt of the Heart*, op. 8 (1928), *Life*, op. 15 (with violin, viola and piano 1928), *From the Depths*, op. 18 (1928), *Silence*, op. 22 (violin, viola and piano, 1934), *The Voice of the Native Soil*, op. 33 for baritone (1951) and op. 35 for mezzo-soprano (1959) and *Harsh Love* for middle voice, op. 38 (1960).

Pícha's choral compositional work is prolific as well:

female choirs *On the Road*, op. 2 (1925), *Love*, op. 11 (1926), *Female Choirs*, op. 27 (1933), *A Small Spring*, op. 24 (accompaniment by violin, oboe, bassoon and piano, 1936), *A Song of Faith*, op. 37 (with four-hand accompaniment, 1960);

male choirs *The Meditation*, op. 4 (1926), *Moments of Humility*, op. 10 (1926), *From a Full Goblet*, op. 13 (1927), *The Artery Throbs*, op. 14 (1927);

mixed choirs *Two Hymns*, op. 12 (1927);

children's choirs with piano accompaniment, op. 28 (1943).

Pícha's numerous and outstanding arrangements of folk songs belong as well to this category.

His most important vocal compositions are the cantata symphonies *Ecce homo* for orchestra, choir and organ, op. 16 (1929, with a new version 1950) and the *Service for the Dead* (Panichida) op. 34 (1956).

Writings

Pícha has written a book of reflections on life and musical creative work entitled *Uncovered Roots* (1929), *The General Instruction on Music* (1949), and *A Short and General Harmony* (1949).

In manuscript form still are *A Musical Ear* (1958) and *A Complete Book of Harmony* (the first version dating from the year 1945).

PIŇOS, Alois

[born Vyškov, 2 October 1925]

Piňos completed the study of forestry engineering and simultaneously studied music, the latter privately at the Brno Conservatory, completing it at the Janáček Academy of Musical Arts, where he was pupil of VILÉM PETRŽELKA and JAROSLAV KVAPIL.

In his early compositional activity the folk song element is predominant, particularly in his vocal works where he attained a sound elemental expression. Later his creative work was marked by the endeavour to arrive at a new content by an independent application of modern compositional principles. At the same time Piňos lays stress on new melodics and new rhythm.

Chamber Music

The results of his endeavours are concentrated particularly in his chamber music compositions: *Sonata* for violoncello and piano (1950), two *Wind Quintets* (1951 and 1959), *Sonata* for viola and violoncello (1959), *Trio* for violin, violoncello and piano (1960), *Suite* for string trio (1960), *Caricatures* for flute, bass-clarinet and piano (1962), *String Quartet* (1962), *Monologues* for wind instruments (1962) and *Lyrical Sketches* and *Conflicts* for violin, bass-clarinet, piano and percussion instruments (1964).

Orchestral Works

Czech Dances (1951), an orchestral *Wedding Suite* (1952), *Concerto* for French horn and orchestra (1953), *Concertino* for orchestra (1963) and a cycle of compositions for orchestra *Abbreviations* and *Two Compositions* for a reciter, flute and violin, set to words by JAN SKÁCEL (1964).

Instrumental Works

A piano suite *In a Summer Camp* (1949), *Passacaglia* for piano (1950) and *Capriccio amaro* for organ (1962).

Vocal Works

Voices: four songs for middle voice and piano *I Have Come to Live,* set to words by LUDVÍK AŠKENAZY (1961 to 1962);

Songs: *Songs on Love* set to words of Slovak folk poetry (1949), *Mountain Songs* (1953), song-cycles *Lullabies* (1956), *A Happy River* (1957), *From the Book of Woods, Waters and Hillsides* (1959) and *Mourning Songs* (1960).

Choral cycles: *The Children's Year* (1951)and the fairy-tale *The Sun, the Moon and the Wind* (1952);

Mixed Choir: *A Slovak Ballad* to words by MILAN KUNDERA (1962);

Cantatas: *Peace* to words by FRANTIŠEK BRANISLAV (1953), awarded a prize in the Jubilee Competition of the Guild of Czechoslovak Composers and the Czech Music Fund (1956).

Instructive Compositions

In addition, Piňos composed three collections of instructive compositions for string chamber ensembles, scenic music and music to pantomimes.

PLAVEC, Josef

[born Heřmanův Městec, 8 March 1905]

Holder of the decoration FOR OUTSTANDING WORK

Plavec was a pupil of JOSEF BOHUSLAV FOERSTER and has oriented himself in the main to vocal music.

Chamber and Instrumental Music

In the instrumental field Plavec has composed a *String Quartet* (1928), a symphonic poem *Summer Moments* (1932), *Summer Overture* (1933), *Meditations* for viola and piano (1934), an *Overture* (1937), an orchestral *Scherzo*

(1939), a *Fantasy* for violin and piano (1941), a *Suite* for piano (1944) and *Variations* for organ (1945).

Vocal Works

In addition to individual choirs, he has composed a number of outstanding choir cycles and songs:

Voices: *Only in Us is Spring* for alto (1928—29), *Three Songs* to words by MARIE PUJMANOVÁ for mezzo-soprano (1939—40), *Dawn* for tenor and soprano (1947), *Voices of Eastern Wisdom* for alto and organ (1952) and *From Tears and Smiles* (1955).

Songs: *Cycle of Songs* to words by JIŘÍ WOLKER (1925 to 1931) and *Three Songs* to words by A. S. PUSHKIN for baritone (1937).

Female choir: *Three Songs of Dawn* (1933).

Male choirs: *The Months* (1928), *Today* (1937), *Words of Steel* (1947) and *Choirs* set to words by JAN NOHA (1962).

Children choirs: two cycle of *Children's Choirs* with piano.

Mixed choirs: *Sub specie mortis* (1935) and *May Greetings to the Nation* (1943—45).

Cantatas: Among the most momentous of the composer's works are the cantatas *Two People* (1931), *We, the Czech and Slovak Peoples* (1938—43) and *The Immortal Village* (1949—50) in memory of the village Ležáky.

Arrangements

Plavec has devoted himself as well to arrangements of folk songs and has made montages of folk songs with orchestra *From the Region of the Iron Mountains* (1948).

Writings

He is an untiring fighter for the development of music education and an outstanding representative of the music scientific school of Zdeněk Nejedlý.

He has written monographs on *František Škroup* (1941), *Otakar Jeremiáš* (1943) and a number of articles on

Zdeněk Fibich, J. B. Foerster and Otakar Ostrčil. Recently, he has enriched the literature on Smetana by following works: *Smetana's Choral Works* (1954) and *Choral Compositions* (1956). He has worked untiringly for the publication of a volume of pre-First World War national songs *Wreath of Patriotic Songs* (1960) and the Czech edition of the book by IGOR BELZA *Czech Classical Music* (1961). He is collaborating in the publishing of a study of Smetana's works.

At present, he is at the head of the cathedra of musical education at the Pedagogical Institute in Prague.

PLICHTA, Jan

[born Kouřim, 1 December 1898]

Holder of the decoration FOR OUTSTANDING WORK

Plichta studied violin in the class of ŠTĚPÁN SUCHÝ at the Prague Conservatory. In 1919 he was appointed concertmaster of the theatre at České Budějovice, became first violinist of the South-Bohemian Quartet and from 1920 teacher at the local Teachers' Training Institute. From the year 1929 he was active at the Ostrava Radio (at first as concertmaster and later as conductor, chief of the orchestra and manager of the music section). In 1936—1951 he was conductor of the Brno Radio Symphony Orchestra. In 1952—57 he was as well regional inspector of music schools at Brno. At present he teaches at the Brno Conservatory (violin, chamber music, orchestral exercises).

His compositional creative work includes four cycles on motifs of Moravian Slovak songs for voice and orchestra (1936—45), a *Serenade* (1938), *Capriccio* (1946), two potpourris of Moravian folk songs for children's choir and orchestra (1947), *A Spanish Melody* (1959) for violin and orchestra and a cycle *From Moravian*

Nooks for woman's voice with piano accompaniment (1962).

His work includes further a *Slovak Dance* (Odzemek) for orchestra (1933), four *Russian Dances* (arranged also for accordion with orchestra, 1945), *Pizzicato* (1959), the musical comedies *Tommy is Getting Married, Three Days of Happiness, From One Pot, Taboo, We Give Away a Million* and *A Rich Bride,* a folk play with songs entitled *The Bud from the Brewery Garden,* the children's fairy-tale song-play and numerous songs and dance compositions.

Plichta instrumented the compositions of JAN MALÁT, KAREL BENDL, ZDENĚK FIBICH, FRANTIŠEK ONDŘÍČEK, HENRY WIENIAWSKI, FERENCZ LISZT and others. He also arranged and revised the viola concertos of JAN VAŇHAL, KAREL STAMIC and ANTONÍN VRANICKÝ. In addition he has also made arrangements of several violin compositions (BACH, CORELLI, TARTINI, VERACINI) for viola.

PODÉŠŤ, Ludvík
[born Dubňany, 19 December 1921]
Holder of the decoration FOR RECONSTRUCTION SERVICES

Podéšť graduated from the Brno Composition School of JAROSLAV KVAPIL. He completed the study of musical science by taking his doctor's degree.

The twenty years he spent in Moravian Slovakia, region of his birth, are reflected not only in his arrangements of folk songs and dances, in songs, song cycles, choirs and community songs, but also in his chamber music and symphonic works.

Stage Works
His musical dramatic work comprises the operettas *Emil and Dynamite, The Film Star,* the operetta elaboration of ZROTAL's play *A Hen and the Sexton* and the operat-

ic *Three Apocryphas* to short stories by KAREL ČAPEK (1957—58) [the last one had its première in Brno 1959 and was produced as well on television and on the radio].

In 1962 Poděšť completed the comic opera *Frolics with the Devil*, according to the play of the same name by JAN DRDA (première in Liberec 1963).

Orchestral Works

Of his symphonic works it is necessary to mention the three-movement *Symphony* (his graduation work of 1947—48), the poem *Raymonde Dien* (1950) in honour of French fighters for peace, two piano *Concertos* (1952 and 1958), *Violin Concerto* (1953), the *Advent Rhapsody* (1956), four orchestral *Suites*, *Concertino* for two cimbaloms and orchestra and the *Rustic Christmas* for narrator and orchestra, set to a story of VLADISLAV VANČURA.

Recently, he has composed a *Concertino* for cimbalom and symphonic orchestra (1963), reworked his *Symphony* (1964), has written symphonic variations *The Seconds of A Day* (1965) and in instrumental creation added *Small Compositions* for piano (in six parts) (1965).

Chamber and Instrumental Music

Poděšť has composed two *String Quartets* (1946 and 1948), *Sonata* for violin (1949), *Sonata* for violoncello (1957) and a number of instrumental compositions, seven song cycles and two cantatas.

In 1965, he composed a *Concertino* for two violoncellos and chamber orchestra.

Film Music

He has done outstanding work as a composer for the films: *Advent, Chinese Spring, Florence 13.30, Florian, Bitter Love, The Master and the Astronomer, A Song for a Penny, Red Glare Over Kladno, A Waltz for a Million, In Streams, Focus, Please!, The Cannon Gone Astray* and *Tomorrow We Dance Everywhere*, as well as music to the films *Please Don't Wake* and *Three Male Choirs*.

355   **PODÉŠŤ**

Lately, he has composed music to two films, viz. *Three Chaps in a Cottage* and *Kinematofor*.

Radio Music

He has also written music for a number of plays, radio performances and for the radio musical comedies *When Nannette Married* and *There Can Be No Feast Without a Cimbalom*.

For the variety music he has written an orchestral cycle *Coloured Postcards* (in four parts) (1964).

Vocal Music

His songs *On the Watch*, *Hello the World!*, *Welcome Among Us!* and *Singing Together* were awarded in the artistic jubilee competition in 1960.

Recently, he composed following chamber songs: a cycle *Quiet Certainties*, set to words of FRANTIŠEK HALAS, *Good-bye and Kerchief*, set to words of VÍTĚZSLAV NEZVAL, and *One Million and One Hundred Thousand*, set to words of JAROSLAV SEIFERT (all of them 1964).

Various

Podéšť significantly influenced the development of the Army Artistic Ensemble Vít Nejedlý (of which he was artistic director from 1953 to 1956) and the musical programmes department of Czechoslovak Television (of which he was the director from 1958 to 1960).

For the Third Spartakiad he composed music to exercises *United Ahead* (1964).

PODEŠVA, Jaromír
[born Brno, 8 March 1927]

Son of a violin-maker, studied composition at the Janáček Academy of Musical Arts under JAROSLAV KVA-

PIL and in 1960—61 under HENRY DUTILLEUX in Paris and AARON COPLAND in New York.

He was lecturer at the Janáček Academy of Musical Arts, secretary of the Guild of Czechoslovak Composers and chairman of its branch at Brno.

Stage Works

His work up to the present is considerably extensive and embraces many genres. In 1963 he completed his opera *If You Leave Me...*, according to the novel by ZDENĚK PLUHAŘ.

Orchestral Works

Of his symphonic compositions mention should be made, in addition to his *First Symphony* (1951), of the three-part cycle of symphonic poems *The Path of the Homeland* (*The Kounic Halls*, *The Red Army Enters the Country*, *The Great March*, 1952—53) of which the first part, the *Kounic Halls* set to the poem of MILAN KUNDERA, received the second prize in the competition at the Festival of Youth in Warsaw 1955; further his symphonic poem *The Meeting of Youth* (1956), a *Triple Concerto* for violin, violoncello, piano and orchestra (1956—57), *Suita Notturna* (1957), a *Sinfonietta* for string orchestra (1959), *Second Symphony* for strings and flute (1960), an overture *The Festival l'Humanité* for strings and brasses (1961).

Chamber Music

He has writen considerable chamber music of importance as four *String Quartets* [No. 1 (1948), No. 2 (1950), No. 3 *You Will Live in Peace* (1951) and No. 4 (1955), inspired by a poem of IVO FLEISCHMANN *From the History of a New Contemporary*, was awarded in the artistic jubilee competition in 1960].

Podešva's further chamber music compositions include a *Sonatina* for clarinet and piano (1948), two *Sonatas* for violin and piano (1948 and 1958, awarded a third

357   **PODEŠVA**

prize in the competition at the Festival of Youth in Vienna), a *Concertino* for trombone and piano (1949), a *Sextet* (1949), a *Poetic Trio* (1954), a nonet *Of Happy Children* (1954—55), a *Sonatina* for violoncello and piano (1960), a *Sonatina* for cornet and piano (1960) and *Three Sonata Studies* for flute and piano (1964).

Instrumental Works

Two *Sonatas* for piano (1951, 1953), *Four Miniatures* for piano (1953), a *Rhapsodietta* for piano (1955), a piano suite *Parisian Seconds* (1961) and a piano cycle *The Piano Tells Nursery Rhymes* (1963).

Vocal Works

Of his vocal creative work mention should be made of the cantata for mixed choir and string orchestra *The New Man* (1949) and of the cantata *The Party Membership Card* (1951), awarded the second prize in the competition at the Festival of Youth in Berlin.

Podešva's choral works include a male choir *To Ostrava* (1950), *Fly, My Dove!* (1951), three male choirs *To the Army of Our People* (1951), three children's choirs *Wild Thyme* (1954), a cycle of male choirs *The Hero's Song* (1954), a mixed choir *Life of Woman* (1957), a vocal poem for male double-choir *The Great Chorus* (1958), two male *Choirs* to poems by OLDŘICH MIKULÁŠEK (1959), a sinfonietta for mixed choir *A Salute to the Universe* (1960) a cycle of songs for choir and piano, *Short Fairy-tales* set to words of KAREL ŠIKTANC (1961), a sinfonietta *Of Nature* fox mixed choir (1962), set to words by MIROSLAV HOLUB, *Farewell Black City*, three female choirs to words by OLDŘICH MIKULÁŠEK (1962) and *Spring Cycle*, six male choirs (1964).

Podešva wrote as well many community songs and chamber music songs, as for instance *The Song of Friendship* (1951), *Forward the Army of Peace!* (1952), a cycle of songs *The Intimate Voice* (1955), *Simple Songs on Prévert* (1959) and *Two Little Songs for Sparks* (1962).

He has composed as well popular valses for variety performances and military songs.

Writings

He has written a book *Contemporary Music in the West* (1961—62).

POKORNÝ, Antonín

[born Škvorec, 18 January 1890]

Holder of the decoration FOR OUTSTANDING WORKS

After completing the secondary school, Pokorný studied composition under EMANUEL JAROŠ, a pupil of Antonín Dvořák, and under VÍTĚZSLAV NOVÁK.

Stage Works

His full-length opera *A Philosopher Story* according to the novel of the same name by ALOIS JIRÁSEK (1957) and the one-act opera *Cyrano's Death* according to EDMOND ROSTAND (1958) are the most significant expressions of Pokorný's creative activity during the recent years.

Instrumental and Chamber Music

His instrumental compositions did not remain without response in musical circles. These works include *Preludes* (1910—15), a *Piano Sonata* in F sharp minor (1916), a *String Quartet* (1918), *Bright Flowers* (1954—56), *Meditation* for violoncello and piano (1954—55), a *Violin Sonatina* (instructive, 1956), *Polonaise* for violin and piano (1957) and a *String Quartet* (1959).

Vocal Works

Of his creative work vocal compositions are of primary importance. He composed several song-cycles which include primarily *Meditations* (*Songs on Death*) to poems

by J. V. Sládek (1945), *A Beautiful Land* to poetry by
Jaroslav Seifert, J. B. Sedlák, Zdeněk Kalista and
Karel Burian (1946), *Trees and People* and *Mozart in
Prague* to poems by Jaroslav Seifert (1955), *The Poet
and Children*, *From the Homeland*, *Songs* set to words by
R. M. Rilke and *Mourning Songs*. The poetry of Petr
Bezruč inspired Pokorný to compose the song *The
Guelder Rose* (1951) and a cycle of *Three Male Choirs*
(*Hrabyň—Below the Mountains—You and I*, 1955), awarded
in the Jubilee Competition of the Guild of Czechoslovak
Composers and the Czech Music Find in 1956) and
female and mixed choirs.

He is as well the author of the melodrama *Follow
Your Heart* to words by Jan Neruda (1917).

Arrangements

He has arranged several albums for children (from
Czech, Italian, French, Russian and German operas
and from the works of Antonín Dvořák).

He is collaborating on the publication of the complete
edition of the works of Antonín Dvořák and Zdeněk
Fibich.

POLÍVKA, Vladimír

[born Prague, 6 July 1896—died Prague 11 May 1948]

Polívka graduated from the piano class of Josef
Procházka at the Prague Conservatory and from the
Master School where he was a pupil in composition of
Vítězslav Novák.

After the First World War, together with the violin
virtuoso Jaroslav Kocián, he made a concert tour
around the world. As a piano pedagogue he was active
in Chicago, Písek and at the Prague Conservatory.

He was chairman of the Association for Contemporary
Music called Přítomnost, regional inspector of musical

schools and chairman of the state commission of examiners for teachers of music.

Stage Works

The climactic point of Polívka's compositional activity was attained by his opera *The Demi-god* (Heracles) to a libretto by OTAKAR FISCHER (1930). He set to music melodramatically *A Ballad in the Eyes of a Stoker* by JIŘÍ WOLKER (1924) and *A Ballad of a Deaf-mute Child* by JIŘÍ KARÁSEK (1936). He also composed scenic music and occasionally ballet music as well.

Orchestral Works

He enriched Czech orchestral literature by a symphonic poem *Spring* (his graduation work in 1918), a *Small Symphony* (1921), *Suite* (1930), *Overture* in D minor (1942) and a *Symphony* (1943, unfinished).

Chamber Music and Instrumental Works

Polívka's chamber music includes two violin *Sonatas* (1918 and 1919), a *Suite* for viola and small orchestra (1933), a *Suite* for viola and wind quintet (1934), a *String Quartet* (1937), *Divertimento* for wind quintet (1939), *Giacona* for viola and piano (1944) and a viola *Sonata* (1945).

Piano compositions occupy a significant place in Polívka's creative work. In addition to large forms represented by the *Concerto* for piano and small orchestra (1934), a *Sonata* (1932) and *Prelude, Passacaglia* and *Fugue* (1936), Polívka's work includes also smaller forms and cycles such as *Days in Chicago* (1926), *Three Impromptus* (1930), *Preludes* (1931), *Bio* (1936), *Landscapes* (1941), *Dances* (1947), and small and instructive compositions [*Merry Music, A Small Suite, Seven New Compositions for Youth*].

Vocal Works

His vocal compositions are numerous and are set to

words both by Czech poets (ADOLF HEYDUK, JOSEF HO-
RA, S. K. NEUMANN, ANTONÍN SOVA and others) as by
foreign authors (J. W. GOETHE, REMY DE GOURMONT,
A. S. PUSHKIN and others). They include the following:
song-cycles *Songs of Venice* (1922), *Festive Cantata* for
mixed choir and orchestra (1930), a male choir *The
Revolution* (1930), *Wings* (1931—32), *The Pacific Ocean and
the Earth from which We Come* for voice, violin, violoncello
and piano (1934), *Malayan Songs* (1935), *Three Female
Choirs* (1923—37) and the mixed choir *Prague* (1939).

Polívka also arranged Czech and American folk
songs.

Writings

He is the author of numerous articles dealing with
music, of essays and publications: *With Kocián Around
the World* (1945) and *Musical America* (1949).

POLOLÁNÍK, Zdeněk

[born Tišnov, 25 October 1935]

Pololáník studied organ at the Brno Conservatory
under JOSEF ČERNOCKÝ and composition at the Academy
of Musical Arts under VILÉM PETRŽELKA and THEODOR
SCHÄFER.

Chamber Music

In his creative work up to the present, chamber
music and symphonic compositions prevail. His chamber
music includes *Variations* for organ and piano (1956),
a *Suite* for violin and piano (1957), a *String Quartet*
(1958), *Toccata* for doublebass, brasses, percussion
instruments, two harps, harpsichord and piano (1959),
Divertimento for strings and four French horns (1960),
Scherzo contrario for violin, bass-clarinet and xylophone

(1961), *Small Mythological Exercises* for string quartet and recitative (1961), *Musica spingenta* (first for doublebass and wind quintet, 1961, second for string quartet and cembalo, 1961, third for bass-clarinet and percussion instruments, 1962).

Orchestral Works

His symphonic work includes a *Sinfonietta* for full orchestra (1958), four *Symphonies* (first for full orchestra, 1961, second for wind instruments, 1962, third for percussion instruments and organ, 1962 and fourth for string orchestra, 1963).

Instrumental Works

Among his instrumental works are *Preludes* for piano (1957), *Variations on two Moravian Songs* for piano (1957), a *Sonata bravura* for organ (1959), a *Sonata gaudia* for organ (1962) and a *Sonata eccentrica* for solo violin (1963).

Vocal Music

In the field of vocal music Pololáník has composed *Four Songs on the End of Spring* for lower voice and nonet (1958), a musical piece *Nabuchodonosor* fox mixed choir, four timpani and three trumpets (1960), a mixed choir with piano *Vávra* (1960) and the mixed choir *Two Spring Echoes* (1960).

In addition, he has also written scenic music to several radio and theatre plays.

PONC, Miroslav

[born Vysoké Mýto, 2 December 1902]

Ponc studied piano at the Prague Conservatory under ALBÍN ŠÍMA and organ under B. WIEDERMANN; he graduated from the Master School of composition under

JOSEF SUK; he studied also abroad with ARNOLD SCHÖN-
BERG and HERMANN SCHERCHEN (Strasbourg, Venice,
Trieste).

He was one of the first pupils and collaborators of
ALOIS HÁBA. From 1924 to 1927 he occupied himself
with experimental composition in connection with
visual and form elements. His musical drawings were
exhibited in the Berlin group of creative artists of the
expressionistic trend "Der STURM" and at the International Theatre Exposition in Magdeburg (1927). He
organized courses in quarter-tone music in Berlin (1927).

At present, he is chief-conductor of the theatre
section at the National Theatre in Prague.

Stage Works

He achieved great success with his witty suite from
the scenic life to COCTEAU's play *The Wedding Guests on
the Eiffel Tower* (1923, première in Prague 1923, in
Strasbourg 1933).

His experiences in conducting ballets had an influence
on his dance pictures *The Pastoral Idyll, Death of Medusa*
and *Šárka* (1932, produced in Prague 1932), on the
three antique ballet pictures *The Fates* (1935, première
in Prague 1935) and on the three intermezzos in
MOLIÈRE's play *Le Malade imaginaire* (1938, produced in
Prague 1938).

Instrumental and Vocal Works

His song cycle *The Gamins' Chansonettes* (1923) has
a grotesque character. Following his *Five Polydynamic
Compositions* for piano, xylophone and string quartet
(1923), he wrote the song cycles *A Bad Dream*, text by
FRANTIŠEK HALAS (1925), *A Black Swan* set to words
by CHRISTIAN MORGENSTERN (1926), the large orchestral
Prelude (1929), *Three Merry Pieces* for wind quintet (1929),
Little Pieces for flute and piano and for violoncello and
piano (1930), a *Concertino* for piano and orchestra
(1930), *the Nonet* (1932) and the *String Trio* (1937).

Quarter-tone System

In the quarter-tone system he has composed the *Overture to an Ancient Greek Tragedy* (1930), produced at the Tenth Festival of the International Society for Contemporary Music in Vienna (1932) and several compositions for string instruments as well as *Etudes* for piano in the quarter- and sixth-tone system.

Film and Scenic Music

Since 1942, Ponc has devoted himself completely to film and scenic music (J. K. TYL, WILLIAM SHAKESPEARE, ancient dramas) and to music for radio montages. He has also composed music to the first Czech puppet film *Freddie, the Ant.*

POSPÍŠIL, Juraj
[born Olomouc, 14 January 1931]

Pospíšil studied first at the City Music Institute at Olomouc, then composition at the Janáček Academy of Musical Arts in Brno, under VILÉM PETRŽELKA, and finally at the High School of Musical Arts in Bratislava under ALEXANDER MOYZES and JÁN CIKKER.

After graduation he was appointed professor of music theory at the Bratislava Conservatory.

As a composer he has mainly oriented his work to instrumental compositions. His most important work in this field includes the symphonic poem *Mountains and People*, op. 4 (1955), a *Sonata* for violoncello and piano, op. 6 (1956), the first *Symphony* for full orchestra, op. 7 (1957), four compositions for chamber music orchestra entitled *Reflections*, op. 8 (1958), five piano compositions *Monologues*, op. 10 (1960), symphonic variations *A Song About Man*, op. 13 (1961) and the second *Symphony* [*Nebula in Andromeda*], op. 19 (1963).

In vocal music he has written a ballad for solos, choir and orchestra *Margita and Besná*, op. 5 (1955).

Pospíšil has published a textbook *The General Theory of Music*.

PRAVEČEK, Jindřich

[born Vyprachtice, 29 June 1909]

After completion of the secondary school, Praveček matriculated at the Master School of the Prague Conservatory as a student of violin in the class of JAROSLAV KOCIÁN, of conducting under PAVEL DĚDEČEK and of composition under GUSTAV ROOB.

In 1931 he became band-master of military orchestras. He was commander of the Military School of Music and chief conductor of the Principal Brass Band of the Czechoslovak Army. He concluded his career as a conductor in the Czechoslovak Army by preparing and executing the entire musical scores of the First Spartakiad. From 1952 to 1955, he was lecturer on instrumentation for brass bands at the Janáček Academy of Musical Arts.

At present, he is devoting himself to work with Folk Art ensembles.

Instrumental Compositions

The intermezzo *Golden Youth*, the tarantella *To the Stars of the Universe* for brass band, the *Serenade* for violin and orchestra, the *Serenade* for bugle-horn and orchestra, *The Czech Dance*, *The Czech Suite*, a *Ballet Valse* and the *Jump-Dance* amply display the author's sense for an individual expression of ideas. *The Valse Fantasy* for piano and orchestra and the *Jubilee Overture* represent a transition to the secondary type of symphonic music.

In collaboration with VLADIMÍR ÚLEHLA he wrote

a pantomime *Héla, The Noon-Ghost* (1944, première at Hradec Králové 1944).

Light Music

¶ Marches: *Orbis, The Equestrian March, The Falcon, Hail to Peace, With Courage Forward, Hail to our Army, With Valour to Victory, At a Victorious Pace* and *The Astronaut*;

¶ polkas: *Little Liboria, Youth—Joy, The Czech Polka*;

¶ valse: *The Autumn Melody*;

¶ gallop: *With Zest to Work*; all these compositions maintain a high standard of musical good taste and are amplified by expressive melodies, freshness of rhythm and colourful instrumentation.

His polka *Ostrava Dances* was awarded in the artistic jubilee competition in 1960.

Various

He has made instrumentation for numerous compositions for orchestra (SMETANA, CHOPIN, DVOŘÁK, TCHAIKOVSKY, DOBIÁŠ, SEIDEL, STANISLAV, KUBÍN, KALAŠ, SHOSTAKOVICH and others).

In collaboration with KAROL PÁDIVÝ, he has written a textbook on instrumentation for brass band.

PŘECECHTĚL, Zbyněk

[born Klagenfurt, Austria, 3 November 1916]

Přecechtěl studied composition at the Prague Conservatory, where he was a pupil of RUDOLF KAREL and JAROSLAV KŘIČKA.

Upon graduation he was active at the theatre of E. F. Burian and after the Second World War continued in his post there. Soon, however, he joined the Czechoslovak Radio in Ostrava as its musical manager.

In addition, during the years 1955—58, he taught at the Pedagogical Advanced School of Music.

Přecechtěl belongs among the foremost composers in Ostrava. His creative work has been influenced by the regeneration of the folk tradition after the war.

Orchestral Works

In this line he worked in his symphonic compositions; it was an *Overture* for full orchestra (1940), *The Manifest* for orchestra and recitative choir (1944), *In the Hills and Dales*, the *Wallachian Folk Songs* for solos, choir and orchestra (1948) and the *Wallachian Dances* (1950). Then followed the symphonic poem *New Ostrava* (1952) and a *Rhapsody* for piano and orchestra (1954).

Stage Works

A ballet *The Fairy-tale About the Dance* (1941, première in Prague 1941), followed by the opera *Savitri*, according to the tale about the faithfullness of woman, from the Indian epos Mahabharatam (1943).

Chamber and Instrumental Music

A *String Quartet* (1942) and a suite *Lights and Shadows* for two pianos (1948).

Vocal Music

The building up of the country in and around Ostrava is reflected in his songs for community singing [*The March of the Miners, Song of Peace, Down into the Pit, The Tractor Sings*], in the small cantata *The Road to Socialism* for male choir and orchestra (1950), in a song suite *Against the Wind* for alto, string octet and two harps (1945), a cycle of five songs *The Songs of Love* for male choir, female choir and orchestra (1955) and *Songs of Life* for female voice and orchestra (1958).

Within the past few years he has devoted himself to the field of variety and song music.

PROVAZNÍK, Anatol

[born Rychnov on Kněžna, 10 March 1887—died Prague, 24 September 1950]

Provazník acquired the rudiments of music theory from his father, choirmaster at Rychnov. After graduation from the Prague Conservatory, Provazník became organist at the St. Vitus Cathedral in Prague. Since 1930 he was attached to the Czechoslovak Radio where his activity was very versatile, being an accompanist, music arranger and composer.

Stage Works

Provazník is the author of two operas, the dance opera *Akaga* (1927, première in Prague 1928) and the lyrical opera *Ghitta* (1921—22) as well as of several operettas [*The Acrobat, The Bonbon King, The Lady with Blue Hair, The Journeys of Venus, Dolly, The Kiss of Love, Bartered Love*].

Orchestral Works and Cantatas

Provazník's musical training had a direct influence on his most important work, namely the variations for solos, choir, organ and orchestra, *Cantatibus organis* (1935, performed at the Salzburg Festival 1936). The following works fall into the same compositional field: a symphonic poem *Judith* (1907), a *Concerto Fantasy* for viola and orchestra (1929), a symphonic *Overture* (1938), a *Symphony* for baritone, mixed choir and orchestra to words by JAROSLAV VRCHLICKÝ's The Legend St. Procopius (1945), the *Cantata of Work* for solos, mixed choir, recitation, piano, organ and full orchestra to words of folk poetry and to verses by J. V. SLÁDEK and SVATOPLUK ČECH (1948), and a *Fantasy* on a national song for violoncello and orchestra (1950).

Popular compositions

In his numerous popular type compositions Provazník displayed a rich scale of media of expression. This genre includes the orchestral suites *In Nature* and *From the Countryside* (1935), *National Dances* for orchestra, *Czech Dances* for mixed choir and orchestra (1945) and *The March* (1948).

To these compositions numerous arrangements of folk songs should be added such as *Czech Songs*, *Songs of Moravian Slovakia*, *Songs from the Country*, many dance compositions, particularly valses (*Coloratura*, *Fantastic*, *Gracious* and the popular *Valse des Amourettes*).

RAICHL, Miroslav

[born Náchod, 2 February 1930]

Raichl studied composition at the Academy of Musical Arts under PAVEL BOŘKOVEC.

His opera *Fuente Ovejuna*, according to LOPE DE VEGA, attracted attention (1957, première in Prague 1959), as well as his two *Symphonies* (1955, 1958), a violoncello *Concerto* (1955—56), *The Revolutionary Overture* (1958) and of his chamber music compositions the second *Piano Sonata* (1962).

He has also composed a number of choir cycles. In addition he has written many songs for community singing, for variety programmes and dance music.

His interest extends as well to political themes. His *Students' Songs*, the song *Congratulation* and the cycle *Six Satirical Songs* received special mention in the artistic jubilee competition in 1960.

In *Three Songs* for baritone with the accompaniment of flute, double-bass, percussion instruments, guitar and piano (1963), based on poems by the Cuban poet NICOLAS GUILÉN, Raichl was inspired by Latin American folk songs.

RAJTER, Ľudovít

[born Pezinok, 30 July 1906]

MERITED ARTIST

Rajter is an outstanding Slovak conductor; he studied at the Bratislava Academy of Music first piano and violoncello (F. KAFENDA, R. RUPNIK) and then composition and conducting at the Hochschule für Musik in Vienna (FRANZ SCHMIDT, JOSEFPH MARX, CLEMENS KRAUSS). After graduation he attended the Master School in Budapest (ERNÖ DOHNÁNYI).

At first he was active as professor of music theory at the City School of Music in Bratislava and later as conductor of the Radio orchestra in Budapest (1932 to 1945).

After his return to Slovakia he became chief conductor of the orchestra of the Bratislava Radio and since the foundation of the Slovak Philharmonic (1949), he has been its conductor, often being in demand as guest conductor abroad. At the High School of Musical Arts in Bratislava he is in charge of the conducting class.

Rajter's creative work gives evidence of a composer growing out of cultivated late romanticism. His most important works include the ballet *Majáles* (Spring students' festival, première in Budapest 1938), an orchestral *Divertimento* (1946), a suite *Janko, the Hero* (1954). In the chamber music genre he wrote two *Wind Quintets* (1946, 1962), two *String Quartets* (E major, C major, 1946) and a *Suite* for four violins (1953).

He is the author of several choral arrangements of folk music: *Songs of Detva* for male choir (1950), *Songs and Dances from Slovak Grob* (1952). He has written as well a choir *Ho, Away!* (1961) for male voices.

REINBERGER, Jiří

[born Brno, 14 April 1914]

Reinberger graduated from organ and composition section of the Brno Conservatory as a pupil of EDUARD TREGLER and VILÉM PETRŽELKA. He continued the study of organ under B. A. WIEDERMANN in Prague and GÜNTHER RAMIN in Leipzig and completed it at the Master School of the Prague Conservatory under VÍTĚZSLAV NOVÁK. Simutaneously he completed the study of law at Brno.

He was active as pedagogue at the Conservatory in Prague and at Brno.

Reinberger ranks among the most prominent organ interpretors of the compositions of J. S. BACH and at present is professor of organ at the Academy of Musical Arts.

His compositions include two *Symphonies* (1938, 1958), three *Organ Concertos* (1940, 1956, 1960), a *Concerto* for violoncello and orchestra (1962), three cycles of songs and several smaller chamber music compositions.

He stimulated a number of Czech composers to write music for organ, was active in the drive for the publication of compositions for the organ of old Czech Masters (*Classici Boemici per organo*, 1953; F. X. BRIXI: *Concerto per organo ed orchestra* 1956) and edited the three-part anthology *Musica Boemica per organo* (1954, 1956, 1958) and a monography *Organs in Czechoslovakia*.

In addition, Reinberger is active in the Guild of Czechoslovak Composers.

REINER, Karel

[born Žatec, 27 June 1910]

Holder of the decoration FOR OUTSTANDING WORK

Although he completed the study of law at Charles University, he devoted himself exclusively to music, studying composition under ALOIS HÁBA and JOSEF SUK at the Master School of the Prague Conservatory. In addition, he studied musical science at Charles University.

He was musical collaborator of E. F. BURIAN and of the gramophone record factory ESTA, editor of the review „Rytmus", musical editor for the magazines Cultural Policy and Free Czechoslovakia, secretary of the Syndicate of Czech Composers, secretary of the Czech section of the Guild of Czechoslovak Composers and chief of the music department of the Central House of Folk Art in Prague. He was active as well in various trade union organizations.

He is chairman of the Council of the Czech Music Fund.

As a pianist Reiner intensively propagated contemporary music both in Czechoslovakia and abroad. At the Opera House of May 5th, he prepared HÁBA's quarter-tone opera *Mother*.

As a composer Reiner had his roots in the principles of HÁBA's school. His works written after 1945 are noted for their melodiousness and well defined balance of conception. He strives for a realistic creative work which would express the feelings, thoughts and aspirations of a socialist man.

Stage Works

Amongst musically dramatic works there are pantomime *Unity* (1933), incidental music to the old French farce *Maître Patelin* (1936, reworked in 1955), *Something for the Fatherland*, according to the play of V. K. KLICPERA (1936) and an opera *The Enchanted Song* (1951).

Orchestral Works

Concerto for violin and orchestra (1937), *Spring Prelude* (1950), *Symphony* (1960), awarded in the artistic jubilee competition 1960, six pictures according to music for the film *Butterflies Do Not Live Here* (1960).

Chamber and Instrumental Music

Nine *Merry Improvisations* for piano (1928—29), piano *Sonata* No. 1 (1931), *String Quartet* No. 1 (1931), *Concerto* for nonet (1933), piano *Sonata* No. 2 (1942), *Sonata brevis* for violoncello and piano (1946), *String Quartet* No. 2 (1947) and No. 3 (1951), *Four Compositions* for clarinet and piano (1954), *Three Compositions* for oboe and piano (1955), *Elegy and Capriccio* for violoncello and piano (1957), *Sonata* for contra-bass and piano (1957), *Violin Sonata* (1959), *Small Suite* for nine wind instruments (1960), piano *Sonata* No. 3 (1961), *Six Bagatelles* for trumpet and piano (1962) and *Two Compositions* for harp and oboe (1962), as well as *Divertimento* for clarinet, harp and chamber orchestra.

Recently, he has composed *Three Compositions* for solo violin (1963), *Symphonic Overture* (1963), *Six Studies* for flute and piano (1963), *Four Compositions* for solo clarinet (1963), *Three Preludes* for organ (1963), *Trio* for flute, bassclarinet and percussion instruments (1964), a *Suite* for harp (1964) and *Three Compositions* for piano (1964).

Vocal Works

Voices: A cycle of four songs for tenor and piano *The Native Land* (1956) and a concert song for tenor and piano *On Land* (1960);

Songs: fourteen *Songs* to Bohumil Mathesius' translations of Chinese poetry (1936, reworked 1946), five *Songs* set to German and Czech verses of K. H. Mácha (quarter-tone, 1936) and the songs *The Woman Tractorist, The Song of School Youth, Oh, Don't Lament!, At the Goal, A Spring Song of Youth, Young People's Dance, Oh Hills, Oh Dales!, The Train of Joy, A Rocket with a Red Flag, Let's Go!, The Sparks, Yankee, No!, The World Growing Young, The Beloved Land* and others.

Female choirs: six two-part *Songs* set to words by J. V. Sládek for female choir and piano (1958);

Male choirs: two male choirs *How I Love You* and *Thou*

My Country (1956); the choir *At the Red Square* (1960) was awarded in the artistic jubilee competition 1960.

Children's choirs: the cycles of children's choirs *The Floral Horse, The Pioneers' Kerchief, Hail to the Republic!* (all were composed in 1962).

Marches: the march of youth *We March Hand in Hand* (1962).

Mass songs: two songs *We Stand Firm* and *The War Atom* were awarded in the artistic jubilee competition in 1960, as well as the march *We Keep Time on the March.*

Film Music

He composed as well music for the films *Glass, The Arctic Sea Calls* and the film that depicted the tragic fate of Jewish children in Terezín Nazi camp *Butterflies Do Not Live Here.*

ŘEZÁČ, Ivan

[born Řevnice, 5 November 1924]

After completing the secondary school, Řezáč studied piano under FRANTIŠEK RAUCH and composition under VÁCLAV DOBIÁŠ. He is senior lecturer at the Academy of Musical Arts (Faculty of Music).

His creative work up to the present includes:

Chamber Music and Instrumental Works

A *String Quartet* (1955), *Sonata* for violoncello and piano (1956), *Four Nocturnes* for violoncello and piano (1960), a *Torso of the Schumann's Monument* for viola and piano (1963) and a *Duo* for violoncello and piano (1964).

Two piano *Sonatas* (1954, 1957), *Piano Trio* in A minor (1958), a *Sonatina* in C major for piano (1959), six piano compositions entitled *Dry Points* (1961), *Allegro* for piano (1963) and *Capriccio* for organ (1964).

375   ŘEZÁČ

Orchestral Works

Concerto for piano and orchestra (1955), two *Symphonies* (1958 and 1961), an *Overture* to MAJAKOVSKY's poem *The Right Thing* [awarded a special prize in the artistic jubilee competition in 1960] (1959), a sinfonietta for violoncello and orchestra *The Return* (1962) which was inspired by a poem of FRANTIŠEK HALAS.

Vocal Works

A *Montage* for children's choir and small orchestra *Greetings to Spring* (1952), and *Four Songs* to words by VÍTĚZSLAV NEZVAL (1959).

•

Řezáč has also written several scenic compositions and music to films (*The Rehearsal Goes on*, *People—Be On Guard*, *Notes from the Gallows*, *June Days*, *This Year in September*, *Trio* and others).

He is active as well in the field of music criticism.

ŘÍDKÝ, Jaroslav
[born Františkov, 25 August 1897—died Poděbrady, 14 August 1956]
LAUREATE OF THE STATE PRIZE

Řídký occupied himself with music from his early childhood. After the First World War he matriculated at the Prague Conservatory where in addition to the harp he studied composition under JAROSLAV KŘIČKA and after graduation continued at the Master School under J. B. FOERSTER.

On completion of his studies he became a member of the Czech Philharmonic where he played the harp and appeared also as conductor. From 1929 he taught music theory and later composition at the Prague Conservatory.

Since 1948 he taught at the section of composition at the Academy of Musical Arts.

Řídký's work belongs to the significant expression of contemporary Czech music. In the symphonic and chamber music field he created works of permanent value, tying in with the tradition of the creators of Czech national music and expanding it by new media of expression.

Orchestral Works

A noteworthy sense for musical structure and a rich melodic fund, stemming from the elemental musicalness of the Dvořák type, are characteristic traits of Řídký's creative activity.

Heading his compositional heritage are his seven *Symphonies*: the *first*, op. 3 (1923), the *second* with obligato violoncello, op. 4 (1925), the *third*, op. 8 (1928), the *fourth*, op. 10 (1928), the *fifth*, composer's most momentous symphonic work, op. 17 (1930—31), the *sixth* "The *Year 1938*", in unfinished sketch, and the *seventh*, op. 47 (1955).

His orchestral works are supplemented by a *Sinfonietta* in C minor, op. 1 (1923), an *Overture* for full orchestra, op. 11 (1928—29) and a *String Serenade* in E major, op. 37 (1941).

Chamber Music and Instrumental Works

The chamber music counterpart of Řídký's symphonies is represented by five *String Quartets* (the first, op. 6, 1926; the second, op. 9, 1927; the third, op. 16, 1931; the fourth, op. 20, 1933; the fifth, op. 34, 1937. These quartets must be supplemented with further chamber music works: *Quintet* for clarinet and string quartet, op. 5 (1926), two *Nonets* [the first, op. 32 (1933—34), the second, op. 39 (1934)]; chamber *Sinfonietta*, op. 40 (1944—45) and a *Piano Trio*, op. 44 (1951).

Řídký felt a particular inclination to violoncello; in addition to a number of small and witty composi-

tions for violoncello with piano he composed a violoncello *Sonata* No. 1, op. 2 (1923), a *Serenata appassionata*,
op. 12 (1929), a violoncello *Concerto* No. 1, op. 14 (1930),
Furiant, op. 15 (1930), violoncello *Concerto* No. 2, op. 36
(1940) and a violoncello *Sonata* No. 2, op. 34 (1948).

His compositions for v i o l i n include a *Concerto*, op. 7
(1927) and a *Joyous Sonatina*, op. 42 (1947).

For p i a n o he wrote several less extensive compositions and a broadly conceived *Piano Concerto*, op. 46
(1953).

Vocal Compositions

Řídký's vocal music is represented by two cantatas
A Winter Fairy—tale to a text by PETR KŘIČKA, op. 33
(1936) and *To The Native Country* to words by FRANTIŠEK
BRANISLAV, op. 38 (1941).

RIMÓN, Jan

[born Teplice, 28 September 1921]

After completing the secondary school he was accompanist at the Jihlava and Teplice theatres and
later pianist in dance orchestras. Since 1962 he has
been a lecturer on the history of jazz and dance music
at the People's Conservatory in Prague.

He has written music for three revues, two suites,
much dance music and chansons [*Time Flies, I Have Not
Seen You for Long, The Episode, Illona, One World, The
World Is Beautiful*, a *Bouquet of Memories, Young Promises,
My Friend Emil, The Water Front* and *Summer Night, Don't
Tell Fairy—tales, A Romantic Tango, The Sun Has Risen
with You, With a Gay Little Song, A Lucky Chance, We
Like to Live, She is Beautiful, Catherine, Elvíra, The Guitar*
and others].

RISINGER, Karel

[born Prague, 18 June 1920]

Risinger studied composition at the Prague Conservatory under JAROSLAV ŘÍDKÝ and at the Master School under JAROSLAV KŘIČKA and ALOIS HÁBA.

He studied the science of music at Charles University and is candidate of the science of art; he devotes himself to composition and to the theory of music.

Stage Works

His creative work includes the operas *The Devil's Brother—in—law* (1952) and *Cinderella* (1955, première in Prague 1958).

Orchestral Works

A symphonic poem *The Song of Peace* (1950), *Concerto* for violin and orchestra (1953), a *Concerto Overture* (1961) and a *Symphony* (1962).

Chamber Music

String Quartet No. 1 (1942), *Trio* for clarinet, French horn and piano (1942), *Trio* for violin, clarinet and piano (1943), *Nonet* No. 1 (1943), *String Quartet* No. 2 (1946), *Sonatina* for oboe and piano (1949), *Nonet* No. 2 (1952), *Puppet Suite* for clarinet and piano (1953), *String Quartet* No. 3 (1956), *Concertino* for clarinet and string orchestra (1959) and *Small Suite* for wind quintet (1960).

Vocal Works

Songs: the following five song cycles occupy a special place in his creative work: *Three Songs* for bass and piano to words by JAROSLAV SEIFERT (1940), *Three Songs* for baritone, violoncello and piano to words by JOSEF HORA (1943), *Three Songs* for baritone, flute nad piano set to texts of ancient Chinese poetry [BOHUMIL MATHESIUS (1944)], *Three Songs* for alto and string quartet to words by ELIZABETH BROWNING (1948) and *Eight Songs* for voices and piano set to Czech folk poetry (1951).

Voices: The ballad *The Ice Queen* for alto and piano (1953).

Choral singing: A *Mass* for choir, orchestra and organ (1944) and *Four Easter Scenes* to the text of the Kralice Bible (1950).

Female choirs: *Three Female Double—choirs* to words by MILAN KUNDERA (1961).

Cantatas: *Lily* (1943) and *Girl and Death*, set to text by MAXIM GORKY (1961).

Writings

Risinger is the author of a large number of theoretical works on music, including *The Musical—theoretical Basis of Intonation* (his diploma work, 1947), *The Musical—theoretical Basis of New Tone—Systems* (1948), *The General Science of Harmony* (1955), *An Outline of the General Musical Functional System of Expanded Tonality* (1957), *Basic Harmonic Functions in Contemporary Music* (1958) and *The Leading Personalities in Czech Modern Musical Theory* (1963).

Risinger is at present a member of the scientific staff of the Institute for Musical Science in the Czechoslovak Academy of Sciences.

ROSINSKÝ, Jozef
[born Bánovce, 6 December 1897]

Rosinský acquired his training in composition in Torino and Rome. He was active as choirmaster and music pedagogue.

Of his very extensive work embracing practically all genres, his attempts at composing a Slovak national opera aroused considerable interest. The Bratislava Opera produced three of his eight operatic works *Mataj*

(1933), *Matuš Čák Trenčiansky* (1936) and *Čalmak* (1940).

His song creative work has been influenced by folk melodies and of these *Ten Lyric Songs* (1942) and *Slovak Lyric Songs* (1946) have been published.

In addition to various chamber music compositions (for violin and piano, *The String Quartet*) Rosinský devotes himself to the writing of choirs, cantatas and arrangements of folk songs. A number of his vocal and organ compositions have appeared in print.

RYCHLÍK, Jan

[born Prague, 27 April 1916—died Prague, 20 January 1964]

Rychlík graduated from the Master School of the Prague Conservatory as a pupil of JAROSLAV ŘÍDKÝ.

He began his compositional work relatively late. Due to the fact that the universities were closed during the German occupation, he had to discontinue his studies and matriculated at the Conservatory. He was prepared for his work as a result of his wide experience in dance orchestras.

Chamber Music and Instrumental Works

In his compositions the chamber music outweighs other genres. This field offers him greatest opportunities for exploration into the possibilities of instruments and for testing the potentiality of uncustomary usage. However, his sense of balance and a sound musicality do not permit excesses of experimentation.

After his early *Sonatinas* for clarinet and piano (1943) his style acquires definite form in *The Small Suite* for two violins and viola (1945) and in *The Suite* for wind quintet (1945), *Arabesques* for violin and piano (1947 to 50), *Trio* for clarinet, trumpet and bassoon (1948), *Divertimento* for three double-basses (1952), *Pictures and Moods*, a children's chamber suite for ten instruments

(1953), *Etudes* for English horn and piano (1953), *Suite* for string quartet (1954) *Serenade* for eight wind instruments (1957), *Omaggi gravi cembalistici* (1960), *Wind Quintet* (1960), and an *African Cycle* for wind and percussion instruments and piano (1961), in which the composer translates effectively and in a manner of discovery the melody and rhythm of African music into a modern chamber music expression.

Rychlík has composed interesting cycles in his *Partitas* for flute (1954) and *Burlesque Suite* for clarinet (1956).

In his *Wind Quintet*, the *African Cycle* and *Relazioni* for alto flute, English horn and bassoon (his last work) Rychlík used the dodccafonic, serial and aleatoric technique.

Orchestral Works

His chamber music is supplemented by two *Preludes* (1944 and 1954), *Partita giocosa* for wind orchestra (1947) and an orchestral composition *In Commemoration of a Dead Friend* (1948).

Vocal Works

His vocal creative work is important as well.

Songs: His *Southern Bohemian Songs* and *Ditties* (1949) are inspired by folk art; similar to these are arrangements of songs from the period of national regeneration, as *The Wreath of Patriotic Songs* (1955) and *A Handful of Songs of the Czech Baroque* (1956). To texts of strolling scholars, Rychlík wrote *The Songs of Roguish Students* (1960).

Children's choirs: *Poking Fun* for children's choir and children's instrumental ensembles (1962).

Mixed choirs: seven choirs for SOPHOCLES' *Oedipus* for mixed choir, recitative and orchestra (1962).

Cantatas: The Christmas carol *Shepherds Rise!* (1945) and the *Herdsman's Calls* (1949).

Madrigals: *The Gallows Madrigals* for mixed choir (1962) set to poems of CHRISTIAN MORGENSTERN.

Various

Children's, mixed and male choirs, extensive incidental and film music (among others the music to the films *The Great Adventure, Music from Mars, The Castaways, Creation of the World* and *In the Penal Zone*) add up to a characterization of Rychlík's musical personality as a composer.

In 1964 he wrote for the Television Conservatory an essay *The Musical Instruments and the People*.

SALICH, Milan

[born Polanka on Odra, 19 May 1927]

Salich studied composition at the Brno Conservatory under THEODORE SCHAEFER and VILÉM PETRŽELKA, at the Prague Conservatory under EMIL HLOBIL and at the Academy of Musical Arts under VÁCLAV DOBIÁŠ, JOSEF STANISLAV, JAROSLAV ŘÍDKÝ and VLADIMÍR SOMMER.

Orchestral and Instrumental Compositions

Salich is the author of four piano *Sonatas* (1958, 1960, two in 1961), a piano *Suite* (1962), two violin *Sonatinas* (1958 and 1961), a *String Quartet* (1959), two *Symphonies* (1961 and 1963), *Wind Quintet* (1962), scenic music and other compositions.

Vocal Compositions

In his creative work he is influenced by the folk song of his native Silesia and by LEOŠ JANÁČEK. He has composed a collection of songs and rhymes for mezzosoprano and piano to words of Moravian folk poetry entitled *Love Abided But Is No More* (1947), *Songs About Love* to words of Moravian and Silesian folk poetry for soprano and piano (1955, given an award in the Jubilee Competition of the Guild of Czechoslovak Composers and the

Czech Music Fund 1956), the cycle of songs to words of Moravian and Silesian folk poetry for soprano and piano *What a Pity, Little Bird* (1957), *Two Ballads* [*The Jealous One* and the *Awaited One from the War*] to words of Silesian folk poetry for male choir (1957), the ballad for mixed choir and piano to words of Silesian folk poetry entitled *The Fighter* (1958), a ballad *In the Black Forest of Polanka* for male choir with a baritone solo (1959), *Five Folk Male Choirs* (1961), a cycle of female choirs with piano accompaniment to words of Silesian folk poetry *A Heavy Burden Bears That Stone* (1961) and a cycle of mixed choirs *From Bezruč's Land* to words by Petr Bezruč (1962).

Salich's vocal work includes two cycles of *Silesian Folk Songs* for voice and piano (1957) and various arrangements of Silesian folk songs from the Bílovec region, published in cooperation with Jaromír Richter under the title *Silesian Folk Songs of the Bílovec Region* (in arrangement for schools, ensembles and choirs, 1962).

He compiles and arranges ethnographic broadcasts for the Czechoslovak Radio and writes articles on folk songs for ethnographic periodicals.

Salich is an outstanding collector of Silesian folk songs (1,500 songs from the Bílovec region) and of folk literature (fairy-tales, legends, sorcery and others) and is a collaborator of the Prague Television for programmes for children and youth.

SARAUER, Alois
[born Netolice, 16 June 1901]
Merited Teacher

Sarauer studied piano and composition at the Prague Conservatory and after graduation he continued his studies with Vilém Kurz and Vítězslav Novák. He was active as a pedagogue at musical schools and at the Brno Conservatory.

He is the author of interesting instructive compositions for piano: *Pictures from the Life of Children, From Youthful Years*, a *Small Piano Suite, From Morning Till Night, Seven Small Pieces, Trifles, Gay Moments, From the Lake Country, To Children, In the Morning Dew, Poetic Variations* and *Four Small Compositions, Morning* and others.

In colaboration with ZDENKA BÖHMOVÁ and ARNOŠTKA GRÜNFELDOVÁ, Sarauer wrote a *Piano School for Beginners*.

ŠATRA, Antonín

[born Prague, 21 February 1901]

Šatra studied composition at the Prague Conservatory under JAROSLAV KŘIČKA and K. B. JIRÁK and conducting under VÁCLAV TALICH. He continued his study of composition at the Master School under J. B. FOERSTER.

He was a teacher of music. In 1937 he joined the Prague Radio, where he worked first in the programme department, later became musical archivist and finally a manager of music.

Orchestral Works

His compositions include five *Symphonies* (first 1930, second 1940—41, third 1958—59, fourth vocal, on texts by FRATIŠEK HRUBÍN, BOHUMIL MATHESIUS and JOSEF HORA for solos, chamber female choir and orchestra 1959—60, and fifth 1961—62), *Prelude, fugue* and *finale* (*Thanksgiving*, 1945—46), a *Comedy Overture* (1949), *Piano Concerto* (1956), *Violin Concerto* (1957) and a *Suite* for orchestra (1960—61).

Chamber Music

He enriched Czech chamber music by two *String*

Quartets (first 1931, second *Music About Man* 1933), *Violin Sonata* (1940) and *Three Aquarelles* for wind quintet (1960).

Vocal Works

He has composed several song cycles such as *Lyrical Songs* for higher voice and piano, set to words by OTAKAR THEER (1925), *Pilgrim's Songs* for higher voice and orchestra to words by KAREL TOMAN and JIŘÍ WOLKER (1932), *Sunset Glow* for baritone and orchestra to words by JIŘÍ WOLKER (1936), *The Woman* for alto and orchestra, set to words by MAURICE MAETERLINCK (1939), *Little Songs and Ballads* for tenor and orchestra, to words by FRANTIŠEK GELLNER (1947), *The Mountains and Man* for tenor and symphonic orchestra (1955), the cantata *The Angel of Death* for female choir, alto, soprano and chamber orchestra, to words by K. J. ERBEN (1947) and a cantata *From Spring to Winter* for soprano, baritone and orchestra (1957).

•

Šatra has written music to a number of radio plays. At present he is working on a musical comedy. From the prevalently lyrical orientation of his earlier compositions, Šatra has attained a contemporary melodic and harmonic expression and structural balance in his latest works.

ŠAUER, František
[born Vienna, 3 December 1912]

Šauer graduated from the Law Faculty of Charles University. In composition he was a pupil of JAROSLAV KŘIČKA.

In 1945—47 he cooperated to a great extent in the founding of the Army Artistic Ensemble Vít Nejedlý. For more than thirty years he has devoted himself to work as a choirmaster and for that reason vocal music prevails in his creative work.

This includes cycles of children's choirs *Skimming Through the World of Children*, a *Children's Corner, Musicians Played to Dance, Sing With Micky, May Songs, We Sing of Peace* and other, songs for pioneers and youth ensembles entitled *To Youth and Pioneers, The Goose-Girl, Pioneers of Peace, A Proud Little Mushroom, The Dandelion, A Merry Day, Czech May, Gottwald's Warriors, In Honour of the Party, With the Soviet Union Forever, Pioneers Take the Lead, Tractors Help.*

Šauer's cycles of female choirs include *The Unfinished Finale* set to words by Fráňa Šrámek and *I Shall Defend Peace.*

The male choirs comprise *Late Spring, On the Road to Peace* and *Already Tomorrow.*

For female, male and mixed choirs Šauer wrote the compositions *The Lovely Highlands* from the Czech-Moravian highland region to words of folk poetry.

Šauer also wrote more than a hundred songs for the Army of which many received awards in the competitions of the Ministry of National Defense and the Central House of the Czechoslovak Army. They include, for instance, *When You Come This Evening* (first prize), *Song of the Frontier Guards* (second prize), *Six Songs* to words of Soviet poets, *Parachutist* and the *Combine Driver, A Song Makes for Gayety* and others.

In Šauer's vocal creative work we find a great number of various songs such as *The Fallen Patriot, The Liberated Fatherland, Sokolovo, The World is Ours, The Strength of Arms, To the Republic for the New Year, Prague—the City of Peace, The Steel Heart of Slovakia, The Song of Joy, Set the Mountains Aflame* and others.

Melodramas, cantata songs and the cantatas as *John the Violinist, Partisan Songs, Prague Fireworks, From Dnieper Beyond the Baikal, The Armies of Peace* and dance songs complete a review of Šauer's vocal work.

He is also the author of piano compositions of instructive character, of a string quartet, a violoncello sonata, scenic music and of a ballet *Niobe*.

To the twentieth anniversary of Slovak national uprising he composed a mixed choir *Freedom Is Not A Simple Gift* to words by MILAN LAJČIAK.

SCHAEFER, Theodor
[born Telč, 23 January 1904]
MERITED TEACHER

Schaefer studied composition at the Brno Conservatory under JAROSLAV KVAPIL and at the Master School in Prague under VÍTĚZSLAV NOVÁK,

He was active as a pedagogue at the Brno Conservatory and at the Palacký University at Olomouc, director of the State Commission of Examiners for teachers of music in Brno and inspector of music schools in Moravia. At present he is professor of composition at the Janáček Academy of Musical Arts and secretary of the Brno branch of the Guild of Czechoslovak Composers.

Stage Works

He composed a cycle of ballets *A Legend on Happiness* which was awarded a prize in the Jubilee Competition of the Guild of Czechoslovak Composers and the Czech Music Fund in 1956.

Orchestral Works

Schaefer's symphonic work is represented by a one-movement *Violin Concerto* op. 4 (1932—33), the symphonic poem *The Wallachian Serenade*, op. 12 (1936), a three-movement *Piano Concerto*, op. 10 (1937—43), a balladic overture *Jánošík*, op. 15 (1939), a one-movement *Diathema* for viola and orchestra, op. 24 (1955—56), by a composition for piano and orchestra *The Barbarian and the Rose*, op. 27 (1957—58) and a four-movement *Diathema* for orchestra, op. 25 (1957—58).

Chamber Music and Instrumental Works

His important compositions include *The Wind Quintet*, op. 5 (1934—35), and the *String Quartet*, op. 21 (1944 to 1945).

Schaefer's compositions for piano include a one-movement *Sonatina*, op. 6 (1935—36), *Romantic Compositions*, op. 7 (1946), *Piano Etudes*, op. 8 (1936—37) and op. 11 (1937—38), *Tema con variazioni* (1936), two series of *Piano Compositions* in easy style op. 13a-b (1936) and the piano suite *Elegy*, op. 20 (1944).

Vocal Works

His vocal work includes a cycle of songs for high female voice with piano accompaniment *Spring Is Coming*, op. 1 (1925—37), a mixed choir *A Letter-Box* to words by Jiří Wolker, op. 3 (1932), *Three Male Choirs*, op. 14 (1939), three female choirs *Libuše's Native Land*, op. 17 (1940), *Love Ballads* in memory of the Lidice tragedy, op. 18 (1943), *A Winter Cantata* for soprano, mixed choir and orchestra, op. 19 (1943—45), and *Two Madrigals* for female choir, op. 26 (1957).

●

His *Wind Quintet* (op. 5) was awarded a prize at the international competition of La Revue Musicale de Paris, 1936.

SCHÄFER, František

[born Břeclav, 3 April 1905]

On completing the secondary school, Schäfer matriculated at the Conservatory in Brno where he studied piano and composition under Jaroslav Kvapil. He continued his study of piano under Vilém Kurz.

For several years Schäfer taught piano at the Brno Conservatory and at present is active in the same field at the Janáček Academy of Musical Arts.

Schäfer is not only an accomplished pianist and pedagogue but also a composer who has enriched Czech piano literature by a number of maturely styled compositions as evidenced by his ten *Preludes*, sixteen *Etudes*, the cycle *Romance*, *A Concerto Allegro* for piano and orchestra (1941), *Five Studies*, *Furiant* (A Czech dance), a *Sonata* in A minor, a *Rhapsody* for piano and orchestra (1943), *Three Sonatinas for Youth*, *Three Sonatinas for Adolescents*, *Three Concerto Sonatinas*, a *Concert Fantasy* to texts of Russian songs and twelve *One-Minute Etudes* for piano (1946—60).

He has composed as well a *String Quartet* in A minor, four *Concertos* with orchestra, one for clarinet, another for flute, another for trombone and the last for French horn, and *Preludes and Fugues* for organ (1945) and a *Fantasy* for violoncello and piano (1949).

SCHNEEWEIS, Jan

[born Holešov, 1 January 1904]

Schneeweis studied philosophy, modern philology and musical science at Charles University and composition at the Master School of the Prague Conservatory under J. B. FOERSTER. He is a secondary school teacher at Beroun near Prague.

Instrumental and Chamber Music

Of his instrumental compositions mention should be made of the *Violin Sonata* (1930), *A Children's Suite* for wind quintet (1955), *Pastorale* for nonet (1945) and *Two Czech Dances* for orchestra (1949). Several of his compositions were awarded prizes in public competitions.

Vocal Works

The main center of interest of his work lies in vocal music. He wrote the song cycles *Christmas* (1929—30), *Five Songs* (1931), *Two Love Songs* (1928 and 1932), *Lyrical Songs* (1929—34), *Nox et solitudo* (1932 and 1935), *Three Psalms* (1938), *On the Eve of the New Spring* (1939), *Three Songs About Prague* (1943 and 1945), *My Home Calls Me* (1945), *Songs of a New Village* (1949), *Four Lullabies* (1961) and *Lamentable Songs* (1962—63).

For children he wrote *Sleighbells* (1928), *About Little Animals* (1955) and *Flowers* (1958).

His choral compositions are numerous and include following works: *Four Children's Choirs* (1928), the cycle *Mother* (1939), *The Months* with wind quintet accompaniment (1952), *The Whistle* with piano or small orchestra (1954), *In Spring* (1953), and *The Green Years* (1960);

For female choir: *Three Female Choirs* (1928 and 1931), *Nocturne* (1940), *A Song of Peace* (1952), a *Lassie from Šumbark* (1956);

For male choirs: *Media vita* (with violoncello obligato, 1937);

For mixed choirs: *Two Mixed Choirs* to words by OTAKAR BŘEZINA (*Nature*, 1929) and *When the Heavens Illuminate our Windows* (1928);

Cantatas: *An Unborn Child* (1936) and the small cantata-legend for solos, female choir and piano (1944) entitled *How the Dove Got its Ribbon.*

Schneeweis composed as well a number of songs for community singing.

Arrangements

He has also made many arrangements of folk songs, as for inst. *Songs of Haná, Highland Songs, Lach, Moravian-Slovak, Wallachian, Czech* (from the region of Beroun), *Silesian, Slovak* and *Ukrainian Songs.*

Writings

His activity in the field of musical science supplements his compositional creative work. He has written two studies dealing with the renowned Czech violinist JOSEF SLAVÍK (1933 and 1956), and in 1945 he revised Slavík's *Violin Concerto* in F sharp minor.

SCHNEIDER-TRNAVSKÝ, Mikuláš

[born Trnava, 24 May 1881—died Bratislava 28 May 1958]

NATIONAL ARTIST

Schneider-Trnavský was a significant composer of the pioneer generation in Slovak musical life before the First World War. After completing the secondary school (together with Zoltán Kodály) he studied organ and composition at the Conservatory in Budapest, Vienna and Prague.

He was active for a short time as choirmaster at Becs-kerek until he settled permanently in his native town as choirmaster of the local Cathedral. After the foundation of the Czechoslovak Republic he held important posts in Slovak cultural life.

Schneider-Trnavský grew out of the Dvořák school of Czech music, enriching his romanticism by elements stemming from Slovak folklore. His expressive melodic talent asserted itself at its best in song compositions, works which met with great social response (some of his songs, especially of a lyrical and hymnal quality, have assumed the character of national songs).

The composer's extensive creative work in the field of church music and his activity on behalf of a reform of Catholic choral singing grew out of his profession.

Stage Works

His only scenic work is the operetta *Bellarosa* (1941, première in Bratislava 1941).

Instrumental and Orchestral Works

His instrumental creative work was influenced by romantic tradition and by his efforts to express the national character; it includes a *Sonata* for violin and piano in G minor (1905), *The Sonatina* for piano (1938), an instructive composition of a witty stylization of folk motifs.

Schneider-Trnavský's orchestral work is represented particularly by his *Dumka and Dance* (1905), a symphonic poem *Pribina's Vow* (1933) and *The Symphony of Recollections* (1956).

Vocal Works

His songs appeared in the cycles *Little Flowers* (1907), *Tears and Smiles* (1909), *From the Heart* (1920) and *Songs About Mother* (1940).

His arrangements for voice and piano were published mainly in a collected edition under the title *Slovak National Songs*.

His harmonizations of folk songs are of similar importance as his arrangements of them. They include the male choirs *Beyond the Hills—Beyond the Vales*, *Mixed Choirs* and others.

The same is true of his arrangements for voice, respectivelly for choir and orchestra which were composed during the most recent period of his creative activity: *The Gemer Brigands' Songs*, *A Medley of Dance Folk Songs*, *Voices of the Tatra Mountains*.

SCHREIBER, Josef

[born Hlavnice, 25 December 1900]

Schreiber studied composition at the Brno Conservatory under Jaroslav Kvapil and Vilém Petrželka and at the Master School in Prague under J. B. Foerster.

He was active as a pedagogue at Opava, Ostrava and Olomouc and as a choirmaster of choral societies at Opava and Ostrava. After 1945 he participated in the reorganization of the Ostrava Opera. At present he teaches the theory of music at Palacký University at Olomouc and at the Ostrava Conservatory.

Instrumental and Orchestral Works

Schreiber's work written within the last few years includes: *Sonata* for solo viola (1959), *Sonatina* for piano (1959), *Four Small Compositions*, for flute and piano(1962) and a *Symphonic Suite* for orchestra and soprano solo (1962).

Vocal Works

He has written song cycles *March* (1936) and *Nights* (1943), a cycle of male choirs *Songs of Ondra Lysohorský* (1940), *Three Songs* set to folk texts for female choir (1959), the female choir *Maple Tree* in commemoration of the partisans killed in the Second World War (1962) and *Autumn and Summer Evenings* (1962).

In 1959 he made an arrangement of *Silesian Folk Songs* for female and male choir.

Writings

He has also written a book on the life and work of ANTONÍN DVOŘÁK and textbooks on the science of harmony and modulation.

SCHULHOFF, Ervín

[born Prague, 8 June 1894—died in a German concentration camp, 18 August 1942]

Schulhoff acquired his musical education in Prague, Vienna, Leipzig, Cologne, Bonn and in Paris. His teachers were JINDŘICH KÁAN, WILLY THERN, ROBERT TEICHMÜLLER and CARL FRIEDBERG (piano), STEPHAN

Krehl, Fritz Steinbach and Ludwig Schiedermair (theory of music), Max Reger and Claude Debussy (composition).

After his return from the war (in 1918) he was active for several years in Dresden, Saarbrücken and Berlin. During this period he studied new trends in musical creative work in Europe and sought his own expressive medium in the small dance form, in the grotesque and in stylization of modern dances.

At the end of 1923 he returned to Prague where he was active as pianist and pedagogue (privately and temporarily at the Prague Conservatory). Later he took an active part in the work of the Liberated Theatre and at the Ostrava and Brno Radio.

Stage Works

This period was represented by his ballet mysterium *Ogelala*, the basis of which was and old Mexican legend elaborated by K. J. Beneš (1924, première in Dessau 1925 and Brno 1927). The tragi-comedy *The Flames*, on a libretto by K. J. Beneš (1927—28, première in Brno 1932) represents momentous creative feat between the two World Wars.

Orchestral Works

The center of gravity of Schulhoff's compositions lies in symphonical works:

First Symphony (1925, première in Berlin 1928);

Second Symphony (1932, première in Prague 1938);

Third Symphony (1935, première in Prague 1950);

Fourth Symphony, called *Spanish* (1936—37); the second part of it he composed for baritone and orchestra to a poem by Ondra Lysohorský, entitled *The Dying in Madrid*;

Fifth Symphony, which was composed after Munich (1938, lost for many years, performed in Weimar 1965);

Sixth Symphony, called *The Symphony of Freedom* (1940 to 1941), in which he elaborated—in the fourth part—

the poem *The Slaves* by ADALBERT CHAMISSO, for choir and orchestra (première Prague 1946).

Seventh Symphony, called *Eroica* (1941) was preserved only in a sketch form;

Eighth Symphony (1942), composed in a concentration camp, remained unfinished.

Besides these he composed two cycles of songs (called also symphonies): *Landscapes*, op. 26 (1918) for mezzo-soprano and orchestra, published by Universal Edition Vienna, and *Humanity*, op. 28 (1919), for alto and orchestra, set to texts by the impressionist THEODOR DÄUBLER (written for the Radio).

Instrumental Music

The *Double Concerto* for flute and piano, accompanied by strings and two French horns (1927) and the *Concerto* for string quartet, accompanied by wind orchestra (1930). Other significant works, highly estimated abroad, see under "International Prizes".

Vocal Works

These include, first of all, the cycle "*1917*", twelve songs of the October Revolution (1933). At that time, Schulhoff arrived at a personal crisis which was resolved in his cantata *Manifesto*, composed on the text of the Manifesto of the Communist Party (arranged by RUDOLF FUCHS), a monumental oratorio for four solo voices, boys' choir, two mixed choirs and full brass band (1933).

Arrangements

During his activity in Ostrava, Schulhoff wrote arrangements of Těšín musical folklore (*Songs and Dances from Těšín*); later he made similar arrangements of the Wallachian, Haná and Chod folklore.

International Prizes

His work is well known abroad; this is shown by following facts: The Mendelssohn Foundation of the

Berlin High School of Music awarded him twice the annual prize—the first time in 1913 for the *piano* and the second time in 1918 for his *Sonata* for piano, op. 22 (1918).

At International Festivals of Contemporary Music he achieved pronounced compositional successes: *Violin Sonata*, op. 7 (1913), in Prague 1924; *Five Pieces* for *String Quartet* (1923), in Salzburg 1924; *String Sextet* (1924), in Donaueschingen 1924; *First String Quartet* (1924), in Venice 1925; *Concertino* for flute, viola and double-bass (1925), in Donaueschingen 1926; *Violin Sonata* (1927), in Geneva 1929; dance grotesque *The Somnambulist*, on a theme by Vítězslav Nezval (1925), in Oxford 1931.

SCHWARZ, Lubor

[born Pozlovice, 5 September 1920]

After completing the secondary school Schwarz graduated from the Master School of the Prague Conservatory and continued his studies in Paris at the Ecole Normale de Musique. At present he is conductor at the Jiří Wolker Theatre in Prague.

He devotes himself to writing scenic and film music and to chamber music compositions. He has also written a one-act ballet *Budulínek* which was awarded a prize in the Jubilee Competition of the Guild of Czechoslovak Composers and the Czech Music Fund in 1956.

ŠEBO-MARTINSKÝ, Teodor

[born Martin, 23 October 1911]

Šebo was originally a private pupil of F. F. Finke in Prague; later he studied composition at the Bratislava

Music and Dramatic Academy under ALEXANDER MOY-
ZES and conducting under JOZEF VINCOUREK.

In 1934—35 he was the leader of the first dance
orchestra of the Bratislava Radio, composing at the
same time: ¶ the swing *Tell Me My Girl*, *Today I Have
My First Rendezvous*; ¶ the chanson *Parting* and making
arrangements.

For the radio he composed the musical *People in a Boat*
and music to radio plays. He was active at the radio for
many years and at present is chief of the gramophone
edition of the State Publishing House of Music.

His recent creative work includes ¶ the dance music
Marita, *So Much Happiness Have I In My Heart*, *Close Your
Lovely Eyes*, ¶ songs for children *We Welcome the New May*
¶ popular orchestral compositions *Mazurka*, *Gay Acrobats*
and ¶ the small cantata *The Partisan*.

His musical *The Cormoran Leaves Tomorrow* is being
prepared for production by several Czechoslovak
theatres, the radio and television.

SEDLÁČEK, Bohuslav

[born Droždín, 13 August 1928]

Sedláček studied at the Brno Conservatory and at the
Janáček Academy of Musical Arts as a pupil of JAROSLAV
KVAPIL.

He was editor of music programmes at the Brno
Radio Station and at present is dramaturgist of the
Brno Variety Radio Orchestra.

His compositions include a *Sonata* for flute and piano
(1949), a *Piano Trio* (1949), a *Sinfonietta* (1949), a *String
Quartet* (1951), *Variations* on a folk theme for piano
(1951), a *Sonata* for violin and piano (1954), and *Moravian Suite* (1954).

In the vocal field he composed *Four Songs* for middle

voice and piano (1949), *Two Songs* with orchestra (1950), a *Lullaby* for male choir (1950) and the cantata *A Song of Peace* (1951).

Sedláček is as well a successful composer of variety music as demonstrated by his *Bulgarian Rounds* (1951), *Variety Suite* (1952), *Little Songs of Wood* (1954), *Ballet Suite* (1958) and many dance compositions, satirical songs and chansons.

He is also the author of the operetta *The Widow From Valencia* and of musical accompaniments to films, as *The Princess with the Golden Star* and others.

SEDMIDUBSKÝ, Miloš

[born Rokycany, 21 February 1924]

Sedmidubský studied composition under KAREL JANEČEK, at first privately and after the Second World War at the Prague Conservatory.

He was conductor of the North-Bohemian Symphonic Orchestra at Teplice and at the Prešov Theatre, music instructor and conductor at the Pilsen Theatre and dramaturgist and later manager of the Czechoslovak Radio. Since 1962 he devotes himself only to composition.

During his work with the Army Artistic Ensemble Vít Nejedlý he wrote a successful Slovak dance fantasy called *Under the Sabres* on the theme of a song sung by young people at Shrovetide.

His larger compositions include a cantata *When the Wood-Hewer Will Awake* (1954—55) to words by PABLO NERUDA, a ballet *Peter and Lucia* (1956—57), a cycle of mixed choirs *Three Loves* (1958—59), set to texts of Slavonic folk poetry, a cantata-concerto-grosso *The Metamorphosis* for five solo voices, concertante wind quintet, solo piano, mixed choir and full orchestra, to a poem by

FRANTIŠEK HRUBÍN (1959—60), *Slovak Rhapsody* for full brass band (1961—62), *Elegy and Scherzo* for violoncello and small orchestra (1961), a seven-part cycle *The Worker's Songs* for bass and orchestra (1961), three mixed choirs *Spring Sonatina* (1961—63), a *Concertino* for violin and orchestra (1962), a *Sonata* for violin and piano (1962), a *String Quartet* (1963), and a one-act opera *Madonna*, according to the novel by SERGEJ MACHONIN (1962, première Pilsen 1964).

Sedmidubský has arranged programme suites from the ballet *Peter and Lucia* as well as from the scenic music to SHAKESPEARE's *Merchant of Venice*. He has also composed a sonata, sonatina and cycle of fugues for piano, a viola sonata and a *Serenade* for chamber orchestra.

•

For his opera *Madonna* he was awarded the STATE PRIZE in the artistic jubilee competition 1965.

SEEHÁK, Jan
[born Prague, 4 April 1910]

Seehák studied composition at the Prague Conservatory in the class of OTAKAR ŠÍN. After completing the course of study at the Conservatory he matriculated at the Master School as a pupil of VÍTĚZSLAV NOVÁK.

He graduated from the Geneva Institut de Rhythmique (founded by EMILE JACQUES DALCROZE) and was as well manager of production of the traditional Swiss festival "Genève chants".

As a composer he has directed his creative work to music for rhythmical exercises and has composed considerable musical accompaniments for the Sokol rallies and the Spartakiads. Many of these are among the best Czech compositions of this genre. They are *The Golden*

Arch for the First Spartakiad; *For Peace, Friendship and Cooperation* as well as music to the military exercises for the Second Spartakiad.

He wrote music also for the Third Spartakiad (1965): *The Chant of Peace*; *The Song—the Resolute—the Prepared*; *The Victory is Ours* and *To the Highest Goals*.

He was also active in the creation of musical patterns for gymnastic exercise formations (Olympic Games in Melbourne in 1956, in Rome 1960, the World Championship in Moscow 1958 and in Prague 1962, and for our participation at the Olympic Games in Tokyo 1964).

Seehák is as well an experienced accompanist and improviser for gymnastic competitions and is the author of a number of marches, dance music, melodrama and scenic music.

SEIDEL, Jan

[born Nymburk, 25 December 1908]

LAUREATE OF THE STATE PRIZE,
holder of the ORDER OF WORK

Seidel was influenced in his artistic growth by two contrary trends which had a potent effect on Czech music before the Second World War: one trend represented by his teacher ALOIS HÁBA and the other by the classical heritage of J. B. FOERSTER. However, he did not lose his individuality under either influence but created a personal musical expression which by its melodiousness is deeply rooted in spontaneous Czech musicalness.

After completing the secondary school and studies at the university, he graduated from the Prague Conservatory (in composition under ALOIS HÁBA and privately with J. B. FOERSTER).

From 1930 to 1945 he cooperated as composer, conductor and pianist at Prague theatres (THE E. F. BURIAN THEATRE, THE NEW THEATRE, THE PRAGUE CHILDREN'S

THEATRE) and took an active part in establishing the Czechoslovak gramophone industry (ESTA) as its artistic adviser, dramaturgist and musical manager. In 1945, he became artistic director of the Gramophone Corporation.

Seidel has also taken a prominent part in the organizational work of the Guild of Czechoslovak Composers and of the Prague Spring Music Festivals.

In 1958—64 he was artistic director of opera of the National Theatre in Prague. He was chairman of the Editorial Council of the Publishing House of the Guild of Czechoslovak Composers PANTON.

Seidel's compositional creative work is many-sided.

Stage Works

In 1964 Seidel finished the full-night opera *Tonka, the Gallows,* set to libretto of LUDĚK MANDAUS, according to the story by E. E. KISCH.

Orchestral Works

Of particular interest is his symphonic composition *Prologue* (1942).

Chamber Music

He composed *The String Quartet* with soprano solo, a *Quartet* in the quarter-tone system, containing a recitation of a poem by FRANTIŠEK HALAS from the collection The Old Women, two *Wind Quintets* and a string quartet *Chrysanthemums.*

Vocal Works and Cantatas

After 1945 Seidel linked up his creative work with the struggle for the victory of socialism, convincing proof of which are his songs *The Song of Freedom* and *Left Foot Forward March!,* belonging, as they do, to the most expressive declaration of the new revolutionary songs (awarded the State Prize).

The ideological and artistic qualities of Seidel's

creative work are characterized by following compositions: the extensive cycle of male choirs *The War-trumpet of Glory* (1946), to text by FRANTIŠEK HALAS, and the cycles *For One's Own Land* and a *Ballad of the Unborn Child* to words by JIŘÍ WOLKER, the cantata *A Challenge to Battle* to the text of a letter written by JAN ŽIŽKA to the people of Domažlice, the monumental cantata-triptych *The Bequest of Julius Fučík* (*People, Be On Guard!*), *The Faithful Resists* and *Yes, We Are With You*.

Seidel's latest period of creative activity has produced a cycle of songs *Happy Journey*, a number of compositions for the Folk Art ensembles, choirs (*Poems About Prague*), a *Cycle* of mixed choirs to text of the romances by VÍTĚZSLAV NEZVAL.

Especially noteworthy is the orchestral song *By the Grace of the Sun*. Inspired by FUČÍK's Notes from the Gallows he composed *The May Overture* (1951), the closing part of which includes the old revolutionary song The Red Banner and, finally, the musical movement for mixed choir and orchestra *A Message to the Living* (1953) set to the text of the poem of FRANTIŠEK HALAS To the Fallen.

Of particular importance are his song cycles *Letters* and *Sweetly Scenting Bouquet*.

Film Music

Seidel's power of expression and of dramatic tension is convincingly evident in his musical accompaniments to the films *Exit for Mr. Habětín, Anna the Proletarian, Darkness, The Godo Soldier Schweik, The Strakonice Bagpiper* (arranged as well into a symphonic suite) and *Kašpar Lén the Avenger*.

Writings

Seidel's literary activity is represented above all by his anthology *The Nation in Song* (one thousand national songs), the two-part *Chap-book* (in cooperation with ALOIS HÁBA and KAREL REINER) and by the *Songs of Home* (second thousand national songs), as well as by the book *Smetana—His Life and Work* [in cooperation with VLADIMÍR POLÍVKA and ZDENĚK NĚMEC (1941)].

Many of his works have been granted awards in Czechoslovak as well as foreign competitions. Seidel has contributed to Czechoslovak musical culture by numerous studies and articles.

For the Library of Czechoslovak National Artists he wrote a monograph on his teacher J. B. FOERSTER (1948) and edited his literary work.

ŠESTÁK (Marek) Jaroslav
[born Libiš, 2 March 1917]

Šesták acquired an elementary musical education at the Teachers' Training Institute in Prague. He studied piano first privately with KAREL HOFFMEISTER and harmony with JAROSLAV ŘÍDKÝ and J. Z. BARTOŠ. In 1955 he completed his study of composition under JAROSLAV ŘÍDKÝ.

He is active now as a pedagogue in Prague.

Dance Music

He has written much successful dance music. In keeping with Czech folk music traditions, he has composed many

¶ polkas: *Bedřichov, Sunday, Libiš, Pensive, The Little Gardener, Hush-a-by, For the Twelve, And Tomorrow Anew, The Deucedly Pretty One, On the Way Home, The White Maypole* and the *Musician*;

¶ mazurkas: *To Little Helen* and *So Charming*;

¶ valses: *The Prettiest Forget-me-not, An Evening Song, Don't Ask the Stars, Tomorrow I Shall Tell You More, Only Those Two*;

¶ marches: *The Imprudent Bumble-bee* and *The Two-part Song*.

Vocal Compositions

Of his popular songs mention may be made of *It Is Christmas*, *White May*, *Neighbourly* (A Czech dance) for bassoon, *To the Golden Wedding* and *The Autodrome*.

Arrangements

Šesták's endeavour to grasp the substance of Czech musical folklore is evident in his orchestral arrangements, such as *Eight Chod Dances*, and in the songs from the collection of LUDVÍK KUBA, as well as in the fifteen *Songs and dances of Hořice* in a piano arrangement by JOSEF FLÉGL.

The Czechoslovak Radio broadcasts Šesták's arrangements of folk songs for choir and orchestra: *Heigho Geese!*, *Shoemakers*, *Twirl and Dance!*, *My Dear*, *In the Yard*, *On the Hill*, *She Wove a Wreath*, *Love, oh Lord, Love*.

Various

Šesták composed music to the women's exercise formations with ninepins and for adolescents taking part in the First Spartakiad; for rhythmic formations *The Fairy-tale* for the Second Spartakiad (from these Fairy-tales the *Marches of Happy Children* and *Happy Days* are played constantly); and music to rhythmic formations *One for All* for the Third Spartakiad (1965) [three *Rhythmic Etudes for Girls* and three *Rhythmic Etudes for Boys* have been selected for preparational work for the Third Spartakiad].

ŠESTÁK, Zdeněk

[born Citoliby, 10 December 1925]

After completing the secondary school, Šesták studied composition at the Prague Conservatory under EMIL HLOBIL and MIROSLAV KREJČÍ and simultaneously musical science at Charles University.

He was active at the Central House of Folk Art in Prague, in the Army Artistic Ensemble Vít Nejedlý and at the Central House of the Czechoslovak Army.

Stage Works

In 1960 he composed the melodrama *Osvětim* to words by SALVATORE QUASIMODO.

Orchestral Works

Up to the present his compositional work includes the following: A symphonic overture *To Fallen Warriors* (1950), a Spanish *Valse Capriccio* for symphonic orchestra (1955), music to a *Pantomime* for symphonic orchestra (1959), *Rhapsodic Fantasy* for violoncello and orchestra (1960), *Rondo* on folk motifs for orchestra (1961), *Epitaph* for symphonic orchestra (1961) and *Balladic Intermezzo* for symphonic orchestra (1964).

To the twentieth anniversary of the Slovak national uprising he composed a *Balladic Intermezzo* for full orchestra (1964), inspired by a partisan song *"Howl the Mountains, Howl!"*

Chamber Music

Two *String Quartets* (1949 and 1953), a children's suite for small orchestra *The Roguish Waterman* (1957), *Cassation* in D sharp for flute, oboe, clarinet, bassoon and French horn (1958), *Suite* for flute and piano (1959), *Two Pieces* for violin and piano (1961), a suite *From Bohemia* for wind orchestra (1962) and a *Concertino* for flute, oboe, clarinet, French horn and bassoon (1964).

Instrumental Music

He has composed an *Impromptu* (1957), *Small Frescoes* for piano (1958) and a *Mischievous Sonatina* for piano (1959).

Vocal Works

Songs: His songs *Bayonet, Charge!*, *Antiaircraft Fighters*,

The Trumpeter, Our Company have become popular with
military artistic ensembles;

Female choirs: two female choirs *Heroic Elegies* (1960);
Children's choirs: a cycle of children *Follow the Sun*;
Mixed choirs: *Two Sonnets* to words by MIROSLAV
FLORIÁN;
Cantatas: a small cantata *A Diune Land* for mixed
choir and two pianos to words by JARMILA URBÁNKOVÁ.

Furthermore he composed a *Vocal Symphony* for mixed
choir and orchestra, set to words by JARMILA URBÁNKOVÁ
(1962) and a *Suite of Czech Folk Songs* for soprano, tenor,
baritone, a boy voice and orchestra (1964).

Various

Of his numerous arrangements of folk songs reference
should be made to the *Pictures from Moravian Slovakia* for
baritone and piano, to *Simple and Fanciful Little Songs*
from the collection of K. J. ERBEN, to a suite of folk
songs for soprano and baritone with orchestra *The Czech
Pilgrimage*, to renaissance *Folk Songs from the Golden
Crown*, for soprano, alto, tenor, baritone and bass with
orchestra, to *Four Gay Songs from Bohemia* for baritone,
female choir-duet, mixed choir and orchestra.

Writings

In his work on the history of music Šesták has concentrated on Czech music of the eighteenth century. He
is now writing a monograph on the composer *Karel
Blažej Kopřiva* (1756—1785).

ŠIMAI, Pavol
[born Levice, 29 June 1930]

Šimai is a composer with manifold interests. He has
received thorough compositional training at first under
PÁL KADOSA in Budapest, then at the High School of

Musical Arts in Bratislava under ALEXANDER MOYZES and JÁN CIKKER and finally with PAUL DESSAU at the Deutsche Akademie der Künste in Berlin.

During his studies he devoted himself to research in Slovak folklore which particularly influenced his early compositional work. Šimai's creative work grows out of an endeavour to arrive at a contemporary expression, capable of attracting a broad circle of listeners.

Stage Works

He is the author of the ballet *Three Spinners* (1956—62), from which he has created two orchestral suites. His dance ballad *The Rebellious Men* (1962) is outstanding due to its originally conceived dance scenes for folkloristic ensembles.

Orchestral Works

In symphonic pictures *Combattimenti* (1963), written to the twentieth anniversary of the Slovak national uprising and in *Victory* (1964) he tried to compound with the thematic of the Second World War; he asserts there his serial compositional procedure.

Chamber Music

In his chamber music compositions, the lyrical and expressive elements are most convincing. Among them are a *Sonatina* for flute and piano (1956), a *Sonatina* for piano (1957), *Introduzione e Allegro* for trumpet, French horn and trombone (1958) and a piano suite *From Slovakia* (1961).

His chamber music melodrama *Mother Speaks* (1959) for female reciter, flute, clarinet, bassoon, guitar and percussion instruments is his most profound, from the point of view of ideas, and is as well the most mature in style.

Vocal Works

The lyrical elements prevail in the *Strophes of Love*

for tenor and piano, set to words by STIEPAN SHCHIPA-
CHOV (1956).

Recently, Šimai has devoted himself successfully to
to the writing of chansons and political songs (*Melancholy,
A Song About Shoe Pegs*).

Film Music

He has also written music to a number of films for
Czechoslovak as well as German production.

ŠIMÍČEK, Joža Eduard

[bon Bernartice, 17 March 1908]

Šimíček is a pupil of F. M. HRADIL. He was active at
the Ostrava Radio Station as a pianist and conductor
and at present is a member of the Ostrava State Philharmonic.

He has composed many marches, dance and variety
compositions and a great deal of scenic music.

He is as well the author of the operetta *A Capricious
Woman*, of the radio musical play *Pancíř and Věra*, of the
music to the cabaret *When Silence is Heard and Unmasked*,
of the orchestral suite *Miners' Merry-making*, two *Hu-
mouresques* and of a *Burlesque* for oboe with orchestra, of
a *Scherzo* for violin with orchestra, the intermezzo
A Ballet of Fire-flies, a cycle of sixteen national dances
for orchestra, and of a song cycle *Patriotic Songs*.

He has arranged as well Wallachian and Soviet songs
for solos, choir and orchestra.

ŠÍN, Otakar

[born Rokytno, 23 April 1881—died Prague, 21 January 1943]

Šín studied composition at the Prague Conservatory as a pupil of KAREL STECKER, continuing his studies under VÍTĚZSLAV NOVÁK.

In 1920 he was appointed professor of theoretical subjects at the Prague Conservatory, gaining distinction as a musical theoretician and pedagogue. He wrote a two-volume *Complete Science of Harmony on the Basis of Melodics and Rhythm* (first edition 1922, second worked over 1933), *The Science of Counterpoint, Imitation and Fugue* (published 1936), *General Science of Music as a Preparation for the Study of Harmony, Counterpoint and Musical Forms* (after Šín's death completed and published by FRANTIŠEK BARTOŠ and KAREL JANEČEK 1949) and many essays and articles on problems of modern harmony.

His compositional work is not extensive but is characterized by an economy of expression, a wealth of suprising harmony and counterpoint brought to a fine art. It includes two symphonic poems *Tilottáma* on themes of JULIUS ZEYER (graduation work, 1908), *King Menkera* (1909, reworked in 1916—18), *Intimate Moods* (1913), *Spring Songs* (1916) for piano, two string quartets (1923 and 1926—28), *Silesian Songs* for female choir (1931), *Sonata* for violoncello and piano (1934), *Radio Overture* (1936), a cycle *A Woman's Songs* for soprano and piano (1936), *A Small Suite* for violin and piano (1937), a festive greeting for French horns *Hunting* (1938) and *Three Czech Dances* for full orchestra (1939, also for nonet).

He is also the author of numerous unconventional compositions for youth: *Little Songs and Dances* for piano, *From Morning Till Dusk* and *On Holiday* for piano, *Five Dances* for piano for four hands, *National Dances* and *Folk Dances* for three-voice children's choir.

SIVÁČEK, Ján

[born Myjava, 27 May 1928]

Siváček completed the study of law and as a student was leader of a dance orchestra. He studied music privately and later attended the class of composition of ALEXANDER MOYZES at the High School of Musical Arts in Bratislava. At present he is on the staff of the Public Education Institute and is active as well as a publicist in the field od dance and jazz music and arrangements.

In his creative work he ranks among composers seeking a modern musical style. His work includes the compositions *It Is May*, *A Song of Happy Days*, *At the Last Stop*, *One of Two*, *The Wild Poppy* and the cycle of chansons *The Episodes*.

For television he has written a musical *That's the Way It Usually Is*.

ŠKVOR, František

[born Varaždinska Toplica, Yugoslavia, 11 January 1898]

Holder of the ORDER OF WORK
and of the decoration FOR OUTSTANDING WORK

Škvor comes from a musical family (his father was a violist in the orchestra of the National Theatre in Prague). He studied piano with the well-known Prague pedagogue ADOLF MIKEŠ and composition under VÍTĚZSLAV NOVÁK.

For many years he conducted the opera of the National Theatre in Prague.

Stage Works

His fondness for children prompted him to write two works for them: In his ballet *Doctor Faust*, according to HEINRICH HEINE (1925, première in Prague 1926) he composed an expressive music as well as in the children's

411   SIVÁČEK-ŠKVOR

opera *The Spring Fairy-tale* to a libretto by J. NYKVAN-
SKÁ (1929).

Orchestral Works

Among his manifold composition he wrote an *Overture* for full orchestra (1923), a symphonic poem *Zvíkov* (1924), a *Serenade* for small orchestra (1925), seven orchestral suites [*From the Children's World* (1933), *In the Puppet Theatre* (1934), *Moravian Slovakia* (1937), *Exotikon* (1938), *Scenes from the Countryside* (1939), *Spring* (1940), and a *Romantic Suite* (1946)], further *Songs and Dances from the Region of Božena Němcová* (1939), *Three Valses* (1940), *Three Painters' Etudes* (1944) and *Variations on Russian National Songs* (1949) are the composer's significant contribution to Czech orchestral creative work. The symphonic music is represented by *The Violin Concerto* (1946), a *Serenade* for string orchestra and harps (1956) and by two *Concertinos* for flute, oboe, clarinet, bassoon and strings (1938 and 1960).

Chamber Music

In the field of chamber music he composed *The Septuor* for oboe, clarinet, bassoon and string quartet (1936), *The String Quartet* in E minor (1954), two *Nonets* (1955 and 1961) and *Duetto* for flute and harp (1964).

Vocal Works

His vocal music includes *Songs of Moravian Hill Dwellers* for soprano, tenor, baritone and orchestra (1938), *Old World Songs* for soprano, tenor and orchestra, set to words by J. V. SLÁDEK (1939), *Echoes of Russian Songs* for soprano, baritone and orchestra (1945), children's choirs *The Whistle* for flute and harp (or piano) to texts of folk poetry (1948), *Moravian National Songs on Love* for alto, baritone and orchestra (1948), *Songs* for children's choir, flute and clarinet (1955), *Six Mixed Choirs* to texts of folk poetry with instrumental accompaniment (1956), *Children's Choirs* set to words by J. V. SLÁDEK (1960), *Echoes of Czech and Russian Songs* to poems by F. L. ČELAKOVSKÝ for female choir with piano accompaniment (1962), *The Summer*, songs for girls choir, flute, clarinet, bassclarinet, harp and piano, to words of folk poetry (1964).

For Czechoslovak State Ensemble of Songs and Dances he composed *The Slovak Csardás* (a dance) and the popular *Karičky* (Slovak folk dance).

Film Music

Music to KAREL PLICKA's film *The Land Sings* and to the historical films *Mikoláš Aleš* and *The Revolutionary Year 1945* testify to Škvor's broad range of creative work.

SLABÝ, Jan
[born Kunštát, 9 March 1904]

Slabý graduated from the Brno Conservatory. In 1928—1946 he was active as conductor in Yugoslavia. At present he is editor at the Brno Radio Station.

During the years he spent in Yugoslavia he composed two cantatas *A Song of the River* (1931) and *Joy* (1936), *The Adriatic Suite* (1933), and many choirs to Yugoslav folk poetry, making arrangements as well of Yugoslav folk songs.

His extensive creative work also includes *The Variety Overture*, a *Fantasy* on a national theme and *A Gay Round Dance* for violin with orchestra, *Pioneers' Suite*, the suite *With Us*, a *Small Suite* for flute and *A Fairy-tale* for violoncello with orchestra.

He devotes himself to arrangements of folk songs and dances of the Highland region and is the author of *Highland Melodies* for violin and orchestra, and of the suite *Highland Pictures*.

Yugoslav themes have reappeared in his songs and dances for violoncello and orchestra and in three orchestral rounds.

Other variety compositions include his *Brno Valses, A Paraphrase* on the folk song *Under the Oak—Behind the Oak* for two pianos and the marches *Prague-Berlin-Warsaw, The Fair 59* and *Faith for Faith*.

SLAVICKÝ, Klement
[born Tovačov, 22 September 1910]

Slavický studied composition and conducting at the Prague Conservatory under K. B. JIRÁK and PAVEL DĚDEČEK and at its Master School under JOSEF SUK and VÁCLAV TALICH.

From 1936 to 1951 he was active at the Czechoslovak Radio in Prague as music lecturer, conductor and manager.

He acquired his basic musical education from his father, a pupil of Leoš Janáček at the School for Organists in Brno.

Orchestral Works and Chamber Music

His great musical talent is combined with his uncompromising artistic approach. Following the *Fantasy* for orchestra and solo piano (1931) he composed two cycles, the orchestral *Moravian Dance Fantasy* (1951) [hitherto the most successful of Slavický's work, representing efficaciously Czechoslovak music abroad] and the effective *Rhapsodic Variations* (1953), which drew on the same inspirational sources of Moravian folk art.

String Quartet (1933), *Trio* for oboe, clarinet and bassoon (1937, performed at the XXI. International Festival for Contemporary Music in Copenhagen) and *Two Com-*

positions for violoncello and piano (1936). He climaxed this group with his *Sinfonietta* (1940). In later years he composed a *Suite* for oboe and piano (1959).

Instrumental Works

Outstanding are *Three Compositions* for piano (1947) for their unusual use of brilliance of sound and the magnificent possibilities of this instrument. He continued in this line with his *Frescos* for organ (1958), the piano sonata *Meditation on Life* (1957—58), the *Partita* for solo violin (1962), the *Invocations* for organ (1963) and *Small Preludes* and *Etudes* for piano (1964).

Instructive Compositions

Within the past few years Slavický has turned his attention to more modest forms. This has resulted in two booklets of successful instructive compositions for the piano *On the Whites and Blacks* and *Piano and Youth* (1958).

Vocal Works

Slavický's musical expression, in its rich harmony and orchestral resonance, has an affinity to SUK and in its tempestuous expressiveness and intrinsic relationship to folk art to JANÁČEK. It, however, has individual character, growing more distinctive in the composer's vocal works.

This is true of his symphonic song composition for higher voice and orchestra entitled *To Nature* (1942) and the cycle *Songs of the Native Land* (1942), the male choir *To My Mother* (1942) and the song-cycle *A Bouquet of Songs* (1944—48). The counterpart of the last two compositions is the double-choir *Lidice* (1945), a memorial to the martyrs of the German occupation.

In the choral suite of Moravian songs *Gallants, Gallants!* (1950) and the little song *Oh, My Little Heart* (1954), Slavický follows up his *Songs of the Native Land*.

His *Madrigals* to folk texts for mixed choir were awarded a special prize in the artistic jubilee competition in 1960.

Recently, he has composed a cycle of songs and rhymes for children's choir and piano, entitled *Children, Happiness and Song* (1962) and *Songs for a Severáček* for children choir and small orchestra (1964).

ŠLIK, Miroslav

[born Zagreb, 25 March 1898]

Šlik graduated from the violin section of the Zagreb Conservatory as a pupil of VÁCLAV HUML. Thereafter, for three years, he was concert-master of the orchestra of the Zagreb National Theatre. He then continued his study of violin under OTAKAR ŠEVČÍK in Prague and later with CARL FLESH and CESAR THOMSON in London.

After many years of concert and pedagogic activity abroad, he has been, since 1948, concert-master of the orchestra of the Prague Smetana Theatre.

Šlik studied composition under FRAN LHOTKA and FRANJO DUGAN in Zagreb and with JOSEPH HOLBROOK in London. Many of his works have been published abroad by outstanding publishing houses.

Chamber Music

He has composed several compositions for violin, five string quartets, a *Sonata* for French horn and piano (1951), *Piano Variations* on his own theme (1956), *Three Pieces for clarinet* and piano (1957), *Caprice Nègre* (1958), a *Small Suite* for three violins, viola, violoncello and piano (1958), two *Albanian Pictures* (*Elegy* and *A Dance*) for string quartet (1959), *Moravian Slovak Fantasy* for two violins and piano (1961), a *Psalm* for string quartet (1962), *From National Melodies* for two violins and violoncello (1962), a *Sonata* for solo violin (1962) and *Two Sonatas* for solo viola (1963).

Orchestral Works

The Medjumurska Suite for full orchestra (1940), and a march *Vivat Spartakiad* for brass band (1959).

Vocal Works

His work also includes a cycle of songs for girls' choir *Summer* (1956), a cycle of songs for mezzosoprano and string quartet *Fished Out of the Vltava* (1959), *Three Songs* for baritone and piano (1961), and an *Egyptian Folksong* (1961).

ŠLITR, Jiří

[born Lhota Zálesní, 15 February 1924]

Šlitr completed the study of law at Charles University, privately studying painting and music. As a painter, song writer and composer he has applied his talents significantly at the Czechoslovak Television from its very beginnings. At the World Exposition in Brussels he appeared on the programme of Laterna Magica 58 and has taken part as well in its tour in the Soviet Union, Poland and Austria.

Since 1956 he has been cooperating with JIŘÍ SUCHÝ in the Prague theatrical productions at Reduta, Theatre on the Balustrade and Semaphor.

Up to the present, he has composed music to the following plays of JIŘÍ SUCHÝ: *Man From the Attic, Such a Loss of Blood, The Paper Blues, Suzanne Is at Home Alone, Suzanne Is Again at Home Alone, Six Wives, Jonah and Tingle-Tangle, Suzanne Is not at Home for Anyone.*

On the topical texts of JIŘÍ SUCHÝ he has composed many satirical songs and chansons of which the most popular are: *A Worn-Out Waistcoat, Yesterday and Sunday,*

A Child of School Age, A Bladder-nut, Heavenly Love, A Cat in the Window, The Moon's Aria, A Lady-bird, A Little Song for Suzanne, A Vain Cousin, A Stupid Sunday, The Tulip, I Lack that Assurance, I Have Bought Myself a Wick, Country Bumpkin, Life is a Struggle, The Butterfly, From my Life, The Blushing One and others.

In addition, Šlitr is the author of music to the dramatised version of the tale *Joe B. Semple is Getting Married* by the American Negro-poet LANGSTONE HUGHES, to the comedy *The Wedding of a Marriage Impostor* by OLDŘICH DANĚK and of musical accompaniments to several short and television films.

A great attention of the public is paid just now to the musical film *If One Thousand Clarinets...*, of which he is the co-author.

SLUKA, Luboš

[born Opočno, 13 September 1928]

Sluka studied composition at the Prague Conservatory under MIROSLAV KREJČÍ and FRANTIŠEK PÍCHA and conducting under BOHUMIL ŠPIDRA and ALOIS KLÍMA. He completed his study of composition at the Academy of Musical Arts under JAROSLAV ŘÍDKÝ and PAVEL BOŘKOVEC.

Sluka belongs to the group of successful young Czech composers and some of his works have already found appreciation abroad.

Up to the present he has written six song-cycles and various chamber music compositions, of which *Sonata* for violoncello and piano (1956) has been played in almost all European countries; this *Sonata* was awarded a silver medal in the competition at the Festival of Youth in Moscow (1957).

Moreover, Sluka has composed a symphonic poem *The Ballad of Orava* (1954), *Variations* (1955), *Nocturnes*

(1957) and a cantata *In the Name of Life* (1959), awarded at the Festival of Youth in Vienna, (1959), musical comedy *The Countess from Belfort* (1962, première at Jihlava 1962), a cycle of piano compositions *Plays and Dreams* (1963), a concerto valse *Liala* for violin and piano (1963) and *The Road of Silence* for organ (1964).

He has also written instructive compositions, choral and scenic music.

His latest symphonic work is *Variation Fantasy* for piano and orchestra.

In the field of film music he is particularly active, having created about 30 scores for films, some of which have met with great success abroad.

He is editing contemporary music at the publishing house PANTON.

SMATEK, Miloš

[born Rovné, 12 August 1895]

Smatek studied music at the Vienna Conservatory where he was a pupil of J. B. FOERSTER. He played the double-bass in the Czech Philharmonic and was conductor at several theatres. Since 1930 he has devoted himself entirely to composition.

Stage Works

His most important work is the opera *Čachtická paní* [Mistress of Chakhtice] (1929—30, première in Bratislava 1931), but has written also scenic compositions such as musical comedy *Bourgeois Nobleman* according to J. B. MOLIÈRE, a folk musical comedy *Untamed Barbara*, a comedy *The Golden Whistle* and the play with songs *Children of Our Village*.

Orchestral Works

Smatek's orchestral work includes *The Workers'*

Symphony, a *Moravian Suite*, a *Suite* on motives from JIRÁSEK's play *The Lantern* for small orchestra, a *Polar Suite* for voices and full orchestra, *The Old Town Suite*, the suite *On the Lužnice River*, overture to a *Musical Comedy*, *The Orava Rhapsody*, *Hussite Fantasy*, *South Bohemian Polka* and the *Strakonice Polka*, *Capriccio* for violin and orchestra, *Concertino* for French horn with orchestra and concerto valse fantasy *Château Mělník* for piano with orchestra.

Chamber Music

In the field of chamber music Smatek wrote *Sonatas* for French horn, oboe, double-bass, a *Wind Quintet*, *Scherzino* for wind quintet, *Three Compositions* for harp, viola and flute.

Vocal Works

His vocal works include *Twenty Lads from the Carpathians* for male choir with orchestra, a ballad *When My Beloved Went to War* for mixed choir and *Lullabies* set to words by J. V. SLÁDEK for female choir.

In addition, Smatek has written many songs for children, pioneers and youth.

Film Music

He also composed music to a number of plays, to the films *Jánošík*, *Jenufa*, *Man from the Unknown*, *He was a Czech Musician*, *The Last of the Mohicans*, *The Iron Old Man*, *The Five Hundred*, *The Lantern*, *At the Empty Shop* and others.

Various

The author's inclination to military music inspired him to write *The March of Tankists*, a *Military Review March*, *The March of Model Riflemen*, *The March of the Antiaircraft Gunners* and others. *The March of Boxers*, *The Skiing Scherzo*, *The Song of a Weir*, *The Sports March* and *The Hunting Valse* are dedicated to sportsmen. Among others Smatek has recently written *The March of the First of May* and *The Dukla March*. His march *The Artists* (written in collaboration with KAREL PEČKE) has achieved world-wide popularity.

SMETÁČEK, Václav
[born Brno, 30 September 1906]
MERITED ARTIST

Smetáček studied oboe at the Prague Conservatory under LADISLAV SKUHROVSKÝ, composition under JAROSLAV KŘIČKA and conducting under METOD DOLEŽIL and PAVEL DĚDEČEK. For several years he was a conductor of the Czechoslovak Radio, now he is chief conductor of the Prague Symphonic Orchestra F. O. K.

As a prominent oboe player and member of the Prague Wind Quintet, which he founded, Smetáček composed considerable chamber music works for wind instruments.

Stage Works
His work as a conductor has stimulated his interest in orchestral music and he composed a ballet *An Evening of a Sultry Day* which was produced by Jarmila Kröschlová's group at the International dance competition in Paris 1932 and in Prague 1933.

Orchestral Works
Of his orchestral works we may mention a festive march *Vivat Olympia* (1937), a balet suite *In the Glade of Nymphs and Satyrs* (1930), a military march *The Guard* (1937) and a *Wedding March* (1948).

Chamber Music
His chamber music work includes the piano cycles *Romantic Moods* (1925), the *Wind Quintet* (1930), *Duettino*

for oboe and French horn (1931), a suite for wind quintet *From Insect Life* (1932) and *Mood Pictures* (1932). He has written a cycle of songs for chambre ensemble and three wind instruments entitled *Little Ivan's Songs*.

In the field of popular music he has composed two polkas [*The Senohraby Polka* and *With Us at Třešť*], a march for brass band *Reveille* and two compositions for wind quintet called *The Davle Polka* and *Perpetuo brillante*.

His work as an arranger and orchestrator is significant as well.

The Polish People's Republic has decorated him with the Officer's Cross of the Order Polonia restituta. In 1958 he was awarded the prize of the City of Prague.

He is a member of the committee of the Prague Spring Music Festival.

SMUTNÝ, Jiří

[born Prague, 1 April 1932]

After completing the secondary school he graduated from conducting section of the Academy of Musical Arts as a pupil of ROBERT BROCK and VÁCLAV SMETÁ-ČEK, studying composition as an external student.

He is accompanist at the National Theatre Opera in Prague. His creative activity is directed towards musical dramatic works as evidenced by his three operatic scherzos *When Two Do the Same*, according to a tale by G. B. BOCCACCIO (1959, première at Ústí on Labe 1960), *The Fortune-teller*, according to a story by KAREL ČAPEK (1961) and *The Budapest Express* after a story by E. E. KISCH (1962), a children's ballet *Two Days on the Moon* (1960, première at Ústí on Labe 1961) and the comic opera *Dalskabáty—The Sinful Village*, according to the comedy by JAN DRDA (1960—61, première Czechoslovak Television 1962).

Smutný has also composed a ballad for middle voice and piano *At The Gate of the Charitable Ones* (1957), a cycle of songs for soprano, violoncello and piano *The Pilgrim* (1958), a cycle of songs for lower voice and piano *Evening Moods* (1959), a chamber music cantata *Internment of Light* (1961), *Three Epigrams* for middle voice and piano (1962), *Three Songs* for tenor and piano (1962), a *Sonata* for two pianos (1962) and music to the television films *The Rogue*, *Close Your Eyes* and *The Mystery of Tone*; furthermore *Three Epigrams* set to words by A. S. PUSHKIN, with the accompaniment of piano (1962), *Concertino piccolo* for chamber orchestra (1963), *Two Impromptus* for flute and piano (1963) and *The Mail Pigeon*, three songs for middle voice and piano, set to words by JAROSLAV SEIFERT (1963).

SNÍŽKOVÁ-ŠKRHOVÁ, Jitka

[born Prague, 14 September 1924]

Snížková studied piano at the Prague Conservatory under JAN HEŘMAN and ALBÍN ŠÍMA and after graduation continued with KAREL HOFFMEISTER. She studied composition at first privately with FRANTIŠEK SPILKA and later at the Prague Conservatory under ALOIS HÁBA. In addition, she graduated from Charles University in musical science and aesthetics.

She appears on concert platforms, composes and in the musical scientific field specializes in Czech music from the fifteenth to the seventeenth century.

Instrumental and Chamber Music

She has written a number of compositions for harp (1944—46), a *Sonata* for viola and piano (1947), three

423   SNÍŽKOVÁ-ŠKRHOVÁ

String Quartets (1948, 1953, 1956), *Trio* for flute, oboe and harp (1955), a *Sonata* for violoncello and piano (1956—57), *Tercetto* for flute, viola and violoncello (1957), a *Sonatina* for flute and piano (1957), a *Small Sinfonietta* for chamber orchestra (1957), *Interludes* for string orchestra and flute (1958), *Sonata* for piano (1959), *Overture* for chamber orchestra START (1959), *Trio* for flute (violin), oboe and violoncello (1961), a *Trio* for violin, violoncello and piano (1961), *Concerto* for two pianos (1962), *Sonatina* for violin and piano (1961) and *Concertino* for piano (1963).

•

Snížková-Škrhová has also written several works in the quarter-tone system for piano and the cycle entitled *The Mosaics for Harp.*

Vocal Works

Arabesques, songs for alto to Arabian folk poetry texts (1950—55), *Nomadic Tribes*, songs for alto set to words of Věra Kubíčková (1951), *Rubaiyat* songs for alto to texts of Persian poetry (1953), *The Portuguese Sonnets* for soprano to words by Elizabeth B. Browning (1953), *Songs to a Little Boy* set to text by Jaroslav Seifert (1954 to 55), *Children's songs* with flute (1955), *The Dove's Necklace*, songs for alto to texts of Arabian poetry (1956), *Panegyricus on Komenský* (Comenius), a choir to a Latin text by Leibnitz (1956), mixed choirs set to text by J. Pátová-Vrchotová (1958—59), *The Song of Songs* (a full-length musical poem for alto, recitative and chamber orchestra with solo harp to the text of Solomon's Songs translated by J. Seifert, 1960) and a *Cantata* for female choir and clarinet *The Eternal Woman* (1962).

Recently, she composed a melodrama *The Miner*, set to words of Petr Bezruč (1963), *Swan Song* for songs and piano, set to words of Petr Bezruč (1963) and *Prague Pictures for Children* for songs and piano, set to words of Jiří Hutina (1963).

Various

She has composed as well a number of instructive works for piano, violin and voice, arranging also several montages of music. She has successfully composed the musical accompaniment to the gymnastic exercises of women *The Sower* for the second Spartakiad.

In addition, she has arranged a selection of works of the 16th and 17th centuries for multiple voices, *Musica polyfonica Bohemiae* (The State Publishing House of Fiction, Music and Art).

SOKOLA, Miloš

[born Bučovice, Moravia, 18 April 1913]

Sokola studied composition at the Brno Conservatory under VILÉM PETRŽELKA and at the Master School of the Prague Conservatory under VÍTĚZSLAV NOVÁK and JAROSLAV KŘIČKA.

For a short time he was administrator of the school of music at Kroměříž. Then for many years he has been a member of the orchestra of the National Theatre in Prague.

Stage Works

The opera, *The Prodigal Son* (1948, première at Olomouc 1963) according to VÁCLAV RENČ's play, shows clearly the composer's convincing dramatic talent.

Orchestral Works

The variation form particularly appealed to Sokola's highly developed logical and imaginative musical thinking. This is evident in his compositions *Passacaglia*, *Toccata* and *Fugue* for orchestra (1943), in the orchestral *Variations* on a theme by VÍTĚZSLAVA KAPRÁLOVÁ (1952), one of the composer's most significant works. In his *Concerto* for violin and orchestra (1952) Sokola combines the virtuosity and experience of a reproductive artist with the creative inspiration and deliberation of a composer. His symphonic poem *The Ninth of May* was awarded the second prize in the artistic jubilee competition in 1960.

Chamber and Instrumental Music

Instrumental music is represented in Sokola's work mainly in the field of chamber music. These compositions include three *String Quartets* (the first in 1944, the second, entitled *The Song of the Highest Tower*, to words by ARTHUR RIMBAUD with a tenor solo, 1946), *Valses* (1953) and *Preludes* (1954), both for piano.

During his studies he composed *Five Miniatures* for piano (1932) and later *Passacaglia, Toccata, Chorale* and *Fugue* for organ (1946).

Vocal Works

He called attention to his compositional ability early in his studies when he wrote *Two Songs* for lower voice and piano, to verses by VÍTĚZSLAV NEZVAL (1932), a song cycle *In Darkness* (1932) and a cantata *A Ballad About a Dream*, set to words by JIŘÍ WOLKER (his graduation work in 1938); his cantata *The Sea* (1945) is inspired as well by WOLKER's poetry. As preparatory compositions for his opera, Sokola wrote two cantatas as well as significant song cycles *Songs About Love* (1941), *Lullabies* (1945) and the male choirs *To a Lucky Girl* (1946); they were followed by the song *The Steamboat* to words by TRISTAN CORBIER for low voice and piano (1946) and a male choir *In One's Own Destiny* to words by JOSEF HORA.

SOMMER, Vladimír

[born Dolní Jiřetín, 28 February 1921]

LAUREATE OF STATE PRIZE

Sommer studied at the Prague Conservatory under KAREL JANEČEK and at the Academy of Musical Arts under PAVEL BOŘKOVEC.

He was senior lecturer at the Academy and at present is an assistant professor in composition at the History of Music Department at Charles University. Sommer was for a time the secretary of the Guild of Czechoslovak Composers. He is active as well in the organizational work of the Authors' Association for Protection of Rights on Musical Works.

Instrumental and Chamber Music

Following a *Sonata* for two violins (1948) and a *Cantata on Gottwald* (1949), Sommer attracted attention with his *Violin Concerto* (his graduation work of 1950), a vigorous work with PROKOFIEV orientation. His compositions for piano include a *Sonatina* (1947), *Three Polkas* (1951) and a *Sonata* (1955) while three *String Quartets* (the first of 1950, the second of 1955—awarded the State Prize 1960, the third of 1963) are his most significant expressions in the field of chamber music.

Sommer's other works include *The Overture* to SOPHOCLE's tragedy *Antigona* (1957) and a *Violoncello Concerto* and a *Symphony Concertante* for two violins, viola, violoncello and chamber orchestra (both works completed in 1963).

He is also the author of accompaniments to films *The Happiness Rained for Them* and *Thirty three Silver Quails*.

Vocal Works

During his studies and later as well, he took a very active part in the work of youth ensembles, enriching their repertoire by songs on the building up of the country and by choirs and dances. The most popular of these are *Heigh-Ho*, *The Stalinists*, *The Youth Song*, *The Flyer's Song*, *May Song*, *Hail the Army*, *Pioneers' Songs*, a cycle of songs for children *It is Good to be on the Earth* (successfully produced abroad as well) and the *Myjava Csardás*.

His three-movement *Vocal Symphony* for alto, choir and orchestra (1958) is truly representative of contemporary Czech music. Its first movement is a meditative passacaglia set to the poetic prose of FRANZ KAFKA, depicting a night watch over a sleeping world, the second movement, substituted for the symphonic scherzo, is based on Raskolnikov's dream from the novel *Crime and Punishment* by F. M. DOSTOJEVSKY and the third slow movement has as its literary background the poem *Death Will Come and Will Have Your Eyes* by CESARE PAVESE.

Further he composed *Three Female Choirs* (1960) and a passacaglia *The Black Man* to words by SERGEI JESENIN for baritone, reciter and orchestra (1964).

•

For his *Vocal Symphony* he was awarded the STATE PRIZE 1965.

SOUKUP, Vladimír

[born Prague, 20 February 1930]

Soukup studied composition privately with ZDENĚK HŮLA and after completing the secondary school he continued his study at the Academy of Musical Arts as a pupil of JAROSLAV ŘÍDKÝ.

He composed a string quartet *Poem About Love* (1954), a *Symphony of Youth* (1954), a *Rhapsody* for violin and piano (1956), a *Wind Quintet* (1957), a *Viola Sonata* (1958) symphonic poems *The Service for the Dead* and *The Oath and Revenge* (1959), giving expression to an antifascist theme; further a concerto for piano and orchestra *An Ode on Youth* (1960—61), and sonets for bass-clarinet and piano *An Apology of Contemporaneousness*: *Galaxy, Hyperbole, Elegy, Rocket, Ode* (1961).

In 1962 Soukup completed his three-movement second *Symphony* and *Sonata* for violin and piano, in 1963 *Cantata Futura*, set to words by VLADIMIR MAJAKOVSKY, and in 1964 *Exotic Songs* for female voice, flute and piano and his *Third Symphony* (Canto allegro).

He devotes himself intensively to musical dramatic work and has produced two operettas on contemporary themes entitled *A Review in Paradise* (1955) and *Lovers and a Trunk Call* (1957—58) and a full-length ballet *François Villon* to his own libretto (1959—60).

At present he is working on a ballet *The Native Land* and on a cantata *On the Road to the Sun* for recitative, choir and orchestra.

He has also written a number of songs for youth and military ensembles.

SPILKA, František
[born Štěkeň, 13 November 1877—died Prague, 20 October 1960]

Spilka studied composition at the Prague Conservatory under KAREL STECKER, KAREL KNITTL and ANTONÍN DVOŘÁK. While a member of Dvořák's class he composed the following works: an orchestral *Rhapsody in* H minor (1896), an *Overture* in E minor (1897), a piano *Sonata* in C sharp minor and several songs.

He was professor and administrative director at the Prague Conservatory.

His versatile creative talent found expression in his activity as choirmaster, composer, pedagogue and writer. As a choirmaster he made his influence felt in the PRAGUE TEACHERS' CHOIR (1908—21), which he founded. In 1928—38 he directed the Prague Singing Ensemble SMETANA.

Together with FERDINAND VACH, founder and choir-master of the Moravian Teachers' Choir, Spilka pioneer-ed in a new choral reproduction which had as an im-mediate result the growth of a rich and technically exacting choral literature that has no analogy elsewhere. Spilka's art of reproduction, in which a deep sensitiveness and extraordinary sense for sound colour was combined with a captivating temperament, stimulated the origin of a Czech choirmaster school. ERICH KLEIBER was one of Spilka's pupils.

Stage Works and Cantatas

Spilka composed a three-cat o p e r a *Ancient Rights* (1915, première in Prague 1917) and a one-act o p e r a *The Birth of Death* (Cain, 1917), an o r a t o r i o *Jan Hus at the Stake* (1907) and a c a n t a t a *Miller's Journeyman* (1947).

Chamber Music

He wrote considerable chamber music, including the following: *Rhapsodic Sonata* in E minor for violon-cello and piano (1945), *Six Sonets* for violin and piano on PETRARCA's theme (1944) and five piano *Sonatas* (1951—54).

Instrumental Works

He enriched Czech piano literature by these cyclic works: *Three Dances of Marianna* (1943), *You and I* (1943), *I Met ...* in two parts (first 1944, second 1945).

Vocal Works

The cycle of songs *Love Letters* for mezzosoprano and baritone with piano accompaniment represents the composer's personal creative expression.

Spilka's choirmaster activity inspired him to write

many compositions for male, female, mixed and chidren's choirs. The choir *The Earth* to words by JITKA SNÍŽ-KOVÁ (1943) is the best known of his male choirs. His choirs "*30. X. 1938*", *Saint Wenceslas* (1944), *Panychida* (*The Service for the Dead*, 1945) and *The Song of Victory* to the texts by JITKA SNÍŽKOVÁ (1946) echo the difficult times of the Czech people during the German occupation.

In numerous arrangements of folk songs for choirs Spilka demonstrates his sense of humour.

Writings

His pedagogic practice resulted in the volume *A Brief Theory of Harmony* (2nd edition 1944) and *Ear Training* (1955), a part of which deals with *Music Dictation* (1944).

SPIŠIAK (Fest), Radovan
[born Spišské Podhradie, 25 June 1900]

Spišiak was a pupil in composition of ZOLTÁN KO-DÁLY at the Music Academy in Budapest.

As a conductor he was active in Transcarpathian Ukraine, in Budapest, Bratislava and since 1945 at the State Theatre at Košice.

His most important work is the ballet *The Carpathian Rhapsody* (Marijka, 1956, première at Košice 1959). From the music of this ballet he composed the *First* and the *Second Carpathian Rhapsody* (1956).

His latest works include a cantata *Heigh, Villages, Villages!* for tenor, choir, reciter and orchestra (1959), *The African Fantasy* for bass, tenor, choir and orchestra (1960) and *Three Pastels* for violoncello and orchestra (1961).

SRNKA, Jiří

[born Písek, 19 August 1907]

LAUREATE OF THE STATE PRIZE

Srnka studied at the secondary school in his native town and at the same time was a violin pupil of OTAKAR ŠEVČÍK. He continued his study of violin at the Prague Conservatory under JAN MAŘÁK and JINDŘICH FELD where he also was a pupil in the composition class of OTAKAR ŠÍN and at the Master School of VÍTĚZSLAV NOVÁK. He studied as well the quarter-tone and sixth-tone system under ALOIS HÁBA.

He was active in Prague as a violinist and later as a conductor at the Liberated Theatre, at the National Theatre and, for some time, at the Czechoslovak Radio. Since 1935 he has devoted himself exclusively to composition. In 1950—53 he was professor of film music at the Academy of Musical Arts.

Orchestral Works

Symphonic *Fantasy* for full orchestra (1932), *Violin Concerto* (1957) and an orchestral *Suite* which he arranged from his music to the films Moon Above the River and The Silver Wind.

Chamber Music

Srnka's instrumental work is represented by a one-movement *String Quartet* No. 1 (1928, his graduation work from the Conservatory), a *Suite* for violin and piano (1929), a *String Quintet* with two violoncellos (1930), *Three Compositions* for violin and piano (1961 to 62) and a cycle of eight compositions for chamber string orchestra *Historical Pictures from the Písek Region* (1963), intended for amateurs.

Vocal Music

First is the song *November*, set to words by OTAKAR THEER, for soprano with piano (1928), male choir

January, to words by KAREL TOMAN (1936), *Three Songs* to words by K. H. MÁCHA for mezzosoprano with piano (1936) and a cycle of children's choirs with chamber orchestra, set to verses by FRANTIŠEK HRUBÍN, entitled *The Children's Year* (1950).

●

Srnka's *Suite* for piano (1933), *Fantasy* for piano (1934), the second *String Quartet* (1936) and *Three Compositions* for piano (1938) were composed in the dodecaphonic system.

In 1935, he wrote two compositions for the quarter-tone piano.

Film Music

Srnka belongs among the foremost Czech composers of music to films.

Music to full-length films: *A Fiery Summer, The Past of Jane Kosinová* (of which the song *Pale-Blue Distances* is still popular), *The Enchantment of May, The Tribune, A Blue Veil, Happy Journey, Fog Over the Bogland, The Foundling Rozina, A Mischievous Bachelor, Foreboding, The Stolen Frontier, Krakatit* (the State Prize in 1948), *White Darkness, The Silent Barricade* (the State Prize to the film collective in 1949), *New Fighters Shall Arise, Action B, At Attention!, Moon Above the River* (the State Prize in 1954), *The Silver Wind; the Hussite trilogy: Jan Hus, Jan Žižka* and *Against All; The Game for Life, The Wolf's Hole; Romeo, Juliet and Darkness; The First Work-Team, The Ardent Heart, The Guest, Golden Fern.*

Music to medium-footage films: *Storm Over China, Prague—Mother of Towns, A Golden Dream.*

Music to short films: *Poor People* (produced by Alex. Hackenschmied), *A Song About Southern Bohemia, The Youth of New Greece, The Codex of Jena,* the Czechoslovak-German co-production film *Mountains and the Sea.*

433

Animated cartoons: *Hansel and Gretel* and a series of *Fairy-tales* according to KAREL ČAPEK.

Television fairy-tales: *Perutinka, The Shepherdess, Little Chimney-Sweep*.

In 1936, Srnka wrote his first musical accompaniment to films [anti-war film *Give Us Wings*]; since then he has composed music to more than 140 films.

He is as well a much sought-after author of scenic music: KAREL ČAPEK—*The Highwayman*; JAN DRDA—*Games with the Devil, Dalskabáty, a Sinful Village*; VIKTOR DYK: *Andrew and the Dragon, Don Quixote's Growing Sagacity*; MILAN JARIŠ: *The Kingdom of God*; VÍTĚZSLAV NEZVAL: *Manon Lescaut*; WILLIAM SHAKESPEARE: *Hamlet, Macbeth, Midsummer Night's Dream*; LOPE DE VEGA: *El Villano en su Rincón*.

ŠROM, Karel
[born Pilsen, 14 September 1904]

Šrom studied law at Charles University in Prague and at the same time composition under KAREL HÁBA.

He became manager of the musical department of the Czechoslovak Radio, editor in the field of music publishing and director of the Czech Music Fund. He wrote a popular little book *Orchestra and Conductor* (1961).

Orchestral Works and Chamber Music

In 1930 he composed his first *Symphony* and in 1934 the orchestral *Suite*, both in the athematic style. In his second *String Quartet* (1941) Šrom chose initially a traditional manner of compositional work together with uncompromising contemporary media of expression, particularly in the field of harmony. His consistent efforts towards a purity of style, unaffected by extraneous elements, reached its climax in the second *Symphony* (1951), noteworthy for its using of the slow and scherzo movements. Then followed the orchestra scherzo *The Goblin* (1953), the symphonic allegretto *A Sigh on Skates* (1957), inspired by a poem of CHRISTIAN MORGEN-STERN, the *Piano Concerto* (1961) and the orchestral suite for small and older children *Hajaja* (1961).

His chamber music consists of a *String Quartet* (1923); twenty years later of *Moments* for piano (1942), *Seven Pieces* (1943) and the *Scherzo Trio* for violin, viola and violoncello (1943); then *Little Minutes* for two pianos (1951) and *Fairy-tales* for nonet (1952).

Vocal Works

His predilection for instrumental works yielded for a short period to his interest in the human voice, resulting in the song cycle *The Face*, set to words by FRANTIŠEK HALAS (1936). Followed *Five Songs* for male choir [folk songs] (1940), to which were later added the songs *The Wooing* for mixed choir and *Little Rosemary* for women's choir.

STANČEK, Ladislav
[born Prievidza, 7 February 1898]

After completing the Teachers' Training Institute Stan-ček was first active as a teacher; later, after graduation from the Brno Conservatory in composition, conducting and organ, he became professor of music at the Teachers' Training Institute in Bratislava, Spišská Kapitula and Spišská Nová Ves.

The finest compositions of his extensive creative work are to be found in the field of c h a m b e r music (composi-tions for violin and piano, piano sonatas, string quartets, particularly the second *Quartet*, in G minor and *The*

435

Dorian Quartet), in music for the organ (an *Overture* in E major, *Preludes, Variations on Slovak Folk Song*) and in song compositions (*Songs* for voice and orchestra, the cycle the *Dead*).

He has made as well many arrangements of Slovak folk songs for voice and piano [*Twelve Slovak Folk Songs*], for choirs [*In Spiš They Sing, Verbovačka in Spiš* (a folk dance), *Song from Prievidza*] and for choir and orchestra (*The Spiš Songs, Slovak Songs* for orchestra).

He has written two cantatas (*A Dove is Flying Over My Land* and *A Festival in the Mountains*) and numerous original choirs for children.

He is as well the author of a collection of essays on music entitled *Chapters On Musical Art*, and of the manual *The Organ, Its History, Construction and Manipulation*.

STANISLAV, Josef

[born Hamburg, 22 January 1897]

LAUREATE OF THE STATE PRIZE,
holder of the ORDER OF WORK

Stanislav was a pupil of J. B. FOERSTER and VÍTĚZSLAV NOVÁK at the Master School of the Prague Conservatory where he also studied piano under ROMAN VESELÝ and KAREL HOFFMEISTER.

On completing his studies he devoted himself to concert activities as a pianist and later as choirmaster. He became deputy-choirmaster of the Prague HLAHOL.

Very early he joined the labour movement where he found fundamental inspirational sources for his compositional creative work and a broad field for cultural activity.

As chief of the musical section of the Workers' Amateur Theatre Union, he organized competitions for community singing, as well as discussions concerning music.

During the German occupation he founded the Union of Czech Musicians, including a music school.

After the liberation, Stanislav made use of his experiences in the revolutionary labour movement for the building up of a new musical life in the Revolutionary Trade Union Movement, at the Central House of Folk Art and in the Guild of Czechoslovak Composers.

From 1948 he is professor at the Academy of Musical Arts (section of musical folklore).

In 1953 he became director of the newly established Institute for Ethnography and Folklore of the Czechoslovak Academy of Sciences.

He was chairman of the composition section of the Guild of Czechoslovak Composers and in 1963 was elected Honorary member of the Guild.

Instrumental and Orchestral Works

Stanislav composed three piano *Sonatas*, music to two pantomimes *Voices over the Taiga* (1933) and *Voices over Turksib* (1933), a number of musical compositions for theatrical plays, a *String Quartet* in C major and a *Sonata* for violin and piano (1933); during the German occupation he wrote *The Red Army Symphony* (1942—44).

Vocal Works

He composed several cycles of songs, as *Alone and Alone*, set to words by FRÁŇA ŠRÁMEK (1927), two social cycles a *Song of the Employed* and *Song of the Unemployed* (both 1935) and a cantata *A Song About Granada* set to words by E. SVIETLOV (1936).

He made a considerable contribution to the repertoire of the Folk Art Ensembles with his revolutionary hymns *Thanks to the Soviet Union* (1945), *The Partisan's Song* to words by VÍTĚZSLAV NEZVAL (1945) and a *Song About a Beautiful Land* (1947).

His cantata *The Mother Earth* set to words by J. ČERNÝ, *The March of Good Crops* set to words by VLADIMIR MAJAKOVSKY and a number of songs for community singing are concerned with the problem of reorientation in our agriculture. He is in fact a pioneer in the community type of song and is a staunch believer in the use of socialist themes in Czech music.

In 1951, he was awarded a State Prize for songs well-known everywhere in our country: *With Song and Laughter* and *With President Gottwald*.

On the occasion of the thirtieth anniversary of the founding of the Communist Party in Czechoslovakia, he wrote the song *Salute to the Party* in the tradition of worker revolutionary songs (he elaborated this song later into a large a cappella mixed choir).

His cycle of songs *Lights in the East* was awarded in the artistic jubilee competition in 1960.

Writings

Stanislav devotes his time to musical theory (in 1957 was published a collection of his critical reviews and essays). He wrote a number of studies on ideology in music. He has often solved in an original manner questions concerned with musical folklore, of great assistance to him having been his experiences acquired on his journeys in Europe, Asia, Indonesia and Africa.

He prepares a monograph on music of black people in Central Africa; for the seminary on Arabian music, which took place in Baghdad (1964), he prepared a treatise on music of a Congo tribe N'Daka; simultaneously he wrote an exposé about the significance of European harmony for Arabian MAQÂMA.

He has written an extensive work about the founder of Slavonic musical folklore, *Ludvik Kuba*. For this book he received in 1965 a STATE PRIZE.

ŠŤASTNÝ, Vincenc

[born Bystrc, 20 January 1885]

Šťastný graduated from the Brno Teachers' Training Institute and Janáček School for Organists. For many years he was a teacher in a suburb of Brno. He was active as pianist and choirmaster (in the Philharmonic Society Beseda at Brno), devoted himself to school education in music and in cooperation with his wife Marie Havelková collected folk songs. In his creative work he made frequent use of folk song elements.

Stage Works

His stage works include *The Fairy-tale About a Golden Key and Living Water* to a text by VILMA SOKOLOVÁ (1914—16) and *A Captive of the Rock-sprites* set to a text by FRANTIŠEK FLOSS (1923).

Orchestral Works

Two works are noteworthy in this field: two *Funereal Marches* (1941) and a *Festival March* (*To the Victors-Liberators*, 1946).

Chamber Music

Chamber music compositions are represented by *Three Compositions* for French horn and piano (1949), *Variations on National Songs* (1950), a *String Quartet* (1951), *National Songs* for tenor and string quartet (1952) and a *Small Suite* for piano quartet (1962).

Instrumental Works

His piano compositions include *Three Etudes* (1906 to 1909), a *Song of the Woods* (1910—14), *Three Valses* (1915—17), *Four Valses* (1941—45), an *Etude* in A major for left hand (1950), *Variations on a Valse Theme* (1952), *Three Concerto Polkas* (1952—53), a *Sonata* (1953), a *Suite* for left hand (1955), *Four Valses* (1955—57), *Three Preludes* (1959), a *Sonatina* (1959), a *Small Suite* (instructive, 1959), a *Prelude and Scherzo* (1959), a *Fantasy* (1960), and *Two Suites* (1960 and 1962).

Šťastný's compositions for organ comprise a number of musical *Sketches* (1937—47), three suites (*Christmas, Romantic* and *Wedding,* 1944—50), *Variations on Old Czech Chorals* (1951), *Variations* and *Improvisations on National Songs* (1955), *Three Compositions* (1956) and *Four Compositions* (1958).

Vocal Works

The composer's vocal compositions include *Children's Songs* with piano (1923), *Christmas Carols* (1947), *A Great Day* set to words by VICTOR DYK (1952), *Christmas Songs* (1953), *Incidental Mixed Choirs* (1923), *Youth Carols* for female choir and organ (1944), the ballad *The Orphan* for solos, female choir and organ or harmonium (1944), the *Victory March of Youth* (second prize in the choral competition of the Czechoslovak Union of Youth in 1950), *Our Land* for mixed choir and organ (1953).

Šťastný's activity as an arranger of the folk songs of Slavonic nations has been very comprehensive, resulting in nearly 1,200 arrangements.

ŠTĚDROŇ, Vladimír

[born Vyškov, 30 March 1900]

Štědroň studied composition at the Prague Conservatory (J. B. FOERSTER) and graduated from its Master School under VÍTĚZSLAV NOVÁK and JOSEF SUK. For many years he served as a judge and then became professor at the Prague Conservatory.

His talent for composing made itself evident very early. At the age of twenty he had already several larger works to his credit, such as the orchestral overture *Fidlovačka* (1916) and *A Fantastic Scherzo* (1920), *Two*

Songs with orchestral accompaniment (1920), the first *String Quartet* (1920), two Melodramas (*The Reeds* and *The Sea*, 1920) and male choirs.

In the years that followed his creative work took on a broader aspect with such compositions as a song-cycle *Dawn* (1920—21), *A Variation Fantasy* to a Moravian folk song for string quartet (1923) and with piano compositions (*Dumka* and *Burlesque* of 1928).

With his symphonic poem *Illusions* (1936) he returns to full orchestral instrumentation while simultaneously his *Small Domestic Suite* (1937) satisfies itself with the intimacy of two violins and viola. Štědroň's refreshing musicalness has its foundation in the folk song and folk dance.

At the beginning of the difficult years of German occupation he stimulated the spirit of the people by a cycle of folk songs and dance arrangements *To One's Native Land* (1939) and by male choir *The Hand Land* (1939). During the war he wrote the second *String Quartet* (1940—45), a cycle of three patriotic songs *On One's Own Land* (1940—45), a *Lullaby quasi una fantasia* for violin and piano (1941—43, also arranged for violoncello and piano) and the choral *Lullaby* with alto solo (1942). His three *Love Songs* were written at considerable time intervals (1941, 1946, 1956).

Of late, dance stylizations and march elements prevail in Štědroň's creative work as illustrated by his *Festive Military March* for brass band (1951), an orchestral *Poetic Polka* (1952), *Folk Dance Fantaisies* (1953); further he composed the male choir *The Miners of Ostrava* (1953), a symphonic overture *Alla marcia* (1954), *Deux Moments Musicaux* (1953), a *Sonatina* for piano (1957) and a poetic polka *Janka* for orchestra (1962).

STEINMAN, Vilém

[born Oplocany, 31 October 1880, died Brno 23 February 1962]

Steinman studied composition as a pupil of VILÉM PETRŽELKA. He held a place of importance in Moravian musical life as an outstanding choirmaster and pedagogue. His activity as choirmaster reached its climax in his work with the organization of the Friends of Art of Choir Singing at Brno.

As a pedagogue he was active in Brno at the Conservatory, at the school for choirmasters attached to the Friends of the Art of Choir Singing, at the Faculty of Pedagogy of Brno University and at the Janáček Academy of Musical Arts. He has trained many successful choirmasters.

In order to meet the constant growth in the exacting claims, constituted by contemporary as well as classical choral literature, he made a systematic study of new trends in the field of choral interpretation. He thus became a pioneer in a new conducting technique (which in his work became a kind of motion-speech) and in an insistence on a consistent choral intonation on the basis of natural tone sequences and new colourful combinations. He laid down his main principles for musical reproduction in a commentary to the publication of the secular choirs of Pavel Křížkovský (*The Compositional Work of Pavel Křížkovský*, published 1949).

As editor of the Choral Archives he helped to popularize old as well as newer choral literature. Steinman's system served as the basis for the Textbook of Conducting and Choral Art by JIŘÍ SVOBODA.

He arranged many folk songs for choirs, wrote a number of instructive choir compositions for practical training of choirmasters, two collections of rhymes, songs, choirs and instrumental compositions, a violin sonata, two violin-cycles with piano accompaniment, orchestral works, a children's opera *Be Prepared!* (1936), music to student theatrical plays and to gymnastic exercises.

ŠTĚPKA, Karel Václav

[born České Budějovice, 31 May 1908]

Štěpka studied music at first at the local music school where he was a pupil of OTAKAR JEREMIÁŠ. He continued the study of composition at the Prague Conservatory under JAROSLAV ŘÍDKÝ and ALOIS HÁBA, completing it at the Academy of Musical Arts.

For several years he was a leading force in the musical life at Soběslav. Since 1939 he has been active in Prague as a teacher of music and as choirmaster. He is now lecturer on old religious hymnal songs at the John Hus Faculty.

His works include a melodrama *The Hands*, set to words by MIROSLAV VALENTA, a song cycle *Offering of Songs* for baritone, accompanied by brass and percussion ensemble, to a text by RABÍNDRANÁTH TAGORE, a mixed choir *The Hands* to words by LADISLAV STEHLÍK (1937), a song cycle *Yearning* for baritone and piano (1939), the children's choir *Three Fairy-Tales* (1942), a rondo for violin and piano *A Romantic Meditation* (1942), a *Suite* for full orchestra (1943), a cycle of mixed choirs *Music* (1945), a *Sonata* for viola and piano in the athematic style (1946), a cycle of three songs from the world of children *The Little Windows* for four women's voices in the quarter-tone system, accompanied by a quarter-tone clarinet (1948), *The Hussite Cantata* for solos, choir, symphonic orchestra and organ set to words by B. V. LOHNICKÝ (1949), a mixed choir *Comenius* (1950), *Meditation on a Hussite Choral* for string quartet (1951), *In the Footsteps of the Hussites*—canto bellicoso for mixed choir, brasses and timpani (1953), a cycle of songs *Summer in South Bohemia* for baritone and piano (1959), *Song to the Beloved* for soprano and piano (1960), a grand march *Trocnov* for full orchestra (1960), a march on the building up of the country *A Victorious Tomorrow* for children's choir, piano and little drum (1962) and a suite for nonet *Budowicia* (1962—63).

Recently, he has written *Rondo* for violin and string chamber orchestra (1963) and *Hussite Cantata* for solos, mixed choir and symphonic orchestra, set to words by B. V. Lohnický (1964).

Furthermore, he wrote several compositions for organ as well as instructive works.

STERNWALD, Jiří

[born Prague, 14 May 1910]

Sternwald was a student of composition at the Prague Conservatory as a pupil of Rudolf Karel. In 1940 he completed his course of study, writing the *Symphonic Overture*. Prior to that, he had composed a *String Quartet*, a *Piano Sonata*, songs and several small compositions.

E. F. Burian gave the young composer the post of musical advisor at his theatre, giving him opportunity of working in the field of scenic music (*Everyone Has Two Tasks, The Foster-Daughter, The Girl Robinson*, a montage of folk poetry *A Year in the Village*).

Sternwald has also written a great deal of incidental music for other theatres. His music and songs to Šamberk's play *The Eleventh Commandment* enjoyed a long run of popularity.

His work for the theatre led him to the film. In succession he has written music to such films as *The Rhythm, Rubber, The Mountain Climbers, Black and White, The Actor's Youth, A Little Story, Return to Life, The Way Out, A Far Journey, Hard as Steel, The Magic Hat, The Northern Harbour, Music from Mars, The Bomb, The Žižkov Romance, Five in a Million, The Ski, The Silon Dress, People Behind the Camera, Transport from Paradise* and to number of short films.

He has been awarded prizes for many of his films. Many of his songs for full-length films have been re-

corded on gramophone records for the radio and published as well (*Goodbye Sorrow*, *The Maiden*, *The Organ-
Grinder*, *The Itinerant Jobber's Song*, *A Million*, *The
Wedding Song*, *Prague Bids You Welcome*, *Trilobit* and
scores of others.

Of his variety programme compositions, mention
should be made of *The March*, *Grande Valse*, *A Suite for
the Films*, *The Postcard* and *The Water-lily*.

STRNIŠTĚ, Jiří

[born Dašice, 24 April 1914]

Strniště studied composition at the Prague Conservatory under RUDOLF KAREL and OTAKAR ŠÍN and attended as well conducting class of PAVEL DĚDEČEK. At the
Master School he continued his study of composition
under VÍTĚZSLAV NOVÁK.

He conducted at several theatres, directed radio
orchestras as guest conductor and recorded on gramophone records. He worked as well in the music department at the Czechoslovak State Film and was active as
dramaturgist and secretary of the opera of the National
Theatre in Prague. At present he is devoting himself
exclusively to composition.

Stage Works

After 1950, on attaining his compositional stride, he
wrote his operetta *The Heroes of the Manor-House*
(1955) which reflects the composer's experiences in the
field of vocal music. In 1962 Strniště completed his
opera *Lan-Ni* (A Long Journey).

Orchestral Works and Chamber Music

He has directed his creative endeavours to various
genres. In the field of symphonic music, he has written

a *Small Serenade* for strings (1953), a *Burlesque* for two pianos and orchestra (1954), *Three Dances*, a *Folk Suite*, a *Legend* (1954), a symphonic poem *Life* (1955), a dance suite *On Friendship* (1957) and the suite *The Evening Meeting* (1957).

Of his chamber music work we may mention the *Sonata* for oboe and piano (1955), his *Romance* for violoncello and strings (1954), which was dedicated to lovers of music, and a *Reminiscence* for violin and small orchestra.

Dance Music

He has also enriched the repertoire of music for variety theatres by the polkas *Eileen*, *The Woman Patriot*, *Eva*, *Jeanne*, *Drahomíra*, and the *Variety Dance*.

Vocal Works

He has written a cantata *To Young Communists* (1949) to words by JAN STERN, cycles of songs *We Have Faith* and *Hold in Contempt* (1946), the *Lyrical Songs* (1953), the *People Chorale* for male choir (1953) and *The Autumn Songs* (1958).

He derived considerable assistance from results attained in the field of community songs (*The Song of the October Revolution*, *Parcel Song*, *Confession to the Party*, *The Salute to Friends*, *The Song of Aeronautics*, *The Pure Land*, *The People*) and of variety songs (*The Green Fountain* and *The Spring Song*). The following songs are intended for the pioneers: *The Pioneers' Flag*, the cycle of children and pioneer songs, the *Pioneer Song* for children's choir and small orchestra and *Our Flag*.

SUCHOŇ, Eugen

[born Pezinok, 25 September 1908]

NATIONAL ARTIST and LAUREATE OF STATE PRIZES

Suchoň belongs among the founders of modern Slovak music. He came from a family of teachers and very early gave evidence of talent as a pianist and composer. He studied at the Bratislava Music and Dramatic Academy under FRICO KAFENDA and JOZEF VINCOUREK. After graduation he attended VÍTĚZSLAV NOVÁK's class at the Master School in Prague.

His first post, up to 1948, was that of a teacher of music theory and composition at the Music and Dramatic Academy, predecessor of the Bratislava Conservatory. In 1947 he was appointed professor of music education at the Pedagogic Faculty of the Bratislava University where he amply demonstrated his interest in the raising of the level of musical knowledge of the broad masses of people. For the purpose of study he edited several scripts on the theory of music.

In 1960 he was forced to discontinue his pedagogic activity for reasons of health but has continued taking part in the work of the agencies and institutions active in Czechoslovak cultural life.

Suchoň's compositional development is marked by a tenacity of purpose and directness. His early opuses are in every respect mature works, each new composition reflecting at the same time an over-all design. This design grows out of a deep understanding of the concrete needs and problems of Slovak national culture.

His creative work does not only aid in the building up of modern Slovak music from the very foundations but endeavours also to give directives to the people as a whole, leading to an understanding of it. The originality of Suchoň's expressive and characteristic style is unthinkable without such an ethical and philosophical basis. Musically it is characterized by distinctive emotionally rich melodics, which, like harmony, makes use of modality, typical for the Slovak folk song. In its form, Suchoň's music unites a dynamic formation with a well-reflected upon and ambitious structure which, however, in no way restrains its spontaneous effect.

His early compositions such as *The Sonata* in A flat major for violin and piano, op. 1 (1930) and *The String Quartet*, op. 2 (1931, worked over 1939), testify to his inclination to a polyphonically graded expression in the late romantic style.

Under the guidance of Vítězslav Novák, Suchoň's style becomes simpler, as demonstrated by his *Small Suite with passacaglia*, op. 3 (1931), with his expressive media broadened by an impressionistic tone quality. This is especially evident in his cycle of songs for mezzo-soprano and piano *Nox et Solitudo*, op. 4 (1932). His *Serenade* for wind quintet, op. 5 (1932—33), better known in its revised version for string orchestra, gives evidence of a growing sense for colouristic modal harmony.

The typically Suchoňesque dramatic character and tendency to monumentality appears in *The Piano Quartet*, op. 6 (1933). After the *Burlesque concertante* for violin and full orchestra, op. 7 (1933, joined to the *Fantasy* in 1948), appears a cycle of four male choirs *About the Mountains*, op. 8 (1933—34), which is one of the basic compositions in modern Slovak choral creative work.

Suchoň's music to Ivan Stodola's drama *King Svatopluk*, op. 10 (No. 1, 1935) was the starting point for the composer's later monumental national opera.

The Balladic Suite, op. 9 (1936, published in Vienna) is one of Suchoň's most important compositions while the *Sonatina* for violin and piano, op. 11 (1937, published in Vienna) which, together with *The Balladic Suite*, has contributed to spreading the fame of the composer abroad, is a more intimate example of a perfect modern chamber music composition.

The climax of Suchoň's development in the thirties,

however, is represented by his cantata *The Psalm of the Sub-Carpathian Land*, op. 12 (1938, published in Vienna) which in a stirring manner speaks of the composer's native country.

During the war Suchoň began to work on his first opera *Krútňava*, completed in 1949 (première in Bratislava 1949). This work signified a fulfilment of the efforts to create a Slovak national opera. Here a story, realistic in character, carries within it a deep ethical meaning. In his music to *Krútňava* the composer's style shows a maturity drawing on folklore elements. This opera very soon acquired an all-national character. It attained considerable success abroad as well.

The Metamorphoses (1953, published in Kassel), written on the composer's own themes, had become in the meantime a new key work in Suchoň's creative activity. Using the form of the suite with variations on the composer's own themes, it deals autobiographically with the fate of his country in the prewar period, during the war cataclysm, up to the days of liberation.

The style of *The Metamorphoses* shows evidence of Suchoň's further development, reflected in his subsequent compositions. Prior to these, the musically educational cycle *Pictures from Slovakia* (1957) came into being, consisting of six collections of piano compositions arranged in a progressive succession.

In 1959 the composer completed his second opera *Svatopluk* (première in Bratislava 1960), a historic opera, the story of which dates back to the beginnings of national history.

The simplification of tonal relations in favour of twelve tones of equal parity becomes even more expressive in the cycle of songs *Ad astra* set to poems by Štefan Žáry (1961), inspired by man's victories in the cosmos.

The cycle of choirs *About Man* (1962, rewarded by M. Schneider-Trnavský prize 1964) is a philosophically penetrating synthesis of the substance of modern man's existence.

Poème Macabre for violin and piano (1963) is a musical transcription of Hviezdoslav's antiwar poetry, of experience and sensibility of a man who lived through two world wars.

The melodrama *Contemplations* for a reciter and piano was composed in 1964, as well as *Rhapsodic Suite* for piano and orchestra, which was written for the Prague Spring Music Festival in 1965.

Together with Miroslav Filip he wrote a *Concise Science of Music* (1961, published in 1964).

SUCHÝ, František

[born Libina, 9 April 1902]

Merited Teacher

Suchý was a pupil in composition of Jaroslav Kvapil and Vítězslav Novák. He is active as a pedagogue at the Brno Conservatory and at the Janáček Academy of Musical Arts.

Due to the fact that he himself is an excellent oboist and experienced instrumentalist, he has oriented most of his extensive creative work to wind instruments.

Chamber Music

This is evident from his *Sonatina* for oboe and piano (1927), a *Quintet* for wind instruments (1928), a *Sonata* for trumpet and piano (1929), a *Concertino* for violin and five wind instruments (1931), a *Small Dance Suite* for wind quintet (1931), a suite *Autumn* for English horn and string orchestra (1931), *Serenade* for wind instruments (1945), a *Concertante Quintet* for wind instruments (1947), *Three Czech Dances* for wind quintet (1952), *Moravian and Slovak Folk Songs* for higher voice and wind quintet (1954), *Sonata* for bassoon and piano (1956) and a *Quintet* for instruments (1958), *Sextet* for oboe, clarinet, bassoon, violin, viola and violoncello (1962) and a *Sonata* for clarinet and piano (1962).

Instrumental Music and Orchestral Works

Concerto for flute with orchestra (1939), *Baroque Concerto* for violin with orchestra (1946), *Concerto* for oboe with orchestra (1950), his symphonic suite *The Highlands* (1958) [received an award in the artistic jubilee competition in 1960], and orchestral *Variations* to the workers' song by KAREL BENDL I am a Czech Worker (1961) as well as three symphonies, four cantatas and scenic music.

Stage Works

For his three-act opera *Maryla* (1956, première in Brno 1961) he received a special award in the artistic jubilee competition in 1960.

SUCHÝ, František Pražský

[born Březové Hory, 21 April 1891]

Suchý studied music under ONDŘEJ HORNÍK and KAREL STECKER and later under ARTHUR NIKISCH at the Master School of Conducting in Leipzig.

He was head-master of a secondary school in Prague and was the first conductor of the Orchestral Association of Prague Teachers.

His work as a collector of songs and his reasearch activity in the field of town-folklore deserve particular attention.

Stage Works

In the field of musical drama Suchý composed an o p e r a *The Miners* (1948—52) and a one-act opera *Love's Wonder*, according to JULIUS ZEYER (1923, première in Ostrava 1925); further a scenic melodrama *Rachel* to the libretto by PAVEL ORSZÁGH HVIEZDOSLAV (1925), a ballet *A Porcelain Kingdom* and a children's ballet-melodrama *School by Play*.

Orchestral Works and Church Music

He composed a *Rococo Suite* (1931), a miners' symphony *The Silver Town* (1933), a *Ballet Suite* for orchestra (1936), *Missa festiva* (1939), an overture *To Our Students* (1947) and *Symphonic Trifolium* (1960).

Chamber Music

The Wind Quintet (1936), a *Nonet* (1934) and *The Vintage Suite* for viola and chamber orchestra (1955).

Instrumental Compositions

Two piano *Nocturnes* (1918) and a *Gay Toccata and Fugue* on a theme of an old students' song for organ (1962).

Vocal Works

Songs: a song-cycle *The Miners* for baritone, flute, viola and piano (1941), a montage of miners' songs for solos, choir and orchestra, entitled *Miners, Smelters, Engineers, Workers* (1947), a montage of folk songs *Mountains-Valleys* (1949) and *Songs for the Pioneers and the Sparks* (1962).

Male choirs: *Aurora* (1910), *Eternal Struggle* (1912), *Prague, the Song of Bohemia* (1941) and a cycle of choirs *The Miners* (1943).

Children choirs: Three three-voice choirs *The Slovak May* for children's voices [also for mixed choir] (1962), awarded a prize.

Cantatas: *The Blessed of a Pure Heart* to words by ANDREJ SLÁDKOVIČ (1930).

Transcriptions and Arrangements

Transcriptions of Czech songs for string quartet,

Roumanian idyllic songs *Doiny*, the *Wallachian Odzemek* (a folk dance), *Dances from the Rye Island* and various arrangements of Czech and Slovak folk songs.

Writings

Suchý has writeen a *Textbook of Singing for Slovak Schools, Tests in Musical Education* and *Musical Tales*.

ŠUST, Jiří
[born Prague, 28 August 1919]
Holder of the decoration FOR OUTSTANDING WORK

Šust studied piano at the Moscow State Conservatory of P. I. Tchaikovsky under J. R. GINSBURG and composition under J. A. DUBOVSKY and S. N. VASILJENKO. After his return from Moscow in 1939, he continued the study of composition at the Prague Conservatory under JAROSLAV ŘÍDKÝ and ALOIS HÁBA. After completion of his studies, he was active as a composer at the Gottwald Film Studio, later as musical dramaturgist of the Czechoslovak Army Film. At present he is chairman of the Board of the Authors' Association for Protection of Rights on Musical Works.

Orchestral Works

Šust has concentrated his creative efforts on orchestral music, such as *Sinfonia* (1941), a symphonic poem *The Way Home* (1946), a *Suite Antiqua* for trumpet, strings, organ and percussion instruments (1948), a *Symphony Of Life and Work* (1949) and *Mourning Music* for oboe, French horns, harp, violoncello and strings (1953). Of his other compositions we refer to a *Romantic Fantasy* for piano and orchestra (1950), a ballet *For Peace* (1951, première at Ostrava 1951) and a *Cantata About Gottwald* for baritone, choir and symphony orchestra (1952).

Chamber Music

In the field of chamber music Šust has composed two *Barcarolas* for piano, three *Duets* for clarinet and bassoon and the suite *The Farm Under the Elms* for four trombones, tuba and little bell, *Sonatina* for piano (1946) and *Allegro* for string quartet (1955).

Film Music

Šust has composed music to more than eighty films, including such popular ones as *The Christmas Dream*, *Dead Among the Living*, *A Week in a Quiet House*, *The Kidnapping* (the collective was awarded the State Prize in 1953), *The Sea-gull is Late*, *Dawn*, *Farewell to Klement Gottwald* (the collective was awarded the State Prize in 1954), *A Tank Brigade*, *Conscience*, *Victory March*, *A Village on the Frontier*, *Frona*, *The Bread of Lead*, *Morale of Madam Dulski*, *The Sons of the Mountains*, *The Hesitating Marksman*, *Safebreakers*, *Golden Spider*, *Gloria*, *The Crossroads*, *People Like You*, *A Column for Africa*, *Theresa*, *The Witness* (the collective was decoreated For Outstanding Work in 1962), *The Fort on the Rhine* and to television film *Prague Saturday Night*.

Vocal Music

Šust has written many songs which are noteworthy for their political texts: *The Spring Song*, *The Maiden's May Feast*, *Youth of the World* (won the highest award at the Fourth Festival of the World Federation of Youth), *The Combine Driver's Song*, *The Song About Love for the Native Land* and a *Song On the Freedom of Mankind*.

The Song to be Sung at a Campfire, *Dusk*, and *Trumpeters Blow Merrily* as well as twenty-four songs *From Spring to Winter* were written for children and young people.

Two Songs set to a text by A. S. PUSHKIN and *The Party Song* to words by JOSEF KAINAR, music to the women's dance, *Life Wins Over Death* for the Second Spartakiad and to the puppet show *Don Rope* for LATERNA MAGICA complete the picture of his work.

SVĚCENÝ, Ladislav

[born Velká Ves, 11 December 1881]

Svěcený studied at the Prague Conservatory and passed the state examinations in voice and piano. He was teacher at the secondary school and was a much sought after accompanist by the pupils of OTAKAR ŠEVČÍK at Písek and of numerous guest artists. At Písek he founded the Philharmonic Society SMETANA. While living at Košice he founded there the choral society FOERSTER and in Prague established the choral society HLAHOL.

Chamber and Instrumental Music

Three Bagatelles for violoncello and piano (1944), *Terzetto* for two violins and viola (1944, arranged for flute, violin and viola in 1960), two string quartets, two suites for wind quintet, *Variations on Czech Folk Songs* for flute and piano or orchestra (1952), a *Concertino* for flute and piano or orchestra (1952), *Concertino* for viola and piano (1955), a *Suite* for string orchestra (quintet) and piano (1960), a *Children's Suite* for flute and piano (1961), a *Trio* for flute, violin and viola (1961) and a *Quintet* for two violins, two violas and violoncello (1963).

Vocal Works

In addition to arangements of folk songs he composed many songs and choirs—female, male and mixed choirs to words by JAROSLAV SEIFERT and FRANTIŠEK NECHVÁTAL, a melodrama *Spalivec* to words by ADOLF HEYDUK (1944), the balladic cantata *The Dove* set to words by K. J. ERBEN (1957), the cantata *The Romance About King Ječmínek* to words by VÍTĚZSLAV NEZVAL (1959) for solos, mixed choir and orchestra and *The Song about Friendship* for mixed choir and piano [or orchestra] (1963).

SVOBODA, Hanuš

[born Příbram, 15 June 1876—died 16 December 1964]

Svoboda graduated from Teachers' Training Institute where he took state examinations in singing, violin, piano and organ. He taught musical subjects at the Teachers' Training Institute at Příbram, Soběslav and in Bratislava where he was also active at the local School of Music. In 1923 he left Bratislava for Prague to take the post of choirmaster.

In addition to the opera *Horymír* and two ballets, he has composed twenty five piano sonatas, thirteen violoncello sonatas, fifteen violin sonatas, six viola sonatas, 36 string quartets, a piano quartet and quintet, four violin concertos, two viola concertos, *Ten Příbram Dances* for symphonic orchestra, two nonets, about three hundred songs for solo voice and two hundred ecclesiastical compositions, including seventeen masses.

SVOBODA, Jiří

[born Třebíč, 23 December 1897]

Svoboda was a composition pupil of J. B. FOERSTER, K. B. JIRÁK and ALOIS HÁBA. He completed the study of musical science at Charles University in Prague.

He was a professor at Teachers' Training Institutes, assistant professor at the Pedagogical Faculty and later at the High Pedagogical School in Brno.

Orchestral and Instrumental Works

Svoboda started with the composition based on jazz, *The Merry-Go Round* (1926); in later years he moved in his development from chamber to symphonic music: *Suite* for piano, dedicated to the antifascit fighter W. LANGHOO (1937), three *Lyric Compositions* for piano (1939), the sonata for piano *"March"* (1939), inspired by the loss of national liberty, *Six Preludes* from the time of German occupation (1941), imbued with protest and defiance against the fascist terror, a *Wind Quintet* (1942), *Impromptu* for violoncello and piano (1942), *Capriccio* for violin and piano (1946), symphonic poem *To the Tragic Anniversary of Munich* for male choir and orchestra to words by S. K. NEUMANN (1949) and a *Symphony* (1951—52).

Vocal Works

In his extensive vocal creative work, VÍTĚZSLAV NEZVAL's texts occupy a predominant position; his work includes the following: the songs *Love* (1919—20), *Three Songs* (1927—28), *Four Songs* (1932) bearing the mark of social protest, *Two Children's Songs* (1936), the song-cycle *Manon* with piano or orchestral accompaniment (1940), the cantata *An Invitation to a Journey* (1950), the male choir *Warning* (1957), *A Ballad About a King and a Wasp* for children's choir with piano accompaniment (1960), and *The Cantata on Prague*, a triptych for solos, mixed choir and orchestra (1961).

Svoboda composed as well a cycle of three songs *A Blue Peace* to words by NAZIM HIKMET, L. HUGHES and RAFAEL CHACÓN NARDI (1957—58). His other compositions include a cycle of two male choirs *To the Native Land* to words from MÁCHA's *May* (1944) and the hymn *The Native Land Sings* to verses by JOSEF HORA (1946), a female choir *A Child's Voice* to verses by KAREL KAPOUN (1960) and a cantata for baritone and full orchestra set to poem by KAPOUN *The World's Model* (1962).

Writings

The three volume work *The Development of Czech and Slovak Music* (in cooperation with JAN TROJAN), *A Textbook of Conducting and Choral Art* (System of V. Steinman, 1952), *Essays from the History of Music* and *Artistic Trends* (for the textbook Music Education) and *Portraits of*

Composers (1956) represent for the time being Svoboda's work as a writer on music. In addition, he writes reviews, glosses and commemorative studies for various periodicals.

SÝKORA, Václav Jan
[born Prague, 10 October 1918]

Sýkora studied composition at the Prague Conservatory under RUDOLF KAREL, piano at the Master School of the Conservatory under JAN HEŘMAN and history and musical science at Charles University.

After the Second World War he was active as a pianist and harpsichordist and since 1946 has taught at the Prague Conservatory. He devotes himself as well to the history of music.

In his compositional work he concerns himself above all with piano music, expressing his ideas in a genuinely modern style. This is demonstrated by his *Fantasy* (1944), *Sonata* in C major (1952), *Polkas* (1955), *Prague Nocturne* (1958), *Variations and Fugue* to a theme by J. L. DUSÍK (1960) and the *Etudes of Higher Effectiveness* (1961).

His further works include *The Psalms* for bass and orchestra (1945), *Two Capricious Legends* for soprano and orchestra (1951), *Impromptu* for violoncello and piano (1952), *Dumky* for oboe and piano (1952), a *Spring Suite* for violin and piano (1954), *Autumn Songs* for voice and piano (1954), a melodrama *The Poet and Other Crafts* (1954) and *Cadences* (1) to the cemballo concerto do minore of JAN ZACH (2) to piano concertos of F. X. DUŠEK and (3) to the concerto of KAREL STAMIC for viola d'amour.

He wrote a monograph on *Jan Heřman* (1956) and on *Fr. X. Dušek* (1958). He has also published the piano works of JIŘÍ BENDA, the piano sonatas of J. L. DUSÍK and the *Piano fugues* of ANTONÍN REJCHA.

TARABA, Bohuslav

[born Sedlčany, 22 November 1894]

By vocation a teacher but Taraba was active as well as music critic and in that capacity contributed to Šalda's rewiev KMEN and to the music magazine DALIBOR. He wrote two books (*The Genius, Both the Lion and the Dove*) and was also a co-founder of the society for contemporary music THE PRESENT TIME and of the publishing house Music Editions.

Stage Works

His musical creative work has developed in a parallel line with his work as a painter. He composed a musical comedy *The Life of the Painter Peter* to his own libretto, according to the novel about PETER BREUGHEL by FELIX TIMMERMANS (1939—45) and a pantomime scene *Cain* (1923).

Melodramas

Songs of Separation to poems by WALT WHITMAN (1923), *The Funeral* (with orchestra) set to words by KAREL ČAPEK (1953—55) and *The Little Joan of Arc* to a text by MARK TWAIN (1956).

Orchestral Works

Two *Symphonies* (1920, 1922), Variations with fugue entitled *The Metamorphoses* (1922), a large counterpointed suite *Life of a Musical Motif* (1948), a *Symphonic March* (1958), a symphonic poem *Your Portrait?* (1959), an *Impromptu* for orchestra with cimbalom (1961) and *Inventions*, ten variations for symphonic orchestra (1964).

Chamber Music

Three Meditations for ten instruments (1922), *Two Compositions* for nonet (1942—43), two *Quartets* (1946 and 1955) and *Sentimental Prelude* for chamber ensemble (1963).

　　　　　　　　　　　　　　　TARABA

Instrumental Compositions

Three Piano Cycles (1914—15) and *A Discourse for Two Pianos* (1961).

Vocal Works

Out of many of his compositions we should mention a female choir *Music* (1920), male choirs *To Beauty and Love*, set to words by JOSEF HORA and CHARLES BAUDELAIRE (1916), a cycle *My Slovakia* (1946—50), *Seeking* to words by R. M. RILKE (1949); the cantatas *To Slovakia*, set to Slovak folk texts (1934), *Jánošík* (1949), *On Horse!* to words by VILÉM ZÁVADA (1950) and *We Go In Your Footsteps, Pilgrim!* to words by JOSEF HORA (1952).

TAUSINGER, Jan

[born Piatra Neamt in Roumania, 1 November 1921]

Tausinger studied at the Bucharest Conservatory under EDUARD LINDENBERG and D. CUCLIN and completed his studies at the Academy of Musical Arts in Prague as a pupil of METOD DOLEŽIL, ROBERT BROCK, KAREL ANČERL, ALOIS HÁBA and PAVEL BOŘKOVEC.

He directed the University Artistic Ensemble which under his leadership became one of the foremost Czechoslovak amateur musical ensembles.

After graduation he went to live at Ostrava where he was active as organizer, pedagogue and artist. He became director of the Ostrava Conservatory and artistic manager of the Workers' Artistic Ensemble of the Vitkovice Iron Works and later was artistic director of the Artistic Ensemble of the Ministry of Interior.

Tausinger's creative work shows the traces of an arduous search for a new expression in the spirit of socialist realism.

Orchestral Works

His orchestral work embraces the symphonic dance *Mateník* (1951, a folk dance in varied rhythm), as well as the *Suite* in classical style for orchestra (1946 to 1947) and the *East Moravian Suite* (1955—56). His other works include the symphony *Liberation* (1950—52), a *Violin Concerto* (1963), *The Flight of Cosmonauts* for full wind orchestra (1963) and a *Violin Concerto* (1964).

Chamber Music

In the field of chamber music Tausinger composed a piano *Sonata* (1948—50) and a viola *Sonata Suite* (1957—59), *Suite* for violoncello (1949) and a *Sonata* for violin and piano (1953—54, inspired by an article by JULIUS FUČÍK on his return from Transcaucasia), a Trio for violin, viola and violoncello *Etudes* (1961), a *String Quartet* (1961—62) and a Duo for flute and violoncello *Etudes* (1962), composed according to the dodecaphonic technique with intentional reservations.

Vocal Works

His first efforts in composing were in the field of song (*Youth as Leader*, *The March of Young Builders*, a *Medley of Czech Peasant Songs*, a montage of Slovak Folk Songs about *Jánošík*, *Roumanian folklore*). In the cycle of children's choirs *The Holidays* (1955) he found a true individual expression. Furthermore in the choral field he composed the male choir *Secret Love* (1957) and female choir *I Shall Always Believe in May* (1958), then incidental songs, scenic music (*The Horn of Plenty* and *The Death of the Mother of Yugovich*), a cycle of mixed choirs *Ilo*, set to words by ARTHUR RIMBAUD (1964), and a cycle of songs *The Love*, set to words of the Japanese folk poetry for voices and piano (1964); furthermore a cycle of children songs *Swan's Feather* with orchestra, set to words by MIROSLAV FLORIAN (1964) and a cycle of male choirs *The Harvest*, set to words by JIŘÍ WOLKER (1964).

Various

Musical accompaniment to pantomime and other scenes for the Artistic Ensemble of the Ministry of Interior (music to the dance pictures *A Shoemaker's Tale* (1960), *The Workers' Quadrille* (1961) *Daybreak* (1961), *Two Roumanian Dances* (1963) and music to the dance scene *Oldřich and Božena* (1963) complete the picture of the composer's creative work up to the present.

TĚŠÍK, Jan
[born Zakřany, 11 January 1922]

Těšík graduated from piano and composition sections of the Brno Conservatory. In composition he was a pupil of VILÉM PETRŽELKA. Since 1944 he has been active at the Brno Radio Station as a pianist.

He is outstanding for his brilliant technique and his natural musicality. He has teamed up with JIŘÍ HUDEC, a brilliant piano duo resulting.

As a composer Těšík has devoted himself successfully to variety and dance music in which he demonstrates a keen imaginativeness and a rhythmic vigour.

He has composed as well a *Piano Sonata* (his graduation work), eight national dances for piano and orchestra, a *Moravian Rhapsody* for violin and orchestra, a nine-movement *Lyrical Suite* for full orchestra, *Six Compositions* for viola and orchestra, *Moravian Dances* for orchestra, *Flute and Rhythm*, a composition for flute and orchestra and *Lyric Suite* for full orchestra.

THOMSEN, Geraldine

[born London, 5 July 1917]

Studied music at the London Royal Academy of Music under BENJAMIN DALE and after his death under ALLAN BUSH. In 1945 she came to Czechoslovakia with her husband, the writer JIŘÍ MUCHA. Her creative work embraces instrumental and vocal compositions.

After completion of her studies, in 1942, she wrote two compositions for piano *Parting and Teasing* and the second *Collection of Czech and Slovak Folk Songs* for baritone and piano (1943), *Sonatina* for viola and piano (1945), *Fantasy* for violoncello and orchestra (1946), *First Sonata* in G minor for violin and piano (1947), an *Orchestral Overture* (1951), a symphonic *Picture of Šumava* (1952), a collection of *Folk Lullabies* for voice and piano (1952), a collection of children's *Pieces* for piano (1953), sixteen variations on a *Scottish Folk Song* for piano (1957), *Sea Scenes* for violin and piano (1958), *Nonet* (1959), two *Women's Choirs* set to words of an anonymous English poet of the sixteenth century (1956 and 1958), *Piano Concerto* (1960), *Second Sonata* for violin and piano (1961) orchestral *Overture* to a ballet (1961), *Sonets* for recitation, flute and harp, set to texts of WILLIAM SHAKESPEARE (1961), and a *String Quartet* (1962).

Recently, she has composed *The Song of Songs* for recitation, flute and harp, Second *String Quartet* (1963), a *Wind Quintet* (1964) and ballet *Macbeth* (1965).

TICHÝ, František

[born Chrudim, 25 March 1898]

Tichý studied organ at the Prague Conservatory under JOSEF KLIČKA and ONDŘEJ HORNÍK and composition under KAREL STECKER and JAROSLAV KŘIČKA.

He was an organist in Prague, a member of dance orchestras, an operetta conductor, a member of the artistic staff of the former gramophone company Ultraphon, chief of the music and recording section of the Gramophone Company (His Master's Voice), assistant conductor of the radio orchestra, manager of light music ensembles (one called by its initials FAT and the second, The Spark) and editor for light music at the Czechoslovak Radio.

He has written about three hundred fifty light and dance compositions of which mention should at least be made of the following: ¶ the intermezzos *Without Pause*, *The Mill-Wheel*, *A Sugar Doll*, *A Summer Breeze*, *A Danse of the Wooden Shoes*, *The March of the Children's Army*; ¶ a valse *Recollections of a Dancing Lesson*, ¶ six sport gallops, *Tanganilla* and *Into Your Little White Hands* (awarded first prize in the competition for the best dance song in 1933).

For full orchestra Tichý composed *A Festive March*, *A Little Romance*, *An Elegic Valse* and the suites *From the Native Region* and *From the Mountains*.

He is also the author of a full-length ballet *Dancing Fairy-tales* (1959—60) to a libretto by JIŘÍ VOLDÁN, five operettas, revue music, music to one of the first Czech sound films *When Strings Moan*, incidental music to the *Hollywood Revue* and others.

Tichý was the first to make gramophone records of BEDŘICH SMETANA's opera *The Bartered Bride*.

TOMAN, Josef
[born Lukavice, 15 April 1894]

Toman studied music at the Prague Institute for the Blind. He studied piano under VÁCLAV ŠTĚPÁN and composition under VÍTĚZSLAV NOVÁK. He became choirmaster first at Červený Kostelec, later at Beroun and appeared, as concert pianist, both in Czechoslovakia and abroad (Nürnberg, Vienna, Budapest). He is also an excellent organist and improvisor.

Toman has composed about seventy compositions among which are autobiographical piano cycles *In the Darkness* and *In the Pursuit of Light, The Idyll, A Ballad*, four *Concerto Valses* and *Trifles* for piano, a *Piano Composition for Left Hand*, compositions for violin and piano such as *A Spring Mood, An Autumn Mood, A Christmas Mood, A Concert Fantasy* and an instructive work *The First Steps of a Young Violinist*, chamber music compositions (three string quartets, two wind quintets), four compositions for symphonic orchestra, *Children's Rhymes* for voice with piano accompaniment, songs, male, female and mixed choirs, church compositions, a *Czech Christmas Mass* for mixed choir, orchestra and organ and a *Christmas Fantasy* for organ and orchestra.

Recently he wrote two mixed choirs, *The Song of Liberty* set to text by FRÁŇA ŠRÁMEK (1960) and *Peace* to a text by FRANTIŠEK BRANISLAV (1960) and a *Trio* for violin, flute and piano (1961).

TOMÁŠEK, Jaroslav

[born Koryčany, 10 April 1896]

Tomášek studied musical science at Charles Univesity. His compositional style shows the influence of the school of VÍTĚZSLAV NOVÁK and his work deals in the main with vocal music.

Chamber and Instrumental Music

In the field of instrumental and chamber music Tomášek has written *Four Piano Compositions* (1916), a *Rondo* for piano for the left hand (1924), a *Sonata* for piano for the left hand (1925) and two *String Quartets*. In 1962, he completed a *Symphonic Rondo* for full orchestra and piano.

Vocal Music

He composed *Two Songs* to words by ANTONÍN SOVA for middle voice and piano (1917—18), *Three Songs* set to words by S. K. NEUMANN for higher voice and piano (1920), a cycle of songs *Miracles and Illusions* (1920—21) for middle voice and piano, to words by FRÁŇA ŠRÁMEK, a cantata *The Christmas Eve Romance* (1921, rewritten 1953), set to text by JAN NERUDA for higher voice and orchestra, a cycle of songs *A Simple Heart*, set to words by FRÁŇA ŠRÁMEK for middle voice and piano (1921 to 1922), a cycle of male choirs *Strings in the Wind* to words by JOSEF HORA (1943), a cantata *A Meditation*, set to the poetry of RABINDRANÁTH TAGORE for middle voice and string quartet (1945—46) and *Three Women's Choirs*, set to words by JOSEF HORA (1946). The cycle of songs *To Woman*, to a text of S. K. NEUMANN and FRÁŇA ŠRÁMEK for higher voice and orchestra (1919—20, orchestrated in 1944—46), represents the first part of a monumentally conceived and vigorously contrasting composition entitled *Songs About Man*, while the second part consists of a cycle of songs *Grief*, set to words by different poets for tenor, soprano, bass and orchestra (1958—59).

•

Tomášek significantly influenced the development of Czechoslovak musical life in his role as a critic, editor of the review TEMPO and organizer, particularly in the Guild of Czechoslovak Composers (he was the first Chairman of the Czech section and the first vice-chairman of the Central Committee), of the Prague Spring Festival of Music and of the Association for the Protection of Rights on Musical Works (as its director).

TONKOVIČ, Pavol

[born Podkonice, 13 January 1907]

After completing the Teachers' Training Institute he studied violin at the Bratislava Music and Dramatic Academy under NORBERT KUBÁT and at the Academy of Pedagogy.

He was active as a teacher, chief of the folk music section at the Košice Radio; in 1948—49 he founded and managed the Slovak Folk Art Ensemble and then became chief editor of folk music and conductor of the folklore ensemble of the Bratislava Radio.

His published works include *Songs of Our People, Songs from Orava, Těrchová Melodies*; he has made contributions to the scientific edition *Slovak Folk Songs*. He has also written a number of studies on Slovak folklore and as an expert directed the production of documentary films dealing with Slovak folklore and folk musical instruments.

As a composer he has concentrated on making arrangements of folklore, in the main for solos, choir and orchestra (*The Šariš Suite, Hojdana Songs* and *Dances from under Babia Gora, Pictures from the Tatra Lowland Country*).

TROJAN, Václav

[born Pilsen, 24 April 1907]

LAUREATE OF THE STATE PRIZE

Trojan studied organ at the Prague Conservatory under B. A. WIEDERMANN, conducting under OTAKAR OSTRČIL and PAVEL DĚDEČEK and composition under JAROSLAV KŘIČKA. He graduated from the Master School under VÍTĚZSLAV NOVÁK and attended as well the section of ALOIS HÁBA for quarter- and sixth-tone music.

He was music producer at the Prague Radio and in charge of its programmes, as well as a teacher of scenic and film music at the Academy of Musical Arts.

During his studies he composed a *String Quintet* (his graduation work at the Master School, 1927) and a *String Quartet* (1929). In these works he demonstrated his outstanding talent and technical aptitude.

Stage Works

His children's opera *The Merry-Go-Round* to a libretto by MARIE CHAROUSOVÁ-GARDAVSKÁ (1936—39, premiére at Ostrava 1960) is an outstanding work in the field of musical drama.

Orchestral and Chamber Music

Trojan's work includes a successful *Wind Quintet* on folk song motifs in classical style (1937), concerto suites from his music to the films *Chap-book*, *The Emperor's Nightingale* and *Bajaja*, from his opera *The Merry-Go-Round* and *Fairy-tales* for accordion and orchestra (1961).

Film Music

Trojan has become well-known throughout the world for his music to films. After the full-length film *Once Upon a Time There Was a King* he devoted himself to writing music to animated cartoon, trick and puppet films of JIŘÍ TRNKA: *The Old Man Planted a Beet-Root*, *The Water Sprite's Mill*, *Chap-book* (a collection of folk songs), *The Emperor's Nightingale*, *The Devil's Mill*, *Bajaja*, *Old Czech Legends*, *The Fortune of the Good Soldier Schweik* and *Mid-Summer Night's Dream*. For the music to the film *Mid-Summer Night's Dream* he was awarded the State Prize in 1960.

Scenic Music

He is a much sought-after author of scenic music: *The Philosophers' Story*, *The Judgment of Love*, *Fireflies*, *Our Swaggerers*, *The Mischievous Stag*, *The Bagpiper of*

Strakonice. He has also composed scenic music to the plays *The Regiment's Mother Molly* and *The Clever Widow*.

Various

Trojan has also applied his ability in the field of general purpose music with which he acquainted himself intimately during his long practice with dance orchestras. Due to their highly artistic quality, his compositions in this field are above the usual level as demonstrated, for instance, by his rumba *The White Moon* from FRAN-TIŠEK HRUBÍN's play A Sunday in August.

In addition, he has written a number of music montages to various occasions for the radio *From Bohemia and Moravia, Humour in Folk Songs, Children's Games, Our Little Songs, Czech Christmas Carols, Folk Songs of the Pilsen Region, Folk Songs from the Giant Mountain Foothills, Little Marching Songs* and others.

International Prizes

In 1962 he received the premium *Mercurio de Oro* awarded by the International Association for Music and Dance in Films CIDALC. In the same year CIDALC awarded Trojan a *silver medal* for all his creative work for films and special premium for his music to the film *Chap-book*.

TYLŇÁK, Ivan

[born Nižní Sinevír, 16 January 1910)]

Tylňák studied composition privately with VÍTĚZ-SLAV NOVÁK. He is teacher of musical theoretical subjects at the Prague Secondary Boarding School for children with defective eye-sight. He has written for them instructive textbooks on harmony, intonation and note-printing for the blind.

In his development as a composer, Tylňák has

proceeded from atonality and a complicated expression to a simple and clear musical utterance.

Compositions

His compositional works include two *Collections* of female choirs (1941 and 1957), a cycle of songs for middle voice and piano entitled *Song for You* (1942), a *Scherzo* for violin and piano (1944), an *Eclogue* and *Burlesque* for clarinet and piano (1945—46), *Four Compositions* for violin and piano (1945—46), two *Wind Quintets* (1947 and 1958), two *String Quartets* (1955 and 1958), *Furiant* (a Czech dance) for violin and piano (1956), a *Quintetto* for flute, clarinet, two violins and piano (1957), a *Sonata* for solo violoncello (1957), a *Rondo* for three accordions (1958), a mixed choir *To the Native Land* set to words by FRANTIŠEK TOVÁREK (1960), a *Divertimento* for flute, two clarinets and French horn (1961), *Three Mixed Choirs* to words by VÍTĚZSLAV NEZVAL (1961), a *Small Concerto* for accordion with orchestra (1962), a cantata *Count With Us* for solos, mixed choir and orchestra to words by RUDOLF KRCH-ŇÁK (1963), songs for community singing [*A Song of Youth*] and a *Sonatina* for flute and piano (1964).

Writings

Intonations and Rhythm (in Braille characters) and *Manual of the Normal Note Transcribing* (for the blind).

UHLÍŘ, Jan
[born Ivanovice, 6 May 1894]

Holder of the decoration FOR OUTSTANDING WORK

His love of music led him first into the ranks of military musicians and during the First World War he conducted a military brass band. From the year 1920 he was active as military band leader at Most and Litoměřice, finally settling in Prague. He studied at the Prague Conservatory and in 1935 graduated from its section of conducting. Thereafter he became commander of the military school of music, inspector of military bands and teacher in instrumentation for brass bands at the Prague Conservatory.

Uhlíř undertook the instrumentation for brass bands of about two hundred compositions (SMETANA, DvoŘÁK, SUK, NOVÁK, JANÁČEK, DOBIÁŠ, HANUŠ, KAPR, KUBÍN, PAUER; from Russian composers TCHAIKOVSKY, MURA-DELI, BLANTER, SHOSTAKOVICH, TULICHOV).

He composed a number of successful ¶ marches as *Smartly Forward, Forward March! Hail to the Victors! Steadily Forward! Hail!, The Rival, The Meteor, Avia, To Men of Work, The Ninth of May, Hail the Flight!, To Sportsmen, The Sporting March, The Infantry Marches, To Our Miners, The Relay Race of Peace.*

He has furthermore composed ¶ polkas *The Woman of Haná, Jaruška, The Capricious Polka*; ¶ waltzes: *A Greeting to Spring, A Dance Roundelay, Domino, A Small Waltz, A Ballet Waltz*; ¶ mazurka *The May Mazurka* and others.

The popularity of the band he conducted prompted him to write all types of compositions, including ¶ the intermezzos *Gay Moments, Reviewing the Troops, Dance Suites, Romance,* the *Ukrainian Dance Kolomyjka,* ¶ the gallops *Electrone* and *For the Start, Folk Merry-making* and others.

ULLRICH, Josef
[born Pilsen, 27 February 1911]

Ullrich received his basic musical preparation from his father, acquiring further musical education at the military school of music in Prague, from NORBERT KU-

BÁT SENIOR at Pilsen, OTAKAR ŠEVČÍK and JAROMÍR HRUŠKA at Písek and from JAROSLAV KOCIÁN and FRANTIŠEK PÍCHA in Prague.

He has set to music the poems of RAYMOND HELI, *The Little Wreath*, *The Kerchief* and *Consolation* and of the poems of FRÁŇA ŠRÁMEK *Advent*, *The Girl*, *Simple Johnny* and others. In the Grand Jubilee Competition of the Guild of Czechoslovak Composers and the Czech Music Fund he was awarded the third prize for his *Valse Capriccio* for violin and orchestra and the first prize of the Ministry of National Defense for his march *Spartakus*.

Of his further compositions we may mention *The Písek March*, *Humoresque* for brass or string orchestra, the intermezzo *Parnasia* for full brass band, the concert waltz *The Fan*, *The Old Town Waltz*, *Mitrovice Polka*, *Daniela Polka*, *The Morning Rays Waltz*, *Tarantella*, a *Romantic Overture*, a waltz with solo trombone *Playful Moments*, a *Mazurka*, *Ball Slippers* for wind quintet, a *Valse Serenade*, *Scherzettino*, a *Dancing Mood* for piano quartet and *Introduction and Rondo* for violin and piano (orchestra).

URBANEC, Bartolomej

[born Krompachy, 12 November 1918]

Originally Urbanec had intended to be a teacher but after graduation from the composition and conducting section of the Bratislava Conservatory (ALEXANDER MOYZES, EUGEN SUCHOŇ and KORNEL SCHIMPL) he began to be active as a military band-master. After the war he continued the study of conducting under VÁCLAV TALICH.

Urbanec is one of the pioneers in the field of creative work for folklore ensembles (The Slovak Folk Art Ensemble, Lúčnica). In performing Urbanec' compositions, these groups crystallized their artistic character and artistic aims.

In 1949—52 he conducted the Slovak Folk Art Ensemble and soon thereafter the orchestra of the Bratislava Radio. For several years he functioned as secretary of the Slovak Guild of Composers.

Within the last few years he has concentrated mainly on composition, with practically all his creative work stemming from Slovak folklore of which he has a thorough understanding and an ability to interpret with great sensitiveness and effectiveness.

For the Slovak Folk Art Ensemble and Lúčnica he has composed a number of songs and dance songs for their repertoire, such as *Periniarky* (songs of women who used to carry feather beds for newlyweds), *Trávnice* (songs of women cutting grass), *Bunkošovy Dance* (a pastoral male dance using the ring-tipped canes of the Orava region), *Kresák* (a folk dance of the Mountaineers' region).

Urbanec has written as well many songs for community singing of which the song *Ho, Up Goes the Sun* has acquired the character of a folk song. In creating songs and choirs characterized by an inclination to lyricism, Urbanec develops the romantic song tradition of MI-KULÁŠ SCHNEIDER-TRNAVSKY (the song cycles *The May Love* 1954, *Songs About the Mountains* 1957, *Four Duets* 1959). This is true as well of his operettas *May Poles* (première Košice 1954) and *Love*.

More recently Urbanec has turned his attention to larger vocal-instrumental compositions [the cantata *Greetings to the Soviet Union* (1957), the oratorio *A Song About Mirko Nešpor* (1960), the radio play with songs *The Ballad of Vojtovej Marina, Musician Zvrtala* (1959)] and the *Concertino* for piano and orchestra (1961) and *String Quartet* (1962).

Urbanec is as well the author of numerous scenic and film compositions and popular symphonic works [*The Bratislava Valses*] and of a reference book on instrumentation for brass band.

473   **URBANEC B.**

URBANEC, Rudolf

[born Dačice, Moravia, 3 December 1907]

After graduation from the Prague Conservatory, Urbanec became band-master of the Czechoslovak Army, later deputy commander of the military school of music in Prague and professor at the Conservatory in Teheran. After the liberation of Czechoslovakia he became head of the brass-band of the Castle Guard.

He is now musical manager and chief editor of light music at the State Publishing House of Music, where he organized a brass-band.

Of his compositions, the following have become widely popular: *Wave*, *Flag of Ours!*, *Catherine*, *The March of Mathausenians* (with Jiří Allan), *Hail!* and a military march song *The People's Army*.

He also wrote *The Flower Polka*, the polkas *A Beautiful Day*, *Why Have You Promised Me Love*, *A Grotesque Polka* for wind quintet and a valse *Spring Blossoms*. Of his other works, we may mention a *Potpourri of English Songs* for brass-band.

He has conducted innumerable brass-band concerts for recordings as well as for radio, the latter gaining him an international reputation. He occupies himself as well with instrumentation for brass-bands.

VACEK, Karel

[born Liberec, 21 March 1902]

Holder of the decoration FOR OUTSTANDING WORK

Vacek was active as a musician in dance and theatre ensembles (The MELODY BOYS, LIBERATED THEATRE in Prague). During the second World War he was conductor of a light music orchestra.

He is the composer of the world-known tango *The Gypsy*, which was recorded under the title *Play to Me*,

Gypsy and played by foremost dance ensembles all over the world (Billy Reid, Billy Cotton, Ambrose, Roy Fox, Titterton, Alfredo Campoli, Don Sesta, BBC Dance Orchestra, Lyton and Johnston, Jack Jackson).

His polkas also enjoy considerable popularity: *Come to See Us, On the Wooded Slope, Beautiful Moments, But No, The Nameless One, The Huntsman, When you Get Married, Playing by Ear, To a Syncope, Muddy Water, At the Weir, The Fifties, The Sixties, For Little Jarmila, Hu and Hu* and a *Carload of Straw*.

Of Vacek's popular valses mention should be made of *When we Meet Again, Before We Part, The Blue-eyed Doll, A Last Penny Had I, Through a Quiet Village, Love without Ire, A Little Song, Monogram, Czech Mountains, The Green Birch Tree, Near Our Barracks, Hi Mummy, Four Pairs of White Horses, The Announcer* and others.

In addition to the famous *Gypsy song*, Vacek composed songs no less popular as *The Story of Youth, Café in Vienna, Come Along Comrade!, Farewell, Comrades!, Tramp Songs*, the hiking song *The Camp-fire*; the foxtrot *Cat's Eyes*; the mazurka *Cinderella* and others.

A number of Vacek's compositions have been published in England, France, Germany, Austria, Switzerland and in the United States.

His polka *To a Syncope* was awarded in the artistic jubilee competition in 1960.

Vacek is editor of the edition Club of Good Wind Music Band in the Publishing House of the Guild of Czechoslovak Composers PANTON.

VACEK, Karel Václav

[born Hřebeč, near Kladno 5 June 1908]

Vacek studied composition privately with OTAKAR ŠÍN and ANTONÍN MODR and graduated from the violin class of the Prague Conservatory.

He was a teacher of singing at secondary schools, head-master of music schools, orchestral artist and director of the Higher Pedagogical Music School in Prague. He led choral ensembles, appeared as conductor and organized various musical activities.

He is now deputy-chief of the director of the Prague Conservatory.

Stage Works

To his native region he dedicated the operetta *At the Picture* (1933).

Orchestral Works

His concert compositions include a fantasy for symphonic orchestra *To the Native Country*, *Romance* for small orchestra and *Rhapsody* for full bras band.

Chamber Music

Bagatelle for trombone, accompanied by strings and a *Bagatelle* for viola with wind quintet accompaniment.

Various Compositions

From the period of his enlistment into a military band he began to compose dance music, which includes ¶ the slow folk valse *Neighbourly*, *When We Were Young* and ¶ the polkas *A South Bohemian*, *Agricultural* and *From Our Countryside*.

Popular became his ¶ overtures *Fantastic*, *South-Bohemian*, *On Building-up the Country* and *Joyous Day*.

He composed as well several ¶ marches: a festive march *A Greeting to the Liberators*, *Hail to the Cable!*, *450 Years of Buštěhrad Town*.

Instructive Compositions

Vacek is the author of forty instructive compositions, as a concert polka for oboe *The Siskin*, an intermezzo for oboe and bassoon *Two Friends*, a fantasy for clarinet on the song *The Little Red Kerchief*, a polonaise for trumpet *Merry Friendship* and *Neighbourly* for trombone with piano accompaniment.

Vocal Works

Voices: *Song of the Kladno Steel-workers* for tenor with small orchestra and other songs as *A Red Dawn*, *The Kladno Glare* and *From Our Mines*.

Songs: a song-cycle *Four-leaf Clover* for soprano, tenor and mixed choir accompanied by a small orchestra.

Cantata *With a Stroke of the Hammer*.

VACEK, Miloš

[born Horní Roveň, 20 June 1928]

Vacek studied organ at the Prague Conservatory and then composition at the Academy of Musical Arts under Frantíšek Pícha and Jaroslav Řídký.

Stage Works

He devoted himself mainly to musical dramatic work. He has composed a historical opera *Jan Želivský* (1953 to 1956), ballets *The Comedian's Fairy-tale* (1957, première in Pilsen 1958) and *Wind in the Hair* (1960, première in Prague 1962, at Cottbus, German Democratic Republic, 1963), *The last Dandelion* to libretto by Jan Mareš (1964), then the musical comedies *The Petrograd Usurer* (1953) and *The Black Madona* or *Hands Up, Mr. Karmín!* (1956), the blues drama *The Night is My Day* (1962, première in Frankfort on Oder 1964), inspired by the fate of the singer Bessie Smith, who died as a victim of rasism, and the comic three-act opera *The Emperor's New Clothes* according to Andersen (1962).

Orchestral Works

His orchestral compositions include a *Sinfonietta*

(1951), *Sketches from a Chinese Notebook* (1952), *The Brigands' Rhapsody* (1952), suites from the film *People of One Heart* and from children's film *The Adventure at the Golden Bay* and two suites from the ballet *The Comedian Fairy-tale*.

Chamber Music

Vacek's chamber music includes a *Suite* for violoncello and piano (1947), a *Suite* for piano (1948), a *Sonatina* for violin and piano (1949), a *String Quartet* (1949), a *Dramatic Prelude* for organ (1958), several smaller compositions for piano and others.

Film Music

Vacek has composed music to many full-length and short films [*The People of One Heart, Lost Footsteps, The Windy Mountain, Life for Jan Kašpar, Brother Ocean, Escape from the Shadow, Then at Christmas, The Unconquered, The King of Šumava, A Respectable Grandfather, A New Story of an Old River, Snowstorm, A Fugitive, A Fascinating Day, A Big Chap, A Procession to the Virgin, The Mystery of a Chinese Carnation*.

He is holder of a Gold Medal awarded him by the Minister of Culture of the Chinese People's Republic in 1954 for his music to the film *The People of One Heart*.

Television Music

He composed music to the cabaret *Whale Comedy*, to the play *Boy* and to the children cabaret *Box full of Adventures*.

Variety Music

Among Vacek's compositions we find as well music for variety ensembles, music for brass bands, various arrangements of folk songs, community songs, compositions for the Spartakiad and incidental pieces of which the best known is the signature tune of the Peace Relay

Races Prague-Berlin-Warsaw and the signature tune of the Czechoslovak film weekly news programme.

Vocal Works

He has composed song cycles *The Aurora* (1947), *The Girl's Motifs* (1947) and the lyrical meditation *On the Highlands* for female voice, violoncello and piano (1948), female choirs *The Spring in the Highlands* (1947) and a cycle of children's choirs with piano accompaniment entitled *Five Fairy-tales for Tommy* (1962).

With the cantata *Stop War!* (1953) he expressed his attitude to the situation in Korea.

VAČKÁŘ, Dalibor

[born Korčula, 19 September 1906]

Son of the popular composer Václav Vačkář was a pupil of OTAKAR ŠÍN and JOSEF SUK in composition.

He has been successful in two branches of art, as composer and writer (pen name Dalibor C. Faltis).

Stage Works

Vačkář has composed two full-length ballets: *Švanda the Bagpiper* (1954, première in Prague 1954) and *A Midsummer Night's Dream* (1957).

Orchestral and Instrumental Works

He has created a number of symphonic compositions: *Four symphonies* [*The Optimistic Symphony*, *The Chosen Land* for alto, choir and orchestra, *The Smoking Symphony* and *The Peace Symphony* (1941—49)], a *Symphonic Scherzo* (1946), a *Sinfonietta* for strings, French horn, timpani and piano (1947), a *Czech Concerto* for piano and orchestra (1953), a *Concerto* in C major for violin and orchestra (1958) and two symphonic movements—

479   VAČKÁŘ D.

Prelude and *Metamorphoses* (1956, arranged as well for piano 1960—61).

Chamber Music

His chamber music work includes *The Smoking Sonata* (piano arrangement of the third Symphony), a *Sonata* for violin and piano (1937), a *String Quartet* (1939), a *Quartet* for piano, oboe, clarinet and bassoon (1950), a *Suite giocosa* for violin, violoncello and piano (1959), a four-movement *Dedication* for violin and piano (1960), a *Concerto* for string quartet (1960), a *Piano Fantasy* on a theme by FRANZ SCHUBERT, The Arch (1962), a *Concerto da camera* for bassoon with small string orchestra and a *Concerto* for trumpet with accompaniment of percussion instruments with keys and double-bass (1963).

Vocal Works

In the field of vocal music Vačkář has composed *The Revolutionary Songs* for male choir (1945) as well as the madrigal *The Song of Songs* (1959—60) for mixed choir.

He has devoted special attention to music for children, as evidenced by his rhapsody on his own text entitled *Children to Grown-ups* for youth ensemble and piano, *Chod Songs* for children's choir and piano, *The Child's Voice*, five songs for children's singing and recitation ensemble and orchestra and a cycle of children's choirs *Daisies*.

For soprano and orchestra he has composed a cycle of songs called *Sheet Lightning* (1943), *Songs of Love* (1944) and *Parents' Songs* (1956) for soprano and tenor with piano, *Little Songs While Sewing* for soprano and piano (1951, also for girls' choir and piano) and *Three Love Songs* (1959).

Various

Vačkář has also composed a large number of compositions for films, dance music, community songs, pioneer songs, a cycle of instructive compositions for piano *The Beautiful Land* (1952) and others.

Together with his father he has published *Instrumentation for Symphonic Orchestra and Brass Band* (1954).

VAČKÁŘ, Václav

[born Dobřejovice, 12 August 1881—died Prague, 4 February 1954]

In composition he was a pupil of VOJTĚCH ŘÍHOVSKÝ and JAROSLAV KŘIČKA.

Vačkář belongs among the most popular Czech composers of marches and dance music. As an instrumentalist (trumpet, bugle) he had considerable experience in military bands, in the brass band of Alexander Schwarz in Russia, in Shibenik, in the Czech Philharmonic in Prague, in the orchestra of the Vinohrady Theatre and in the Šak Philharmonic. He was band master with the theatrical society of Josef Faltys, of the town band at the Dalmatian island Korchula and in Cracow.

Orchestral and Instrumental Music

Vačkář composed the *Moravian Slovak Overture* (1910), *Legends* for symphonic orchestra and organ (1915), symphonic poem *Robinson's Longings* (1920), grotesque overture to the film comedy *A Deceitful Little Cat* (1926), a *Comical Prelude* (1933), *Dance Suites* (1935), the suites *Pictures from Czech Fairy-tales* (1940), *Czech Overtures* on motifs of folk songs (1943).

Popular Music

He has written many

¶ marches, the most popular of which are: *Rivière, The Gallant, Awakening, Liberation, The March of the Hussites, Enthusiasm in One's Soul, The March of the*

Huntsmen, Glory to the Victors, Bratislava, In Vino Veritas, A Country Lass, Around Hradec, Full Steam Ahead, The March of the Anvil, The March of Work, The Prague March, The First of May, Victory of Work, For Freedom, Trumpeters of Peace, March of the Defenders of Peace, Song of the Anvil, So I Swear;

¶ valses: *Evening on the Sea, It Was in May, By the Light of the Moon, A Song of Love, A Dream of Love, A Still Night, On the Waves of the Morava River, Play of Lights, When the Heart Aches, In a Little Green Wood, Don't Forget that I Love You, A Rose from Slovakia*;

¶ polkas: *Confused Recollections, A Black-haired Girl, Herdsman's Love, In that Countryside, A Little Pearl, Youth-Joy, Blue Eyes, The Old Prague Polka*;

¶ mazurkas: *In Dreams, Grandfather Said So* and others.

•

Vačkář was the author of a serenade *A Recollection of Zbiroh*, of a musical picture *Storm on the Sea*, of two idylls for cornet (bugle) *Evening on the Sázava River* and the *Pancíř Guard*, of a polka for flute *A Dance of Sprites*, of a polka for clarinet *A Chatterer*, of characteristic compositions for clarinet, trumpet and trombone (clarinet, bugle, euphonium) *Three Brothers, A Dream Under the Moravian Slovak Sun* for violoncello (violin), *Humoresques, Menuet*, four *Moravian Slovak Dances* (1908, 1934—35).

Vocal Music

Three Songs for baritone and symphonic orchestra, set to a poem by ANTONÍN KLÁŠTERSKÝ (1918), *Three Capricious Songs* for female choir (1921, reworked 1950) and several medleys of folk songs [*Youth, Good Hunting!, Moravian Songs*] and others.

VALAŠŤAN-DOLINSKÝ, Ján

[born Békéscsaba, Hungary, 15 February 1892—died Nitra, 2 March 1965]

Holder of the decoration FOR OUTSTANDING WORK

Valašťan combined his compositional activity with educational work in the field of music and public enlightenment. He has written many arrangements of folk songs for children [*Heigh-Ho Under Kriváň!*, *My Song-book*] as well as original compositions for choir [*Let's Solemnize Solemnly*].

However, his most important compositions include the cycle of songs *Hviezdoslav's Shoots* for middle voice and piano and the cycles of mixed choirs *From Our Hills and Dales*, *Chats With the Unknown*, the male choirs *To All of You* and the *Čaba folk songs*.

His arrangements of folk songs for young violinists *The Golden Violin* enjoy particular popularity.

VALDAUF, Karel

[born Trhové Sviny, 25 October 1913]

Valdauf graduated from the military school of music in Prague. He studied composition privately with JAROSLAV ŘÍDKÝ and conducting with BOHUMIL ŠPIDRA and PAVEL DĚDEČEK, passing the state examination in conducting of choirs and orchestras.

He was active in the field of military music and in various musical ensembles. In 1942 he founded the VALDAUF orchestra which became one of the most popular Czechoslovak musical ensembles.

Valdauf is the author of many successful ¶ polkas: *Without You*, *Two Loves*, *The Photograph*, *I To You*, *To Our Countrymen*, *Little—So Little*, *My Distress*, *The Motorist's Polka*, *Hasten Not Youth*, *Unwelcome*, *Under One*

Roof, Tell Me, The New Year's Eve Polka, That's a Habit, I Like You, The Only Wish, Fifty and *The Moon in Love.*

His ¶ valse songs include *When Our Paths Meet, When You Marry Another, Grandmother Smile!, My Home, A False Love, When a Woman Tells the Truth, How Many Years of Love, After Ten Years, Why Am I Homesick, Perhaps You Will Remember, Take Me Into Your Confidence, Happiness in Song, You to Me, An Evening Confession, Enchanted Wedding Day, In the Milky Way;* ¶ the mazurkas: *For Grandfather, Come Dear Old Thing;* ¶ waltz *We Like to Be Together.*

Valdauf's ¶ march songs are also famous, as for instance: *Dont' Cry My Dear, The Orlice Mountains, The Spotted Little Hen, For Liberty, Fly the Flag!* and others.

He arranged several medleys of his own compositions and of compositions of other authors.

VÁLEK, Jiří
[born Prague, 28 May 1923]

Válek graduated from the Master School of the Prague Conservatory under JAROSLAV ŘÍDKÝ. At the Faculty of Pedagogy at Charles University he completed his studies, qualifying as a teacher for secondary schools; in 1951 the degree of Doctor of Philosophy was conferred upon him.

After occupying the post of secretary of the Guild of Czechoslovak Composers he became editor-in-chief of the Czechoslovak Radio in Prague, the department of transmissions for youth, and later, the editor-in-chief of the editorial division of the Central House of the Czechoslovak Army.

At present he is the editor-in-chief of PANTON, the publishing house of the Guild of Czechoslovak Composers.

Orchestral Works

He started his symphonic works with a *Sinfonietta* (1947) and composed three *Symphonies*: the first, *The Year 1948* (1948—49), the second, *Rustica* for string orchestra (1962), the third, *Meditations of an Optimist*, for soprano, tenor and full orchestra, set to words by S. K. NEUMANN (1962—63). His other orchestral composition is the symphonic poem *The Water-dam* (1959).

Recently, he has composed the fourth *Symphony* and *Dialogues about Life*, according to WILLIAM SHAKESPEARE (1965).

Chamber and Instrumental Music

During his studies he wrote two compositions for violin and piano (1940—41), two *String Quartets* (the first—*Daisies*, the second, both 1945) and a *Suite* for flute, clarinet and piano (1946).

In later years he composed the third string quartet, *The Rumburk Revolt*, on a theme of a poem by MILAN JARIŠ (1960), *Sonata eroica* for trumpet (1960; in 1962 instrumented for trumpet and string orchestra) and three nocturnos for chamber string orchestra and solo viola *Prague at Night* (1962—63).

Among others he has written the first piano sonata *The Year 1942* (1943), the first *Violin Sonata* (1946—47), the first *Viola Sonata* (1948), the second piano sonata *Cosmonautic* (1961), the second viola sonata *Tragic* (1961) and the second violin sonata *The Revolt*, on the theme of a poem by MICHAIL LUKONIN (1962).

Vocal Works

Voices: seven monologues *About Love* for soprano and piano (1959, in 1962 reworked for soprano, harp, piano and string quartet);

Songs: first song-cycles set to texts of Chod folk poetry (1947), the *Song of the Five Year Plan* to words

by Ivan Skála (1951) and *Glory Ye Nameless Ones*
set to words by Vilém Závada (1958);
   Female choir *The Cosmic Sonatina* (1962);
   Cantatas: *May* to words by Josef Hora (1951) and
cantata for children's choir and small orchestra *How
Many Suns*, set to words by František Hrubín (1962).
   Válek's creative work in the field of songs for community
singing is extensive (pioneer songs, dance songs, songs
for ensembles of all types, chansons). Many of them
were awarded prizes in all-national competitions and
recorded on gramophone records [*When the Train Disappears at the Bend, The Distant Beloved, A Song about the
Skies*].

Writings

   Válek devotes himself to the scientific and critical
appraisal of new Czech music. He has written a monograph *The Origin and the Significance of Ostrčil's opera
Jack's Kingdom* (1952) and *Radim Drejsl, Life and Work*
(1957). He is the author of many reviews and articles.

International Prizes

   Of Válek's work to receive the greatest acclaim is the
dance song *Calls of the Sea-gulls* and *Not a Cloud on the
Horizon* (awarded a medal and a prize in the competition at the Festival of the World Federation of Youth,
Vienna 1959).

VIGNATI, Miloš

[born Přerov, 28 April 1897]

   Vignati studied law at Charles University and
simultaneously composition privately with J. B. Foerster in Prague and with Vilém Petrželka in Brno.
Later he graduated from the Faculty of Philosophy at

Brno University, where he received the degree of graduate pedagogue in the field of musical education. At present he is professor at the Kroměříž branch of the Brno University.

He took an active part in the development of musical life in central Moravia. In addition to his work as chairman of the Olomouc branch of the Guild of Czechoslovak Composers he was active as conductor, choirmaster, pianist and author.

Orchestral Works

He wrote numerous outstanding orchestral and instrumental compositions including the orchestral suite *To Young Pioneers* (1944), *Bulgarian Frescoes* (1955), a *Fantasiette* for clarinet and orchestra (1962), and a *Suite* for French horn and orchestra (1964).

Chamber Music

Vignati devotes himself particularly to chamber music as testified to by his *Terzetto* for two violins and viola (1940), *Partita* for two violins (1943), a *Folk Suite* for violoncello and piano (1945), *String Quartet* No. 1 (1949), *Three Pastorals* for string quartet (1953), a *Sonata* for violin and piano (1954), *Sonatina rustica* for violoncello and piano (1961), *Partita* for flute nad viola (1962), *Poetical Pieces* for flute and harp (1962), *String Quartet* No. 2 (1962), a *Nonet* (1963), *Small Suite* for clarinet and piano (1963), *Three Poetical Pieces* for flute and harp (1964), *Balladic Sonatina* for violin and harp (1964) and *Melodies* for violin and piano (1964).

Instrumental Works

Fantasia marittima for piano (1937), *Sonata quasi ballata* for solo viola (1941), *Revolutionary Sonata* for piano (1944) and *August Preludes* for piano (1962).

Vocal Works

Voices: a cycle of four *Songs* set to words of RABIN-

DRANÁTH TAGORE for soprano and orchestra (1933), ten *Songs from Carpatho-Ukraine* for soprano and piano (1931), a cycle of songs *Hear, My Beloved* for soprano and orchestra (1945), *Soldiers' Songs* for baritone and piano (1953), *Love Songs* for alto and piano (1954), the cycle of love songs *Intimate Meetings* for soprano and string quartet (1957), *Songs from Beyond the Mountains* for high voice and piano (1958), *Recruits' Songs* for baritone and piano (1958), and *Nenia eroica* for baritone, violin, viola and violoncello, inspired by the last letter of PATRICE LUMUMBA (1961).

Songs: The cycle of children's songs *The Magic World* with piano accompaniment (1959) and the satirical song *The Career* (1960) were awarded in the artistic jubilee competition in 1960.

Female choirs include *Songs from the Carpathians* (1931), *Songs from the Luhačovice Woods* (1937) and the cycle *Early Spring* (1947).

Male choirs: *The Song of the Native Land* set to words by JAROSLAV SEIFERT, *Three Boon Companions* to words of Chinese poetry (1943), *A Greeting to Moscow* (1948), a choral cycle *For a New Tomorrow* (1950), *Why?* to words by JOSEF HORA (1952), *The Harvest* to words by MARIE KRATOCHVÍLOVÁ (1956), *Four Moravian Poems* (1956) and *Three Choirs* set to words by VÍTĚZSLAV NEZVAL (1958).

Children's choir: *Four Children's Choirs* (1959) and *The Children's Kaleidoscope* (1963).

Cantata *What is Good and What is Evil* to words by VLADIMIR MAJAKOVSKY (1960).

Melodrama: a cycle of children's melodramas fairy-tales *Scanty of Words* set to words by KAREL ŠIKTANC (1961).

He is as well the author of songs and march songs for youth, of scenic music, songs for community singing and of instrumental compositions.

VILEC, Michal

[born Bardějovská Nová Ves, 6 August 1902]

Vilec was a pupil of ZOLTÁN KODÁLY in composition at the Conservatory of Music in Budapest.

Initially he was active as a theatrical conductor in Bohemia and Austria, later as a musical pedagogue at Prešov, a member of the staff of the Košice Radio, conductor of the Košice Orchestra and in 1955—62 director of the Bratislava Conservatory.

His compositional work was a synthesis of the romantic tradition and impressionism, according to the example set by KODÁLY.

Chamber Music

At first he concentrated chiefly on chamber music, composing a *Sonata* for violoncello and piano (1936) and a *Fantasy* for violin and piano (1936). After the Second World War his work shows the influence of the East Slovakian folklore. His arrival in Bratislava marks an intensification in his compositional activity. In the forefront appear again chamber music works including *The Bagatelles, Intermezzo, Children's Games* for piano, a *Piano Trio* (1960) and a *String Quartet* (1962).

Creative work for youth is of particular interest to Vilec (*Little Compositions* for two violins and piano, *Let's Play, Summer Notes* for various wind instruments and piano).

Orchestral Works

Of Vilec's orchestral compositions the most significant are: a *Divertimento* for strings and piano for four hands (1957), *Preludio eroico*, a symphonic poem in honour of the fifteenth anniversary of the Slovak National Uprising (1959).

Vocal Works

Five Songs for voice and piano (1937) and a song

cycle *Lofty Summer Skies* for middle voice and piano (1961).

Writings

In collaboration with Mikuláš Moyzes he has written a modern two-volume *Piano School* and is the author of *The Theory of Harmony*.

VIPLER, Vlastislav Antonín
[born Bílá Třemešná, 12 June 1903]
Holder of the Order of Work

Vipler graduated from the section of composition and conducting at the Prague Conservatory as a pupil of J. B. Foerster, Jaroslav Křička and K. B. Jirák. His graduation work was the *String Quartet* (1923).

After completing his studies he became theatre conductor at Košice and from 1936 conductor for the radio. Since 1939 he has been conductor of the orchestra of the Czechoslovak Radio in Prague.

Vipler has written a number of songs, choirs and small instrumental and orchestral compositions. Of his extensive creative work in the field of operetta, *The First Waltz*, *At the Holy Hillcock* and *The Children of Moravian Slovakia* have gained popularity. His latest (the twenty-third) operetta is *The White Officer*.

He is also the author of music to several sound films and his waltz *Daisies* is equally popular.

Of his more extensive orchestral compositions we may list the suites *Pictures Taken During One Week* (1949), *To Children* (1949), *A Happy Day* (1950), *A Variety Suite* (1953), *Blossoms and Smiles* (1954), *From the Czech Paradise* (1956), *A Postcard from Poděbrady* (1961) and *Five Miniatures* (1962) as well as two symphonic preludes *Welcome, Friends!* (1952) and *Friendship* (1961),

Rhapsody (1962), *Invitation*, valse intermezzo for orchestra (1963), *Marcia festiva* for symphonic orchestra (1963) and *Valse Burlesque* for flute and piano [or orchestra] (1964).

VLACH-Vrutický, Josef

[born Vrutice, 24 January 1897]

Vlach graduated from the Prague Conservatory and its Master School in the class of J. B. FOERSTER. He was for many years active as choirmaster and conductor in Yugoslavia.

Stage Works and Cantatas

He composed an opera *The Village Magistrate of Kozlovice*, op. 20 (1930), a ballet *Arja*, op. 68 (1941) and an oratorio Rex Pacis [*The King of Peace*] (1943—52).

Orchestral Works

He is the author of numerous compositions, the most noted of which are the *Symphonic Prelude and Fugue* on a Saint Wenceslas Choral for orchestra, op. 50 (1939), *Ballet Suite*, op. 61 (1940), *Third*, op. 114 and *Fourth Slavonic Rhapsodies*, op. 116 (both 1955), a balladic *Symphony*, op. 118 (1956), a suite *Carnival Pictures*, op. 119 (1957), a *Comedy Overture*, op. 122 (1958), *Suita giocosa*, op. 126 (1959), a *Concert Overture*, op. 127 (1960), a *Symphonic Triptych*, op. 128 (1961) and *Moments musicaux* for orchestra, op. 129 (1961).

Chamber and Instrumental Music

String Quartet No. 1, op. 32 (1936), *Toccata and Fugue* for organ, op. 63 (1940), *Partita* for solo violin, op. 66 (1941), *Capriccio, Giacona* and *Fugue* for two violins op. 67 (1941), *String Quartet* No. 2, op. 115 (1951), *String Quartet* No. 3, op. 123 (1958), *String Quartet* No. 4, op. 130 (1962).

Vocal Music

In the popular and folk vein Vlach-Vrutický has written *Love Songs*, op. 5 (1924), *Simple Motifs*, op. 14 (1934), *The Hymn of Liberty* for baritone, mixed choir and orchestra, set to words by Džıvo Gundulić, op. 31 (1936) and *The Christmas Cantata*, set to folk poetry, op. 104 (1950).

Dance Music

Vlach has composed twelve national dances (1937 to 39), *A Romantic Valse*, op. 52a (1942) and a *Ballet Valse*, op. 52b (1942).

•

He has written as well poems, dramas, essays and articles on music.

For his *Partita* for solo violin he received honourable mention at the International Competition of Composers at Vercelli [Italy] (1957).

VODÁK, Josef
[born Slatina, 19 March 1927]

Vodák graduated from the composition section of the Prague Conservatory as a pupil of Emil Hlobil and Miroslav Krejčí and continued studying at the Academy of Musical Arts under Pavel Bořkovec. A *Symphony* (1949) and *Concertino* for piano and orchestra (1954) were his graduation works. At present he is music manager at the Czechoslovak Television.

His further compositions include *The String Quartet* (1954), a *Scherzo* for symphonic orchestra (1955), a *Fantasy* for viola and orchestra (1955—56), *Four Songs* set to old Chinese poetry for alto and piano (1957), second *Symphony* (1957), a cycle of three male choirs *The Earth* to verses of Otakar Březina (1957—58), a *Duo* for two violins (1959), a *Sonata* for violin and piano (1959—60), *Miniatures* for brass band, piano and timpani (1960), a cycle of children's choirs *Flowers Along the Road* with piano (1961), *The Dramatic Suite* (1962) and *Two Etudes* for symphonic orchestra (1963) and an *Octet* (1964).

Vodák wrote as well instructive compositions for piano [*A Child Plays*] and for violin and piano [*Five Little Compositions*].

VODRÁŽKA, Karel

[born Drachov, 2 December 1904]

After completing his studies at the Teachers' Training Institute he was active as a pedagogue. During his stay at Soběslav he was taught the rudiments of harmony and counterpoint by EMANUEL RATAJ. Later he held the post of regional cultural inspector in Prague; he was also director of the Prague Symphonic Orchestra F. O. K.

He has written songs, choirs, melodramas, scenic music (for the Institute of Art Education and the Central Marionette Theatre), the *Marionette Suite* for wind quintet (1947), *Two Bogland Dances* for orchestra (1941), a *Scherzo in an Ancient Style* (1944), a *March of Young Sportsmen* (1952), a symphonic poem *To the Stars* (1959), *Instructive Variations* for small orchestra (1960) and the comic opera *King Lávra* (1956).

He has also composed for brass band a symphonic picture *Prague Barricades* (1954) and a *Sinfonietta* (1959). Recently he has written a *Cantata About Prague* (1961) and a jazz cantata *Democracy—Freedom* set to words by BERTOLD BRECHT (1962).

Vodrážka writes variety and dance compositions as well. Several of his works have been given prizes in various competitions.

VOGEL, Jaroslav

[born Pilsen, 11 January 1894]

MERITED ARTIST, holder of the ORDER OF WORK

Vogel acquired his musical education by OTAKAR ŠEVČÍK (violin) and VÍTĚZSLAV NOVÁK (composition); he then studied at the Academy of Music in Munich (VICTOR GLUTH) and at the Paris Schola cantorum (VINCENT D'INDY). In an endeavour to free himself from the academic influence of the Munich and Paris composition schools, he entered the Master School of the Prague Conservatory prior to the end of the First World War and studied composition in the class of VÍTĚZSLAV NOVÁK, graduating in 1919, his graduation work being a *Rondo* for violin and orchestra to which were added the *Carnival Suite* for orchestra, and *Sonatina* for clarinet and piano and songs.

He became conductor of the opera at Pilsen and in 1927—43 was chief of opera at Ostrava, then as conductor at the National Theatre in Prague. He is now the chief conductor of the Philharmonic at Brno.

Stage Works

In the period covering Vogel's work as conductor at Ostrava, his first operatic work came into being, a one-act tragic opera *Mareja* to his own libretto, according to the social theme of a story by ANTONIUS BETTRAMELLI (1922, première at Olomouc 1923). In 1924 he wrote his second opera, a one-act musical comedy *Master Jíra*, according to a story by ZIKMUND WINTER, *The Italian King and a Czech Needlewoman* (première in Prague 1926). The three-act opera *Jovana*, dating from 1935—37, is based on a story by MIČUN PAVIČOVIĆ, the libretto by RODA-RODA and the composer (première at Ostrava 1939). In 1963 Vogel completed his opera *Hiawatha*.

As a result of his long tenure as a conductor in Moravia he became attached to Moravian musical folklore. This prompted him to elaborate numerous folk songs of Těšín and Moravian Slovakia (the cycles *Love-Love*, *The Brigands' Songs* and *A Little Swallow*).

Writings

Vogel's activity as a lecturer is both important and meritorious, contributing as he has to a fuller knowledge and understanding of the operatic heritage of LEOŠ JANÁČEK. His lectures, articles and addresses suplied the material for a valuable study called *Leoš Janáček as Dramatist* (1948) and for the monograph *Leoš Janáček— His Life and Work* (1958, in 1962 published in English), which was awarded by the Guild of Czechoslovak Composers.

VOLDÁN, Jiří
[born Prague, 20 March 1901]
Holder of the decoration FOR OUTSTANDING WORK

Voldán studied harmony under ZDENĚK HŮLA. He began to compose his first songs during his university studies and it was then he wrote his one-time popular song *The Clover Smelled Sweet—the Ears Were Ripening*. He also wrote a number of songs for the Prague cabaret THE RED SEVEN.

After the cabaret had closed its doors, he embarked upon a journalistic career but this did not prevent him from composing his gay and tuneful songs. Many of his verses were dedicated to youth.

His translations contributed to the popularization of foreign dance music in Czechoslovakia. He translated, for instance, the songs of I. J. DUNAJEVSKY from the film *The Whole World Laughs*, *The Circus*, *Children of Captain Grant*, the popular *Sulika*, *The Little Field* of L. K. KNIPPER and others.

In dance music he composed ¶ polkas as the *Double-*

bass Polka, *Musical Polka*, and ¶ the waltz *Hay Waggons are Leaving the Fields*; he wrote then his musical anti-war poster *We Want Peace*.

He also wrote the libretto for the children's ballet *The Dancing Fairy-tales* by F. A. TICHÝ.

His translations of literature, particularly Soviet literature, as well as his texts for dubbing of foreign films complete the picture of his abundant activity.

VOMÁČKA, Boleslav

[born Mladá Boleslav, 28 June 1887—died Prague, 1 March 1965]

MERITED ARTIST, holder of the ORDER OF WORK

Vomáčka graduated from the Faculty of Law of Charles University. As a composer he ranks among the most significant representatives of the school of VÍTĚZ-SLAV NOVÁK.

At the very beginning of his creative work he wrote a number of compositions which showed evidence of a striving for a new musical expression. They caused a stir in Czech musical circles.

Stage Works

In his first opera *The Water Sprite*, to a libretto by Adolf Wenig, according to the ballad by K. J. ERBEN (1934—37, première in Prague 1937), Vomáčka endeavoured to achieve a musical atmosphere expressing both a fairy-tale and a ballad character as the theme itself demanded.

In the historical opera *Boleslav*, on a libretto by MILAN JARIŠ, (1955, première in Prague 1957) the composer dealt with the probable reasons for the conflict between Prince Wenceslas and his Brother Boleslav and its consequences for the Czech State. Inspired by a monumentally conceived model, he embarked on a search for a clean-cut melodic expression, particularly in the vocal sections.

In his third opera *Waiting for a Husband*, set to his own libretto, according to the comedy by F. X. SVO-BODA (1956), Vomáčka brings to the forefront the comedy as a theme for an opera. He applies here in full measure a sense of musical humour relatively rare in his creative work.

Chamber and Orchestral Compositions

His musical expression is shown in the three-movement *Sonata* for violin and piano, op. 3 (1912), a cycle of four compositions for piano entitled *The Quest*, op. 4 (1913), a symphonic poem *Youth* for mixed choir and orchestra, on words of ANTONÍN SOVA, op. 20 (1914—16, instrumented 1930), a cycle of three compositions for piano *Intermezzo*, op. 6 (1915—17) and a one-movement *Sonata* for piano, op. 7 (1917).

The Second World War opened up new vistas with new significant musical expressions. The *Piano Sonata quasi fantasia*, op. 40 (1942) recalls the horror during Heydrich reign of terror and impressions from the period of the Nazi occupation and of the Prague revolution in May, 1945, influenced *The Symphony* in F major, originally entitled *The Czech Eroica*, op. 47 (1944—46).

Vocal Works

After the First World War he embarks on the path of simplification in musical expression and for an emotionally inspired melodic line. This is evident in his song cycles *"1914"*, op. 11 (1920) and *The Return from the Battlefield*, op. 13 (1922—28), to which the two male choirs *Outcries*, set to words of VICTOR DYK, op. 9 (1918) and two male choirs *Painful Memories*, to words by KAREL TOMAN, op 21 (1929) should be added.

The poetry of JIŘÍ WOLKER with his revolutionary social aspect, growing into a vision of a new social order, strongly affected the foremost Czech composers, among them Vomáčka as well. This manifested itself, in his *Ballad about the Eyes of a Stoker* for male choir op. 18 (1924—27), in the dramatic cantata *The Lighthouse Keeper* for solos, mixed choir and orchestra, op. 24 (1931—32), in the mixed choir *The Ballad of a Dream*, op. 27 (1933) as well as in the male choir *S. O. S.*, set to a poem by Petr Křička, op. 17 (1927), expressing the feeling of solidarity of people the world over.

The Second World War and its aftermath brought his several choirs; they were the male choir *The Prague May*, to a poem by František Hrubín, op. 49 (1945); in memory of the battles fought in Slovakia he composed the overture *Dukla*, op. 48 (1947—48) and the military cantata *The Banner of Peace Over Dukla*, to words by Jaroslav Moucha, for bass, mixed choir and orchestra, op. 55 (1951). A cycle of four songs with orchestra (piano) *A New World Shall Arise*, set to words by Marie Kratochvílová, op. 57 (1950—51), a cantata *The Partisan Bojka*, to words by Milan Jariš for mixed choir and orchestra (1952), and a number of songs, marches and dances give expression to the thoughts and sentiments of man in our era.

In 1958 and 1959 he composed a male double-choir *Young Love*, to words by Antonín Sova, a cycle of songs *Seven rondeaux*, set to poems by Jaroslav Seifert, a cantata *Under the Banner of Communism* for tenor, bass, mixed choir and orchestra to words by Julius Fučík, op. 73, three duets *Early Spring* and three female choirs *May Sun*.

Writings

Vomáčka has done significant work as musical critic, editor of the Papers of Hudební Matice (Musical Review) and the musical journal The Tempo and has been active as organizer of musical activities.

He has written as well on the life and work of *Josef Suk* (1922) and *Stanislav Suda* (1933) and edited (with

Stanislav Hanuš) a *Memorial Volume* in honour of the sixtieth anniversary of the birthday of *Vítězslav Novák* (1930).

VOMÁČKA, Jaromír

[born Dašice, 23 March 1923]

Vomáčka attended a special course (conducting) at the Prague Conservatory. He was a member of dance orchestra of LADISLAV HABART, a pianist in the variety ensemble LIŠÁCI [*The Sly Old Foxes*] and a pianist and actor at the Prague theatre NA ZÁBRADLÍ [*on the Balustrade*]. At present he is a pianist at the LATERNA MAGICA (an experimental film studio) in Prague.

He has composed considerable successful dance music including the following: ¶ the foxtrots *Smile at Me*, *A Little Black Cat*, *Yesterday I Was Seventeen*, *I Am In Love*, *A Little Boy Went for a Walk*, *In Our Village*, *Dandelions Are Already in Blossom*; ¶ the slow rock *Sooner Than Flowers Blossom in the Meadow* and others.

His most popular compositions are ¶ the slow foxtrot *Blow Out the Lanterns*, ¶ the song *Merry Christmas* and ¶ musical comedy *More Beautiful than Galatea*.

Vomáčka is also the author of several scenic compositions to films *(Don't Wake, Please!, A Comedy with a Handle, Marie)* and is a competent arranger of dance music.

VORLOVÁ, Sláva

[born Náchod, 15 March 1894]

Holder of the decoration FOR OUTSTANDING WORK

Vorlová was a pupil of the school of VÍTĚZSLAV NOVÁK and JAROSLAV ŘÍDKÝ. A broad creative fantasy, fortified by a profound understanding of joy and pain, found its expression in her creative work which today is considerably extensive.

Stage Works

Vorlová gave expression to her sensibility for the dramatic field in the fairy-tale opera *The Golden Bird* (1950), in the singspiel *Rosemary* (1952, première at Kladno 1955), in the historic singspiel *The Náchod Cassation* (1955) and in the one-act opera *Two Worlds* (1958).

In 1960, she arranged a melodramatic triptych from the scenic music to Hviezdoslav's drama *The Game-keeper's Wife*.

Orchestral Works

To Czech concerto literature Vorlová contributed a *Fantasy* for violoncello and orchestra (1940), a *Pastoral Concerto* for oboe and orchestra (1952), a *Concerto* in A minor for trumpet and orchestra (1953), a *Moravian Slovak Concerto* for violin and orchestra (1954), a *Concerto* in D minor for clarinet and orchestra (1957), a *Concerto* in B flat minor for flute and orchestra (1959), a *Concerto* for bass-clarinet and strings (1961) and *Double Concerto* for oboe, harp and orchestra (1963).

In orchestral works as well, Vorlová has demonstrated her sense for the expressiveness of musical themes and for their moulding into larger forms. This is evident in her *First Symphony* (1948), a suite of eight symphonic pictures *Božena Němcová* (1951), *Three Czech Dances* (1953), *Dances of Doudleby* (1955), a symphonic composition *Memento* (1957), *Thuringian Dances* (1957) and *Kybernetic Studies* for symphonic orchestra (1962).

Chamber Music

Her chamber music work includes four *String Quartets*, a *Nonet* in F major (1944), *Miniatures* for bass-clarinet and piano (1962), a *Serenade* for oboe and harp (1962), a *Serenata Desta* for flute, bass-clarinet and piano

(1962), *Four Sketches* for four harps (1963), *Sonata lirica da tre* per violino, viola o chitarra (1964) and *Kaddish*, an arrangement of a Hebrew melody for bass-clarinet and piano (1964).

Instrumental Music

Of her numerous instrumental compositions we refer at least to nine preludes for piano entitled *Colourful Notes* (1944), thirty variations for piano *The Crossroad's Variations* (1946), instructive compositions *Little Animals at the Piano* (1951), a cycle of five compositions for two pianos *Charades* (1953), a *Fantasy* on a Czech folk song of the fourteenth century for solo viola (1953), a *Pantoum* for harp (1959), children's études for piano for four hands *Gay Intervals* (1961) and *Sketches* for four harps (1963).

Vocal Works

In the vocal field Vorlová has composed five song-cycles with piano accompaniment, a four-movement cantata *The Little Land*, to her own text, for solo, mixed choir and full orchestra (1941—42), a cycle of ten songs to her own texts for female choir with orchestral accompaniment, entitled *White Skies* (1942—43), a full-length symphonic epos *Songs of Gondwana* for solos, mixed choir and full orchestra (1948—49) and the symphonic ode *We, the People of the Twentieth Century* for male, female, mixed and children's choirs and orchestra (1959). Further the oratorio *Magellan of the Universe* for solos, children's and mixed choirs and full orchestra (1960), a cycle of nine songs *Maliniarky* for girls' choir, set to words by P. O. HVIEZDOSLAV (1961), a cycle *The Gypsy's Songs* for baritone and piano (1961) and music to a recitation programme of Gypsy poetry *The Gypsy's Heart*, for voice, violin and cimbalom (1961).

VOSTŘÁK, Zbyněk

[born Prague, 10 June 1920]

Vostřák graduated from the section of conducting at the Prague Conservatory under PAVEL DĚDEČEK. Simultaneously he studied composition privately with RUDOLF KAREL, whose opera *The Golden Hairs of the All-Wise Grandfather* Vostřák arranged and instrumented after the author's death.

He was active as a pedagogue at the Prague Conservatory and at the Academy of Musical Arts, but at present he devotes himself exclusively to conducting and composition.

Stage Works

The main branch of Vostřák's compositional work is musical drama. He composed the comic opera *The Four-horned Rohovín*, according to V. K. KLICPERA, op. 12 (1947—48, première in Olomouc 1949), *The King's Mint Master*, according to the play The Miners of Kutná Hora by J. K. TYL, op. 18 (1951—53, première Prague 1955), *The Prague Nocturne*, according to FRANTIŠEK KUBKA, op. 23 (1957—58, première Ústí on Labe 1960), and *The Broken Pitcher*, according to the comedy by HEINRICH KLEIST, op. 25 (1960, première in Prague 1963 and at the Radio Diffusion Paris 1964).

These works amply prove Vostřák's dramatic talent and his sense for an appropriate linking up of the musical expression with stage action.

His ballets have met with notable response not only at home but abroad as well. They are *The Primrose*, according to SVATOPLUK ČECH, op. 10 (1944—45), *A Philosophers' Story*, according to ALOIS JIRÁSEK, op. 13 (1949, première Prague 1949), *Little Victoria*, according to BOŽENA NĚMCOVÁ, op. 15 (1950, première Prague 1950, Neustrelitz, German Democratic Republic, 1963) and *Snow White*, libretto by J. ROY, op. 20 (1955, première Prague 1956, awarded the second prize at the

Jubilee Competition of the Guild of Czechoslovak Composers and the Czech Music Fund, 1956). The three last mentioned works have been arranged by the composer into orchestral suites.

Orchestral and Instrumental Works

The *Czech Festive March*, to text by FRANTIŠEK HALAS, op. 4 (1939), falls into the period of his studies with RUDOLF KAREL. His further creative work includes the *Serenade* in G major for small orchestra op. 5 (1940), *The Prague Overture*, op. 6 (1941), the *Polka Suite* op. 19 (1954) *Emotions*, improvisations for seven instruments, op. 32 (1964) and *Elements* for string quartet, op. 35 (1964).

Vocal Works

His song cycle *Short Dreams*, *Two Songs* for soprano, op. 1 and 5 (both 1937) and *Two Intimate Songs* for alto, op. 3 (1939) were composed during his studies with RUDOLF KAREL. His further compositions include *The Paradise Ballad* for alto, op. 7 (1942), *Farewell to Spring* for soprano, op. 8 (1942), the ballad *Where is Mummy*, *op.* 9 (1946), *The Psalms*, seven biblical songs for bass, op. 21 (1956) and *Cantata* set to words by FRANZ KAFKA for mixed choir, wind and percussion instruments, op. 34 (1964).

Film Music

He wrote music to full-length films *Ninety Minutes of Surprise* and *Young Years*.

Dodecaphonic Works

From 1960 Vostřák has devoted his attention to composing dodecaphonic and serial works: the song cycle *Until Sleep Comes*, set to words by FRANTIŠEK HALAS, op. 26 (1961), *Contrasts* for string quartet, op. 27 (1961), *Crystallization* for twelve wind instruments, op. 28 (1962), *Two Japanese Madrigals* for women's voices, op. 29 (1962), a *Recollection* for solo violin, op. 30 (1962) and *Three Essays* for piano, op. 31 (1962).

International Prizes

For opera *The Broken Pitcher* he was awarded a prize in the radio competition of UNESCO in 1962.

His *Three Sonets*, based on WILLIAM SHAKESPEARE, for voice and chamber orchestra, were awarded the second prize in the International composers' competition of the Società Italiana da Musica Contemporanea (1963).

VRÁNA, František

[born Bystřice, Moravia, 14 November 1914]

Vrána acquired a solid basis in composition at the Brno Conservatory in the class of VILÉM PETRŽELKA. He continued the study of composition at the Master School of the Prague Conservatory under JOSEF SUK and VÍTĚZSLAV NOVÁK and simultaneously studied piano under the guidance of VILÉM KURZ.

Since 1939 he was active first as a pianist at the Czechoslovak Radio and now occupies the post of its music manager.

Vrána is mainly the composer of instrumental works.

Orchestral Works

His symphonic music is represented by the *Overture* (1939), *Concerto* for piano and orchestra (1957), *Sinfonia giocosa*, a musical reflection of the composer's impressions of his native region (1956) and the *Second Symphony* (1962—63).

Chamber Music

His compositional career was inaugurated by a series of chamber works, the first of which was a *String Quartet*

(1936), which he composed while still at the Conservatory, and the second *String Quartet* (1937), *Concerto* for piano and string instruments (1941), *Fables* for bass and wind quintet (1962) and *Prelude and Scherzo* for violin and piano (1963).

Instrumental Compositions

Besides two *Concerto Etudes* for organ and several small violin and piano compositions he has written a number of cycles imbued with a keen sense for instrumental effectiveness, such as *The Piano Sonata* (1938), a *Prelude and Passacaglia* for piano (1938), *Concertino* for piano (1939), a *Prelude* for piano (1940), *Sonatina* for viola (1940), *Violin Sonata* (1942), *Suite* for violoncello (1943), *Sonata* for violoncello (1944), a *Concertino* for viola (1944) and *Intermezzo* for organ (1962).

Vocal Music

His lyrical cycles of songs are closely correlated to his instrumental works. They include *Four Songs*, set to words of children's poetry (1936), *Dawn* (1938) and *Fate* (1943), *The Songs of the Artisans* (1948) and *Six Songs* to texts by JAROSLAV SEIFERT (1953), *Three Madrigals* set to words by ROBERT BURNS (1958) and *Male Choirs* to words by A. S. PUSHKIN (1962).

VYCPÁLEK Ladislav

[born Prague, 23 February 1882]

MERITED ARTIST, LAUREATE OF THE STATE PRIZE

Vycpálek studied composition under VÍTĚZSLAV NOVÁK. From 1907 to 1942 he held a post at the Prague University Library, where he re-organized and managed its musical department.

He wrote musical criticisms and reviews for the MUSICAL REVIEW and LUMÍR and contributed incidental articles to The Papers of the HUDEBNÍ MATICE (Musical Publishing House) and to the reviews TEMPO and RHYTHM.

In the thirties he was a member of the advisory board of the National Theatre in Prague and in 1936 became a member of the artistic management of its opera. In 1947 he was elected chairman of the Guild of Czechoslovak Composers.

Chamber and Orchestral Music

During the period when he abandoned the impressionistic and decadent tonalities—so characteristic for the beginning of the twentieth century—and strived for a new orientation in his creative work, he composed a *String Quartet*, op. 3 (1909) and a piano cycle *On the Path*, op. 9 (1911—14); later he continued in this direction by *Sonata* in D major—*Praise of the Violin*, op. 19 (1927—28), *Duo* for violin and viola, op. 20 (1929), *Suite* for solo viola, op. 21 (1929) and *Suite* for solo violin, op. 22 (1930). After the war he composed a fantasy *Courage, My Heart!*, op. 30 (1950, a piano and orchestral version). In his latest creative period he has written a four-movement piano suite *At Home*, op. 38 (1959).

Vocal Works

From the very beginning, Vycpálek inclined to vocal creative work. His style rapidly acquired maturity and individual characteristics as evidenced in many of his song cycles, as for inst. *Quiet Conciliation*, op. 1 (1908—09), *Lights in the Darkness*, op. 4 (1910), *Anticipations and Visions*, op. 5 (1910—16) and *Festivities of Life*, op. 8 (1912—13). In his arrangements of Moravian folk songs *From Moravia*, op. 11a (1910—11), *Moravian Ballads*, op. 12 (1915) and *The War*, op. 13 (1915) he endeavoured to penetrate to the emotional core and poetic foundation of folk songs.

In his choir arrangement *The Orphan*, op. 11b (1914)

he was inspired by a cycle of paintings of MIKULÁŠ ALEŠ. In the cycle *War*, Vycpálek gives expression to his abhorrence of war while the male choir *The Vagrants*, op. 10 (1914) is a confession of his social attitude.

His vocal creative work achieved a climax in the cycle *In God's Palm*, op. 14 (1916), based on a poem by VALERIJ BRJUSOV.

Shortly before the foundation of the Czechoslovak Republic (in 1918) he wrote the choirs *Our Spring* and *The Present Fight*, op. 15 (1918).

At that time Vycpálek matured artistically and ideologically in a powerful synthesis of his creative efforts in the cantata *Concerning the Last Things of Man*, op. 16 (1921), based on words of two Moravian folk songs. It is the first section of his outstanding oratorial work to which belongs also the cantata *Blessed is that Man*, op. 23 (1933) and the *Czech Requiem*, op. 24 (1940). In these last three works Vycpálek declares his creed of life.

The cycle of songs *On Parting*, op. 25 (1945) is akin to his oratorio works.

In addition to two variation fantasies on songs of the Hussite period he turned to choirs and folk songs arrangements exclusively. They are the choir arrangement *From the Czech Homeland*, op. 29 (1949), *Out of the Depths*, op. 31 (1950), *Let Us Not Perish*, op. 32 (1951), *The Voice of Hus*, op. 33 (1951, revised in 1953), *Love Unrequited*, op. 34 (1954), two female *Duets* set to words of folk poetry, op. 35 and 36 (both 1956), *The Voice of Bezruč*, op. 37 (1958), *A Clumsy Fellow*, a jocose female choir with piano accompaniment, op. 39 (1960 to 61), two mixed choirs *Oh Love!*, op. 40 (1961—62) and two female choirs with piano *Czech Songs*, op. 41 (1961—62).

He was an honourable member (chairman) of the Artistic Union, of the Guild of Czechoslovak Composers, of the Philharmonic Society, of the Brno Beseda (Union).

In 1962, he was awarded the first degree STATE PRIZE for his compositional work.

VYCPÁLEK L.

VYCPÁLEK, Vratislav

[born Rychnov, 30 July 1892—died Prague, 9 October 1962]

Vycpálek acquired the rudiments of musical art from his father, Josef Vycpálek, an outstanding collector of folk music. He was active as a secondary school teacher. Due to his knowledge of musical folklore he was of considerable assistance to the Folk Art Ensembles, particularly the Prague Ensemble of Songs and Dances of Josef Vycpálek.

Vycpálek's creative work includes a cycle of songs *Prague Motifs* to words by JAN NERUDA (1943), *The Heart and Clouds* to words by S. K. NEUMANN (1945), songs *The Birth of Lenin* to words by STIEPAN SHCHIPA-CHOV, *Ours is the Day!*, *A Song on Thälmann*, *With the Army of Peace*, a *Salute to the Red Army*, a cycle of songs for children's choirs *Spring—Summer—Autumn—Winter* (1945) a small cantata for mixed choir *The Promise* (1949), a cycle od songs for children *To Kids* (1940—41), *Songs of the Gay* to words by JAN ALDA (1950) and *In the Sun* to words by K. V. RAIS (1952), *Songs of Jan Jeník of Bratřice* (1956) as well as a cycle od mixed choirs *To the Native Land* (1960).

Vycpálek is the author of many cycles of folk song arrangements, as, for instance, *Czech Dances* from the collection of Josef Vycpálek, *Moravian Lullabies*, *Songs of Vožice*, *From the Hradec Region*, *Songs from Jičín*, *Songs of Southern Bohemia*, *From Chrudim*, choir montages *Cotter's Songs*, *Songs from Javornice* and others.

He has written a number of notable musicological treatises, the most important of which is the monograph on *Jan Malát* (second edition in 1946).

VYHNÁLEK, Ivo

[born Prague, 7 March 1930]

Vyhnálek graduated from the composition section of the Academy of Musical Arts of JAROSLAV ŘÍDKÝ and from the quarter-tone class of ALOIS HÁBA.

He worked in the music division of Czechoslovak Radio. Now he is director of musical programmes of the Czechoslovak Television.

His graduation work was a *Fantasy* for full orchestra (1953—54). He has written as well *Variations* for piano (1950), two *String Quartets* (1952 and 1955), the opera *Mandragora*, according to theme by NICOLA MACCHIAVELLI (1958, première in Prague 1959), the television opera *Notes from the Gallows* (1960—61, première Czechoslovak Television 1961) and scenic music to numerous radio and television plays.

WOLF, Alois

[born Vienna, 10 February 1914]

Wolf graduated from the military school of music in Prague. After five years service in regimental bands, he returned to civilian life and played in dance and light music orchestras.

He is an experienced composer and arranger of dance and jazz music. His ¶ slow-foxes *To Speak to Her, I Know a Beautiful Fairy-tale* and *Only About You* achieved popularity as well as his ¶ foxtrots *Jap, The Mistral, a Race With Rhythm* and *I Have a Name-day*, and his ¶ swings *The Cyclone, Berbera, C minor, Jupiter, Laughter, Your Eyes* and the *Boccacio-Stomp*.

After 1945 he wrote, among others, ¶ the slow-foxtrots: *At Parting, It May Happen, It Keeps On Raining* and *Christmas in the Mountains*; ¶ the foxtrots: *At the*

Breast Tape, A Strange Thought, Rhythm Around B, Why Are You Afraid?, A Fully Blue Day, The Signal and *Eight Oar Sculls*; ¶ the characteristic foxtrots: *The Slalom, The Locomotive, The Little Paper Devil, At the Airport* and *A Visit From the Orient*; ¶ the swings: *The Aquarelle, I Only Turned Around, Don't Ask About Love* and *I Ask Your Eyes;* ¶ the blues *The Old House in the Suburb;* ¶ the tango *Little Susanne;* ¶ the waltzes: *It's Not Written in Books, Milano* and *The Thistle.*

Wolf has also composed several compositions for solo instruments with orchestral accompaniment: *A Night Party* for clarinet, *The Stomp in C* for guitar, *The Happy Trumpet* and *A Song About Autumn* for trumpet, *Irene* for tenor saxophone, *Serenade* for trombone, *Evening in the Club* for electric keyboard and *Reminiscence*, a concertino for violoncello.

The following compositions complete a survey of Wolf's work: A Spanish dance *La Danza*, The Luhačovice *Habanera*, a dance suite *Three Cities*, a concerto valse *The Magic Skates*, a characteristic composition *A Recollection of Dobrošov* and *Children's Songs.*

ZAHRADNÍK, Zdeněk

[born Lomnice, 3 June 1936]

Zahradník studied composition at the Academy of Musical Arts under VÁCLAV DOBIÁŠ. He was lecturer on vocal music at the Advisory Section of Folk Art of the City House of Culture in Prague. At present he is editor at the archives of the Czech Music Fund.

In his creative work up to the present programme music prevails. This is evidenced by his three symphonic pictures *May* (1958), the three-movement *Sinfonietta* for full orchestra (1959), the three-movement *Suite* for strings, the motto of which is one of the Cosmic Songs by Jan Neruda (1959), a *Cantata* according to the closing part of the epos *Madame Curie* by Marie Pujmanová (1960), a cycle of melodramas *Enchanted by Life* set to verses by Jiří Šimánek (1960), full-length melodrama *May* to a poem by K. H. Mácha, for string quartet, harp, piano and recitative (1961—62), the choirs *The Thirteenth of February* to a text by Jarmila Urbánková and *You, the Living!* to a text by Čestmír Hrubeš, three melodramatic vocal compositions *Songs About Little Victoria* for soprano, recitative and piano trio set to verses by Jaroslav Seifert (1962), a nine-movement piano trio *A Song About Little Victoria* (1962) and a cantata *Spring Tidings* for solos, choir, recitative and orchestra to a pocm by S. K. Neumann (1962).

Of Zahradník's other works, mention may be made of a *Sonatina* for clarinet and piano (1956), a *Clarinet Quintet* (1957), a *Quartettino* for violin, viola, violoncello and harp (1961), *Three Female Choirs* to verses by Jan Skácel (1961), *The Symphonic Allegro* (1961—62), *Three Characteristic Sketches* for violin and piano (1962), *Moments*, three compositions for viola and harp (1964), *A Bloom at the Roadside*, a one-movement sonata for string sextet (1964) and a *Sonata* for violin and piano (1964).

In addition, Zahradník has composed several cycles of songs, small instrumental compositions and scenic music.

ZELENAY, Pavol
[born Zohor, 15 April 1926]

Zelenay studied originally at commercial school, playing at the same time in student dance orchestras. At present he is a member of the dance orchestra Tatra Revue in Bratislava. He is active as well in the field of dance and jazz music where, as composer, he belongs to the progressively oriented branch of Slovak composers and arrangers of music.

He has composed dance music, chansons, and popular orchestral pieces [*My Ideal, The Old Man and The Blues,* the orchestral *Aurora Borealis* from the suite *The Geophysical Year;* the foxtrot The *Glorious Day* and *It is Nice to Love;* the slow fox *I Don't Believe You Love Me.*

He has written an informative booklet *How to Play Dance-music* (1964).

ŽELEZNÝ, Lubomír
[born Ostrava, 16 March 1925]

Železný studied composition in his native town under JOSEF SCHREIBER, at the Prague Conservatory under KAREL JANEČEK, at the Academy of Musical Arts under PAVEL BOŘKOVEC and for a short time also with K. B. JIRÁK.

Up to the present he has composed a *Sonata* for flute and piano (1943), a *Trio* for flute, viola and violoncello (1946), a *Quartet* for flute, violin, viola and violoncello (1948), a *Polka* for piano (1949), *Songs* to folk texts (1949), two *Gavottes* for orchestra (1954), a *Concerto* for violin and orchestra (1958—59), a *String Quartet* (1959 to 60), a *Symphony* (1961—62) and others.

In 1951—56 he arranged songs for various ensembles (The Army Artistic Ensemble Vít Nejedlý and others).

ZELINKA, Jan Evangelista
[born Prague, 13 January 1893]
Holder of the decoration FOR OUTSTANDING WORK

Zelinka acquired the rudiments of musical education from his father, the Prague choirmaster JAN EV. ZELINKA, and completed the study of composition under

OTAKAR OSTRČIL. His prolific creative activity embraces all fields of musical forms.

Stage Works

Of Zelinka's numerous melodramas, the full-length scenic melodrama *Heart on a Fishhook* to a theme by EMIL ZOLA is the most significant (1932, première in Brno 1938). Other musical dramatic forms are represented by the ballet pantomime *A Glass Doll* (1927, première in Prague 1928), one-act operas *The Innkeeper's Little Daughter* (1921, première in Prague 1925) and *The Departure of Don Quijote* (1936), the full-length operas *The Ninth Meadow* (1930, première in Prague 1931), *The Stubborn Cobbler* (1940, première in Prague 1944), *The Wailing Wind* (1947, première in Pilsen 1950), *Shrovetide Night* (1950), *Love's Woe and Laughter* according to CARLO GOLDONI (1958), *A Fanciful Spring* (1960), *Marriage* according to GOGOL (1950, worked over 1962) and opera suite *The Big Shadow* (1963).

An informatory survey of Zelinka's musical dramatic work must be supplemented by a reference to his satirical short opera *A Wooden Horse* (1962) and to his operettas *Under a Green Bough, The Holidays of Jaroslav Hašek, A Shop on the Square* and *Spring with the Shakespeares*.

Orchestral Works

The symphonic field is represented by an *Overture to a Renaissance Comedy* (1919), a *Dramatic Intermezzo* (1935) and the suites *Weekend* (1939); then, after the war *Au Revoir* (1950), two series of *Folk Dances* (1950), *Sinfonia Rustica* (1956), *A Slovak Summer* (1959) and *Musichetta primaverale* (for chamber orchestra, 1962), and suite *Satiricon* (1964).

For variety orchestra Zelinka has composed a suite *The Czech Summer* (1959), a small symphonic poem *The Polka is Coming* (1961), and a symphonic intermezzo-scherzo *A Little Spa* (1962).

Chamber Music

Zelinka's chamber music creative work is also extensive. It includes numerous instrumental sonatas, suites and fantasies as well as cyclic works for chamber music ensembles: the wind quintet *Air Free of Charge* from the year 1933, *Capriccio* of 1937, *Cassation* for nonet (1943), the organ *Small Suite* (1945), *Vigilie* (1948), a piano trio *Late Summer* and a piano quintet *A Song About a Southern River* (1949) and further compositions such as *Lullabies* for piano (1949), *Nenie-Eulogy* (1956) and the *Toccatina di primavera* (1960).

Vocal Works

His extensive vocal work, based on a rich melodic fund of a pronouncedly lyrical type, includes

songs and song cycles: *A Lad* (1921), *Paradise of the Heart* (1922), *Songs about Summer*, *The Earth and the Sun* (1924), *Lullabies* (1928), *The Heavenly Ballad* (1953), *Songs about a Painter* (1955), *Poet and Other Crafts* (1957), a *Song of Propaganda* and *Cultural Stimulation*, *Echoes of a Czech Home*, *A Black Heart* (1961), *About Wine, Life and Sallow Trees* (1962);

male choirs: *The Pilgrim* (1920—21), *Black Love* (1937), *A Wandering Singer* (1960);

female choir *A Quiet Message* (1960);

mixed choirs: From Wolker's *Guest of the House* (1960), *Children and the Sea* (1960), from Hrubín's *Mánes' Months* (1960);

cantatas: a small lyrical cantata *A Weeping Child* (1928—29), *A Cantata Full of Love* (1932), *A Small Folk Cantata* (1956), *A Sunny Cantata* (1956), *Slovakia* (1961), two cantatas for solo voice and accompaniment: *A Plastic Raincoat* (for bass baritone, 1960), and *Dancing Lessons* (for tenor, 1961), *Cantata gastronomica* (1962).

Film Music

He has created as well a great deal of scenic music,

music to the full-length film *A Red Lizard* and to short films *The Slippers of Miss Pauline*, *Prague at Night*, *An Assistant or an Enemy* and *The Tax Morale*.

ZELJENKA, Ilja

[born Bratislava, 21 December 1932]

Zeljenka is the most vigorous and original personality among young Slovak musicians. As a secondary school student he studied music theory for a short time with JÁN ZIMMER and piano with RUDOLF MACUDZINSKI. It was not, however, till his attendance in the composition class of JÁN CIKKER at the High School of Musical Arts, that he began to study music systematically.

He was active as a dramaturgist of the Slovak Philharmonic and since 1961 has been advisor for symphonic music at the Czechoslovak Radio in Bratislava.

During his years of study he wrote many compositions of note, as for instance *The Bagatelles* for piano (1955), indicating as they do the development of the composer's musical expressive media, showing the influence of S. S. PROKOFIEV. Of importance as well are the *Suite* for small orchestra (1952), the first *Piano Quintet* (1953), *First Symphony* for full orchestra (1954) and the *Dramatic Overture* (1955).

Film Music

After graduation Zeljenka began to devote himself intensively to film and scenic music. He composed music to more than thirty documentary, three full-length and two medium-footage films, enabling him to verify experimentally the elements of contemporary compositional technique and thus to speed up the crystallization of his own expression. His development aims at increasing economy in the use of the media of expression and at attaining a maximum of effectiveness.

These attempts have led him to the use of the principle of serial organization and to experimentation with synthetic music (electronic and concrete).

Instrumental and Orchestral Works

His most significant works, written during this evolutionary process, are: a *Ballad* for choir and orchestra on folk poetry (1957), a *Sonata* for piano (1958), a *Piano Suite* (1958), second *Piano Quintet* (1959, peformed at the Festival of International Society for Contemporary Music in Amsterdam 1963), the cantata-melodrama *Oswiecim* for two reciters, two choirs and orchestra (1960) and *Seven Compositional Studies* for chamber music ensemble (1962). The *Second Symphony* in C major for string orchestra (1960) deviates to a certain extent from preceding works by its neoclassical tendency.

Of compositions, using synthetic sound, the music to the films *"65 Millions"*, *The Sun in the Net*, the ballet *Cosmos* and several improvisations are noteworthy.

In 1964, his *String Quartet* was performed at the Bienale in Venezia and at the Warsaw Autumn. His aleatoric *Structures* for symphonic orchestra (1964) attracted a great attention.

His last work are his *Metamorphoses* xv., according to OVIDIUS NASO, for nine instruments and reciter, which were ordered by the Festival Musical Bienale in Zagreb (1965).

ZICH, Jaroslav

[born Prague, 17 January 1912]

Zich started his study of composition with his father, OTAKAR ZICH, a noted composer and aesthetician, completing it at the Master School of the Prague

Conservatory in the class of J. B. FOERSTER. He attended Charles University as well, graduating from the section of musical science.

From the year 1937 he was musical manager, lecturer and programme director at the Czechoslovak Radio. In 1952 he was named assistant professor and in 1959 professor of instrumentation and aesthetics at the music faculty of the Academy od Musical Arts.

He was also active as pianist, especially in the ZICH PIANO TRIO, together with the violinist LUDVÍK NĚMEČEK and his brother OTAKAR ZICH who played violoncello (1935—50).

He composed *Eclogue*, *Nocturne* and *Pastorale* for piano (1929—32), a cycle of songs with orchestra *A Passing Guest*, set to words by VIKTOR DYK (1932), a *Duo* for violin and violoncello (1932), a *String Quartet* (1932), a melodrama with orchestra *The Helgoland Romance*, to words by JAN NERUDA (1934), *Mateník* (a Czech folk dance in variable rhythm) for violoncello and piano (1935), *Three Folk Songs* from Southern Bohemia for male choir (1940), *At a Village Dance* (nine dances on folk motifs for octet, 1940).

After the war he composed *Folk Songs* of the Krumlov district for middle voice and piano (1945), *Two Songs* for piano (*Lullaby* and a *Summer Motif*, 1950), a mixed choir *Morning Song*, set to words by František Branislav (1951), *Rhapsody* for violoncello and orchestra (1956) and *Wind Quintet* (1965).

In his musical scientific work, Zich concentrates upon questions of instrumentation [*The Instrumentation of Smetana's Dalibor* (1957), *Smetana's Tábor and Blaník interpreted by V. Talich* (1964)] and of interpretation [*Media of Interpretative Musical Art* (1959) and *The Communicating Ability of Music* (1964)].

ZIMMER, Ján

[born Ružomberok, 16 May 1926]

Zimmer acquired his musical education at the Bratislava Conservatory studying organ (Jozef Weber), piano (Frico Kafenda) and composition (Eugen Suchoň) and attended as well the High School of Music of Ferencz Liszt in Budapest (composition with Ferencz Farkas). In 1949 he also graduated from the composition section of the Salzburg Seminary in American Studies (David Diamond).

Initially Zimmer was active as accompanist of the Bratislava Opera, joining later the staff of the Czechoslovak Radio and in 1948 became professor of theoretical subjects at the Bratislava Conservatory.

Since 1952 he has concentrated exclusively upon composition and has become one of the most prolific of contemporary Slovak composers.

Zimmer himself is a piano virtuoso (on concert platforms he appears, however, solely as an interpreter of his own works), and is constantly intrigued by the problem of a new use of the expressive possibilities of both solo piano and of the piano with orchestra. The development of his style found its basis in a synthesis of the neoclassical interpretative form with expressive sound quality.

Now Zimmer focuses his attention on seeking new paths in symphonic works, including compositions for piano.

Stage Works

In his scenic two-act work *Oidipus*, op. 48 (1963) he has, for the first time, turned to the operatic field.

Orchestral Works

Zimmer wrote five *Simphonies*: No. 1, op. 21 (1955), No. 2, op. 26 (1958), No. 3, op. 33 (1959), No. 4, op. 37 (1959) and No. 5, op. 44 (1961) [the No. 4 is with mixed choir]. Further he composed five *Piano Concertos* with orchestra: No. 1, op. 1 (1949), No. 2, op. 10 (1952), No. 3, op. 29 (1958), No. 4, op. 36 (1960) and No. 5 op. 50 for left hand (1962).

He attained the most convincing formulation of his intent in the third and fifth *Symphony* and in the fourth *Piano Concerto*, indicating a symphonic conception of the PROKOFIEV and BARTÓK type.

Notable, for their compositional line, are his concertante compositions as the *Concerto grosso* for strings, two pianos and percussion instruments, op. 7 (1951), *Concerto* for violin and orchestra, op. 15 (1953), *Rhapsody* for piano and orchestra, op. 18 (1954), *Concertino* for piano and strings, op. 19 (1955), and *Concerto* for organ and orchestra, op. 27 (1957).

Zimmer's works of a programme character include the first symphonic suite *The Tatras* for full orchestra, op. 11 (1952), the second suite *The Tatras*, op. 25 (1956), the *Festive Overture* written on the occasion of the liberation of Bratislava, op. 22 (1955) and the symphonic poem *Strečno*, op. 34 (1958), one of the most profound works inspired by the Slovak National Uprising.

In 1965 he finished his sixth (one-movement) *Symphony Improvisata*.

Chamber Music

His chamber music compositions, as his orchestral works, are outstanding for their striving for a firm, often counterpointal plastic form and for a dramatic expression. They include *Sonata* No. 1 for two pianos, op. 16 (1953), *Sonata* No. 2, op. 35 (1959), while the second *Sonata* for piano, op. 45 (1961) shows the influence of the serial technique.

Vocal Music

Cantatas: symphonic poem for mixed choir and orchestra *Peace*, op. 14 (1952—53) and the cantata for male choir and orchestra *The Uprising*, op. 17 (1954).

Film Music

Music to films holds an important place in Zimmer's creative work. For his music to the documentary film *The Town of Spiš* he received a prize in the competition category (1963).

ZRNO, Felix

[born Prague, 2 October 1890]

MERITED TEACHER

Zrno studied composition under VÍTĚZSLAV NOVÁK. His keen interest in musical education brought him to the Research Institute of Pedagogy and later to the Advanced Pedagogical School in Prague. Zrno's interest in musical education has left its mark on his compositional activity. For children he has written song-books, chorals, instructive compositions, music to fairy-tales and children's melodramas.

Chamber Music

His compositions in this field include a *Suite* for viola and piano (1946), a *Nonet* (1946), *Variations on a Folk Song* for viola and piano (1952), a *Scherzo* for violoncello and piano (1952), two *Terzettos* for two violins and viola, five *String Quartets*, *Three Czech Dances* for two violins, violoncello and piano (1952), three *Wind Quintets*, a suite for violin and wind quintet, *Wandering of Folk Musicians* (1956), *Impromptu* for flute and piano (1959), a *Sonatina* for viola and piano (1961), *Prelude and Rondo* for violoncello and piano (1961), *Suite* for wind quintet (1962) and piano quartet *In Memory of Božena Němcová* (1963).

Orchestral and Instrumental Works

A symphonic picture *Resurrection of Spring* (1921), rhapsody for orchestra *The Voice of Darkness* (1942), three *Violin Sonatas* (1946), and *A Ballad* in the form of *Variations* for piano (1958), then recently a *Suite* for solo viola (1964), a *Rhapsody* for solo violin (1964) and a *Rhapsody* for solo violoncello (1964).

Vocal Works

His long service as choirmaster and collaborator in the field of choral music found expression in his

female choirs: *The May Ballad* (1940), *A Lassie from Šumberk* (1950), *Two Simple Motifs* (1958), four choirs set to folk texts (1960), *The Oath* (1960), *Mother's and Father's Day* (1962);

male choirs: *All Souls' Day* (1919), *A Song about Dobuše* (1920), *Šárka* (1921), *Lullaby* (1958), five male choirs to folk texts (1960); *The Pilgrim* (1961) and *Once* (1962);

mixed choirs: *The Night* (1932), *A Ballad About a Beggarwoman* (1935), *A Beautiful Land* (1944), *Kalina and Mohelnice* (1951), *Peace of the Home* (1959) and three mixed choirs set to folk texts (1960);

choral cycles: *Beyond The Sea* (1929), *In the Park* (1933), *Two Simple Motifs* (1960).

He furthermore composed songs and song cycles, the folk oratorio *The Eternal Saga* for solos, choirs and orchestra (1940) and the cantatas *The Song of the Love of Life* for baritone, choir and orchestra (1956) and *Remember* for mixed choir and orchestra (1959) make up his vocal creative work.

He has also written a three-act opera *Klimba* (1934 to 36).

Writings

Zrno has written many articles about the problem of musical education in schools at all levels, *Methodics of Musical Education* at the Public Schools and *A Basic List of Compositions* for Performances at Schools at All Levels. *His Sketches Both Musical and Non-Musical* (1959) are a contribution to the history of musical education.

ZRNO

CZECHOSLOVAK MUSIC INSTITUTIONS AND ORGANIZATIONS

1

ORGANIZATIONS OF CREATIVE AND CONCERT ARTISTS AND MUSICOLOGUES

The Guild of Czechoslovak Composers

(Svaz československých skladatelů), Praha I, Valdštejnské nám. I.

This Guild is a selective organization of creative composers, musicologists and concert artists and is divided into three sections: *composition, musicology and critics and concert artists*. The Group of Violin-makers has been attached to the concert artists section.

The Guild publishes the fortnightly Hudební rozhledy (Musical Review); in the book section of this review, a collection of articles and essays Hudební věda (Musicology) is published, dealing with musical science.

Previews of new compositions, organized by the Guild, present the elemental and developing tendencies of contemporary music in the most varied forms and genres.

The Guild of Slovak Composers

(Sväz slovenských skladateľov), Bratislava, Sládkovičova II.

The Guild, with the same tasks, publishes the monthly Slovenská hudba (Slovak Music).

The Czech Music Fund

(Český hudební fond), Praha 1, Besední 3.

The Fund ensures and promotes the development of musical creative work; it has archives and lending library of musical materials; this section is located at Praha 1, Pařížská 13.

Music Information Centre

(Hudební informační středisko — HIS), Praha 1, Pařížská 13.

It propagates the works of contemporary Czechoslovak composers and publishes a bulletin "Music News from Prague".

The Slovak Music Fund

(Slovenský hudobný fond), Bratislava, Gorkého 19.

It has the same tasks as the Czech Music Fund.

The Union of Czechoslovak Theatrical and Film Artists

(Svaz československých divadelních a filmových umělců), Praha 1, Valdštejnské nám. 3.

This Union deals with creative and artistic problems and stimulates creative activity in all fields of theatrical and film work. It publishes The Theatrical and Film Yearbook (Divadelní a filmová ročenka), The Theatrical and Film Newspaper (Divadelní a filmové noviny) and the magazine The Theatre (Divadlo).

Dilia, Czechoslovak Theatrical and Literary Agency

(Československé divadelní a literární jednatelství), Praha 2, Vyšehradská 28.

Dilia is the agent of all authors of scenic creative work, makes copies of and lends their works. It protects their copyrights, acting as their agent abroad as well. It publishes News of the Theatrical and Literary Agency (Zprávy Československého divadelního a literárního jednatelství).

The Slovak Theatrical and Literary Agency

(Slovenské divadelné a literárné zastupiteľstvo), Bratislava, Československé armády 31.

OSA, Authors' Association for Protection of Rights on Musical Works

(OSA, Ochranný svaz autorský), Praha 6, Československé armády 20.

The OSA is a correlating organization for authors of musical works and texts. It protects their copyrights as well.

SOSA, The Slovak Authors' Association for Protection of Rights on Musical Works

(Slovenský autorský sväz), Bratislava, Živnostenská 1.

OSVU, Protective Association of Concert Artists

(Ochranné sdružení výkonných umělců), Praha 1, Míšeňská 9.

The OSVU protects the rights of solo artists and conductors in the use of sound recordings.

The Prague Spring

This is the first Czechoslovak international music festival founded after the war in 1946 by the Czech Philharmonic on the occasion of its fiftieth anniversary.

The Prague Spring linked up with the old Prague tradition and developed into an artistic event of world renown. Its motto reads: "*Through music to peace and to friendship among nations*".

Each festival is concerned with a different but unifying thematic content while retaining the traditional scheme: it is inaugurated with *Smetana's* cycle of symphonic poems "My Country", commemorating the anniversary of the composer's death (May 12th), and concludes with a hymn of the brotherhood of man, the *Beethovens' Ninth Symphony*, with *Schiller's* Ode to Joy.

A customary component part of the Prague Spring consists of regularly alternating international competitions for young artists.

2

MUSIC EDUCATION

Lower Schools of Music

The creative artistic work of youth and workers is developed in schools, extra-curriculum organizations, cultural institutions and in work clubs; it finds its outlet in competition and reviews which are organized yearly on a national scale in three types of categories (district, regional and state). The competitions stimulate youth and the workers to artistic activity in their spare time. Simultaneously these competitions serve as a means to the selection of those who demonstrate the prerequisites and talent for further specialized study.

Secondary Schools of Music

The Prague Conservatory was founded in 1811. It was mainly a Violin School which made this artistic institution renowned throughout Europe, producing such artists as *Josef Slavík*, *Otakar Ševčík*, *František Ondříček*, *Jan Kubelík*, *Jaroslav Kocián* and others.

Of no less renown was the School of Composition, particularly due to the work of *Antonín Dvořák*, his pupils *Vítězslav Novák*, *Josef Suk*, *J. B. Foerster*, *Jaroslav Křička*, *Alois Hába* and others.

Conservatories

are in Praha 1, na Rejdišti 1,
     Plzeň, Smetanovy sady 9,
     Brno, kapitána Jaroše 45
       (branch in Kroměříž, Pilařova 7),
     Ostrava, Hrabákova 1,
     Bratislava, Rybné náměstí 7,
     Košice, Leninova 93,
     Žilina, Engelsova 6.

High Schools of Music

After the Second World War, the Czechoslovak High School of Music (Academy of Musical Arts) linked up with the tradition of the Prague Conservatory. Many students from abroad have come to study at these schools.

The Academy of Musical Arts

(Akademie musických umění), Praha 1, Alešovo nábřeží 12
(chancellery) has following faculties:
Theatrical, Praha 1, Karlova 26,
Film and Television, Praha 1, Smetanovo nábřeží 2,
Music, Praha 1, Alešovo nábřeží 12.

The section of the theory of music publishes a periodical volume Living Music (Živá hudba), containing works of members of the Music Faculty.

The Janáček Academy of Musical Arts,

Brno, Komenského náměstí 6, publishes a periodical volume (Sborník), containing contributions by members of the Academy.

The High School of Musical Arts,

Bratislava, Štúrova 7.

Faculties of Musicology

CHARLES UNIVERSITY,

Faculty of Philosophy, Department of the History of Music, Praha 1, Břehová 17.

This department includes an Institute of the History of Czech Music and publishes Miscellanea musicologica.

COMENIUS UNIVERSITY,

Faculty of Philosophy, Bratislava, Gondova 2.

PURKYNĚ UNIVERSITY,

Faculty of Philosophy, Musical Scientific Seminar, Brno, Grohova 7.

The last named publishes a periodical Musicologie, which deals with musical science and criticism.

PALACKÝ UNIVERSITY,

Faculty of Philosophy, Department of Musical Science and Education, Olomouc, Křížkovského 10.

3

MUSICAL ENSEMBLES

Symphonic Orchestras

The Czech Philharmonic,

Praha 1, Alešovo nábřeží 12. This is an artistic institution, the basis of which is the symphonic orchestra The Czech Philharmonic. Component parts of this institution are The Czech Choir, Kühn's Children Choir, The Smetana Quartet, The Czech Nonet and the soloists *Josef Suk*, *Ladislav Jásek*, *Josef Chuchro*, *Jan Panenka* and *Věra Soukupová*.

The Prague Spring International Music Festival is affiliated with this institution.

The Slovak Philharmonic,

Bratislava Fučíkova 3. This is an artistic institution, the basis of which is the symphonic orchestra The Slovak Philharmonic. Its component parts are The Choir of the Slovak Philharmonic and the soloists *Tibor Gašparek*, *Albín Berka* and *Michal Karin*.

The Symphonic Orchestra of the Capital City of Prague (FOK),

Praha 1, Obecní dům 5. It has a concert division and The Quartet of the City of Prague. It publishes a program periodical Concert Life.

The State Philharmonic,

Brno, Komenského náměstí 8. The Janáček Quartet and the soloist *František Hanták* are associated with this orchestra.

The State Philharmonic,

Ostrava, Gottwaldovo 147. This institution has an affiliated mixed choir, The Ostrava Quartet and the soloist *Ilja Hurník*.

The Moravian Philharmonic,

Olomouc, Slovenská 5. This institution has an affiliated mixed choir Žerotín and the Dvořák Quartet.

The Carlsbad Symphonic Orchestra,

Karlovy Vary, Lázně III, Náměstí československo-sovětského přátelství 5. This ensemble is affiliated with the Karlovarský (Carlsbad) Choir and the soloist *František Smetana*.

The Philharmonic of the Workers,

Gottwaldov, Dům umění. Affiliated are the mixed choir Dvořák and The Pioneers' Choir.

The North-Bohemian Symphonic Orchestra,

Teplice Lázně, Školní 8. The soloist of the ensemble is *Stanislav Knor.*

The City Symphonic Orchestra,

Mariánské Lázně (Marienbad), Dům Casino. The soloist is *Ivan Moravec.*

Chamber Music

The chamber music ensembles Pro arte antiqua (for historical instruments) and Ars rediviva (oriented to Baroque music) devote themselves to the reproduction of old music.

A considerable part of the repertoire of Czechoslovak chamber ensembles—The Prague Chamber Orchestra Without Conductor, The Czech Chamber Orchestra, The Chamber Orchestra of Bohuslav Martinů (Brno) and The Slovak Chamber Orchestra (Bratislava)—is composed of old music. The New Singers of Madrigals and Chamber Music concentrate considerably on vocal polyphony.

Chamber ensembles are of particular importance in the Czechoslovak musical world, the most outstanding of which are the Smetana, Janáček, Vlach, Novák and Dvořák Quartets and the Quartet of City of Prague as well as the Czech, Prague and Suk Trio, the Czech Wind Quintet of the Philharmonic and the Czech Nonet.

Radio and Television

Radio and television programs are important mediums for the presentation of contemporary creative work as well as that of the classics. They contribute to a more profound knowledge of music and thereby to the aesthetic education of the listeners.

The Czechoslovak Radio,

Praha 2, Vinohradská 12.

includes following units: The Symphonic Orchestra, The Radio Choir, The Children Choir, The Vlach Quartet and the Dance Orchestra.

THE BRATISLAVA STATION

includes The Symphonic Orchestra, The Dance Orchestra, The Folk Music, The Orchestra and the Choir of Folk Art and the Children Choir.

THE BRNO STATION

has the Great String Orchestra and Radio Orchestra of Folk Instruments (Broln).

Other stations have following orchestras: The Ostrava Radio Orchestra, The Pilsen Radio Orchestra and The Košice Radio Orchestra.

The Czechoslovak Radio publishes a weekly Czechoslovak Radio and Television.

Film

The Film Symphonic Orchestra,

Praha 1, Ve Smečkách 22.

An important part in such a complex artistic work as is the film, is represented by music. By producing Czechoslovak films a special attention is paid to the creation of a dramatically effective and artistically convincing musical accompaniment. Music of this type is the work of outstanding Czech and Slovak composers, many of which have gained international success.

Songs and Dances

The Czechoslovak State Ensemble of Songs and Dances,

Praha 1, Pohořelec 23. This ensemble includes vocal and dance units and an orchestra of the symphonic type.

Czechoslovak State Ensemble of Song and Dance and **The Slovak Folk Artistic Ensemble (SLUK)**

which concentrate their creative activities on the presentation of a re-evaluated cultural heritage, served as their model.

The Dukla Ukrainian Folk Ensemble,

Prešov, Leninova 44.

Lúčnica,

Bratislava, Dunajská 48, an ensemble of high and secondary school students; it has vocal, dance and orchestral units.

The Army Artistic Ensemble Vít Nejedlý,

Praha 1, Pohořelec 120. This ensemble has a male choir, a dance unit, an orchestra of a symphonic type and a variety music group. In addition to programs of military songs and dances, it arranges choral, symphonic and chamber music concerts.

The Artistic Ensemble of the Ministry of Interior,

Praha 1, na Perštýně 12.

Amateur Ensembles

After the Second World War, many amateur ensembles sprung up, setting themselves the task of reviving the traditional song and dance culture of the Czech and Slovak people.

Popular Music

Traditional Czech musicianship finds expression as well in an important social branch—popular music. The most significant representatives in this genre, such as *Karel Vlach, Karel Krautgartner, Gustav Brom* and others take their stimuli from the newest trends of dance and jazz music, and endeavour to arrive at their own stylized expression.

Competitions for new dance music contribute to the raising of the standard and actuality of this creative work.

The Association of Musical Youth, The Circle of the Friends of Music and The Circle of the Friends of Modern Dance and Jazz Music have an important status in musical life and culture of the country.

The Spartakiads

A review of results of the Czechoslovak physical training movement are the Spartakiads. The individual performances are there thematically concerned with modern events and are moulded into monumental gymnastic and musical tableaux.

4

THEATRES WITH MUSICAL REPERTOIRES

In Czechoslovakia, there are twelve permanent opera houses. The number of performances and the percentage of Czech and Slovak operas in the repertoire of the opera houses places Czechoslovakia among the nations with the most mature opera culture. Only in Prague, two opera houses play ten months each year, with as many as three performances daily.

The National Theatre

Praha 2, Národní 2.

This is the leading theatre of Czechoslovak theatrical art; it has three ensembles: *dramatic, operatic* and *ballet,* as well as a chamber music ensemble The Novák Quartet.

The National Theatre in Prague, built by the Czech people through their own efforts, was opened on June 11, 1881. The inaugural performance was *Smetana's* opera "Libuše", representing a monumental apotheosis of the history of the Czech nation. The theatre was destroyed by fire on August 12, 1881, but rose again from the ruins in a newer and even more beautiful form.

At the festive opening on November 18, 1883, *Smetana's* "Libuše" was again presented in order to symbolize the mission of these hallowed halls *"where moral truths and beauty are to be presented to the Czech nation".*

The National Theatre has heard Czech singers of international fame, such as *Emmy Destin, Karel Burian, Otakar Mařák, Vilém Zítek* and others.

The Slovak National Theatre

Bratislava, Gorkého 4.

This is the leading theatre in Slovakia and has three ensembles: *dramatic, operatic,* and *ballet.*

The State Theatrical Studio,

Praha 1, Smetanovo nábřeží 26, is an association of ensembles of small groups (SEMAFOR, REDUTA and others).

The State Theatre, Brno
The State Theatre, Ostrava
The Theatre J. K. Tyl, Pilsen
The Theatre Oldřich Stibor, Olomouc
The Theatre of F. X. Šalda, Liberec
The Theatre of Zdeněk Nejedlý, Ústí-on-Labe
The South-Bohemian Theatre, České Budějovice
The Silesian Theatre, Opava

The State Theatre, Košice
The Theatre of J. G. Tajovský, Banská Bystrica
The Theatre of Jonáš Záborský, Prešov

The Music Theatre in Karlín, Praha 8, Křižíkova 10
The Theatre of Music, Praha 1, Opletalova 5
The Theatre of Music, Ostrava, Gottwaldovo 23
The Theatre of Music, Bratislava, Nedbalova 14

5

CULTURAL AND SCIENTIFIC
INSTITUTIONS

The National Museum

Praha 1, Václavské náměstí 68.

This is the central museum in the field of natural and social sciences. It has a *section of music* (Praha 1, Velkopřevorské nám. 4) and a *theatrical section* (Praha 1, Václavské nám. 68). It publishes The Magazine of the National Museum (Časopis Národního musea).

In affiliation with the ensemble of the Society of the National Museum are The Prague Chamber Orchestra Without Conductor, the chamber ensemble Pro arte antiqua and The New Singers of Madrigals and Chamber Music.

The Memorial of National Literature

(Památník národního písemnictví), Praha 1, Strahov.

This is the central museum of Czech literature. It includes two museums, of *Bedřich Smetana* and *Antonín Dvořák*.

The Smetana Museum,

Praha 1, Novotného lávka, in which all the documentary material on the life and work of the founder of Czech modern music has been assembled, was opened in 1936. The building in which the Museum is situated occupies an important place in the development of Czech neorenaissance architecture.

The Dvořák Museum,

Praha 2, ke Karlovu 20, is situated in the summer palace called "America". This building was the first work of the famous Prague architect of the Baroque era *Kilián Ignác Dintzenhofer.*

Bertramka,

Praha 5, Mozartova 169, is a memorial to *Wolfgang Amadeus Mozart* and to *František Xaver Dušek* and his wife *Josephine.*

The Moravian Museum,

Brno, Náměstí 25. února, includes an Institute of the History of Literature, Music and Theatre (Brno, Smetanova 14) and publishes The Magazine of the Moravian Museum (Časopis moravského musea).

The Slovak National Museum,

Slovenské národné muzeum, Martin, is the central ethnographic museum in Slovakia.

The State Library—The University Library,

Praha 1, Klementinum, has a music division; it publishes the Czechoslovak Bibliography.

The People's City Library

(Městská knihovna), Praha 1, Vackovo náměstí 1, has a *music section* (The Library of Bedřich Smetana) as well as a *theatrical* and *film section.*

The Czechoslovak Academy of Sciences

(Československá Akademie věd—ČSAV), Praha 1, Národní 3.

The ČSAV includes The Institute of Musical Science, Praha 1, Valdštejnské náměstí 4. It publishes studies dealing with musical sciences.

The Slovak Academy of Sciences

(Slovenská Akademia ved—SAV), Bratislava, Vajanského nábřeží 12, includes The Institute of Musical Science, which publishes studies dealing with musical sciences.

THE CABINET FOR THE STUDY OF WORK
OF ZDENĚK NEJEDLÝ,

Praha 1, u Sovových mlýnů 2.

THE INSTITUTE FOR ETHNOGRAPHY
AND FOLKLORISTIC SCIENCE

of the Czechoslovak Academy of Sciences, Praha 2, Lazarská 8.

THE INSTITUTE FOR ETHNOGRAPHY
AND FOLKLORISTIC SCIENCE

of the Czechoslovak Academy of Sciences, Brno, Grohova 7.

THE ETHNOGRAPHIC INSTITUTE

of the Slovak Academy of Sciences, Bratislava, Klemensova 27.

THE THEATRICAL INSTITUTE,

Praha 1, Valdštejnské nám. 3. The Bratislava office of this Institute (Vajanského nábřeží 2) is the documentation centre of Czechoslovak contemporary theatrical art.

The Central House of Folk Art,

Praha 1, Sněmovní 7, is a specialized institute in the field of amateur artistic activity.

6

PUBLISHING AND PROMOTIONAL INSTITUTIONS

The State Music Publishing House

(Státní hudební vydavatelství), Praha 1, Palackého 1, publishes musical works and publications dealing with music; recordings and the manufacture of gramophone records falls as well within its activity.

It has a branch office in Bratislava, Obráncov mieru 8a.

Panton, Publishers for the Guild of Czechoslovak Composers,

Praha 1, Besední 3 and Bratislava, Sládkovičova 11.

The Publishing House Orbis,

Praha 2, Vinohradská 46, publishes popular instructive, theatrical, film and other literature.

Artia,

Praha 2, ve Smečkách 30, is a foreign trade corporation for the imports and exports of cultural works. It publishes literary works on art and specialized subjects as well as fiction (including the production of gramophone records), destined for exportation.

Pragokoncert,

Czechoslovak Musical and Theatrical Agency, Praha 1, Valdštejnská 10.

Concert and Theatrical Office,

Bratislava, Leningradská 5.

Appendix

II

RECORDINGS OF CONTEMPORARY CZECH AND SLOVAK MUSIC

In making up this list, a special attention has been paid to compositions contained in the preceding survey of younger Czech and Slovak composers. At the same time an emphasis has been laid on folk music, songs and dances as well as on new songs and new dances, anchored recently in the repertoires of contemporaneous musical performances.

The soloists and musical and vocal ensembles grown up and ripened in a tradition of long standing, ensure a true interpretation of the composer's intentions.

The cited records can be obtained at *Artia*, Praha 1, ve Smečkách 30.

AIM Vojtěch Bořivoj

To the Sons of Melantrich, a male choir [M. Navrátil]

ALBRECHT Alexander

Sonatina for eleven instruments

AMBROS Vladimír

What Brought the Year, eleven children songs for two voices [O. Bereza]

ANDRAŠOVAN Tibor

Slovak Workers' Songs (folk poetry), for solo, choir and orchestra
Detva Merry-making (folk poetry), for solos, choir and orchestra
Three Songs from Terchová (folk poetry), for solos, choir and orchestra
The Fair of Radvaň (folk poetry), a series of songs and dances for solos, choir and orchestra
At the Foot of the Crone Hill, a song about Orava Dam for choir and orchestra [M. Rúfus]

BABUŠEK František

Prelude for string orchestra

BÁRTA Lubor

Concerto for viola and orchestra
Concerto for piano and orchestra
Fire, a children choir with accompaniment [V. Mikeš]

BARTOŠ Jan Zdeněk
String Quartet No. 5 (May the whole World be a Garden)
String Quartet No. 6 (Miniature)
Chamber Symphony No. 2
The Flag is Flying down the Pole, a children choir with accompaniment [L. Sedláčková]

BARVÍK Miroslav
My Dearest, male choir [A. Surkov]
Dukla for solos, choir and orchestra [Š. Ladižinský]

BÁZLIK Miroslav
Five Songs for alto, flute, violoncello and piano [B. Mathesius]
Three Pieces for fourteen instruments

BAŽANT Jiří
Beautiful Metamorphoses for orchestra

BERG Josef
Nonet for two harps, key and percussion instruments

BLÁHA Václav
Children Choirs (Cabinet-maker—Jacob, Little Jacob—Bumble-bee—The Earthworm was dancing) [M. Veselý]

BLATNÝ Pavel
Suita for wind instruments

BLAŽEK Zdeněk
The Highlands, selections from the opera (libretto J. Zatloukal)
Mud, a children choir [J. Čarek]

BOHÁČ Josef
Going on Holidays, a children choir [M.Sedloň]
Children's Laughter, a children choir [E. Sojka]
It is awaiting us, a song for choir and orchestra [E. Sojka]

BOŘKOVEC Pavel
Sonata No. 2 for violin and piano
String Quartet No. 1
String Quartet No. 4
String Quartet No. 5
Concerto grosso for two violins, violoncello and orchestra with piano obligato
Symphony No. 2
Rat-Catcher, a ballet
The Flag of the Republic, children choir [J. Seifert]

BOROVIČKA Antonín
The nicest Corner, a polka for orchestra

BROŽ František

Chromatic Variations for accordion and orchestra
Spring Sonata for viola and piano

BURGHAUSER Jarmil

A Servant of Two Masters, a suite from a ballet
Carolina and the Liar, a selection from the opera (libretto L. Mandaus)
Seven Reliefs for full orchestra

BURIAN Emil František

Maryša, selected scenes from the opera (libretto according A. and V. Mrštík)
War, selected parts from the folk play with songs and dances (folk poetry)
An Overture to Socialism for orchestra
String Quartet No. 3
I Know the Country near the Pole for solo, choir and orchestra [Vítězslav Nezval]
Children Songs, a cycle for a voice and nonet [Vítězslav Nezval]

CHLUBNA Osvald

Slovak Nocturne for cimbalom and orchestra
The Fountains of Brno, a symphonic poem
Miners'Ballad, a male choir [J. V. Sládek]

CIKKER Ján

Resurrection, a complete opera (libretto according L. N. Tolstoi)
Juro Jánošík, a selection of scenes and dances from the opera (libretto Štefan Hoza)
Sinfonietta for orchestra
Morning, a symphonic poem
Summer, a symphonic poem
Concertino for piano and orchestra
Slovak Suita for orchestra
Reminiscences, a suite for orchestra
The Meeting, a youth dance for choir and orchestra
Starry Night, a dance from Eastern Slovakia for choir and orchestra

DOBIÁŠ Václav

Quartettino for string quartet
Sonata for piano, string instruments, wind quintet and timpani
Symphony No. 2
Nonet *About My Homeland*
Pastoral Wind Quintet
Poetic Polkas for piano
Dreams, a cycle of songs with piano (Songs of the Old China) [B. Mathesius]
The Unique Prague, a cycle of songs with orchestra [M. Pujmanová]

The Litle Spring Song, a children choir [J. Havel]
The Slavonic Linden, a male choir [J. V. Sládek]
Stalingrad, a cantata [J. M. Novák]
Build-up Your Country, Thus You Strengthen the Peace, a cantata
   [František Halas]
Never Alone, a song with orchestra ([A. Tvardowski—I. Štuka]
Spring Song, solo, choir and orchestra [V. Závada]
Song for the Communist Party, cantata [V. Nezval]

DOBRODINSKÝ Bedřich
Baroque Suite for harp

DOUBRAVA Jaroslav
Sonata for piano
Don Quijote, a suite from the ballet
King Lávra, a suite from the ballet

DREJSL Radim
My Country, the Beautiful, a song for solo, choir and orchestra
   [M. Zachata]
Song of a Streamlined Airplane Pursuer, a march for choir and orchestra
   [M. Zachata]
A Day Abloom, a march for choir and orchestra [M. Zachata]

DUSÍK Gejza
A Song of the Native Country from the operetta The Potters' Ball
   [P. Braxatoris]
Potpourri from Melodies of Gejza Dusík
Potpourri from operettas of Gejza Dusík

DVOŘÁČEK Jiří
Morning Monologues, a cycle of songs for baritone with orchestra

EBEN Petr
Sunday Music for organ
Suita balladica for violoncello and piano
Concerto for piano and orchestra
Six Love Songs on medieval texts for voice, harp and piano
Epitaf His Ego, a male choir [Ovidius]
On the Grass, fifteen children choirs with wind quintet
   [František Hrubín, J. Čarek]
The Twig is Getting Green, a cycle of children choirs with accompa-
   niment [J. Seifert, J. Čarek, P. Bojar, V. Čtvrtek, O. Kryš-
   tofek]
About Swallows and Girls, a cycle of choirs (folk poetry)
Love and Death, a cycle of mixed choirs (folk poetry)
Old Enchantments of Love (folk poetry), a small cantata

FELD Jindřich
Concerto for violoncello and orchestra
Two Compositions for violoncello and orchestra
Concerto for flute and orchestra

Furiant for symphonic orchestra
Ocarina intermezzo with orchestra

FELIX Václav

Linden Alley and *Meeting with the Family*, two songs from the cycle
The Battlefield for baritone and orchestra [S. K. Neumann]
Which of Us, a children choir with accompaniment [J. Pražák]
Daddy's Songs, a cycle of choirs [F. Hrubín, D. Kurzová]

FERENCZY Oto

String Quartet No. 1
Finale for orchestra
Hurbanesque, overture for orchestra to a theme of a revolutionary
song from the year 1848
Serenade for flute, clarinet, bassoon, harp, violin and string orchestra
Merry-making, a dance picture from the Šariš region for full orchestra
Three mixed choirs [Pavol Országh-Hviezdoslav, J. Kostra,
Štefan Žáry]
Recruitment (Verbunk), a male choir [Štefan Žáry]

FIALA Jiří Julius

Cavatina for violoncello and orchestra
Love, oh God, Love, a paraphrase on a folk song for violin and
orchestra
Pond of Talín, a paraphrase on a folk song for violin and orchestra
Con amore, a serenade for orchestra
Valse in E flat major for orchestra
A little Town in a Palm, an overture to a film, for orchestra

FISCHER Jan F.

Romeo, Juliet and Darkness, a selection of scenes from the opera
[libretto by the composer according to Jan Otčenášek]
Valse from the ballet *Eufrosina*
A Little Song for Friends for solo, choir and orchestra [J. Hořec]
Nights over Prague, a song for solo, choir and orchestra [M. Za-
chata]

FIŠER Luboš

Sonata No. 1 for piano
Sonata for violin and piano

FLEGL Josef

Among Little Hens, tempo di mazur for wind quintet

FLOSMAN Oldřich

A Dream about Violin for violin and piano

FOLPRECHT Zdeněk

Bolero for orchestra
Concertino for nine instruments
Suite of Czech, Moravian and Slovak Songs and Dances for solos and
orchestra (folk poetry)

FRIED Alexej

The Devil Passed through the Town, a selection of songs from the musical comedy [H. Philip]
The Rose of Friendship, a children choir [M. Zikán]
Song of Peace, a children choir with orchestra [I. Bureš]

GREGOR Čestmír

One of Us, a symphonic picture

GROSSMAN Saša

Russian Dance No. 1 in D minor, arrangement for wind orchestra
Russian Dance No. 7 in F minor for orchestra
A Solitary Tree, song for solo, choir and orchestra [K. Boušek]

HÁBA Alois

Mother, complete opera
String Quartet No. 9 (Small)
String Quartet No. 11 (in sixth-tone system)
String Quartet No. 12 (in quarter-tone system)
String Quartet No. 13, Astronautical (in half-tone system)
String Quartet No. 15 (in half-tone system)
Nonet No. 1 (twelve-tone, in athematic style)
Nonet No. 3
New Land, overture to an opera
What is Good and What is Bad, a children choir with accompaniment of clarinet, trumpet and piano [Vladimir Majakovsky]
Michurin, a children choir with flute [Stephan Shchipachov]

HÁBA Karel

String Quartet No. 3
Folk Songs for Nurseries, a children choir with accompaniment (folk poetry)
Christmas Carols, for solos, children choir and orchestra (folk poetry)
Children are Singing, a selection from a cycle of children choirs with accompaniment [L. Balcar]

HANUŠ Jan

The Flames, scenes from the opera-rhapsody
Salt is Worth More than Gold, first suite from the ballet
Othello, first and second suite from the ballet
Symphony No. 2 in G major
Concert Symphony in C minor for organ, harp, timpani and string orchestra
Suita drammatica for string quartet [meditations to the motives of Aeschylus' *Prometheus*]
Sonnets to texts of renaissance poets for alto and piano
At the Camping Fire, a children choir with accompaniment [František Branislav]
Plant the Trees!, a children choir with accompaniment [F. Branislav]
Young Doves (folk poetry), a choir
Czech Year, suite for children choir, piano and orchestra (folk poetry)

HAVELKA Svatopluk

Symphony No. 1
The Praise of Light, cantata [S. K. Neumann]
Once, We Shan't be Little, a children choir with orchestra

HERTL František

March of the Builders for orchestra

HIRNER Teodor

Greetings to Moscow, a small cantata [A. Plávka]

HLOBIL Emil

Symphony No. 1
Sonata for violin and piano
String Quartet No. 2
Quartet for cembalo, violin, viola and violoncello
Summer in Giant Mountains, a suite
Folk Merry-making, a suite

HOLOUBEK Ladislav

Daughter of Mine, a cycle of songs with orchestra [V. Mihálik]

HORKÝ Karel

Captain Šarovec, a scene from the opera [libretto F. Kožík]
A White Birch Tree, Sister of Mine, a small cantata for mezzosoprano
and female choir [I. Kupec]

HURNÍK Ilja

Concerto for oboe and orchestra
Ondráš, music from the ballet
Moments musicaux for eleven wind instruments
Esercizii for flute, oboe, clarinet and bassoon
Sonata da camera for flute, oboe, violoncello and cembalo
Four Seasons of the Year, a suite for chamber orchestra
The Musicians, a chamber suite set to verses by F. Branislav
Quail, a song with orchestra [F. Branislav]
Lullaby for Little Thomas, a song with orchestra [I. Hurník]
Children Terzettos for three solo children voices, flute, harp and
double-bass [F. Branislav]
The Sun is Smiling, a children choir with accompaniment [I. Hurník]
Sun-Warmed Field Boundary, a children choir with accompaniment
[J. Čarek]
I'll plant an Apple-tree, a children choir with accompaniment
[I. Hurník]
Little Songs about Work, a children choir with accompaniment
[J. Zaoral, M. Hemzáčková]
Choirs about Mothers, a cycle of mixed choirs (folk texts)
Fairy-tale about the Princess Little Frog, recital with orchestra

Fairy-tale about a Big Sugar-beet, recital with orchestra
Maryka, a cantata (folk poetry)

HURT Jaroslav

Curtain Up, an overture to the operetta

ILLÍN Evžen

Bolero from the suite *Carnival*

IŠTVAN Miloslav

Piano Trio
String Quartet
Ballad about the South, three symphonic frescos

JAROCH Jiří

Symphony No. 2
Spring Valse for orchestra
Children Suite for nonet
The Old Man and the Sea, a symphonic poem [Ernest Hemingway]

JEREMIÁŠ Otakar

The Brothers Karamazov, a selection of scenes from the opera [F. M. Dostoievsky]
Charles the Fourth, a melodrama with orchestra [Jan Neruda]
Macbeth and the Witches (from the piano sketch of B. Smetana)
Spring Overture for orchestra
The Song of the Native Land, a cantata [Josef Hora]
The Lord of Ours Commands not to Fear, a Czech Hussite hymn for orchestra
The Love, a cycle of songs with orchestra [Petr Křička, Jaroslav Vrchlický, Jan Neruda]
Steadily Forward!, a march [Jan Neruda]
Ostrava, a male choir [Petr Bezruč]
First Medley of Folk Songs for children choir and orchestra
Second Medley of Folk Songs for children choir and orchestra

JEŽEK Jaroslav

Bugatti-step for piano
Sonata for piano
Jeppe from the Hill, a suite from the scenic music to the play of Ludvig Holberg

JINDŘICH Jindřich

My First of May, a song with orchestra [Jan Neruda]
Little Children Songs from Chod Region, a children choir with piano (folk poetry)

JIRÁK Zdeněk

The March of Artists, a gallop from the suite At the Circus
The Way to School, a children choir with accompaniment [P. Šoltész]

JIRKO Ivan

Sonata for piano
Sonata for violoncello and piano
Concerto No. 3 in G major for piano and orchestra

JUCHELKA Miroslav

In the Whirl of the Dance for orchestra
The Dance of Highlanders for oboe and orchestra
Carnival Valse for orchestra
Humouresque from the Serenade for string instruments and harp
The Way of Red Stars, a choir with orchestra [O. Blažek]
Song against War for solos, choir and orchestra [K. Šiktanc]
The Laughing Soldier, a song for solo, choir and orchestra [Š. Ladi-
    žinský]

JUROVSKÝ Šimon

Knights' Ballad, a suite from the ballet
The Humming Hill, a cantata [P. Horov]
Song of Peace, a cantata [V. Mihálik]
The Dance of Orava for orchestra
Let Us Tie together our Hands, a song for solo, choir and orchestra

KABELÁČ Miloslav

Symphony No. 4 in A major
Fantasy No. 1 and 2 for organ
Mystery of Time, a passacaglia for orchestra
Don't Retreat!, a cantata (folk texts)
Six Lullabies for a voice, female choir and instrumental ensemble
    (folk poetry)
It is Drizzling, a children choir with piano (folk poetry)

KAFENDA Frico

Three Piano Compositions

KALABIS Viktor

Symphony No. 2 (Sinfonia pacis) for full orchestra
Concerto for violin and orchestra
Concerto for piano and orchestra
String Quartet No. 2
Chamber Music for string instruments
Divertimento for wind quintet
Snowman, a children choir with piano [V. Čtvrtek]

KALACH Josef

Serenade for string orchestra

KALAŠ Julius

Miller's Wife from Granada, a selection of scenes from the operetta
    [libretto K. Konstantin, K. Hrnčíř]
Tarantella for orchestra
Nightingale and the Rose, a symphonic poem according to Oscar
    Wilde

KÁLIK Václav

Intermezzo for violin and piano
Sonata for violin and piano
A Highland Region, male choir [Antonín Sova]
Heart, a male choir [Jaroslav Vrchlický]
Prague, a male choir [Jaroslav Vrchlický]
Return Home, a male choir [Otakar Theer]
Evening, a male choir [J. V. Sládek]
Clouds, a mixed choir [Jan Neruda]
Bridge, a mixed choir [Jiří Mahen]
Spring Day, a mixed choir [J. Šulc]
September, a mixed choir [Jaroslav Seifert]
Home, a mixed choir [J. V. Sládek]

KAPR Jan

String Quartet No. 3
String Quartet No. 6 with a baritone solo [R. Pandulová]
Home, a selection from the piano cycle
Fantasy for violin and piano
About Mariners' Dreams, a choir from the cycle Dreams and Plans
   [Jaroslav Seifert]
Serenade for orchestra
In the Soviet Country, a cantata [Vítězslav Nezval]
A New Little Star, a children choir with accompaniment
   [M. Handlířová]

KAPRÁL Václav

Lullabies, a cycle of songs for voice and orchestra (folk poetry)

KAPRÁLOVÁ Vítězslava

Partita for string orchestra and piano
Military Sinfonietta

KARDOŠ Desider

Symphony No. 2 (About My Native Land)
Symphony No. 3
Symphony No. 4 (Piccola)
Concerto for orchestra
Eastern Slovak Overture for orchestra
Preludium qua si una fantasia for organ
Heroic Ballad for string orchestra
Peace Cantata [P. Horov]
Greetings to a Great Country, a cantata [J. Brezina]
Dances from the Zemplín Region (folk poetry) for choir and orchestra
Morena (folk poetry), a composition for choir and orchestra
A Hymn of Free Youth for solos, choir and orchestra [M. Lajčiak]
We'll Help the Nightingale, children choirs for the smallest with
   orchestra [E. Petrík]
A Song of Happy Children, a children choir with accompaniment
   [S. Cónová]
My Native Country, mixed choir [M. Rázusová-Martáková]

KAREL Rudolf
Godmother Death, scenes from the opera [libretto Stanislav Lom]
Three Hairs of the All-Wise Grandfather, scenes from the opera of the
   same name (libretto: the composer)
Military March for orchestra

KAŠLÍK Václav
Brigands' Dances from the ballet *Jánošík*

KINCL Antonín
Dance, Dance Around!, a medley of folk songs for wind orchestra

KLÍMA Alois
Concerto Polonaise, arranged for wind orchestra

KLUSÁK Jan
Pictures for twelve wind instruments
First Invention for wind instruments
Third Invention for string instruments

KOLMAN Peter
Partecipazioni for twelve instruments
Four Pieces for orchestra

KOPELENT Marek
String Quartet No. 3
Nenie, chamber music composition with flute

KORTE Oldřich F.
Sinfonietta for full orchestra
Sonata for piano

KRAUTGARTNER Karel
Students' Suite for orchestra

KREJČÍ Iša
The Tumult in Ephesus, selection of scenes from the opera [libretto
   J. Bachtík, according to William Shakespeare]
Symphony No. 2 in C sharp
Serenade for orchestra
String Quartet No. 2 in D minor
String Quartet No. 3
Divertimento (Cassation) for flute, clarinet, trumpet and bassoon

KREJČÍ Miroslav
The last Captain, a selection of scenes from the opera [libretto
   E. Klenová, according to Alois Jirásek]
New Year Polka for orchestra

KRESÁNEK Josef
Orchestral Suite No. 2

KŘIČKA Jaroslav

Variations for harp to a *Mozart theme,* composed for the Prague
   harpplayer Josef Häusler
Mourning flourish of trumpets for wind instruments
Idylls and Medallions for string quartet with recital of *"Grandmother"*
   by Božena Němcová
Northern Nights, a cycle of songs with orchestra [K. Balmont—
   P. Křička]
Spring, the little Lad, three recitatives with orchestra set to children
   prose from the reader „Morning"
Three Fables with piano [Němcová—Afanasjov]
Album from the Old School, a cycle of songs with piano (composer)
Our Mrs. Božena Němcová, a cycle of songs with orchestra [F. Halas]
Sunny Songs, a cycle of songs with orchestra [J. Čarek]
Blue Sky, a children choir [František Hrubín]

KŘIVINKA Gustav

Sonata for solo violin
In Memory of a Comrade, a male choir [K. Kapoun]
The Song, a male choir [K. Kapoun]

KUBÍN Rudolf

Concerto for clarinet and orchestra
Ostrava, a symphonic poem from a cycle of the same name
In the Beskids, a symphonic poem from the cycle Ostrava
It Is Worth-while to Live, a cycle of songs with orchestra
   [E. F. Burian]

KUČERA Václav

Dramatas for nine instruments

KUNC Jan

Ostrava, a male choir [Petr Bezruč]

KUPKA Karel

Picassiada, partita for full orchestra

KUPKOVIČ Ladislav

Octagon for chamber orchestra
Sketch for six players

KVAPIL Jaroslav

String Quartet No. 4
Burlesque for flute and orchestra
From the Hard Times, symphonic variations
The Fairy-tale of May, a scene from the opera of the same name
   [libretto F. Kožík]

LANGER Alfons

Bolero for orchestra
Nocturno for orchestra
Panorama, a potpourri from melodies of Alfons Jindra

LEOPOLD Bohuslav

Tarantella for orchestra
Plays of Butterflies, an intermezzo for orchestra

LUCKÝ Štěpán

Wind Quintet

MÁCHA Otmar

Slovak Rhapsody for orchestra
Kalamajka and *Peasant Dance* [two dances from the cycle Moravian
   Dances], arranged for wind orchestra
Night and Hope, a symphonic poem
Children Choirs [Jaroslav Seifert, František Halas]

MALOVEC Jozef

Two Parts for chamber orchestra

MARTINŮ Bohuslav

Sketches of Dances for piano
Sonata No. 1 for piano
Duo for violin and piano
Sonata No. 3 for violin and piano
Three Madrigals for violin and viola
Sonata No. 1 for violoncello and piano
Sonata No. 3 for violoncello and piano
Piano Trio in D minor
Five short pieces, piano trio
Grand Trio, piano trio in C major
Bergerettes, piano trio
String Quartet No. 4
String Quartet No. 5
Concerto da camera [String Quartet No. 7]
Sextet for two violins, two violas and two violoncellos
Nonet
Toccata e due canzoni for chamber orchestra
Parables for orchestra
Frescos of Pieva della Francesca for orchestra
Lidice Memorial, symphonic commemoration
Sinfonietta La Jolla for chamber orchestra and piano
Sinfonietta giocosa for chamber orchestra and piano
Incantations for piano and orchestra
Piano Concerto No. 3 for piano and orchestra
Concerto for violin and orchestra
Concerto for oboe and orchestra
Concerto for two string orchestras, piano and timpani
Symphony No. 5
Fantasia concertante [Symphony No. 7]
Madrigals (Part-Songs) for female and mixed voices
The Bouquet, a cycle of compositions for solos, choir and orchestra
   (folk poetry)
The Opening of Wells, chamber cantata
Selection of male and female choirs (folk poetry)

Juliette (or the Key to Dreams), an opera to composer's own libretto, according to a play by G. Neveux

MATĚJ Josef

Sonata da camera for oboe and chamber orchestra
Concerto for trombone and orchestra
Halí, belí, and *Folk Songs* for children choirs with flute and piano (folk poetry)

MIHULE Jiří

Swaggerer (folk dance) for orchestra
Always Merrily (speedy dance) for orchestra

MIKULA Zdenko

Oriešany Merry-making (folk poetry) for solos, choir and orchestra
A Bulgarian Dance for orchestra

MODR Antonín

Poděbrady Polkas No. 1 and 2 for orchestra
Neighbourly Polka for orchestra

MOYZES Alexander

Wind Quintet B flat major
Sonatina giocosa for eleven string instruments
Overture *Jánošík's Lads*
Suite *Down the River Váh*
Suite *Dances from the Hron Country*, for orchestra
Suite *Dances from the Gemer Country*
Symphony No. 1 in D major
Symphony No. 4 in E flat major
Symphony No. 7
In Autumn, a cycle of songs with orchestra
Three Maiden, Hop, Hop, Hop! (folk poetry), a male choir
The She-mowers (folk poetry), a female choir
Hey, Maple Band (folk poetry) for solo, mixed choir and orchestra
Blow, My Dear Wind (folk poetry) for solo, mixed choir and orchestra
The Songs from the Zvolen Region (folk poetry) for mixed choir and orchestra
The Merry-making in Detva Region (folk poetry) for mixed choir and orchestra
They are singing, playing, dancing (folk poetry) for solos and orchestra
Balladic Cantata [J. Poničan]

MÓŽI Július

Terchova Modifications for folk musical band
Terchova Band of Musicians for folk musical band
Spinning-time (folk poetry) for choir and orchestra
The Songs from Tekov (folk poetry) for solos, choir and orchestra

NEJEDLÝ Vít

Victory Shall Be Ours, festive march
Dramatic Overture for orchestra

Czech National Songs (folk suite) for small orchestra
"*150,000.000*" male choir [Vladimir Majakovsky]
A selection of scenes from the opera *The Weavers*, according to
  Gerhart Hauptmann [completed by Jan Hanuš]

NEUMANN Věroslav

The Harvest Song, children choir with orchestra [N. Zabilová—
  J. V. Svoboda]
Frontier-guard Song for solo, choir and orchestra [R. Franz]
The Song for our Guests, mixed choir with orchestra [E. Sojka]
Happiness without Charge, a march for mixed choir and orchestra
  [J. Hořec]

NIKODEM Bedřich

Meditation for a string orchestra
Longing, a valse for string orchestra
A Potpourri of dance melodies
The Storks, children choir with orchestra [H. Janustewska—
  J. V. Svoboda]
We Are Going for an Excursion, children choir with orchestra
  [J. Hořec]

NOVÁK Jan

Capriccio for violoncello and orchestra
Concertino for wind quintet
Balletti for nine instruments
Bridal Shirt, a suite from a dance ballad for orchestra [according
  to K. J. Erben]
Passer Catulli, a musical pun for bass and nonet [according to Gaius
  Valerius Catullus]
Four Songs from the play *Total Cockcrow* [L. Kundera]

NOVÁK Milan

Lezginka for orchestra
A Joyous Song for children choir and orchestra [M. Ferko]

OČENÁŠ Andrej

Concertino for flute and piano
Highland Song, a suite from the ballet of the same name
Ruralia Slovacca, a symphonic poem
To My Generation, a cantata [M. Kratochvílová]

PÁDIVÝ Karol

On the Banks of the Orava River, a valse for wind orchestra
A Slovak Dance for wind orchestra

PÁLENÍČEK Josef

Choral Variations for violoncello and piano

PÁLKA Dušan

Small Swimmers, a children choir [E. Sojka]
A Potpourri of dance melodies

PARÍK Ivan
Sonata for solo flute
Songs about Falling Leaves for piano

PAUER Jiří
Sonatina for violin and piano
Sonata for violoncello and piano
String Quartet No. 1
Wind Quintet
Concerto for bassoon and orchestra
Concerto for French horn and orchestra
Scherzo for full orchestra
Two grotesques *The Matrimonial Counterpoints* [according to
  S. Grodzieńska]
The Chattering Snail, a complete one-act opera, according to Oriental
  fairy-tale [J. Hloucha]

PEČKE Karel
The Artists, a march for wind orchestra [co-author Miloš Smatek]

PETR Zdeněk
Tomorrow, a song for choir and orchestra [Vladimír Dvořák]

PETRŽELKA Vilém
Moments of Intimacy, a cycle for violin and piano
Pastoral Sinfonietta
This is My Land, a male choir [J. Zatloukal]

PÍCHA František
Sonata in D minor for violin and piano
Polka from Říp for orchestra
The Modest, a neighbourly dance for orchestra
A Small Fountain, little songs and rhymes (folk poetry), for solo,
  female choir and accompaniment
Peat-bogs are Singing, a series of songs from Southern Bohemia
  (folk poetry), for solos, choir and orchestra

PLAVEC Josef
Eight Children Choir Songs with piano [H. Kohoutová]

PLICHTA Jan
Slovak Dance (Odzemek) for orchestra

PODÉŠŤ Ludvík
Odzemek, a Moravian dance with orchestra
Gypsy Dance, a Moravian dance with orchestra
Tremulous Dance, a polka for wind orchestra
Sentry, a song for solos, choir and orchestra [R. Franz]
A Song without great Words for solo, choir and orchestra [I. Štuka]

PODEŠVA Jaromír
Sonata for violin and piano
String Quartet No. 4 (From the Story of a New Contemporary)

A Little Song of Young Fruit-growers, children choir with orchestra
[J. V. Svoboda]
Sinfonietta of the Nature for four male choirs [M. Holub]

POLOLÁNÍK Zdeněk

Variations for organ and piano
Musica spingenta
    first for doublebass and wind quintet,
    third for bass-clarinet and percussion instruments

POSPÍŠIL Juraj

Marginal Notes for wind quintet

PRAVEČEK Jindřich

Concerto polonaise for wind orchestra
The Autumn Melody, a valse for wind orchestra
At a Victorious Pace, a march for wind orchestra

PROVAZNÍK Anatol

Indian Song for violin and piano

RAICHL Miroslav

Symphony No. 2
Students' Songs for choir and orchestra [Karel Šiktanc]

REINER Karel

Sonata No. 3 for piano
Sonata for violin and piano
Come, Sparks, Come out!, a children choir with accompaniment
    [J. Havel]
The Great World, a song for children choir with orchestra
    [E. Sojka]
We Are Driving the Time, a choir with orchestra [E. Sojka]
That is the Party, a choir with orchestra [E. Sojka]

ŘEZÁČ Ivan

Piano Trio in A minor
An Overture to Majakovsky's poem *The Right Thing*

ŘÍDKÝ Jaroslav

Piano trio
Nonet No. 1
Funereal Fanfare for wind ensemble
Festive March for orchestra
Serenade for string orchestra
Overture for full orchestra
Concerto for piano and orchestra
Concerto No. 2 for violoncello and orchestra
Lenka, polka for orchestra
Milada, polka for orchestra

RYCHLÍK Jan

Chamber Suite for string quartet
African Cycle for nonet

ŠATRA Antonín

Sonata in G major for violin and piano

ŠAUER František

Playing Guitar, children choir with accompaniment [F. Branislav]

SCHNEIDER-TRNAVSKÝ Mikuláš

Sonata in G minor for violin and piano
A Comedy Overture for orchestra
Bellarosa, the operetta—overture and selection of scenes [libretto
    I. Jakubek]

SCHREIBER Josef

Children Choirs (folk poetry) [J. Filgar]

SEIDEL Jan

Happy Journey, a cycle of songs with piano accompaniment
A Song of Young Tourists, children choir with accompaniment
    [M. Soukenková]
Beat your Drum, Little Drummer!, children choir with accompaniment
    [B. Bobek]
Christmas Carols (folk poetry) for children choir with accompaniment
To Prague, a male choir from the cycle *The War-trumpet of Glory*
    [František Halas]
Wild-Rose, a male choir [J. Červený]
Forward, No Step Backward!, a song for solo, choir and orchestra
    [B. Bobek]
For Country of Mine, a song for solo, choir and orchestra [J. Ostaš]
A Meeting, song for solo, choir and orchestra [B. Bobek]
The May Overture for choir and orchestra
Prague—Moscow—The Peace, a festive song for choir and orchestra
    [B. Bobek]
A Song about a Decisive Step for choir and orchestra [J. Sekera]
The Third Lightning, a song for choir and orchestra [Išidi Ašada
    —K. Holubec]
A Message to the Living, a cantata [František Halas]
The Bequest of Julius Fučík (People, Be on Guard!), a monumental
    cantata-triptych [Julius Fučík]
Music to the film *The Bagpiper from Strakonice*
Concerto No. 2 for oboe and orchestra

ŠIMAI Pavol

Victory, a composition for piano and orchestra
The Mother Speaks, a discourse about peace for recital and solo
    instruments

ŠKVOR František

Mourning Sonnet for wind ensemble
The Country Sings (folk poetry), a suite from the film of the same name [K. Plicka]
Nursery Rhymes on folk poetry for children ensemble with accompaniment
Songs, a cycle of children choirs with accompaniment (folk poetry) [J. V. Sládek]
Children Songs (folk poetry), a cycle of children choirs with flute and clarinet [J. Čarek]

SLAVICKÝ Klement

Three Compositions for piano
Frescos for organ
Rhapsodic Variations for orchestra
Moravian Dance Fantasies for orchestra
Hey, Sweetheart of Mine (folk poetry), a cycle of songs with piano
Swains, Swains!, a suite of Moravian songs about love (folk poetry) for solos, female choir and orchestra

SLUKA Luboš

Sonata for violoncello and piano

SMATEK Miloš

Strakonice polka for orchestra
Slovak Dance for orchestra
The Artist, a march for wind orchestra [co-author Karel Pečke]

SMETÁČEK Václav

In the Glade of Nymphs and Satyrs, a ballet suite

SOKOLA Miloš

Three Compositions for organ
Orchestral Variations on a theme by Vítězslava Kaprálová

SOMMER Vladimír

String Quartet in D minor
Antigona, an overture to Sophocle's tragedy
Concerto in G minor for violin and orchestra
It is Good to be on the Earth, a cycle of children choirs with piano [F. Hrubín, V. Nezval]
The Autumn Morning, mixed choir [Zdeněk Fibich]
Vocal Symphony for mezzosoprano, reciter, choir and orchestra [Franz Kafka, F. M. Dostoevski, C. Pavese]

SRNKA Jiří

Concerto for violin and orchestra (Dramatic)
The Moon above the River, a suite from the film of the same name [Fráňa Šrámek]
Child's Year, children choirs with piano—a selection [František Hrubín]

⊙ RYCHLÍK - SRNKA

ŠROM Karel

Fairy-tales for nonet

STANISLAV Josef

Sonata No. 2 E minor for piano
Sonata No. 3 for piano (These are your Brothers)
Sonata for violin and piano
Song of the Unemployed (from a social cycle) for voice and piano
Lullaby for voice and piano [J. Hrnčíř, K. Ston]
The Song of a great Hope, mixed choir [J. Černý]
A Song about Granada, a cantata [E. Svietlov]

ŠTĚDROŇ Vladimír

Variation fantasies on Moravian songs for string quartet

STERNWALD Jiří

Water-lily, a valse, for orchestra

STRNIŠTĚ Jiří

Valse caprice for orchestra
Polka for orchestra
The Spring Earth, a song for voice and orchestra [E. Sojka]

SUCHOŇ Eugen

Sonatina for violin and piano
Fantasy and Burlesque for violin and orchestra
String Quartet
Serenade for string orchestra
Balladic Suite for full orchestra
Metamorphoses, a symphonic suite
Ad Astra, a cycle of five songs for soprano and orchestra [Štefan Žáry]
Nox et Solitudo, a cycle of songs with orchestra [Ivan Krasko]
The Mountains, a cycle of male choirs
In that Manor of Terchova (folk poetry), a choir with orchestra
How Beautiful You Are, mixed choir [P. Horov]
About Man, a cycle of mixed choirs [Ján Smrek]
Three Lyric Songs (Man and Love) from the above cited cycle About Man [Ján Smrek]
The Psalm of the Subcarpathian Country, a cantata [J. Zatloukal]
Krútňava, the complete opera [libretto of the composer and Štefan Hoza, according to M. Urban]
Svätopluk, the complete opera [libretto Ivan Stodola, composer and J. Krčméryová]
The Pictures from Slovakia, a cycle:
  Highland suite for piano,
  Sinfonietta rustica for orchestra,
  I Am Small, children choir with recitation,
  When the Wolves Met, children choir with recitation,
  The Falcon flew over for solo, recitation and mixed choir

ŠUST Jiří

A Small Dove, children choir with accompaniment [S. Nová]

TICHÝ František
Dance of Wooden Shoes, a valse intermezzo for wind orchestra

TOMÁŠEK Jaroslav
Sonata for piano for left hand

TROJAN Václav
The Destroyed Cathedral, a composition for accordion
Tarantella for accordion
Wind Quintet on folk song motifs in classical style
Tarantella for orchestra (from the broadcast play Niccolo Paganini)
Vrtena, polka for orchestra
Fairy-tales for accordion and orchestra
The Regiment's Mother Molly, overture for a play with songs
Bethlehem, Christmas carols to the puppets' film by Jiří Trnka
The Emperor's Nightingale, a suite from the puppets' film by Jiří Trnka
Prince Bajaja, suite from the puppets' film by Jiří Trnka
Chap-book (a collection of folk songs), suite from the puppets' film by Jiří Trnka
The War with Lucko, a scene from the music to the puppets' film by Jiří Trnka "*Old Czech Legends*"
The Good Soldier Schweik, overture to the puppets film of the same name by Jiří Trnka
Songs from Pilsen Region (folk poetry) for voice and wind quintet
A Selection of National Songs for children choir and orchestra (folk poetry)
A Chap-book of Folk Songs for solos and orchestra (folk poetry)
The Merry-Go-Round, a selection of scenes from the children opera [libretto by M. Charousová-Gardavská]

UHLÍŘ Jan
Compositions for full orchestra:
Electrone (gallop), *To Men of Work* (march), *A Greeting to Spring* (waltz), *Reviewing the Troops* (intermezzo), *Romance* (intermezzo), *A Dance Roundelay* (valse), *A Valse from a Dancing Suite.*
Compositions for string orchestra:
Domino (waltz), *Folk Merry-making* (gallop), *Polka from the Dance Suite*, *Steadily Forward, Forward March!* (march)
Compositions for wind orchestra:
Ballerina (intermezzo), *Czech Polka, The Woman of Haná* (polka), *Meteor* (march), *Forward March!*, *Polonaise from a Dance Suite*, *Reviewing the Troops* (intermezzo), *On Start!* (gallop), *Rival* (march)

ULLRICH Josef
Valse capriccio for violin and orchestra
Compositions for wind orchestra:
Humoresque (intermezzo), *Parnasie* (intermezzo), *The March of Písek, Spartakus* (march)

⊙ ŠROM-ULLRICH

URBANEC Bartolomej

Bunkošovy Dance (a pastoral male dance using the ring-tipped canes—Orava Region) for orchestra
Periniarky (song of women who used to carry feather beds for newlyweds—folk poetry), mixed choir with orchestra
The Picture of Heart, children choir with accompaniment [M. Ferko]
The Evening in Žaluží (folk poetry), for solos, choir and orchestra
Greetings to the Soviet Union, a cantata for solo, choir and orchestra [J. Poničan]
Our Spring, a song for solo, choir and orchestra [J. Poničan]
May-pole, a selection of scenes from a play with songs [J. Poničan]

URBANEC Rudolf

Grotesque Polka for wind quintet
Caterina, a march for wind orchestra
The Flower Polka for wind orchestra

VACEK Karel Václav

Compositions for wind orchestra:
For Little Jarmila (polka), *Neighbourly Valse*, *A Bright Morning* (valse).
The Highland Polka from Šumava for string orchestra
In Woody Country, polka for string orchestra

VACEK Miloš

We'll Live together a Song for choir with orchestra [Jan Noha]

VAČKÁŘ Dalibor

Sonata for violin and piano (a dedication)
The Heart in the Palm, a concerto valse for orchestra
Prelude and *Metamorphoses* for full orchestra
Švanda the Bagpiper, dances of several nations from the ballet of the same name
The Songs from Chod Region (folk poetry), a cycle of children choirs with piano accompaniment
Small Songs to Sewing, a cycle of female choirs with piano accompaniment [Jaroslav Seifert]
Head up!, a march for wind orchestra

VAČKÁŘ Václav

Czech Overture on motifs of folk songs for orchestra
Moravian-Slovak Dance No. 2 for orchestra
Compositions for wind orchestra:
Rivière (march), *A Dream of Love* (waltz), *A Fairy-tale* (song), *Swain* (march), *A Remembrance on Zbiroh* (serenade), *Tempo* (march), *Victorious Return* (march), *Building Trade Polka*

VALDAUF Karel

Compositions for string orchestra:
Eve is leading (polka), *There is no more Love* (valse), *Autumn Polka*, *Under the same Roof* (polka), *A Little Speckled Hen* (polka)

VÁLEK Jiří

When the Train Disappears at the Bend, children choir with accompaniment [Jaroslav Seifert]
We'll Dance a Round, children choir with accompaniment [J. V. Svoboda]
Parting with the Army, a song for solo, choir and orchestra [O. Kryštofek]

VILEC Michal

To a newly-born Citizen, a choir

VIPLER Vlastislav Antonín

Daisies, a concerto valse for wind ensemble

VODRÁŽKA Karel

Gopak and *Polka* from the symphonic picture *Prague Barricades* for wind orchestra

VOMÁČKA Boleslav

Narcissus, a song with piano [Antonín Sova]
The Soldier in the Field, a song with piano [Fráňa Šrámek]
Commemorating the Dead, a song with piano accompaniment [Otakar Theer]
Return from the Battlefield, a song with piano [Fráňa Šrámek]
Ahead, Pioneers!, children choir with accompaniment [F. Semeráková]
Spring is Coming, a cycle of children choirs [A. Jaroš]
The Ballad of a Dream, a male choir [Jiří Wolker]
S. O. S., a male choir [Petr Křička]
The Ballad About the Eyes of a Stoker, a male choir [Jiří Wolker]
Genista, a male choir [K. Toman]
A Summer Drummer, female choir [Fráňa Šrámek]
One-movement *Sonata* for piano
Sonata for violin and piano

VOSTŘÁK Zbyněk

Philosophers' Story, a selection from a ballet
Little Victoria, a suite from a ballet
The King's Mint Master, a scene from an opera (libretto J. Bachtík, according to J. K. Tyl]

VYCPÁLEK Ladislav

Suite for solo violin
Suite for solo viola
Sonata in D major (Praise of the Violin), for voice, violin and piano
Moravian Ballads for voice and piano (folk poetry)
The Orphan, a ballad for voice and orchestra
Lullaby, female choir [J. V. Sládek]
A cantata *Concerning the Last Things of Man* (Moravian folk poetry)
Courage, My Heart!, two variation fantasies for orchestra on hymns and songs sung in the Bethlehem Chapel

ŽELEZNÝ Lubomír
String Quartet

ZELJENKA Ilja
String Quartet
Piano Quintet No. 2

ZIMMER Ján
Symphony No. 1
Ten Small Children Compositions, a piano cycle